Celebrity Access

The Directory

by Thomas Burford

Burford, Thomas G.
   Celebrity access:the directory:or How and where to write the rich and famous/Thomas G. Burford.--1993-94 rev. ed.
   p. cm.
   ISSN: 1057-9427
   ISBN: 0-9619758-3-0

   1. Motion pictures actors and actresses--Directories. 2. Entertainers--Directories. 3. Celebrities--Directories. 4. Autographs--collectors and collecting. I. Title. II. Title: How and where to write the rich and famous.

   PN1998.A1B79 1993   791'.092
                                                    QBI92-20213

Cover design by D. Brent Hauseman
Book design/editing by Catherine Burford

CONTENTS

ACKNOWLEDGMENTS

I would like to thank all those who gave me support, friendship, and encouragement -- Catherine Burford for her hundreds of hours of work on this book, locating my many mistakes and correcting them, and especially for reformatting *The Directory* to make it better than it has ever been; Ralph Jones and his new bride Laura & Dan Bowman (for helping my schedule allow for enough time to get this done), good friends Janice and Wayne Racek, Bob and Terri Farrell, Hank Clark, Joe Wormall, Anthony S. Alfiero, Michael J. Amenta, Lawrence Edge, Ivar Johansen, Jurgen Schwarz, Matthew Seitz, Michael Stevens, Dennis Vance, Jim Weaver, Roger Christensen, Jeanne and Tim Hoyt, Joe and Karren Kraus, Yvonne Craig, Ralph Vogel, Jim Chrisler, and my friend here, Nellu at Nellu's Antiques. Also a big thanks to John Goddard of Village Music with the most incredible selection in the world. These are very special people. They all contributed freely to us. God bless you all.

A massive personal contribution to my book was done by Allen Stenhouse, Richard Harrington, and Roger Adams. You guys are the best. You put in a lot of hours and we hope the time was worth the rewards. See you all in the mail soon.

And my best wishes to all my new friends who helped by sending in "good" addresses for *The Directory*, and informing me of the ones which were no longer current. Without them this book wouldn't have as much useful information as it does. These thoughtful people sent in address return labels from their envelopes, and postal "Return to Sender" labels with the address, which had come back undelivered. We encourage everyone's help!

If we've forgotten anyone, it was truly unintentional. So, to all of you, my thanks. I hope for continued friendship.

INTRODUCTION

Philography, or in common parlance, autograph collecting, is an almost perfect hobby -- it can be done at home in your spare time, it requires no expensive equipment, and takes up a minimum of space. Receiving your first response will not only be very exciting, it will easily make your investment in this book well worth while. **Warning!** This book is only intended for you to have fun writing your favorite stars, <u>do not</u> go visit them. We do not list or identify home addresses, so these people may have their well deserved privacy. You may find that if you attempt to visit these addresses you may very well be arrested for trespassing, invasion of privacy, or held by private security. Respect the individuals privacy. These addresses are mostly business addresses, and will not allow access to the general public.

Most of the addresses listed in this book are of well-known actors and actresses, however, there are also entries for selected people in politics, science, and the arts. The book is **not** cluttered with the addresses of corporations and fan clubs: they are listed only if they have something to send for a celebrity.

This book is one of the best philography tools you can get your hands on. It includes information beyond that offered by any other books in this field. In addition to providing the expected "good" addresses, this book provides "bad" addresses to avoid, and our individual descriptive notes and "V Date", which indicates when contact was last made with that celebrity.

The "bad" addresses are those from which we have confirmed letters will be returned to the sender. They are listed as "good" in many other publications, and therefore just keep circulating. You will find that we have included known bad addresses even when we do not have a good one for a celebrity. We hope this will save the reader from frustration and the waste of valuable time and money.

Thomas Burford

LIVING A CLASSIC MOVIE
by JAN WAHL

The last word I would use about Hollywood today is "magic". Sure there are special effects which Griffith and DeMille could have only have dreamed of, there are multi-million dollar budgets which Capra and Wilder would have loved, there are huge salaries for stars that more than likely have the spirits of Gable and Crawford green with envy. But for all this, the magic of Hollywood is "Gone with the Wind".

Today we have realism in movies and in acting. This I find ironic since films are an art form that gives us a perspective on reality, not reality itself. Show me a vision, not that which I can see myself. Give me your way of seeing life's textures and its characters. Film is a perfect art form for a subjective view.

The glamour has gone along with the magic. Our movie stars were once our royalty, and now they only have the wealth of royalty. Lombard was a madcap joy, bringing a sense of glamour with her. She was part of the dream factory which turned mortals into stars. Yet Lombard's film acting is so natural we identify and relate to her mostly through the film image. That kind of talent and style is what many of today's stars should learn from.

Glamour is one of those wonderful characteristics which can be altered to fit a unique individual. Garbo gave a severe, almost masculine look to herself off camera, yet it worked in contrast to that remarkable face. Dietrich also played the masculine/feminine contrast to great effect. Gish gave us the delicate waif, while Lupe Valez was wild and exotic. Glamour doesn't get more unique than the powerful image created by Katherine Hepburn, or the no-nonsense approach by that career girl of the movies, Roz Russell. Perhaps their studios protected these ladies and others from ugly photographs, just as today's photographers try to capture the natural beauty, avoiding the bland and ordinary.

The word glamour doesn't exactly bring to mind Sean Penn, Dustin Hoffman, or Tom Hanks, but the men who were movie stars of Hollywood's "Golden Era" were an even match for their glamourous counterparts. The rugged masculinity of Gable, the clipped elegance of Grant. Look at the boyish charm of Stewart and how he contrasts with the grace and flow of Astaire! Remember the half-lidded romance promised by the eyes of Boyer, or the full-out sexuality of Gary Cooper?

It all appealed to both sexes. The women wanted the men, and the men wanted to be like these men. Women often copied their favorite female stars in ways far more than cosmetic. Men admired these ladies or enjoyed the challenge of the ones with sparkling wit.

As Myrna Loy reminds us in her autobiography, *Being & Becoming*, none of these images would have been possible without the lighting and make-up experts, as well as the cameramen who were the "Citizen Kane's" of their craft. This is one of the reasons I deplore colorization. It brings these glorious illusions down to earth, to the one place they don't belong - reality.

So I live in an old movie. I can surround myself with alert, direct dames like Jean Arthur and Susan Hayward, the dash and sophistication of Tyrone Power and Errol Flynn. It's a world of interesting words, lovely images which are uplifting and enriching. With the help of my radio show I can help perpetuate, along with other lovers of film and the stars, the high standards we have set for ourselves. We rejoice at the Hollywood that will never die. Our great and glamourous stars will be with us always. Not just in our films but in our hearts.

Jan Wahl won an Emmy award in 1977 for writing and producing for the documentary "They Still Say 'I Do'" on ABC-TV. She currently hosts a talk show, "Jan Wahl's Hollywood Calling", for the San Francisco Bay Area radio station KNBR.

AUTOGRAPH CARE AND PRESERVATION
by Joe Kraus

There is probably nothing more exciting for an autograph collector than to finally obtain that one long-sought-after piece. At the same time, there is nothing more depressing than to find a similar prize destroyed because it did not receive proper care. While there is no magic wand to create the elusive autograph or document you are seeking, there is help at hand to preserve and care for the autographs already in your collection.

Benjamin Franklin may have summed up the necessity of proper care in one statement. "For want of a nail," he said, "the shoe was lost; for want of a shoe the horse was lost; and for want of a horse the rider was lost; being overtaken and slain by the enemy, all for want of care about a horseshoe nail."

Collectors have many choices in how and where to store and preserve autographs. These can range anywhere from a bank vault to a shoe box placed under the foot of a bed. But it seems as soon as a collector thinks he or she has done it the way he or she wants, someone comes along with a new idea. Then it is out with the old, and in with the new. In the end it doesn't matter a great deal what you do, for what works for one person may not work all that well for another. Because of this one shouldn't dwell so much on what **to** do, but rather what **not** to do.

Do not, for instance, ever use paper clips, rubber bands, glue, staples, or tape on your autographs, not even around the corners of the paper. And never laminate your autographs. Never use varnish or shellac, or spray anything over an autograph -- even the advertised plastic sprays which are said to protect documents. The value of such sprayed material is lost, not to mention the long-term damage to the autographed item. Do not ever use the kind of "stick-'em-down album" that you see in five-and-dime and camera supply stores. Again, while it may seem that this is the answer to all your problems, your autographs can in time become permanently stuck, and in addition, the acid sometimes goes right through the paper of the photograph or document, appearing as yellow lines on the surface. Rather, place your collection into three-ring binders, between acetate sheets. Clear plastics can pose a danger, as many plastics are acidic. One way to spot a danger is to rub your fingers over the sheets. If they feel oily -- stay away. Don't ever leave your autographs exposed to sunlight regardless whether you are outside, or inside with direct light reaching your collection. The light, in time, will fade your signatures. Be concerned as well with extremes of heat or cold, and with wet or damp places, as these may cause your collection to warp, mildew or even melt!

Always be concerned about floods or fires. For storage, find a waterproof and fireproof container and store your albums within the house or other similar location, not in a garage, attic, or basement. But even within a house, place your collection on a shelf or in a closet, not on the floor. If you store autographs in three-ring binders, place them on a shelf as you would a book, not face down with other heavy albums on top. The pressure could cause certain inks, such as the dry erase and metallic marker types, to lift off. Give each album space and room to breathe. Remember also, that there are many pests, such as insects, worms, and mice or rats, which can, given the opportunity, damage or completely destroy your collection.

Another concern is burglary. While most burglars would not know what to do with an autograph collection, it still might get taken just as a curiosity. Do what you would do with any other valuable. Photographing or videotaping is the most common and accurate method used, and is recommended by insurance companies. It is best, as well, to keep a running record of your collection should part or all of it be destroyed, damaged or stolen. Most homeowners' or renters' insurance policies have provisions in which you can list your collection. Insurance firms, however, are highly skeptical of the exaggerated prices many collectors place on these types of valuables. An updated letter from an acknowledged dealer on his/her letterhead will be needed for your files and the insurance firm's records. This letter should give a general description of your collection and place a value on it.

Bank vaults, while many think them secure, might cause another problem. Ventilation is essential. Keeping your manuscripts and autographs in an airless environment can be harmful. Store autographs in a clean, dry place where air can freely circulate.

Should you frame autographs and hang them on your wall, make sure they hang well away from direct sunlight. Also make sure they are matted, not under straight glass. A mat will keep the autograph away from the glass and safe from sticking against the glass.

Mats should be acid free and for mounting use only acid-free tape. Glass in frames should be non glare document glass. Plexiglass UF-3 filters out ultraviolet rays. This will prevent much of the fading that you could get from using regular glass.

Before framing an item, however, it is best to encapsulate it. Encapsulation is the process in which autographs are sealed at all four edges between two pieces of acid-free Mylar (bonded together using acid-free adhesive backings such as polyester transparent tape). What this does is form a protective envelope around your autograph. Over this place your mat.

Exercise care and caution when handling autographs. Protect them from tears or creasing, greasy fingers or spilled soda pop. In short, use good common sense and your autographs will remain in excellent repair.

----

*Joe Kraus is currently editor/publisher of **Child Stars Magazine** in Stockton, CA. He is a former editor of the **U.A.C.C./Pen & Quill Magazine** and former editor/owner of **Autograph Collectors Magazine**.*

AN OPEN LETTER TO FANS
by Yvonne Craig

One evening, whilst sitting at dinner with Tom, we began talking about fans and what I liked about hearing from them, what worked, and what was intrusive or frightening about encounters with them. It was then that Tom suggested that I write it down and he'd put it in his book. So, though I wouldn't presume to speak for all actors on this subject, perhaps I can give you some guidelines which might apply to others as well.

1) I am always gratified to hear from fans especially since the bulk of my work was done rather a while back. When I was shooting "Batman" I received no fan mail personally and must assume that either Fox Studios or ABC-TV was intercepting and answering it for me. I currently answer all requests for autographs personally as I believe do most of us "oldies but goodies" actors who are not actively involved in shooting a series at this time. However, because I have a busy life and try to allocate just a few hours a month to this task, it is impossible for me to answer extensive questions. It also helps if fans will send a S.A.S.E. for my reply, and if they enclose a photo they'd like signed, all the better. Reminder: when you request an 8X10 photo from any celebrity, please send an envelope that will accommodate it. I can't tell you how often I receive a request for a signed photo accompanied by a S.A.S.E. that is letter size! Also if you want it personalized (I do so unless specifically requested not to), you need to mention that person's name. For instance I get letters saying "I was such a "Batman" fan and now my daughter is as well. Could you send her a photo and one for me?" They then sign their name which means they get a personalized photo but their daughter does not because I don't know what the child's name is. Disappointment! Also, after giving it a lot of thought, I recently decided not to respond to any more post cards which are pre-printed so that they read: "Dear --- (this is filled in with my name by the sender) I have been a fan of yours for a long time. Please send an autographed photo. Sincerely," or one which contains an obvious formula like: "I've been a big fan of yours for so long. You are the best there's ever been. Can I have an autograph?" This sort of formula on a card could apply to anyone, is easy to spot, and is probably sent out to a number of people at the same time. Finally, many stars give their autograph with ease through the mail, and I'm sure a simple "thank you" would be appreciated if they used their own photo, postage, and envelope.

2) Some of us do personal appearances, and that's a perfect time to ask those questions you wanted to have answered by mail. I usually allocate time during any personal appearance for just such a "Question & Answer" period. It lasts at least an hour each day of the appearance.

I find that often the same people raise their hands again and again, but I have to assume they're asking things about which the more timid are equally interested so I kind of go with whatever happens. What I really hate is to get up and say "Does anyone have anything they'd like to ask?" and be met by a sea of implacable faces, with no raised hands. This is where I just have to wing it in regard to what you guys might find interesting, only to be met as I leave the stage by sixteen people who DO have questions but were too shy to speak up.

3) The following are some guidelines that you might keep in mind:

a. Most performers are as shy or shyer than you are. We use acting as a means to creatively overcome this but the condition still exists. So its very uncomfortable to have someone whisper and point in our direction but very nice to have that person come up and say "I enjoyed you in -----".

b. It's flattering to have someone write a note of appreciation to you via normal channels -- that is to say via the address you find in this book or through SAG, AFTRA, AEA, or our manager or agent. It is unnerving to have someone track you down and/or show up at your home uninvited. We all tend to be a bit paranoid since the murder of Rebecca Shaeffer.

c. We are generally NOT like the characters we play. It's good to be convincing as a character but less fun when someone physically accosts you for some misdeed of a character you've been successfully portraying.

4) I guess the most important thing to keep in mind when dealing with celebrities is actually what you keep in mind in life in general: Treat others as you'd like to be treated. But bear in mind that what I'm saying is from a relatively "low profile" point of view. I'm sure if this chapter were being written by Cher or Madonna or Bruce Willis there would be more than a few lines directed at crowds infringing on one's space as well as how not to ask for autographs during someone's dinner or while in the Ladies/Mens room. However: Treat others as you'd like to be treated still should cover it.

Yvonne Craig is an actress, well-known for her role as "Batgirl" in the popular television show "Batman," which aired in the late 1960's. She has appeared in numerous films, including "The Young Land," "It Happened at the World's Fair," "Kissin' Cousins," "By Love Possessed," "One Spy Too Many," and "In Like Flint." She has also made many guest appearances on TV series. She currently resides and works in the Los Angeles Area.

CONTACTING CELEBRITIES THROUGH THE MAIL
by Thomas Burford

Celebrities! We place them on pedestals, and often forget that they are people with feelings and emotions like the rest of humanity. For autograph collectors, this is an especially important point to remember. When you write to your favorite stars, remember to treat them with intelligence and dignity.

A "truly authentic" autograph is the one which is obtained by you "in person". This kind of contact also leaves you with the memory of meeting the celebrity in person and having a unique one-on-one experience. If you are fortunate enough meet a celebrity in person, remember that he or she is entitled to a private life just as you and I are. Before approaching a celebrity, think about where you are. Because of someone's complete lack of manners, a very famous movie star now refuses to sign for anyone after being asked for an autograph in a rest room. There is a time and place for everything, and that was certainly neither the time nor place.

If you see that a celebrity is trying to remain inconspicuous, he or she may not appreciate your intrusion, and you may not get your autograph. But if you approach stars calmly, without drawing attention to them, (they will appreciate your doing this) and politely ask them to sign something, they probably will. If you have a clean plain-white unfolded card or piece of paper, use it. These make the best examples for framing. Most fans are caught off guard, so any reasonable article to sign on will do in a pinch. Many stars have told me in interviews they don't like paper and pen thrust into their faces, so please use good manners. They also dislike intrusions during meals or when with family.

Since the chances of finding stars in person are slim for most of us, we must rely heavily on the mail. The rest of this article will be devoted to giving the best instruction we can for learning the proper way to collect autographs by mail.

Our most powerful tool for increasing the chance of an autograph is the "self-addressed-stamped-envelope" or S.A.S.E., as it is most commonly referred to. The S.A.S.E. must have enough postage to insure its return without expecting the celebrity to pay any of it for you. This should accompany any letter you send. Your address should be printed clearly on the envelope if you expect any kind of a response. A complete address and zip code is critical on **anything** you mail. Remember to always put your address on your envelope, on your S.A.S.E., on your letterhead, and on whatever photo you send so it doesn't get mixed up with someone else's. (When writing on any photo's reverse surface, use only the slightest pressure, as the pen may leave an impression which could show through on the front surface.) A celebrity will frequently return your S.A.S.E. with your request as their way of "saying thank you for remembering". The size of your S.A.S.E. will be decided by what your request is. If you send a 4x5 inch index card, your S.A.S.E. should be large enough for it to be returned without having to fold it in any way. If you send a photograph, include a S.A.S.E large enough, and with enough postage for it to be returned in the best possible condition. To further insure that any damage will be minimal, we also recommend the use some sort of cardboard backing between which the photograph can be inserted. This gives your photograph a certain amount of rigidity while passing through the mail.

Some stars will send signed photos without any S.A.S.E. or photographs sent to them. These stars are becoming fewer and fewer every day. Because of the enormous cost involved for photos, postage, envelopes (and secretaries' salaries!), and the fact that the bonanza days of studios and their contract players are long gone, your contributions will be needed more in days to come. **Do not send anything return-receipt requested, certified, or by any other way in which a celebrity would have to sign or take responsibility for. The item will almost certainly be refused.**

The response/return time for your request will vary, and depends on many factors. How current is the address at which you are writing the celebrity? Perhaps the individual has moved (and stars move with great frequency). The mail may need to forwarded, or perhaps there is no forwarding address. Celebrities are generally very busy people. The individual may be away on vacation, living at his or her summer or winter home, out on a movie location, on the road with a concert tour or stage production, or is perhaps ill. The possibilities are endless. All these could be reasons for slowing the response to an autograph request. The reason could also be that the photographs were mislaid, misfiled, sent to a wrong address, or even temporarily lost. We have known of cases in which items have been returned after an elapse of two years. Whatever the reason, **they are not responsible** for anything you send. By following this advice you may be surprised to find an occasional extra photo tucked into your envelope -- some of the stars are very generous this way. We should further mention, for those of you who will be writing to people overseas, to purchase an I.R.C. (International Reply Coupon). These are used to exchange for postage in foreign countries. You should be able to purchase the coupons at your own Postal Main Branch, and they are fairly inexpensive. Two to four are usually enough.

Writing a good letter to a celebrity could make the difference between a minimal response and the response you've always wanted. When writing you should be polite, patient, and respectful. It never hurts to say "please", and "thank you". You might even consider **not** being over familiar with a celebrity by calling him or her by first name. In our opinion, your letter should be hand written and on clean paper. (Please do type the letter if your handwriting is hard to read!) One should be as original as possible, for the celebrities have seen every possible type of fan letter you could imagine. A sure fire way of having your mail thrown in the garbage is to photocopy a letter, and hand-write the name of the person you are writing to at the beginning. This also applies to letters printed on computers, form letters (these are obvious), and envelopes with the address on an address label. The later appears to be part of a mailing service or list to them.

The letter should be short and to the point. Usually one page on one side until you know the celebrity wishes to continue writing to you in the future. Long letters may never be completely read if the celebrity isn't interested in personally responding. Since in most cases a secretary or assistant screens the mail, the content and length may decide if the celebrity ever sees it. Don't expect a personal response from the celebrity, as there are so many requests from fans it is not possible to attend to them all. You may however be one of the chosen few to receive that one-in-a-million letter. Sometimes persistence has paid off. After several letters to a hard to reach person, she finally responded. This doesn't always work and it could backfire on you. Be careful and courteous in each letter so as not to upset the celebrity. If the purpose of the letter is an autograph get right to the point in the first paragraph. (You can mention how you would prefer an authentic autograph from the individual, but time will tell whether your request will be honored.) This gives the celebrity the option of fulfilling your request and reading the rest of the letter later. An intelligent letter is always recommended. Don't talk about collecting a lot of stars, as the individual should be the center of attention in the letter, not other celebrities. The rest of the letter should be used to show the celebrity your knowledge of him or her, and his or her career. This is where you would also critique, praise, or comment. But if you are rude or disrespectful you can expect you mail to go unanswered, and the items you sent may be thrown away or even torn up and returned.

Many celebrities don't answer their mail personally. It is frequently answered by secretaries, agents, and fan mail services on the behalf of the celebrity, with all good intentions. But it is disheartening to fans to discover that their autographs were signed by someone other than the celebrity. There are also other types of items sent out by the celebrities' offices which are explained in greater detail in another chapter. Some of these are, photos with signature stamps, mechanical signatures, and signature imprints. More celebrities are sending these every day. Regardless what is sent, **save everything** for someday it will be collectable, and will be your direct contact with your past. It will be fun in a few years to look back on these items to see the changes. You may find some surprises.

What should you send? We have several do's and don'ts. Don't ask for more than one photo and send no more than three for signing. If your have asked for a free photo from a celebrity be aware that some offices keep track of what they send out. They may write and tell you they already honored your request months before. Most celebrities will automatically inscribe a photo to the requester. Should you want one as a gift for a friend it is not unusual to request one signed to your friend. If you want an un-inscribed photo you may run into problems as the celebrity may suspect you want it for other reasons. It is not a good idea to send gifts of food for obvious reasons, but tokens of appreciation are sometimes accepted. Don't send money unless you are asked to formally order an item from them which you want. The celebrities who do send photos send whatever they happen to have on hand. It could be rude to make an unreasonable request for a specific item. You may however mention that you are looking for a particular item and ask if they could tell you where you could find one. When you send anything for an autograph (ie. books, album covers, first day covers, and sheet music) don't over wrap it. They won't fight it to open it. Don't send anything you can't afford to loose. If you have a rare or hard to get item, you should keep it, as it could disappear quickly and mysteriously. We suggest you keep records of what you mail out, when you mailed it, and any follow-up letters you may have sent. Occasionally the celebrity will try to help you locate a lost item if you can furnish specific information on when, where, and what you lost.

Reference material with the history of films and celebrity biographies, as well as books on autograph collecting, can be found at your local library and book stores. We have included a reference section in this book to help you locate clubs, papers, and magazines which promote autograph collecting and interests in film, sports, and other areas. Many of these publications print facsimiles of signatures to help you identify ones you may receive in the mail. If you require further authentication there are several dealers who advertise in these publications and would be willing to help you. I highly recommend that you check on the reputation of any dealer before sending off your prize possession. A reputable dealer won't mind the inquiry. Many are members of fine organizations that have an ethics board and work to protect the integrity of autograph collecting.

A final note on our Postal System. Though the Post Office tries to do its best to move our mail, it does occasionally make mistakes. We have seen letters returned from addresses we know were and are good. Agencies which represent celebrities often make many of the cancellations you see on your return mail. These labels are just like the ones the Post Office uses when mail is undeliverable. Since you won't know who stamped your letter with one of these we recommend checking the address again along with any information you can decipher on the envelope. Sometimes the Post Office will attach a yellow "Return To Sender" sticker on the envelope. Always read this carefully. Most will have a forwarding address on them, even though the forwarding order has expired.

There are many reasons why one would collect autographs and we will always encourage novices to not be disappointed with failure the first few attempts. We have all suffered setbacks at one time or another, and **we** are still always looking forward. Autograph collecting is so widely diversified in its different fields, and virtually cost free to begin (it requires no special equipment), that it is fun, educational, and rewarding.

All the best of luck.

(The following is an actual letter from a dedicated fan to a celebrity; it is an example of an effective bit of letter-writing. Only the names and film titles have been changed.)

Rex King
123 Main St.
Elmwood, CA 12345

Mr. John Smith
321 Main Rd.
Miami, FL 10101

Dear Mr. Smith,

I had to write after seeing "Star Gate" again. You were so cool throughout the film. I've often wanted to write for an autographed photo but I've never been sure whether you would personally see my letter. I've had disappointment in the past with secretaries signing photos, and even mechanically produced signatures. As a true fan I realize major celebrities with busy schedules, like you must have, sometimes do not have the luxury of answering everyone that writes. I hope I am one of the lucky ones.

The film that touched my heart more than anything else you have ever done was "Blue Windows". Everyone around me was crying when it appeared you had died in the last scene. I have to confess when I saw your face reappear, I too was standing on my seat in applause. What a fine and happy ending. I've been trying so hard to find and see everything you've made. You are the best.

I've searched for a long time for photos from "Burford's Dozen" to send you for signing, but so far no luck. In the mean time, I've enclosed a couple 3" x 5" index cards with a self addressed, stamped envelope for your convenience. Would you kindly sign them for me? I would like to thank you in advance for any consideration you may show me.

Respectfully Yours,

Rex King

AUTOGRAPHS, HANDWRITING, AND FORGERY
by Dr. Michael Zanoni

Handwriting and signatures are representations of ideas and identity that convey a person's uniqueness. Possessing the original signature of some significant individual is to have a powerful symbol of all which that person has accomplished.

The collector of contemporary autographs faces very different questions regarding authenticity than does the antiquarian. Very old writings were all executed by hand using instruments and paper which are relatively distinct as to era. The collector of old writings has many signs, symptoms and clues to reveal simulated or forged documents. But the collector of modern writings, particularly the beginning hobbyist, is confronted with numerous sources and methods of simulation.

Handwriting is executed by a combination of conscious and unconscious processes. This is why handwriting takes on unique characteristics. The person who tries to simulate another's signature must consciously execute the appearance and letter-forms of the handwriting. Unless the simulator has specific artistic talent, attempts to replicate another's signature will introduce various defects which are readily apparent.

Since many years of observation, training, and experience are required to become an expert handwriting examiner, this short article cannot prepare someone to render opinions about authenticity. But the information presented will assist in the evaluation and selection process performed by every autograph collector.

SIMPLE FORGERIES

Sometimes called "normal writing simulations", these are situations where someone executes another's signature using their own normal handwriting. You may also hear these called "secretarial signatures" in the situation where a public figure or celebrity has one person whose job it is to sign photos and comply with requests for autographs. These signatures will appear very natural and lifelike because they are, in fact, natural writing. In order to differentiate between secretarial and genuine autographs, one must have access to several samples of known writings. But even this can be difficult, since many public figures have more than one person providing secretarial autographs!

TRACED FORGERIES

There are several ways of producing a traced forgery, and all will show similar symptoms. The simplest way of making a tracing is by the use of light shining through the paper. The paper which is to bear the forged signature is placed over a genuine signature. These are then placed on a light-box or a window, and the image of the genuine signature is traced over. The tracing may be done with a pen, in which case the forger has only one opportunity to make a correct replica. Or the tracing may be done very lightly with a pencil. In this case, additional attempts at producing an acceptable replica can be made. The thin pencil line is then later traced over with ink. A third way of producing a traced forgery is particularly popular with photographs. A photocopy of a genuine signature is placed over the photo which is to carry the replica writing. A fine point ball-pen or pencil is used to trace over the genuine signature. The pressure creates an indentation in the emulsion of the photograph. This indentation is then traced over with a pen, giving the appearance that a ball-pen was used to sign a genuine signature.

Even the best traced forgeries will show the common characteristic of "lifelessness" when compared to genuine writings. When compared to original signatures, tracings generally do not show the dynamic qualities of original writings. Other symptoms and signs may also be observed. Tracings are executed slowly, therefore the ink line will appear uniform and perhaps even heavy. There may be many pen-lifts not present in a genuine signature. Loops and curved lines will often show what is called "deviation from the anticipated curve". This is when the line diverts or wavers from the form or direction one would assume it to normally take. This deviation occurs when the forger carefully tries to follow the pattern signature, but is unable to see the full sweep of the original writing because the hand or pen is in the field of view. Tracings first made with a pencil and then inked over will show the shiny remains of pencil graphite when examined under low magnification. Inked impressions on photographic emulsions will often show either parallel and conflicting impressions if inked with a ball-pen, or may show illogical impressions when inked over with a fiber tip or nibbed pen. But be careful about mistaking the tremor of age and disability for the carefully contrived appearance of a traced forgery.

ARTISTIC FORGERIES

These simulations are the most difficult to identify. They involve what is essentially a drawing of a signature. The forger studies and practices replicating genuine writing. The simpler and more angular the writing, he easier it is to produce an acceptable replica. Also, the closer the genuine writing is to the manner of writing of the forger, the easier it is to produce a simulation. Detection of a good artistic forgery may require examination of dozens of known signatures. In these cases, the examiner often looks for subtle variations between the known and questioned signatures where the forger's personal writing style may not have been completely suppressed.

IMPRESSIONING DEVICES

So-called "rubber stamp" impressions may be made by a rubber-like latex substance, from a silkscreen process in which ink is forced through a pattern embossed on a fabric strip, or by a porous plastic that delivers ink by capillary action.

Signatures produced by "rubber-stamps" are often readily identified, but in some cases (particularly on photographs) careful examination is required to be certain.

Rubber stamps on paper are often readily detectable. Under magnification, one can see the evenness of the ink, the lack of shading, and the absence of any stroke characteristics introduced by changed pen angle. There may also be marks from places where the rubber backing holding the impressioning typeface has not been fully cut away. Sometimes, there will be a "splotchy" appearance to the ink like due to the typeface being worn, dirty, or from the ink being moist. You may also notice that a pattern from the fabric or sponge surface of the stamp-pad has carried over to the signature.

In replica signatures made with porous surface stamps there will not be the usual characteristics of a fabric pattern, but the giveaway is often the even nature of the ink line and under magnification one may sometimes note that the ink line is composed of numerous dots and not a smoothly flowing line.

It is often difficult to determine if a signature on a photograph has been produced by a stamp replication process. On a matte surface print the stamped signature may lose its conspicuous characteristics. On glossy surface photos, particularly with water-soluble inks on older non-resin coated paper, it is possible for the glazed surface of the paper to lose its glossy characteristics and have the rubber stamp appear as if it is pressed down into the emulsion such as would occur with a ball pen. The signs to look for here are the even nature of the ink line and a total lack of embossing and the reverse of the photo.

PHOTOGRAPHS OF AUTOGRAPHED PHOTOGRAPHS

A common problem for autograph collectors is the autographed photograph which is in reality a photograph of an autographed photograph. (Try saying _that_ real fast!) This situation arises when a celebrity places an actual autograph on a picture, which is then re-photographed to make a large number of prints. Quite often, the actual autograph will include some phrase or wording, such as "Yours forever" or "Thanks for your interest and support". It may be that an actual autograph appears on a photograph of another photograph with further wording. But it is very common to find photographs of autographed photographs that have an apparently original dedication or inscription above a signature that is actually part of the photographic image. Someone may have obtained a promotional photo containing a signature, and then placed an inscription above the photographic signature. If the inscription has a writing style similar to the signature, one could easily assume that all writings were by the celebrity.

LITHOGRAPHED SIGNATURES

This is a problem very similar to photographs of autographed photographs. It is not uncommon for a celebrity to utilize promotional pictures that are reproduced by offset or lithographic processes, and are not truly photographs. Quite often, a fan may obtain a genuine autograph on one of these pictures. But equally often, the reproduction also contains a signature of the celebrity which is difficult to differentiate from an actual writing produced by a fiber tipped pen. Careful examination under magnification may be required to determine whether the signature is written or placed there by the printing press. A genuine signature will usually have at least one place where lines cross and the ink has some changed characteristic (more or less shiny, slightly different color, edge of ink line noticeable) not present in a printed signature. Experience is a good teacher in these cases.

THE AUTOPEN

This is a mechanical device that produces a replica of a genuine signature by following a template. These are used in situations where a signature must appear on literally hundreds of documents daily. Generally, autopen signatures have a consistent and almost lifeless line quality with little or no shading. The ink may be fiber tip or rolling ball. These are normally seen in modern governmental appointment certificates and routine politically bases correspondence. Some celebrities also use autopen devices, although they are more common in political and governmental usage. The concept of the autopen goes back to the pantograph-like devices popular in the early 1800's for making duplicate correspondence.

PHOTOCOPIES

Development of the electrostatic photocopy machine revolutionized business operations and added another method for producing replica signatures. This is especially the case since the increased popularity of the fiber-tipped pens. Differentiation between an original signature and a photocopy of an original signature can be difficult. Generally, the best photocopy is on paper having a smooth surface and low rag content (cotton) content. A photocopied signature on textured 100% rag content bond paper will probably be readily identifiable under low magnification as a photocopy. But the same signature copied onto paper specifically manufactured for photocopy use may be almost indistinguishable from an original signature executed with black fiber tip pen. This is one area where experience and observation are the best teachers. There are several slightly different processes for bonding the copy toner to the paper, therefore the product of different manufacturers should be examined to gain experience. Some processes will make the writing line appear like it is melted and sitting into the paper surface. It is also easy to confuse the microscopic splatter made by a fiber-tip pen as it forms looping strokes with excess photocopy toner that has been fused onto the paper near the writing line.

Photocopied signatures are often seen on personal letters purportedly written by celebrities. A secretary will type some brief personal text and then run the letter through a photocopy machine to add a replica of a genuine signature.

EQUIPMENT

The examination of most writings, and the detection of the more common varieties of forgery, requires very little equipment. The most useful tool is a magnifier of the type used for examining 35mm slides. These can be obtained at most camera stores for less than ten dollars. This viewer consists of a transparent round plastic base which supports a lens of about 8 power. The viewer rests directly upon the surface to be examined, thus does not require focusing. A small pen-light is sometimes useful to provide oblique illumination when examining indentations in paper.

A second type of useful optical tool is the pocket microscope. This is a device smaller than a pack of cigarettes which consists of a battery powered illuminating lamp and a compound lens assembly of about 40 power. These are available from Radio Shack for less than ten dollars. This device is useful for examining lines in detail, determination of the type of writing instrument used, and for inspection of suspicious signatures for half-tone dots (which would indicate that it had been made by printing press rather than pen).

Very little other equipment is required, and seldom (if ever) will an autograph collector need something that magnifies more than 40 times. But overall, the best piece of equipment is experience.

Dr. Michael Zanoni is a licenced private investigator in San Mateo County, California. He has testified in court as an expert many times about handwriting, forgeries and questioned documents.

HOW TO USE THIS BOOK

(Except for Address #1 these are examples only)

Burford, Thomas
20 Sunnyside Ave.
Mill Valley, CA 94941
Actor/Writer <----------

The **primary addresses** are identified by the listing of the celebrity's claim to fame located here.

V:04/06/91 <------------

This is the "**V**" **verification** date. This date is when we last made contact with the celebrity, or his/her representative at this address, or we received a response.

Burford, Thomas
327 Main St.
Smalltown, CA 94999
Alternate <----------------

Sometimes the celebrity has more than one address (i.e., his/her home, East or West Coast, or overseas agents, publicists, etc.). This address would be a second choice if the celebrity is away from his/her primary address.

Burford, Thomas
192 Center Ave.
Sun City, CA 99099
Forwarded <--------------

Mail is occasionally **forwarded** from one agency or home to another. This is a third address at which one might locate the celebrity.

Burford, Thomas
555 Wildwest Ln.
Upstate, CA 90909
L.R.U. <--------------------

"**L.R.U.**" stands for "**Letter Returned Un-delivered**". This does not necessarily mean that the celebrity is **not** at this address. It is simply a warning to the reader that we have attempted writing this address one or more times and had no reply. We don't recommend using it, as you may lose all that you send there.

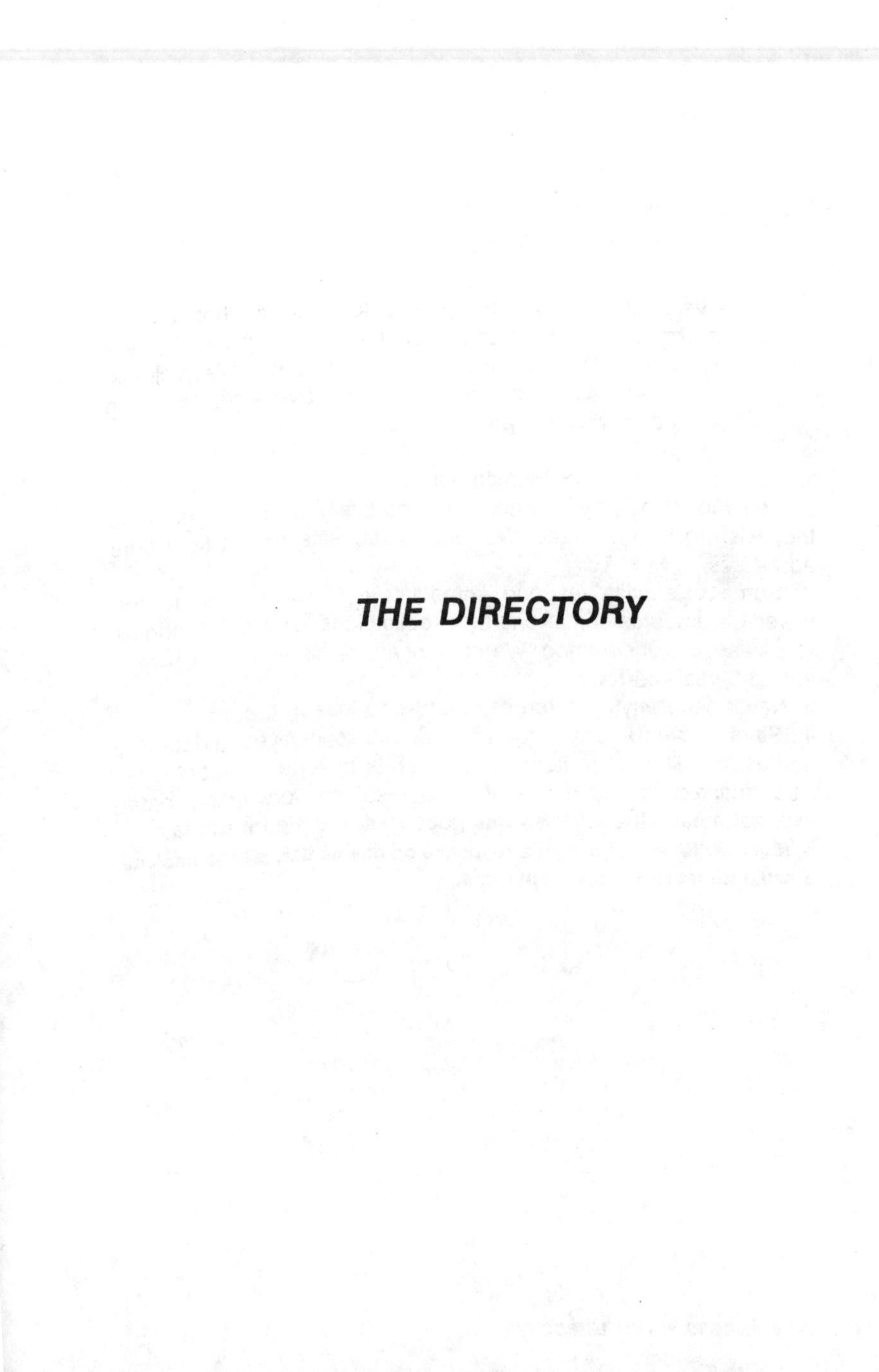

THE DIRECTORY

Every effort has been made to ensure that all the information in this book is accurate and up-to-date. We apologize for any typographical errors, misspellings, duplicate listings, or the unfortunate oversight of listing someone who has passed away.

Remember

1. We try to list only those whom respond easily, and at an address they wish to be contacted. We respect requests to not list home addresses.

2. Some celebrities respond immediately. However due to the incredible amounts of mail and other obligations, a wait of 6 months to a year isn't uncommon. We have heard of cases in which mail took 3-5 years to return.

3. Never send anything you can't afford to lose in the mail.

4. Stars move or change agents & representatives a lot. So, addresses will change frequently, which is beyond our control. A letter marked "no longer at this address" or "forwarding order expired" means the address **was** good, but you tried it too late.

5. **If you write us and expect a response on any matter, please enclose a self-addressed stamped envelope.**

A

A DIFFERENT WORLD
Carsey-Werner Company
P.O. Box 1-710
14755 Ventura Blvd.
Sherman Oaks, CA 91403
Production Company V: 03/26/93

A&E Network
235 E. 45th St.
New York, NY 10017
Network HQ V: 01/21/93

1800 Century Park E.#
Los Angeles, CA 90067
Alternate V: 01/21/93

ABC Film/Tape Library
1717 DeSales St. N.W.
Washington, DC 20036
Archive V: 01/20/93

ABC News Archives
47 West 66th St.
New York, NY 10012
Archive V: 03/20/93

ABC-TV News
c/o Newsroom
1926 Broadway
New York, NY 10023
Production Company V: 01/12/93

147 Columbus Ave.
New York, NY 10023
Alternate V: 02/10/93

47 W. 66th. St.
New York, NY 10023
Alternate V: 03/12/93

ABC-TV/Capitol Cities
77 W. 66th St.
New York, NY 10023
Production Company V: 01/11/93

4151 Prospect Ave.
Los Angeles, CA 90027
Alternate V: 01/02/93

AFH Management
7250 Beverly Blvd. #102
Los Angeles, CA 90036
Talent Agency V: 07/02/92

AFTRA
6922 Hollywood Blvd. 8th Fl.
Hollywood, CA 90028
Actors Union V: 01/13/93

ALL MY CHILDREN
ABC-TV
320 W. 66th St.
New York, NY 10023
Viewer Services V: 12/15/92

AMAZING LIVE SEA MONKEYS
425 S. Flower St.
Burbank, CA 91502
Production Company V: 03/18/93

AMERICAN DETECTIVE
300 S. Lorimar Plaza
Burbank, CA 91505
Viewer Services V: 12/15/92

ANGEL STREET
Warner Bros. TV
4000 Warner Blvd.
Producers Building 3, Rm. 124
Burbank, CA 91522
Production Company V: 01/03/93

ANOTHER WORLD
c/o NBC-TV
79 Madison Ave., 5th Fl.
New York, NY 91523
Production Company V: 01/21/93

AS THE WORLD TURNS
524 W. 57th St.
New York, NY 10019
Production Company V: 03/18/93

Aaker, Lee
P.O. Box 1595
Reseda, CA 91337
Actor V: 01/02/92

Aames, Willie
901 Birmingham Ave.
Los Angeles, CA 90049
Actor V: 02/13/93

Aaron Spelling
1041 N. Formosa Ave.
W. Hollywood, CA 90046
Producer V: 07/09/92

Abbott, Diahnne
460 W. Ave. 46
Los Angeles, CA 00065
Actress V: 02/12/92

Abbott, Jim
c/o NY Yankees
Yankee Stadium
Bronx, NY 10451
 Baseball V: 03/30/93

Abbott, John
6424 Ivarene Ave.
Los Angeles, CA 00068
 Actor V: 06/12/92

Abdul, Paula
14755 Ventura Blvd. #1-710
Sherman Oaks, CA 91403
 Actress V: 04/13/92

P.O. Box 885288
San Francisco, CA 94188
 Forwarded V: 12/10/92

Abdul-Jabbar, Kareem
2131 Century Park Ln. #205
Los Angeles, CA 90067
 Basketball V: 12/10/92

1875 Century Park East #1200
Los Angeles, CA 90067
 Alternate V: 02/25/92

Abercrombie, Ian
1080 N. Gardner
Los Angeles, CA 90046
 Actor V: 03/13/93

Abrams Artists
9200 Sunset Blvd. #625
Los Angeles, CA 90069
 Talent Agency V: 01/05/93

Abrams-Rubaloff-Lawrence
8075 West 3rd St. #303
Los Angeles, CA 90048
 Talent Agency V: 01/05/93

Abruzzo, Ray
20334 Pacific Coast Hwy.
Malibu, HI 90265
 Actor V: 03/13/93

Abzug, Bella
2 Fifth Ave.
New York, NY 10011
 Politician V: 03/13/93

Academy Entertainment
9250 Wilshire Blvd.
Beverly Hills, CA 90212
 Publicity V: 01/10/93

Academy Magazine
P.O. Box 5465
San Jose, CA 95150
 Entertainment V: 01/04/93

Academy of Motion Picture A&S
8949 Wilshire Blvd.
Beverly Hills, CA 90211
 Archive V: 01/20/93

Academy of Television A&S
4605 Lankershim Blvd. #800
N. Hollywood, CA 91602
 Archive V: 03/14/93

Ackerman, Forrest
2495 Glendower Ave.
Los Angeles, CA 90027
 Actor V: 03/13/93

Ackroyd, David
12425 Otsego St.
N. Hollywood, CA 91607
 Actor V: 03/13/93

Acquanetta
4415 N. Arcadia Lane
Phoenix, AZ 85018
 Actress V: 03/21/93

Acton, Loren
3251 Hanover St.
Palo Alto, CA 94304-1191
 Astronaut V: 02/24/92

Actors Equity Assoc.
6430 Sunset Blvd. Ste. 1002
Los Angeles, CA 90028
 Actors Union V: 01/03/93

Acuff, Roy
P.O. Box 4623
Nashville, TN 37216
 Singer V: 07/01/92

Adair, Deborah
P.O. Box 1980
Studio City, CA 91604
 Actress V: 11/11/92

Adams, Cindy
1050 Fifth Ave.
New York, NY 10028
 Actress V: 03/14/93

Adams, Don
6310 San Vicente Blvd. #407
Los Angeles, CA 90048
 Actor V: 03/14/93

Adams, Edie
8040 Ocean Terrace
Los Angeles, CA 90046
Actress V: 02/02/92

Adams, Julie
5915 Corbin Ave.
Tarzana, CA 91356
Actress V: 04/12/92

7060 Hollywood Blvd. #610
Hollywood, CA 90028
Alternate V: 02/15/92

Adams, Mason
900 Fifth Ave.
New York, NY 10021
Actor V: 03/14/93

Adams, Maud
15301 Ventura Vlvd. #345
Sherman Oaks, CA 91403
Actress V: 03/13/93

133 S. Lasky Dr. #105
Beverly Hills, CA 90212-1706
L.R.U. V: 01/02/92

12700 Ventura Blvd.#350
Studio City, CA 91604
L.R.U. V: 12/12/92

Adams, Stanley
9526 N. Fairway Blvd.
Sun Lakes, AR 85224
Medal of Honor V: 07/12/92

Adamson, James C.
c/o NASA
LBJ Space Center
Houston, TX 77058
Astronaut V: 04/21/92

Addams, Dawn
c/o Eric Glass
28 Berkely Square
London W1X 6HD, England
Actress V: 01/21/92

Adderly, Herb
9 Pelham Rd.
Philadelphia, PA 19119
Football V: 05/22/92

Addison, John
1948 Palisades Dr.
Pacific Palisades, CA 90272
Composer V: 05/22/92

Adjani, Isabelle
Boite Postale 475-07
F-75327 Paris, France
Actress V: 02/23/93

Presse 1, Adjani
B.P. 475-07
F-75327 Paris, France
Alternate V: 02/28/92

2 Rue Gaston de St. Paul
75016 Paris, France
Forwarded V: 04/21/92

Adler, Lou
3969 Villa Costera
Malibu, CA 90265
Actor V: 03/14/92

Adler, Matt
1923 Talmadge St.
Los Angeles, CA 90027
Actor V: 03/14/93

Adler, Stella
1015 Fifth Ave.
New York, NY 10028
Actress V: 03/14/93

Adorf, Mario
Perlacher Str. 28
D-(W) 8022 Grunwald
Germany
Actor V: 12/10/92

Adrian, Iris
3341 Floyd Terr.
Los Angeles, CA 90068
Actress V: 12/12/92

Adult Ent. Hall of Fame
11142 Fleetwood St. #10
Sun Valley, CA 91352
Hall Hqtrs. V: 01/17/93

Agar, John
639 N. Hollywood Way
Burbank, CA 91505
Actor V: 12/12/92

Agence Cineart
(f. Cineart J. Nainchrik)
34 avenue Champs Elysees
F-75008 Paris France
Talent Agency V: 03/20/93

Agency for Performing Arts
9000 Sunset Blvd. #1200
Los Angeles, CA 90069
Talent Agency V: 05/21/92

Agents Artistiques
Georges Beaume/Guy Bonnet
4 rue de Ponthieu
F-75008 Paris France
Talent Agency V: 03/20/93

Agentur Mattes
Merzstr. 14
D-(W) 8000 Munchen 80, Germany
Talent Agency V: 03/15/93

Agentur Paltz
Ortlindestr. 6/X
D-(W) 8000 Munchen 81, Germany
Talent Agency V: 02/27/93

Agentur Ute Nicolai
Schorlemerallee 16
D-(W) 1000 Berlin 33, Germany
Talent Agency V: 03/20/93

Aghayan, Ray
9314 Lloydcrest Dr.
Los Angeles, CA 90069
Costume Designer V: 03/14/93

Agnew, Spiro T.
78 Columbia Dr.
Rancho Mirage, CA 92270
Politician V: 03/14/93

Agutter, Jenny
6882 Camrose Dr.
Los Angeles, CA 90068
Actress V: 01/15/92

45 Poland St.
London W1, England
Alternate V: 05/23/92

388/396 Oxford St.
London W1 9HE, England
Alternate V: 02/21/92

c/o Cach Haunes
Parracombe, Barnscape
N. Devon, England
Forwarded V: 05/05/92

Aidman, Charles
525 N. Palm Dr.
Beverly Hills, CA 90210
Actor V: 07/02/93

Aiello, Danny
4 Thornhill Dr.
Ramsey, NJ 07446
Actor V: 03/14/93

Aiello, Danny, contd
10000 Santa Monica Bl. #305
Los Angeles, CA 90067
Alternate V: 01/04/92

Aimee, Anouk
10 ave. George V
Paris, 75008 France
Actress V: 01/09/93

Aimee Entertainment Assoc.
13743 Victory Blvd.
Van Nuys, CA 91401
Talent Agency V: 01/02/93

Aja
c/o Five K Sales Co.
9420 Reseda Blvd., #836
Northridge, CA 91324
Adult Films V: 03/03/93

Akers, Thomas D.
c/o NASA
LBJ Space Center
Houston, TX 77058
Astronaut V: 02/12/93

Akins, Claude
1927 Midlothian Dr.
Altadena, CA 91001
Actor V: 03/14/93

151 El Camino Dr.
Beverly Hills, CA 90212
Alternate V: 01/07/92

805 S. Hudson Ave.
Pasadena, CA 91106
L.R.U. V: 01/02/92

Alabama
c/o Morris
818 19th Ave. S.
Nashville, TN 37203
Band V: 01/14/93

P.O. Box 529
Ft. Payne, AL 35967
Alternate V: 03/14/93

Alberghetti, Anna Maria
2337 Benedict Canyon Dr.
Beverly Hills, CA 90210
Actress V: 01/21/93

Albert, Eddie
719 Amalfi Dr.
Pacific Palisades, CA 90272
Actor V: 02/03/92

Albert, Edward
151 El Camino
Beverly Hills, CA 90212
Actor V: 03/01/93

Albert, Herb
c/o A&M Records
1416 N. La Brea Ave.
Hollywood, CA 90028
Musician V: 01/12/93

Albright, Lola
P.O. Box 6067
Glendale, CA 91225
Actress V: 03/14/93

Alcaide, Chris
502 N. Cerritos Rd.
Palm Springs, CA 92262
Actor V: 12/23/92

Alda, Alan
c/o Bregman Prod.
641 Lexington Ave.
New York, NY 10022
Actor V: 01/02/92

c/o Bregman Prod.
100 Universal City Plaza
Universal City, CA 91608
L.R.U. V: 01/05/92

Alda, Antony
15 Seaview Dr. N.
Rolling Hills, CA 90274
Actor V: 03/14/93

Alden, Ginger
4152 Royal Crest Pl.
Memphis, TN 38138
Actress V: 09/02/92

Aldred, Sophie
235-241 Regent St.
London W1A 2JT, England
Actress V: 06/22/92

Aldrin, Edwin "Buzz"
c/o Starcraft Enterprises
233 Emerald Bay
Laguna Beach, CA 92651
Astronaut V: 01/11/93

UofND, Box 8216, Univ.Sta.
Grand Forks, ND 58202
Alternate V: 01/17/92

400 Maryland Ave. S.W.
Washington, D.C. 20546
Forwarded V: 07/02/92

Aletter, Frank
5430 Corbin Ave.
Tarzana, CA 91356
Actor V: 03/14/93

Alexander, Brandi
c/o Evil Angel Video
12229 Montaque St.
Arleta, CA 91331
Adult Actress V: 01/21/93

P.O. Box 113
Hollywood, CA 90078
Alternate V: 01/17/93

Alexander, Daniele
c/o Mercury Records
66 Music Square W.
Nashville, TN 37203
Musician V: 01/25/93

Alexander, Jane
c/o Morris Agency
1350 Ave. of the Americas
New York, NY 10019
Actress V: 11/11/92

RR2 Gordon Rd., Rt.2
Carmel, NY 10512
L.R.U. V: 10/04/92

Alexander, Terence
c/o Brunskill
169 Queen's Gate, Ste.8A
London SW7 5EH, England
Actor V: 03/02/92

Alexis, Kim
111 E. 22nd St.
New York, NY 10023
Model V: 08/04/92

Alfonso, Kristian
Box 93-1628
Hollywood, CA 90093
Actress V: 05/25/92

201 N. Robertson Blvd.#A
Beverly Hills, CA 90211
Alternate V: 02/01/92

Alfonso, Kristian, con'd.
1873 Sunset Plaza
Los Angeles, CA 90069
Forwarded V: 01/02/92

Ali, Muhammad
P.O. Box 187
Berrien Springs, MI 49103
Boxing V: 03/03/93

Ali Akbar Khan
215 W. End Ave.
San Rafael, CA 94901
 Musician V: 04/01/92

Alien Productions
8660 Hayden Pl.
Culver City, CA 90230
 Production Company V: 02/02/93

Alive Films
8271 Melrose Ave.
Los Angeles, CA 90046
 Production Company V: 03/03/93

All Girls Prod.
500 S. Buena Vista
Burbank, CA 91521
 Production Company V: 02/02/93

All Talent Agency
2437 E. Washington Blvd.
Pasadena, CA 91104
 Talent Agency V: 09/07/92

Allan, Jed
c/o 'Santa Barbara'
3000 W. Alameda Ave.
Burbank, CA 91523
 Actor V: 01/02/92

Allen, Andrew M.
c/o NASA/LBJ Space Center
Houston, TX 77058
 Astronaut V: 01/20/93

Allen, Chad
12049 Smokey Ln.
Cerritos, CA 90710
 Actor V: 03/14/93

Allen, Corey
8642 Hollywood Blvd.
Los Angeles, CA 90046
 Actor V: 02/12/92

Allen, Debbie
607 Marguerite Av.
Santa Monica, CA 90403
 Singer V: 03/14/93

4024 Radford Ave., Bl.#3
Studio City, CA 91604
 Alternate V: 01/04/92

Allen, Ginger Lynn
8228 Sunset Blvd. # 212
Los Angeles, CA 90046
 Actress V: 03/14/93

Allen, Joseph P.
c/o NASA/LBJ Space Center
Houston, TX 77058
 Astronaut V: 03/03/93

Allen, Karen
122 E. 10th St.
New York, NY 10013
 Actress V: 07/01/92

Allen, Marty
5750 Wilshire Blvd. #580
Los Angeles, CA 90036-3697
 Actor V: 08/16/92

Allen, Rex
Lone Star Ranch
Box 1111
Sonoita, AZ 85637
 Actor V: 02/15/93

P.O. Box 430
Sonoita, AZ 85637-0430
 Alternate V: 02/20/93

Allen, Sian Barbara
1622 Sierra Bonita Ave.
Los Angeles, CA 90046
 Actress V: 06/21/93

Allen, Steve
Meadowlane Ent.
15201 Burbank Bl. #B
Van Nuys, CA 91411
 Comedian V: 01/13/93

16185 Woodvale Rd.
Encino, CA 91436
 Alternate V: 03/01/93

Allen, Tim
c/o 'Home Improvements'
500 S. Buena Vista St.
Burbank, CA 91521
 Actor V: 11/11/92

8961 Sunset Blvd. #C
Los Angeles, CA 90069
 L.R.U. V: 07/23/92

Allen, Woody
130 W. 57th. St.
New York, NY 10019
 Director V: 03/03/93

930 5th Ave.
New York, NY 10018
 Alternate V: 03/14/93

Allen Talent Agency
260 S. Beverly Dr., 2nd Fl.
Beverly Hills, CA 90212
Talent Agency V: 06/04/92

Allende, Ferdnando
P.O. Box 4232
Aspen, CO 81612
Actor V: 02/14/93

Alley, Kirstie
9320 Wilshire Blvd., 3rd Fl.
Beverly Hills, CA 90212
Actress V: 03/01/93

c/o Paramount
5555 Melrose Ave., Ball. #105
Hollywood, CA 90038-3149
Alternate V: 04/02/92

10390 Santa Monica Blvd.
Los Angeles, CA 90025
L.R.U. V: 06/01/92

Alliance Entertainment
8439 Sunset Blvd. #404
Los Angeles, CA 90069
Production Company V: 03/05/93

Allison, Bobby
Rt. 1, Box 365
Austinville, VA 24312
NASCAR Driver V: 03/03/93

5254 Pit Road South
Harrisburg, NC 28075
Alternate V: 03/02/92

140 Church St.
Hueytown, AL 35020
Forwarded V: 03/02/92

Allison, Davey
140 Church St.
Hueytown, AL 35020
NASCAR Driver V: 03/02/92

115 Dowelle St.
Charlotte, NC 28208
Alternate V: 03/02/92

Allison, Donnie
140 Church St.
Hueytown, AL 35020
NASCAR Driver V: 03/02/92

Allyson, June
1651 Foothill Rd.
Ojai, CA 93020
Actress V: 03/12/93

Alonso, Maria Conchita
1999 Ave. of the Stars #2850
Los Angeles, CA 90067
Actress V: 03/01/93

9455 Eden Dr.
Beverly Hills, CA 90210
Alternate V: 02/17/93

Alt, Carol
163 John St.
Greenwich, CT 06831-8514
Actress V: 08/16/92

Altman, Jeff
151 El Camino
Beverly Hills, CA 90211
Actor V: 03/11/93

Alvarado Agency
8150 Beverly Blvd. #308
Los Angeles, CA 90048
Talent Agency V: 04/04/92

Amblin Entertainment
Universal Studio, Bl. 477
Universal City Plz.
Universal City, CA 91608
Production Company V: 01/02/93

Ambrosio/Mortimer & Assoc.
9150 Wilshire Blvd. #175
Beverly Hills, CA 90212
Talent Agency V: 02/29/92

Ameche, Don
5422 N. 78th Pl.
Scottsdale, AZ 85250-6817
Actor V: 12/30/92

633 Ocean Ave.
Santa Monica, CA 90402
L.R.U. V: 02/23/92

Amendola, Tony
c/o Michael Bloom
9200 Sunset Blvd. #710
Los Angeles, CA 90069
Actor V: 02/23/93

Amer. Museum of Moving Image
34-12 36th St.
Astoria, NY 11106
Archive V: 03/20/93

Amer. Museum of Natural Hist.
Dept. of Library Services
Central Park West at 79th St.
New York, NY 10024
Archive V: 03/20/93

Amer. Archives of Factual Film
Iowa State University Library, I.S.U.
Ames, IA 50011
 Archive V: 02/18/93

American Cinematographer
P.O. Box 2230
Hollywood, CA 90078
 Magazine V: 01/01/93

American Film Inst.
2021 N. Western Ave.
Los Angeles, CA 90027
 Institute Office V: 01/21/93

American Film Magazine
6671 Sunset Blvd. #1514
Hollywood, CA 90028
 Publishers V: 01/23/93

American Guild/Variety Artists
4741 Laurel Canyon, Bl. #208
N. Hollywood, CA 91607
 Actors Union V: 01/21/93

American Horse, George
15010 Ventura Blvd. #219
Sherman Oaks, CA 91403
 Actor V: 03/01/93

526 S. Reese Pl.
Burbank, CA 91506
 Alternate V: 01/22/92

American Indian Registry
3330 Barham Blvd. #208
Los Angeles, CA 90068
 Main Offices V: 02/13/93

American League HQ
350 Park Ave.
New York, NY 10022
 Production Company V: 01/22/93

American Movie Classics
P.O.Box 999
Woodbury, NY 10112
 Network HQ V: 03/01/93

2450 Broadway #500
Santa Monica, CA 90405
 Alternate V: 02/22/93

Ames, Ed
1457 Claridge Dr.
Beverly Hills, CA 90210
 Actor V: 07/18/92

Ames, Leon
1015 Goldenrod Ave.
Corona del Mar, CA 92625
 Actor V: 04/01/93

23388 Mullholland Dr.
Woodland Hills, CA 91364
 Alternate V: 01/15/92

Ames, Rachel
c/o "General Hospital"
4151 Prospect Ave.
Hollywood, CA 90027
 Actress V: 04/01/92

12711 Hacienda Dr.
Studio City, CA 91604
 L.R.U. V: 01/02/92

Ames, Trey
15760 Ventura Blvd. Ste. 1730
Encino, CA 91436
 Actor V: 04/01/93

c/o Universal Studios
100 Universal City Plaza
Universal City, CA 91608
 L.R.U. V: 02/02/92

Amis, Suzi
131 Rodeo Dr. #300
Beverly Hills, CA 90212
 Actress V: 07/01/92

Amos, John
431 W. 162nd St.
New York, NY 10032
 Actor V: 04/01/93

Amos, Wally
P.O. Box 897
Kailua, HA 96734
 Businessman V: 02/11/92

7181 Sunset Blvd.
Los Angeles, CA 90046
 Forwarded V: 02/15/92

Amsel-Eisenstadt-Frazer
6310 San Vincente Blvd. #407
Los Angeles, CA 90048
 Talent Agency V: 10/01/92

Amsterdam, Morey
1012 N. Hillcrest Rd.
Beverly Hills, CA 90210
 Actor V: 03/01/93

Ana-Alicia
c/o Century Artists
9744 Wilshire Blvd. #308
Beverly Hills, CA 90212
Actress V: 03/01/93

c/o CBS-TV
7800 Beverly Blvd. #206
Beverly Hills, CA 90212
Alternate V: 02/02/92

Anders, William A.
c/o NASA
LBJ Space Center
Houston, TX 77058
Astronaut V: 03/03/93

Anderson, Barbara
4345 Enoro Dr.
Los Angeles, CA 90008
Actress V: 10/04/92

Anderson, Carl
2924 Pacific Ave.
Venice, CA 90291
Actor V: 04/01/93

Anderson, Daryl
5923 Wilbur Ave.
Tarzana, CA 91356
Actor V: 06/05/92

Anderson, Erika
c/o Gersh Agency
232 N. Canon Dr.
Beverly Hills, CA 90210
Model V: 02/13/93

Anderson, Harry
1420 N.W. Gilman Blvd.
Suite 2123
Issaquah, WA 98027-5333
Actor V: 04/01/93

Anderson, Jo
c/o ICM
8942 Wilshire Blvd.
Beverly Hills, CA 90211
Actress V: 04/13/92

Anderson, John
P.O. Box 2977
Hendersonville, TN 37077
Singer V: 01/11/93

Anderson, Lois
50 Catalpa
Mill Valley, CA 94941
Artist V: 03/10/93

Anderson, Loni
Sandy Hook Prod.
20652 Lassen #98
Chatsworth, CA 91311
Actress V: 06/01/92

1001 Indiantown Rd.
Jupiter, FL 33456
Alternate V: 10/30/92

Anderson, Louie
8033 Sunset Blvd. #605
Los Angeles, CA 90046
Comedian V: 04/02/92

Anderson, Lynn
4925 Tyne Valley Blvd.
Nashville, TN 37220
Singer V: 04/21/92

Anderson, Mary
1127 Norman Pl.
Los Angeles, CA 90024
Actress V: 04/01/93

Anderson, Melissa Sue
20722 Pacific Coast Hwy.
Malibu, CA 90265
Actress V: 01/19/92

Anderson, Melody
10433 Wilshire Bl.#1203
Los Angeles, CA 90024
Actress V: 04/13/92

Anderson, Paul
P.O. Box 52S, 1603 McIntosh St.
Vidalia, GA 30474-0525
Olympian V: 07/01/92

Anderson, Richard
10120 Cielo Dr.
Beverly Hills, CA 90210
Actor V: 01/19/92

Anderson, Richard Dean
16030 Ventura Blvd., #380
Encino, CA 91436
Actor V: 06/21/92

8942 Wilshire Blvd.
Beverly Hills, CA 90211
Alternate V: 03/12/92

1122 S. Robertson Blvd.
Los Angeles, CA 90035
Alternate V: 01/21/91

Anderson, Richard Dean, contd
c/o Paramount TV "MacGyver"
5555 Melrose Ave.
Los Angeles, CA 90038
 Forwarded V: 12/07/92

Anderson, Sam
2611 N. Beachwood Dr.
Los Angeles, CA 90068
 Actor V: 02/21/93

Andreas, Christine
c/o "Another World"
79 Madison Ave., 5th Fl.
New York, NY 10012
 Actress V: 06/15/92

Andretti, Mario
53 Victory Ln.
Nazareth, PA 18064
 Race Driver V: 02/21/92

Andrews Sisters
14200 Carriage Oaks Ln.
Auburn, CA 91436
 Singers V: 01/05/92

Andrews, Anthony
c/o Duncan Heath
162 Wardour St.
Paramount House
London W1V 3AT, England
 Actor V: 02/23/92

Andrews, David
888 Seventh Ave. #1602
New York, NY 10019
 Actor V: 01/12/92

Andrews, Julie
P.O. Box 666
Beverly Hills, CA 90213
 Actress V: 05/02/92

Andrews, Maxene
14200 Carriage Oak Ln.
Auburn, CA 95603
 Singer V: 01/11/93

Andrews, Patti
c/o Weschler
9823 Aldea Ave.
Northridge, CA 91354
 Singer V: 01/11/93

Andrews, Tige
4914 Encino Terrace
Encino, CA 91316
 Actor V: 07/07/92

Andrews, Tige, contd
15010 Ventura Blvd. #219
Sherman Oaks, CA 91403
 Alternate V: 03/31/92

Angel
c/o Intropics Video
7131 Owensmouth Ave. #104B
Canoga Park, CA 91303
 Actress V: 04/02/92

Angel, Vanessa
853 7th Ave. #9-A
New York, NY 10019
 Actress V: 06/21/92

c/o APA
9000 Sunset Blvd.
Los Angeles, CA 90069
 Alternate V: 11/11/92

Angel City Talent
8228 Sunset Blvd. #311
Los Angeles, CA 90046
 Talent Agency V: 10/01/92

Angelyne
P.O. Box 3864
Beverly Hills, CA 90212
 Actress V: 03/03/93

Anger, Kenneth
6028 Barton Way
Los Angeles, CA 90038
 Actor V: 02/11/93

Anglim, Jennifer
3257 Primera Ave.
Los Angeles, CA 90068
 Actress V: 04/21/92

Anglim, Phillip
2404 Grand Canal
Venice, CA 90291
 Actor V: 01/04/93

Animation Magazine
P.O. Box 25547
Los Angeles, CA 90025
 Publishers V: 01/21/93

Anka, Paul
140 Tropicana Ave. E.
Las Vegas, NV 89109
 Singer V: 06/06/92

Ann-Margret
435 N. Bedford Dr. #1000
Beverly Hills, CA 90210
 Actress V: 03/03/93

2707 Benedict Canyon Rd.
Beverly Hills, CA 90210
Alternate V: 02/29/92

Annabella
1 Rue Pierret
92200 Neuilly, France
Actress V: 08/08/92

Annis, Francesca
c/o Agency
22 Grafton St.
London, England
Actress V: 02/21/92

Ansara, Michael
4624 Park Mirasol
Calabasas, CA 91302
Actor V: 09/04/92

Anselmo, Nickole
c/o Dallas Cowboys
One Cowboys Parkway
Irving, TX 75063-4945
Cheerleader V: 08/08/92

Anspach, Susan
473 16th St.
Santa Monica, CA 90402
Actress V: 03/11/92

Answer Fan
1112 First St. #134
Coronado, CA 92118
Mail Service V: 02/23/93

Ant, Adam
P.O. Box 866
London SE1 3AP, England
Singer V: 03/03/93

Anthology Film Archives
32-34 Second Ave.
New York, NY 11106
Archive V: 03/20/93

Antin, Steve
6909 Clinton St.
Los Angeles, CA 90036
Actor V: 07/29/92

Anton, Susan
16830 Ventura Blvd. #1616
Encino, CA 91436
Actress V: 02/17/92

1853 Noel Pl.
Beverly Hills, CA 90210
Forwarded V: 11/24/92

Antonio, Lou
530 Gaylord Dr.
Burbank, CA 91505
Actor V: 03/02/92

Apodaca Agency
2049 Century Park E. #1200
Century City, CA 90067
Talent Agency V: 10/01/92

Applegate, Christina
c/o Lynn
4527 Park Allegra
Calabasas, CA 91302
Actress V: 03/01/93

P.O. Box 900
Beverly Hills, CA 90213
Alternate V: 04/04/92

c/o Fox TV
10201 W. Pico Blvd.
Los Angeles, CA 90035
Forwarded V: 04/02/92

11223 Sunshine Terrace
Studio City, CA 91604
Forwarded V: 03/05/93

Aprea, John
c/o "Another World"
Fifth Floor
79 Madison Ave.
New York, NY 91523
Actor V: 07/21/92

Apt, Jerome
c/o NASA/LBJ Space Center
Houston, TX 77058
Astronaut V: 05/22/92

Arbus, Allan
2208 N. Beverly Glen
Los Angeles, CA 90025
Actor V: 01/04/93

Arbus, Loreen
8841 Appian Way
Los Angeles, CA 90046
Actress V: 03/13/93

Archer, Anne
13201 Old Oak Lane
Los Angeles, CA 90049-2501
Actress V: 06/01/92

Archer, Dave
P.O. Box 150180
San Rafael, CA 94915
Artist V: 08/08/92

Archer, Dave, contd
c/o Swanson Gallery
3040 Larkin St.
San Francisco, CA 94109
Alternate V: 12/12/92

Archer, Tasmin
39 St. Oswalds Terr.
Guiseley/Bradford, England
Singer V: 03/20/93

Archerd, Army
442 Hilgard Ave.
Los Angeles, CA 90024
Commentator V: 02/21/92

Archibald, Dottie
10372 Tennessee Ave.
Los Angeles, CA 90064
Actress V: 04/01/92

Archive Photos
530 W. 25th St. 6th Fl.
New York, NY 10001
Photo Archives V: 02/27/93

Argenziano, Carmen
853 Kemp St.
Burbank, CA 91505
Actor V: 09/09/92

Arista Films
16027 Ventura Bl.#305
Encino, CA 91436
Production Company V: 02/21/93

Arista Records
6 W. 57th St.
New York, NY 10019
Company Offices V: 01/21/93

Arkin, Adam
9460 Hidden Valley Rd.
Beverly Hills, CA 90210
Actor V: 03/02/93

50 Ridge Dr.
Chappauqua, NY 10514
L.R.U. V: 10/10/92

Arletty
14 Rue de Rimusat
75016 Paris, France
Actress V: 10/10/92

Armani, Giorgio
650 Fifth Ave.
New York, NY 10019
Designer V: 10/10/92

Armatrading, Joan
27 Queensdale Place
London W11 45Q, England
Singer V: 05/24/92

Armed Forces TV/Radio
10888 La Tuna Canyon Rd.
Sun Valley, CA 91352-2098
Production Company V: 02/01/93

Arms, Russell
2018 Davis Way
Palm Springs, CA 92262-2020
Actor V: 04/02/92

Armstrong, Bess
1518 N. Doheny Dr.
Los Angeles, CA 90069-1104
Actress V: 07/14/92

Armstrong, Jim
c/o King Features
216 East 45th St.
New York, NY 10017
Cartoonist V: 03/21/93

Armstrong, Neil
P.O. Box 436
Lebanon, OH 45036
Astronaut V: 04/03/92

1739 N. State St. Rt.123
Lebanon, OH 45036
Alternate V: 03/02/93

Armstrong, R.G.
3856 Reklan Dr.
Studio City, CA 91607
Actor V: 04/21/92

c/o Contemporary Karma
132 S. Lasky Dr. #B
Beverly Hills, CA 90712
Alternate V: 10/01/92

Armstrong, Tom
c/o King Features
216 East 45th St.
New York, NY 10017
Cartoonist V: 02/03/93

Arnaz, Lucie
560 Tigertail Rd.
Los Angeles, CA 90049
Actress V: 01/02/92

470 Main St., Ste.K
Ridgefield, CT 06877
Alternate V: 11/19/92

Arnaz, Lucie, contd
Wilder #214
5555 Melrose Ave.
Los Angeles, CA 90038
Forwarded V: 01/07/92

40 W. 57th. St.
New York, NY 10019
L.R.U. V: 01/02/92

Arnaz, Jr., Desi
P.O. Box 60684
Boulder City, NV 89006
Entertainer V: 08/15/92

c/o Success
Box 2000
Ojai, CA 93023
Alternate V: 02/20/92

Arngrim, Allison
1340 N. Poinsetta Pl. #422
Los Angeles, CA 90046
Actress V: 03/01/92

Arnold, Debbie
12 Cambridge Park
East Twickenham
Middlesex TW1 2PF
England
Actress V: 04/23/92

Arnold, Eddy
P.O. Box 97
Brentwood, TN 37027
Singer V: 02/01/92

Arnold, Roseanne
14755 Ventura Blvd. #1-170
Sherman Oaks, CA 91403
Actress V: 03/01/93

c/o Carsey-Werner
'Roseanne'
4024 Radford Ave.
Studio City, CA 91604
Forwarded V: 12/07/92

12916 Evonton
Los Angeles, CA 90049
L.R.U. V: 07/23/92

Arnold, Tom
14755 Ventura Blvd. #1-170
Sherman Oaks, CA 91403
Actor V: 03/01/93

Arquette, David
616 N. Gower
Los Angeles, CA 90004
Actor V: 01/12/93

Arquette, Lewis
616 N. Gower
Los Angeles, CA 90004
Actor V: 12/31/92

Arquette, Rosanna
1201 N. Alta Loma Rd.
Los Angeles, CA 90069
Actress V: 06/02/92

9056 Santa Monica Blvd.
Hollywood, CA 90069
Alternate V: 05/21/92

8966 Sunset Blvd.
Hollywood, CA 90069
L.R.U. V: 01/02/92

9830 Wilshire Blvd.
Beverly Hills, CA 90212
L.R.U. V: 07/01/92

Arrington, Buddy
c/o NASCAR
1811 Volusia Ave.
Daytona Beach, FL 32015
NASCAR Driver V: 03/02/92

Arthur, Bea
2000 Old Ranch Rd.
Los Angeles, CA 90049
Actress V: 02/20/92

c/o Witt/Thomas/Harris
'Golden Palace'
846 N. Cahuenga Blvd. Bl.G
Hollywood, CA 90038
Alternate V: 01/17/93

Arthur & Associates
9363 Wilshire Blvd. #212
Beverly Hills, CA 90210
Talent Agency V: 05/21/92

Artist Network
12001 Ventura Pl., Ste.331
Studio City, CA 91604
Talent Agency V: 04/23/92

Artists Agency
10000 Santa Monica Blvd. #305
Los Angeles, CA 90067
Talent Agency V: 07/29/92

Artists First
8230 Beverly Blvd. #23
Los Angeles, CA 90048
Talent Agency V: 01/02/93

Artists Group
c/o Artists Group
1930 Century Park W. #403
Los Angeles, CA 90067
Talent Agency V: 02/23/93

Artists Management Agency
4340 Campus Dr., Ste. 212
Newport Beach, CA 92660
Talent Agency V: 05/21/92

Artmedia
10 ave. George V
F-75008 Paris, France
Talent Agency V: 02/27/93

Arvesen, Nina
c/o "Y & R"
7800 Beverly Blvd.
Los Angeles, CA 90036
Actress V: 06/15/92

Asbury, Martin
c/o King Features
216 E. 45th St.
New York, NY 10017
Cartoonist V: 03/11/93

Ash, Angel
c/o 5K Sales
9420 Reseda Blvd., Ste. 836
Northridge, CA 91324
Adult Films V: 01/17/93

Ashbrook, Dana
2634 N. Beachwood Dr.
Los Angeles, CA 90068
Actor V: 02/12/93

Asher, Jane
c/o The Globe Theatre
Shaftsbury Ave.
London W1, England
Actress V: 09/09/92

c/o Chatto
Prince of Wales Theatre
Coventry St.
London SW1, England
Alternate V: 12/14/92

Ashford, Matthew
10925 Hesby St.
N. Hollywood, CA 91601
Actor V: 04/09/92

Ashford & Simpson
254 W. 72nd St., Ste. 1A
New York, NY 10023
Singers V: 07/09/92

Ashley, Elizabeth
9010 Dorrington Ave.
Beverly Hills, CA 90211
Actress V: 04/07/92

c/o "Evening Shade"
Bldg. 5
Room 104
4024 Radford Ave.
Studio City, CA 91604
Forwarded V: 05/15/92

Ashley, Jennifer
200 N. Robertson Blvd. #219
Beverly Hills, CA 90211
Actress V: 03/01/92

Ashley, John
18067 Lake Encino Dr.
Encino, CA 91316-4433
Actor V: 03/12/93

Ashton, John
22625 Town Crier Rd.
Woodland Hills, CA 91364
Actor V: 04/22/92

Ashworth, Lauren
c/o Dallas Cowboys
One Cowboys Parkway
Irving, TX 75063-4945
Cheerleader V: 08/08/92

Askin, Leon
625 N. Rexford Dr.
Beverly Hills, CA 90210
Actor V: 03/02/92

P.O. Box 124
Beverly Hills, CA 90213
Alternate V: 02/13/92

Askwith, Robin
388-396 Oxford St.
London W1 9HE, England
Actor V: 03/20/92

Asner, Ed
3855 Lankershim Blvd.
N. Hollywood, CA 91604
Actor V: 07/18/92

4348 Van Nuys Blvd. #207
Sherman Oaks, CA 91403
Alternate V: 06/26/92

3575 W. Cahuenga Blvd. #570
Los Angeles, CA 90068
Forwarded V: 02/08/93

Aspin, Les
Dept. of Defense
The Pentagon
Washington, DC 20301
Secretary/Defense *V: 01/31/93*

Assante, Armand
RD#1, Box 561
Campbell Hall, NY 10916
Actor *V: 04/01/93*

Assia, Lys
Hotel Marionlyst
DK-3000 Helsingor
Denmark
Singer *V: 01/19/93*

Assoc. of Space Explorers
35 White St.
San Francisco, CA 94109
Space Society *V: 01/21/93*

Assoc. of Talent Agencies
9255 Sunset Blvd. #318
Los Angeles, CA 90069
Listing *V: 03/17/93*

Ast, Pat
1336 ¾ N. June St.
Los Angeles, CA 90028
Actress *V: 03/03/93*

205 E. Beverly Dr. #210
Beverly Hills, CA 90212
L.R.U. *V: 12/08/92*

Astin, John
P.O. Box 49698
Los Angeles, CA 90049
Actor *V: 01/02/92*

Astin, Mackenzie
P.O. Box 385
Beverly Hills, CA 90213
Actor *V: 04/01/93*

Astin, Sean
438 Norwich Ave.
Van Nuys, CA 91401
Actor *V: 02/22/93*

c/o Byron Ltd.
4354 Laurel Canyon Blvd. #301
Studio City, CA 91604
Alternate *V: 02/08/93*

Atkins, Chet
1013 17th St. South
Nashville, TN 37212
Singer *V: 01/12/92*

Atkins, Christopher
3751 Sunswept Dr.
Studio City, CA 91604
Actor *V: 01/16/93*

Atkins, Doug
5312 E. Sunset Rd.
Knoxville, TN 37914
Football *V: 03/17/92*

Atkins & Associates
305 South Crescent Hts. Blvd.
Los Angeles, CA 90048
Talent Agency *V: 01/02/93*

Atkinson, Rowan
c/o Jones
47 Dean St.
London W1, England
Actor *V: 06/03/92*

Atlanta Braves
P.O. Box 4064
Atlanta-Fulton County Stad.
Atlanta, GA 30312
Team Office *V: 03/21/93*

Atlanta Falcons
Suwanee Road & I-85
Suwanee, GA 30174
Team Office *V: 02/07/93*

Atlantic Group
8255 Sunset Blvd.
Los Angeles, CA 90046
Production Company *V: 07/22/93*

Atlantic Records
9229 Sunset Blvd., Ste. 710
Los Angeles, CA 90069-2474
Studio HQ *V: 01/02/93*

Attenborough, Richard
Old Friars, Richmond Green
Surrey, England
Director *V: 01/14/92*

Atterbury, Malcolm
605 N. Camden Dr.
Beverly Hills, CA 90210
Actor *V: 02/05/93*

Attkisson, Sharyl
One CNN Center
P.O. Box 105366
Atlanta, GA 30348
Reporter *V: 11/11/92*

Auberjonois, Rene
448 S. Arden Blvd.
Los Angeles, CA 90020
Actor V: 12/11/92

c/o Marion Rosenberg
8428 Melrose Pl., Ste.C
Los Angeles, CA 90046
Alternate V: 02/23/93

Aubrey, James
16161 Ventura Blvd. #402
Encino, CA 91436
Producer V: 02/02/93

Auel, Jean M.
P.O. Box 430
Sherwood, OR 97140
Writer V: 05/21/92

Auer Talent Agency
8344 Melrose Ave., Ste. 29
Los Angeles, CA 90069
Talent Agency V: 09/07/92

Auerbach, Red
P.O. Box 8607
Boston, MA 02114
Sports Coach V: 04/05/92

Aumont, Jean-Pierre
259 W. Channel Rd.
Santa Monica, CA 90402
Actor V: 05/21/92

4 alle des Brouillards
F-75018 Droue-sur Drouette
France
Alternate V: 06/07/92

Austin, Patti
641 Fifth Ave.
New York, NY 10022
Singer V: 03/11/93

c/o Newley Assoc.
245 Fifth Ave.
New York, NY 10016
L.R.U. V: 02/02/92

Austin, Teri
4245 Laurel Grove Ave.
Studio City, CA 91604
Actress V: 03/11/93

Autry, Alan
1930 Century Park W. #403
Los Angeles, CA 90067
Actor V: 11/11/92

Autry, Gene
5858 Sunset Blvd.
P.O. Box 710
Hollywood, CA 90078
Actor V: 09/21/92

c/o Gene Autry Hotel
4200 E. Palm Canyon Dr.
Palm Springs, CA 92262
Forwarded V: 02/03/93

3171 Brookdale Rd.
N. Hollywood, CA 91604
L.R.U. V: 03/24/92

Avalon, Frankie
6311 De Soto Ave. #1
Woodland Hills, CA 91367
Actor V: 05/25/92

Avery, Margaret
P.O. Box 3493
Los Angeles, CA 90078
Actress V: 01/14/93

Avila, Leticia
c/o Dallas Cowboys
One Cowboys Parkway
Irving, TX 75063-4945
Cheerleader V: 08/08/92

Axton, Hoyt
P.O. Box 614
Tahoe City, CA 95730
Singer V: 01/12/93

3135 Cedarwood Dr.
Tahoe City, CA 95730
Forwarded V: 07/15/92

Aykroyd, Dan
11288 Ventura Blvd. #371
Studio City, CA 91604
Actor V: 03/14/93

3960 Laurel Canyon Blvd. #371
Studio City, CA 91604
Alternate V: 03/01/93

8955 Beverly Blvd.
Beverly Hills, CA 90211
Forwarded V: 05/05/92

c/o D.E.A.-Warner Bros.
4000 Warner Blvd.
Producers 2
Suite 1104
Burbank, CA 91522
Forwarded V: 01/17/92

Ayres, Lew
675 Walther Way
Los Angeles, CA 90049
Actor V: 07/23/92

Ayres, Lois
c/o Five K Sales Co.
9420 Reseda Blvd., #836
Northridge, CA 91324
Adult Films V: 03/03/93

Azaria, Hank
c/o "Hermans Head"
500 S. Buena Vista St.
Burbank, CA 91521
Actor V: 11/11/92

Azinger, Paul
4520 Beat Tree Blvd.
Sarasota, FL 34241
Golfer V: 02/04/92

Aznavour, Charles
4 ave. De Lieulee
Gallius, 78 France
Actor V: 11/12/92

Azzara, Candy
1155 N. La Cienega Blvd. #307
Los Angeles, CA 90069
Actress V: 03/15/93

B

B-52's
P.O. Box 506
Canal Street Station
New York, NY 10013
Musical Group V: 03/15/93

B.O.P.-L.A. Talent Agency
1467 N. Tamarind Ave.
Los Angeles, CA 90028
Talent Agency V: 06/04/92

BACK TO THE FUTURE
Universal Cartoon Studios
100 Universal City Plaza
Building 473, Room 108
Universal City, CA 91608
Production Company V: 03/18/93

BBC-TV Center
Wood Lane
London, W12 8QT, England
Network HQ V: 02/27/93

BDP &/Associates
10637 Burbank Blvd.
N. Hollywood, CA 91601
Talent Agency V: 11/21/92

BEVERLY HILLS 90210
P.O. Box 884044
San Francisco, CA 94188
Production Office V: 12/10/92

BLOSSOM
c/o Witt/Thomas/Harris
846 N. Cahuenga Blvd., Bl. K
Hollywood, CA 90038
Production Company V: 01/17/93

BOB
Paramount Television
5555 Melrose Ave.
Mae West Building, Rm. 107
Los Angeles, CA 90038
Production Company V: 03/15/93

BOB HOPE SPECIALS
Hope Enterprises
3808 Riverside Dr.
Burbank, CA 91505
TV Program V: 03/23/93

BOLD AND THE BEAUTIFUL
7800 Beverly Blvd., Ste.3371
Los Angeles, CA 90036
Production Company V: 12/19/92

BROOKLYN BRIDGE
5555 Melrose Ave.
Building 329, Rm. 113
Los Angeles, CA 90038
Production Company V: 03/15/93

Babbitt, Bruce
Dept. of the Interior
1849 C St., N.W.
Washington, DC 20240
Secretary/Interior V: 01/31/93

Babcock, Barbara
530 W. California Blvd.
Pasadena, CA 91105-1636
Actress V: 03/15/93

1244 11th Street #A
Santa Monica, CA 90401
Alternate V: 05/01/92

211 S. Beverly Dr. #201
Beverly Hills, CA 90212
L.R.U. V: 01/02/92

Babilonia, Tai
933 21st St. #6
Santa Monica, CA 90402
Ice Skater V: 03/15/93

8730 Sunset Blvd., 6th Fl.
Los Angeles, CA 90069
Alternate V: 02/21/92

2331 Century Hill
Los Angeles, CA 90067
Forwarded V: 02/03/93

Bacall, Lauren
1 W. 72nd St. #43
New York, NY 10023
Actress V: 07/01/92

c/o Turner Pictures
1888 Century Park E.
Los Angeles, CA 90067
Alternate V: 06/14/92

Bach, Barbara
La Rocca Bella
14 ave. Princess Grace
Monte Carlo, Monaco
Actress V: 03/14/93

Bach, Catherine
14000 Davana Terrace
Sherman Oaks, CA 91403
Actress V: 03/14/93

Bacharach, Burt
658 Nimes Rd.
Los Angeles, CA 90077
Composer V: 03/13/93

Bacon, Kevin
Interscope Communications
10900 Wilshire Blvd. #1400
Los Angeles, CA 90024
Actor V: 03/14/93

194 Riverside Dr. #7B
New York, NY 19925
L.R.U. V: 06/01/92

Badgley, Conner
9229 Sunset Blvd. #607
Los Angeles, CA 90069
Talent Agency V: 04/04/92

Badler, Jane
10000 Santa Monica Blvd., #305
Los Angeles, CA 90067
Actress V: 01/02/92

Baer, Parley
4967 Bilmoor Ave.
Tarzana, CA 91356
Actor V: 03/13/93

Baer Jr., Max
10433 Wilshire Blvd. #103
Los Angeles, CA 90024-4613
Actor V: 03/13/93

Baez, Joan
P.O. Box 1026
Menlo Park, CA 94026
Singer V: 01/11/92

Baggetta, Vincent
3928 Madelia Ave.
Sherman Oaks, CA 91403
Actor V: 03/11/93

Bagian, James P.
c/o NASA/LBJ Space Center
Houston, TX 77058
Astronaut V: 03/03/93

Bailey, F. Lee
1275 K St. N.W., Ste. 800
Washington, DC 20005
Lawyer V: 03/02/93

Bailey, Jim
1326 N. Fairfax Ave.
Los Angeles, CA 90046
Actor V: 03/11/93

Bailey, Joel
6550 Murietta Ave.
Van Nuys, CA 91401
Actor V: 03/11/93

Bain, Conrad
1230 Chickory Lane
Los Angeles, CA 90049
Actor V: 12/12/92

Baio, Scott
11662 Duque Dr.
Studio City, CA 91604
Actor V: 06/21/92

Baker, Anita
804 N. Crescent Dr.
Beverly Hills, CA 90210
Singer V: 08/16/92

Baker, Buck
NC Motor Speedway, Box 500
Rockingham, NC 28379
NASCAR Driver V: 03/02/92

Baker, Buddy
c/o NASCAR
1811 Volusia Ave.
Daytona Beach, FL 32015
NASCAR Driver V: 03/02/92

Baker, Carroll
c/o Agent
22 Grafton St.
London W1, England
Actress V: 01/21/92

155 E. 44th St.
New York, NY 10017
L.R.U. V: 04/02/92

Baker, Colin
Grafton House, #42/43
2-3 Golden Square
London W1R 3AD, England
Actor V: 02/06/92

Baker, Diane
P.O. Box 691501
Los Angeles, CA 90069
Actress V: 06/16/92

Baker, Ellen S.
c/o NASA
LBJ Space Center
Houston, TX 77058
Astronaut V: 09/01/92

Baker, Joe Don
10000 Santa Monica Blvd. #305
Los Angeles, CA 90067
Actor V: 03/30/93

Baker, Kathy
c/o Intl. Mngmt. Grp.
1 Erieview Plaza
Cleveland, OH 44114
Golf V: 11/23/92

Baker, Lisa Ann
1239 S. Glendale Ave.
Glendale, CA 91205
Actress V: 12/01/92

Baker, Michael A.
c/o NASA/ LBJ Space Center
Houston, TX 77058
Astronaut V: 04/27/92

Baker, Roy Ward
c/o Leading Artists
60 Saint James St.
London SW1, England
Director V: 05/02/92

Baker, Scott T.
c/o "General Hospital"
4151 Prospect Ave.
Hollywood, CA 90027
Actor V: 03/01/92

Baker, Terry
1800 Orranco Bldg.
1001 S.W. 5th Ave.
Portland, OR 97204-1162
Football V: 05/15/92

Baker, Tom
235/241 Regent St.
London, W1A 2JR England
Actor V: 02/14/92

c/o Burnett, Ste. 42
Grafton House, 2 Golden Sq.
London W1, England
Alternate V: 03/21/92

Bakker, Jim
Federal Medical Center
2110 Center St. E.
Rochester, MN 59901
Evangelist V: 06/05/92

Bakker, Tammy Faye
P.O. Box 690788
Orlando, FL 32869
Evangelist V: 03/06/92

Bakula, Scott
247 S. Beverly Dr. #102
Beverly Hills, CA 90210
Actor V: 04/01/92

c/o Belisarius
"Quantum Leap"
100 Universal City Plz.
Universal City, CA 91608
Alternate V: 08/01/92

Balding, Rebecca
20011 Winnetka Place
Woodland Hills, CA 91364
Actress V: 03/10/93

Baldwin, Adam
151 El Camino Dr.
Beverly Hills, CA 90212
Actor V: 03/11/93

Baldwin, Alec
9830 Wilshire Blvd.
Beverly Hills, CA 90212
Actor V: 03/11/93

Baldwin, Alec, contd
c/o Bloom
233 Park Ave. South, 10th Fl.
New York, NY 10003
Alternate V: 03/12/93

9200 Sunset Blvd., #710
Los Angeles, CA 90069
Forwarded V: 12/02/92

Baldwin, Gerald
3400 Cahuenga Blvd.
Los Angeles, CA 90068
Producer V: 03/01/93

Baldwin, Stephen
c/o Semm
22 W. 19th St., 8th Fl.
New York, NY 10011
Actor V: 03/12/93

P.O. Box 447
Camilus, NY 13031-0447
Alternate V: 05/04/92

Baldwin, William
9200 Sunset Blvd., Ste. 700
Los Angeles, CA 90069
Actor V: 03/12/93

Baldwin Talent
1801 Ave. of the Stars #640
Los Angeles, CA 90067
Talent Agency V: 02/29/92

Bale, Christian
c/o Pine Files Ltd.
6A Wyndham Place
London W1H 1TN, Engalnd
Actor V: 02/21/92

Balenda, Carla
c/o Rutter
15848 Woodvale
Encino, CA 91316
Actress V: 03/12/93

Balin, Marty
436 Belvedere St.
San Francisco, CA 94117
Singer V: 07/30/92

P.O. Box 347008
San Francisco, CA 94134
Alternate V: 02/26/92

Ball Talent Agency
8075 W. Third St. #550
Los Angeles, CA 90048
Talent Agency V: 02/29/92

Ballantine, Carl
6767 Forest Lawn Dr. #115
Los Angeles, CA 90068
Actor V: 03/02/92

10850 Riverside Dr. #501
N. Hollywood, CA 91602
L.R.U. V: 01/02/92

Ballard, Christine
11501 Chandler Blvd.
N. Hollywood, CA 91601
Actress V: 03/13/93

Ballard, Donald E.
801 NE 98th Terrace
Kansas City, MO 64155
Medal of Honor V: 03/17/93

Ballard, Dr. R. D.
Oceanographic Inst.
Woods Hole, MA 02543
Scientist V: 02/21/93

Ballard, Kaye
1204 3rd Ave. #152
New York, NY 10021-5102
Actress V: 03/13/93

211 E. 70th St. #20-C
New York, NY 10021-5102
Forwarded V: 03/09/92

Ballesteros, Serviano
Padrena
Santander, Spain
Golfer V: 01/19/93

Ballesteros, Seve
Ruiz Zorrilla 16-20J
39009 Santander, Spain
Golfer V: 01/22/92

Ballou, Mark
9348 Civic Center Dr.
4th Fl.
Beverly Hills, CA 90210
Actor V: 01/15/93

145 Ave. of Americas
2nd Fl.
New York, NY 10013
Alternate V: 11/12/92

Balsam, Martin
27 W. 72nd St.
New York, NY 10011
Actor V: 03/14/93

Baltimore Orioles
Memorial Stadium
Baltimore, MD 21218
Team Office V: 07/21/92

Banarama
3 Barnston Towers
Heswall, Wirral
Merseyside L6O 2WF
England
Musical Group V: 02/11/93

Bancroft, Anne
2301 La Mesa Dr.
Santa Monica, CA 90405
Actress V: 01/21/92

P.O. Box 900
Beverly Hills, CA 90213
Alternate V: 02/01/92

Banks, Jonathan
909 Euclid St. #8
Santa Monica, CA 90403
Actor V: 02/03/92

c/o Cannell Prod.
7083 Hollywood Blvd.
Hollywood, CA 90028
Alternate V: 02/22/92

Bannock, Russell G.
11 Doncliffe Dr.
Toronto, Ont., Canada M4N 2E5
War Hero V: 07/21/92

Bannon, Jack
5832 Nagle Ave.
Van Nuys, CA 91401
Actor V: 12/13/92

Barbeau, Adrienne
P.O. Box 1334
N. Hollywood, CA 91604
Actress V: 07/01/92

Barber, Glynis
22 Morley House/314 Regent St.
London W1, England
Actress V: 03/23/92

c/o James Sharkey Mgmt.
15 Golden Sq., 3rd Fl.
London W1R 3AG, England
Alternate V: 06/06/92

Barbera, Joseph R.
3400 Cahenga Blvd.
Los Angeles, CA 90068
Animator V: 03/03/93

Bardot, Brigitte
La Madrique
83990 St. Tropez, France
Actress V: 06/01/92

71 Ave. Paul Doumer
Paris 16, France
Forwarded V: 04/12/92

Bare Facts
c/o Craig Hosoda
P.O. Box 3255
Santa Clara, CA 95055
Video Guide V: 12/10/92

Barkdoll, Phil
c/o NASCAR
1811 Volusia Ave.
Daytona Beach, FL 32015
NASCAR Driver V: 03/02/92

Barker, Bob
c/o Goodson Prod.
5750 Wilshire Blvd.
Los Angeles, CA 90036-3697
TV Host V: 11/11/92

1851 Outpost Dr.
Los Angeles, CA 90069
Alternate V: 11/11/92

Barker, Ronnie
c/o Zahl
57 Great Cumberland Place
London W1H 7LJ, England
Actor V: 09/29/92

Barker Productions
c/o Bob Barker
9201 Wilshire Blvd. #201
Beverly Hills, CA 90210
Production Company V: 03/17/92

Barkin, Ellen
8787 Shoreham Dr.
Los Angeles, CA 90069
Actress V: 03/14/93

40 W. 57th St.
New York, NY 10019
Alternate V: 11/11/92

3007 Lake Glen
Beverly Hills, CA 90210
L.R.U. V: 06/01/92

Barnes, Binnie
838 N. Doheny Dr. #B
Los Angeles, CA 90069
Actress V: 02/13/92

Barnes, Binnie, contd
9200 Sunset Blvd. #801
Los Angeles, CA 90069
L.R.U. *V: 01/02/92*

Barnes, Julian
c/o "Y & R"
7800 Beverly Blvd.
Beverly Hills, CA 90036
Actor *V: 06/15/92*

Barnes, Priscilla
3500 W. Olive Ave. #1400
Burbank, CA 91505
Actress *V: 03/15/93*

Barnett, Jerry
P.O. Box 145
307 N. Pennsylvania St.
Indianapolis, IN 46206-0145
Cartoonist *V: 06/17/92*

Barnum, Jr., H.C.
3903 Sabal Palm Ct.
Brandon, FL 33511
Medal of Honor *V: 12/17/92*

Baron, Blaire
1930 Century Park W. #403
Los Angeles, CA 90067
Actress *V: 02/23/93*

Barr, Doug
515 S. Irving Blvd.
Los Angeles, CA 90020
Actor *V: 04/21/92*

Barr Talent Agency
P.O. Box 69590
Los Angeles, CA 90069
Talent Agency *V: 10/01/92*

Barrett, Alice
NBC-TV/"Another World"
79 Madison Ave., 5th Fl.
New York, NY 91523
Actress *V: 06/15/92*

Barrett, Majel
P.O. Box 691370
Los Angeles, CA 90069
Actress *V: 06/10/92*

10615 Bellagio Rd.
Los Angeles, CA 90077
Alternate *V: 10/09/92*

9147 Leander Pl.
Beverly Hills, CA 90210
Forwarded *V: 05/04/92*

Barrett, Rona
1122 Tower Rd.
Beverly Hills, CA 90210
Celebrity *V: 03/14/93*

P.O. Box 1410
Beverly Hills, CA 90213
Alternate *V: 03/13/92*

Barris, Chuck
17 E. 76th St.
New York, NY 10021-1720
Producer *V: 03/14/93*

Barry, Dan
c/o King Features
216 East 45th St.
New York, NY 10017
Cartoonist *V: 11/18/92*

Barry, Gene
622 N. Maple Dr.
Beverly Hills, CA 90210
Actor *V: 02/01/92*

Barry, Sy
c/o King Features
216 East 45th St.
New York, NY 10017
Cartoonist *V: 03/03/92*

Barry, Jr., Philip
12742 Highwood St.
Los Angeles, CA 90049
Actor *V: 03/14/93*

Barrymore, Drew
P.O. Box 1305
Woodland Hills, CA 91364
Actress *V: 02/20/92*

3960 Laurel Canyon Bl. #189
Studio City, CA 91604
Alternate *V: 12/21/92*

4355 Ventura Canyon
Sherman Oaks, CA 91403
L.R.U. *V: 12/10/92*

Bartel, Paul
7860 Fairholm Dr.
Los Angeles, CA 90046
Actor *V: 03/10/93*

2265 Westwood Blvd. #2619
Los Angeles, CA 90064
Alternate V: 03/10/93

Barton, Bill
333 Continental Blvd.
El Segundo CA 90215-5012
Barbie Creator V: 07/02/92

c/o Mattel Inc.
5150 W. Rosecrans Ave.
Hawthorne, CA 90250
L.R.U. V: 07/01/92

Barton, Peter
2265 Westwood Blvd. #2619
Los Angeles, CA 90064
Actor V: 03/10/93

c/o "Y & R"
7800 Beverly Blvd.
Los Angeles, CA 90036
Forwarded V: 03/21/92

Barty, Billy
4502 Farmdale Ave.
N. Hollywood, CA 91602
Actor V: 01/14/92

Baryshnikov, Mikhail
c/o American Ballet Theatre
890 Broadway
New York, NY 10003
Dancer V: 11/12/92

Baseball Commissioner
350 Park Ave.
New York, NY 10022
League Office V: 03/19/92

Baseline
838 Broadway
New York, NY 10003
Infotainment V: 03/30/93

Basinger, Kim
3960 Laurel Canyon Bl. #414
Studio City, CA 91604-3709
Actress V: 07/01/92

4833 Don Juan Pl.
Woodland Hills, CA 91367
L.R.U. V: 07/01/92

P.O. Box 1305
Woodland Hills, CA 91364
L.R.U. V: 07/01/92

Basquette, Lina
Shadow Knoll Apts., #1
Wheeling, WV 26003
Actress V: 02/01/92

Bassett, Laura
9720 Regent St. #8
Los Angeles, CA 90034
Actress V: 03/09/93

Bassey, Jennifer
P.O. Box 80
Fremont, CA 94536
Actress V: 01/04/93

Bassey, Shirley
Villa Capricorn
55 Via Campione
6816 Bissone, Switzerland
Singer V: 04/01/92

Batchler, Emelia
14811 Mulholland Dr.
Los Angeles, CA 90024
Beauty Queen V: 12/12/92

Bateman, Jason
2623 2nd St.
Santa Monica, CA 90402
Actor V: 01/11/93

Bateman, Justine
3960 Laurel Canyon, Ste.193
Studio City, CA 91604-3709
Actress V: 02/14/92

c/o Agency
40 W. 57th St.
New York, NY 10019
Alternate V: 01/02/92

c/o Agency
8942 Wilshire Blvd.
Beverly Hills, CA 90211
Forwarded V: 07/07/92

P.O. Box 5533
Santa Monica, CA 90405
L.R.U. V: 01/02/92

Bates, Alan
122 Hamilton Terr.
London NW8, England
Actor V: 03/29/92

c/o The Globe Theatre
Shaftsbury Ave.
London W1, England
Alternate V: 05/03/92

Bates, Kathy
c/o Smith & Assoc.
121 N. San Vicente Blvd.
Beverly Hills, CA 90211
Actress V: 11/11/92

Batiuk, Tom
c/o King Features
216 East 45th St.
New York, NY 10017
 Cartoonist V: 01/12/93

Batliner, Gerard
Am Schragen Weg2
FL-9490 Vaduz Liechtenstein
 Politician V: 02/15/93

Bauer, Jamie Lyn
3500 W. Olive #1400
Burbank, CA 91505
 Actress V: 02/01/93

10653 Riverside Dr.
N. Hollywood, CA 91602
 Alternate V: 08/15/92

Bauer, Michele
P.O. Box 480265
Los Angeles, CA 90048
 Actress V: 03/26/93

Bauman, Jon "Bowzer"
3168 Oakshire Dr.
Los Angeles, CA 90067
 Singer V: 03/07/93

Bauman-Hiller & Assoc.
5750 Wilshire Blvd. #512
Los Angeles, CA 90036
 Talent Agency V: 11/11/92

Baxter, Meredith
151 El Camino
Beverly Hills, CA 90210
 Actress V: 03/07/93

Bays, Michael
5028 Shirley Ave.
Tarzana, CA 91356
 Actor V: 03/07/93

Beach Boys
P.O. Box 84282
Los Angeles, CA 90073
 Musical Group V: 05/21/92

Beacham, Stephanie
31538 Broad Beach Rd.
Malibu, CA 90265
 Actress V: 03/08/93

9255 Sunset Ave. #505
Los Angeles, CA 90069
 L.R.U. V: 03/02/93

Beal, John
205 W. 54th St.
New York, NY 10009
 Actor V: 05/22/92

Beals, Jennifer
40 W. 57th St.
New York, NY 10019
 Actress V: 10/01/92

Bean, Alan
c/o NASA
LBJ Space Center
Houston, TX 77058
 Astronaut V: 07/03/92

26 Sugarberry Circle
Houston, TX 77024
 Alternate V: 03/30/93

Bean, Orson
9255 Sunset Blvd. #515
Los Angeles, CA 90069
 Actor V: 07/13/92

Bearse, Amanda
4177 Klump Ave.
N. Hollywood, CA 91602
 Actress V: 03/08/93

1907 Lucille Ave.
Los Angeles, CA 90039
 Alternate V: 03/01/92

c/o Fox TV
10201 W. Pico Blvd.
Los Angeles, CA 90035
 Forwarded V: 01/12/92

Beart, Emmanuelle
c/o Artmedia
10 Ave. George-V
F-75008 Paris, France
 Actress V: 02/11/93

Beasley, Allyce
c/o P.A.A.
400 S. Beverly Dr., #216
Beverly Hills, CA 90212
 Actress V: 02/04/92

2415 Castilian Dr.
Los Angeles, CA 90068
 Alternate V: 03/08/93

Beathe, Bob
Box 4580/Airport Bus. Ctr.
402-D Pacific Ave.
Aspen, CO 81611
 Commentator V: 03/05/92

Beatty, Ned
2706 N. Beachwood Dr.
Los Angeles, CA 90027
Actor V: 01/14/92

c/o Tri Star Pictures
3400 Riverside Dr.
Burbank, CA 91505
Actor V: 12/17/92

Beatty, Warren
2029 Century Park E. #300
Los Angeles, CA 90067
Actor V: 03/03/93

1849 Sawtelle Blvd. #500
Los Angeles, CA 90025
Alternate V: 03/24/92

Dressing Room #105
5555 Melrose Ave. #800
Hollywood, CA 90038
Alternate V: 06/15/92

13671 Mulholland Dr.
Beverly Hills, CA 90210
Forwarded V: 11/20/92

Beck, Jeff
11 Old Square
Lincolns Inn
London WC2, England
Singer V: 06/13/92

Beck, John
c/o NBC-TV "Santa Barbara"
3000 W. Alameda Ave.
Burbank, CA 91523
Actor V: 01/02/92

Beck, Kimberly
9229 Sunset Blvd. #311
Los Angeles, CA 90069
Actress V: 03/03/93

Beck, Marilyn
P.O. Box 11079
Beverly Hills, CA 90213
Celebrity V: 03/10/93

2132 El Roble Ln.
Beverly Hills, CA 90210
Forwarded V: 03/10/93

Becker, Boris
c/o Le Rocca Bella
24 Ave. Princess Grace
Monte Carlo, Monaco
Tennis V: 12/10/92

Beddoe, Joyce
397 Avenida Castilla #A
Lauguna Hills, CA 92653-3774
Actress V: 11/11/92

2316-A Via Puerta
Lauguna Hills, CA 90291
L.R.U. V: 11/11/92

Bedelia, Bonnie
1021 Georgina Ave.
Santa Monica, CA 90402
Actress V: 04/24/92

Bee Gees
1801 Bay Rd.
Miami Beach, FL 33139
Musical Group V: 05/21/92

Beery Jr., Noah
P.O. Box 108
Keene, CA 93531
Actor V: 02/20/93

Bega, Leslie
6451 Deepdel Place
Los Angeles, CA 90048
Actress V: 03/09/93

Begley Jr., Ed
3850 Moundview Ave.
Studio City, CA 91604
Actor V: 03/09/93

c/o Imagine
Bldg.2, Floor 2
4024 Radford Ave.
Studio City, CA 91604
Alternate V: 01/07/93

c/o NBC
3000 W. Alameda
Burbank, CA 91523
Forwarded V: 04/02/92

Beilina, Nina
400 W. 43rd St. 7D
New York, NY 10036
Violinist V: 06/14/92

Bel Geddes, Barbara
15 Mill St.
Putnam Valley, NY 10579
Actress V: 12/01/92

Belafonte, David
829 S. Bundy Dr.
Los Angeles, CA 90049
Actor V: 03/09/93

Belafonte, Sharl
c/o Behrens
3546 Longridge Ave.
Sherman Oaks, CA 91403
Actress V: 06/14/92

Belefonte, Harry
888 7th Ave. #1602
New York, NY 10019
Singer V: 01/15/92

Belita
Rose Cottage
42-46 Crabtree Lane
London SW6 6LW, England
Actress V: 01/04/92

Bell, Greg
110 12th Street
Logansport, IN 46947
Actor V: 06/10/92

Bell, Joy
c/o NBC-TV
c/o "Another World"
79 Madison Ave., 5th Fl.
New York, NY 91523
Actress V: 06/15/92

Bell, Lauralee
c/o "Y & R"
7800 Beverly Bl. #3305
Los Angeles, CA 90036
Actress V: 07/28/92

Bellaver, Harry
116 Summit Dr.
Tappan, NY 10983
Actor V: 01/12/92

Belli, Melvin
900 Montgomery St.
San Francisco, CA 94111
Lawyer V: 03/01/93

Bellson, Louie
P.O. Box 2608
Lake Havasu City, AZ 86405-2608
Drummer V: 03/10/93

Bellwood, Pamela
7444 Woodrow Wilson
Los Angeles, CA 90049
Actress V: 03/02/92

Belmondo, Jean-Paul
5 rue Clemont-Marot
F-75008 Paris, France
Actor V: 01/17/93

Belmondo, Jean-Paul, contd
77 Ave. Donvert Rochefort
75 016 Paris, France
Alternate V: 07/24/92

c/o Artmedia
10 ave. George V
Paris, 75008 France
Forwarded V: 03/21/92

Belson & Klass Assoc.
144 S. Beverly Dr. #405
Beverly Hills, CA 90212
Talent Agency V: 11/21/92

Belushi, James
9830 Wilshire Blvd.
Beverly Hills, CA 90212
Actor V: 05/21/92

1888 Century Park E., Ste.1400
Los Angeles, CA 90067
Alternate V: 01/12/92

3400 Riverside Dr., 11th Fl.
Burbank, CA 91505
Forwarded V: 04/21/92

Benatar, Pat
5721 Bonsall Rd.
Malibu, CA 90265
Singer V: 02/28/92

Benavidez, Roy
1700 Byrne St.
El Campo, TX 77437
Medal of Honor V: 06/07/92

Bench, Johnny
661 Reisling Knoll
Cincinatti, OH 45226
Baseball V: 03/02/93

617 Vine St. Ste. 1307
Cincinati, OH 45202
Alternate V: 08/14/92

Benchley, Peter
35 Budinot St.
Princeton, NJ 08540
Writer V: 03/06/93

Bender, Sheldon
c/o Cincinnati Reds
Riverfront Stadium
Cincinnati, OH 45202
Sports Great V: 04/01/92

912 Virginia
Hamilton, OH 62704
Alternate V: 03/02/93

Benedict, Dirk
1637 Wellesley Dr.
Santa Monica, CA 90406
Actor V: 03/10/93

Benedict, Paul
P.O. Box 451
Chilmark, MA 02535
Actor V: 03/06/93

Benetar, Pat
8801 Eton Ave. #48
Canoga Park, CA 91304-1681
Singer V: 02/01/93

Benjamin, Richard
719 N. Foothill Rd.
Beverly Hills, CA 90210
Actor/Director V: 01/02/92

P.O. Box 900
Beverly Hills, CA 90213
L.R.U. V: 01/02/92

Bennett, Bruce
2702 Forrester Rd.
Los Angeles, CA 90024
Actor V: 06/14/92

Bennett, Clay
c/o King Features
216 E. 45th St.
New York, NY 10017
Cartoonist V: 03/11/93

Bennett, Hywell
3rd Fl.,15 Golden Square
London W1R 3AG, England
Actor V: 02/28/92

Bennett, Tony
101 W. 55th. St.
New York, NY 10019
Singer V: 01/11/92

Bennett, Tracie
9 Newburgh St.
London W1V 1LH, England
Actress V: 02/04/92

Bennett Agency
6404 Hollywood Blvd. #410
Los Angeles, CA 90028
Talent Agency V: 02/01/93

Benning, Annette
2029 Century Park E. Ste.300
Los Angeles, CA 90067-2900
Actress V: 03/30/93

Benson, Jodi
c/o "The Little Mermaid"
500 S. Buena Vista St.
Burbank, CA 91521
Actress V: 11/11/92

Benson, Robby
15760 Ventura Blvd. Ste.1730
Encino, CA 91436
Actor V: 03/06/93

4830 Brewester Dr.
Tarzana CA, 91352
L.R.U. V: 02/03/93

Benson Agency
8360 Melrose Ave. #203
Los Angeles, CA 90069
Talent Agency V: 03/22/93

Benton, Barbi
8560 Sunset Blvd.
Los Angeles, CA 90069
Actress V: 03/19/93

P.O. Box 7114
Pasadena, CA 91109
L.R.U. V: 08/08/92

P.O. Box 549
Carbondale, CO 81623
L.R.U. V: 08/08/92

Bentsen, Lloyd
Dept. of the Treasury
1500 Pennsylvania Ave., N.W.
Washington, DC 20220
Politician V: 03/09/93

Beradino, John
1719 Ambassador Drive
Beverly Hills, CA 90210
Actor V: 06/14/92

c/o "General Hosp."
4151 Prospect Ave.
Hollywood, CA 90027
Alternate V: 03/01/92

c/o "General Hosp."
1438 N. Gower
Hollywood, CA 90028
Forwarded V: 07/02/92

Berenger, Tom
P.O. Box 1842
Beaufort, SC 29901-1842
Actor V: 01/27/92

Berg, Patty
P.O. Box 9227
Ft. Meyers, FL 33902
Golf V: 07/02/92

Bergen, Candice
c/o "Murphy Brown"
Bldg. 3A, Rm. 21
4000 Warner Blvd.
Burbank, CA 91522
Actress V: 07/01/92

1134 Miradero
Beverly Hills, CA 90210
L.R.U. V: 01/02/92

Bergen, Frances
1485 Carla Ridge Dr.
Beverly Hills, CA 90210-2214
Actress V: 03/05/93

Bergen, Polly
1400 Devlin Dr.
Los Angeles, CA 90069
Actress V: 03/05/93

200 E. 42nd St.
New York, NY 10018
L.R.U. V: 06/01/92

Bergere, Lee
2385 Century Hill
Los Angeles, CA 90067
Actor V: 03/04/93

Bergin, Patrick
8 Harley St.
London W1N 2AB, England
Actress V: 05/26/92

Bergman, Ingmar
Box 27127
S-10252 Stockholm, Sweden
Director V: 03/04/93

Bergman, Peter
4799 White Oak Ave.
Encino, CA 91316
Actor V: 03/04/93

c/o "Y & R"
7800 Beverly Blvd.
Beverly Hills, CA 90036
Alternate V: 05/09/92

Berjer, Barbara
NBC-TV/"Another World"
79 Madison Ave., 5th Fl.
New York, NY 91523
Actress V: 06/15/92

Berkley, Elizabeth
6212 Banner Ave.
Los Angeles, CA 90038
Actress V: 03/04/93

Berkoff, Sheryl
12401 Sarah St.
Studio City, CA 91604
Actress V: 12/01/92

Berle, Milton
10750 Wilshire Blvd. #1003
Los Angeles, CA 90024-4470
Actor V: 12/12/92

151 El Camino Dr.
Beverly Hills, CA 90212
Alternate V: 01/10/92

711 N. Alpine Dr.
Beverly Hills, CA 90210
L.R.U. V: 08/08/92

Berman, Shelley
268 Bell Canyon Rd.
Bell Canyon, CA 91307
Actor V: 03/03/93

7500 Devista Dr.
Beverly Hills, CA 90211
L.R.U. V: 01/02/92

Bernard, Crystal
Wilder RM.101
5555 Melrose Ave.
Hollywood, CA 90038
Actress V: 01/07/92

Bernard, Jason
c/o "Hermans Head"
500 S. Buena Vista St.
Burbank, CA 91521
Actor V: 11/11/92

Bernard, Robyn
c/o "General Hospital"
4151 Prospect Ave.
Hollywood, CA 90027
Actress V: 03/01/92

Bernhard, Sandra
151 El Camino
Beverly Hills, CA 90212
Actress V: 03/01/93

3500 W. Olive Ave. Ste.1500
Burbank, CA 91505
Alternate V: 12/10/92

Bernhardt, Kevin
9300 Wilshire Blvd. Ste.410
Beverly Hills, CA 90212
Actor V: 03/03/93

Bernsen, Collin
401 N. Poinsettia Pl.
Los Angeles, CA 90036
Actor V: 03/03/93

Bernsen, Corbin
2114 Kew Dr.
Los Angeles, CA 90046
Actor V: 04/12/92

c/o Fox TV
'L.A. Law'
P.O. Box 900
Beverly Hills, CA 90213
Forwarded V: 01/12/92

1145 Gayley Ave. #309
Los Angeles, CA 90024
L.R.U. V: 01/02/92

Bernstein, Jay
P.O. Box 1148
Beverly Hills, CA 90213
Producer V: 03/03/93

Bernstein, Kenny
1105 Seminole
Richardson, TX 95080
Race Driver V: 12/12/92

c/o King Racing
103 Center Lane
Huntersville, NC 28078
Alternate V: 03/02/92

Berra, Yogi
19 Highland Ave.
Montclair, NJ 07042
Baseball V: 11/08/92

Berry, Chuck
Berry Park
Buckner Road
Wentzville, MO 63385
Musician V: 06/14/92

Berry, Fred
11020 Ventura Blvd. Ste.203
Studio City, CA 91604
Actor V: 03/02/93

Berry, Ken
4704 N. Cahuenga Blvd.
N. Hollywood, CA 91602
Actor V: 03/02/93

Berry, Ken, contd
1900 Outpost Dr.
Los Angeles, CA 90068
Alternate V: 11/14/92

Bertelli, Angelo
22 Springdale Ct.
Clifton, NJ 07013
Football V: 11/13/92

Bertinelli, Valerie
15760 Ventura Blvd. #700
Encino, CA 91436
Actress V: 09/09/92

Berwanger, Jay
1245 Warren Ave.
Downers Grove, IL 60515
Football V: 04/04/92

Berzon Agency
336 E. 17th St.
Costa Mesa, CA 92627
Talent Agency V: 02/28/93

Bess, Gordon
216 East 45th St.
New York, NY 10017
Cartoonist V: 03/14/92

Bessel, Ted
1454 Stone Canyon Road
Los Angeles, CA 90077
Actor V: 06/14/92

Best, Kevin
P.O. Box 1164
Hesperia, CA 92345
Actor V: 03/02/93

c/o "General Hospital"
4151 Prospect Ave.
Hollywood, CA 90027
Forwarded V: 03/01/92

Bestwicke, Martine
131 S. Sycamore Ave.
Los Angeles, CA 90036
Actress V: 03/02/93

Bethune, Zina
3096 Lake Hollywood Dr.
Los Angeles, CA 90068
Actress V: 03/03/93

Bewes, Rodney
Heath at Paramount House
162 Wardour St.
London W1V 3AT, England
Actor V: 02/01/92

Bey, Turhan
Paradisgasse Ave. 47
Vienna 1190 XIX, Austria 7
Actor V: 03/03/93

Beyer, Troy
3800 Barham Blvd.
Los Angeles, CA 90068
Actress V: 03/03/93

Beymer, Richard
9744 Wilshire Blvd. #308
Beverly Hills, CA 90212
Actor V: 03/03/93

Bhutto, Benazir
Lankana, Pakistan
Politician V: 07/03/92

Bialik, Mayim
300 W. Alameda Ave.
Burbank, CA 91523
Actress V: 03/03/93

846 N. Cahuenga Blvd.
Hollywood, CA 90038
Alternate V: 01/17/92

1419 Peerless Pl. Ste.120
Los Angeles, CA 90035
Alternate V: 03/04/93

500 S. Buena Vista St.
Burbank, CA 91521
Forwarded V: 11/11/92

Bierdz, Thom
1435 N. Stanley Ave.
Los Angeles, CA 90046
Actor V: 03/04/93

Bierschwale, Eddie
1811 Volusia Ave.
Daytona Beach, FL 32015
NASCAR Driver V: 03/02/92

Biggs, Richard
728 W. 28th St.
Los Angeles, CA 90007
Actor V: 03/04/93

Bigley Agency
19725 Sherman Way #200
Canoga Park, CA 91306
Talent Agency V: 01/17/92

Bikel, Theodore
1131 Alta Loma Rd.
Los Angeles, CA 90069
Actor V: 03/04/93

Bikoff Agency
621 N. Orlando Ste.8
W. Hollywood, CA 90048
Talent Agency V: 12/12/92

Billboard
P.O. Box 2071
Mahopac, NY 10541-9855
Music Magazine V: 03/21/93

Billingslea, Beau
"General Hospital"
4151 Prospect Ave.
Hollywood, CA 90027
Actor V: 06/15/92

Billingsley, Barbara
800 San Lorenzo St.
Santa Monica, CA 90405
Actress V: 03/05/93

9200 Sunset Blvd. #909
Los Angeles, CA 90069
Alternate V: 04/06/92

Billingsley, Peter
11350 Veentura Blvd.
Studio City, CA 91604
Actress V: 03/05/93

Billingsley, Ray
c/o King Features
216 E. 45th St.
New York, NY 10017
Cartoonist V: 03/11/93

Binoche, Juliette
1 place de l'Ecole
F-75001 Paris France
Actress V: 03/20/93

Bionca
c/o Five K Sales Co.
9420 Reseda Blvd., #836
Northridge, CA 91324
Adult Films V: 03/03/93

Bird, Billie
9224 Sunset Blvd. #515
Los Angeles, CA 90069
Actress V: 03/05/93

Bird, Larry
c/o Boston Celtics
151 Merrimac St.
Boston, MA 02114-4714
Basketball V: 01/12/93

Bird, Norman
c/o London Management
235/241 Regent St.
London, W1A 2JT England
Actor V: 03/30/93

Birn, Laura Bryan
c/o "Y & R"
7800 Beverly Blvd.
Beverly Hills, CA 90036
Actress V: 06/15/92

Birney, David
20 Ocean Park Blvd. #11
Santa Monica, CA 90405
Actor V: 03/05/93

Bishop, Joey
534 Via Lido Nord
Newport, CA 92663
Actor V: 06/06/92

Bishop Museum
1525 Bernice St.
P.O. Bos 19000-A
Honolulu, HI 96817-0916
Archive V: 03/20/93

Bissell, Whit
23388 Mulholland Dr.
Woodland Hills, CA 91364
Actor V: 03/06/93

Bisset, Jacqueline
1815 Benedict Canyon Dr.
Beverly Hills, CA 90210
Actress V: 07/01/92

8942 Wilshire Blvd.
Beverly Hills, CA 90211
L.R.U. V: 06/01/92

Bixby, Bill
200 N. Robertson Blvd. #223
Beverly Hills, CA 90211
Actor V: 06/03/92

15155 Galaxy Way #2160
Los Angeles, CA 90067
Alternate V: 03/06/93

c/o "Blossom"
500 S. Buena Vista St.
Burbank, CA 91521
Alternate V: 11/11/92

Black, Clint
P.O. Box 299386
Houston, TX 77299
Singer V: 01/16/93

Black, Clint, contd
8033 Sunset Blvd. Ste.2641
Los Angeles, CA 90046-2427
Alternate V: 03/06/93

Blackman, Honor
235-241 Regent St.
London W1A 2JT, England
Actress V: 12/12/92

c/o Michael Ladkin
2A Warwick Place N.
London SW1V 1QW, England
Alternate V: 02/04/92

Blackwell, Ewell
20 Moy Toy Lane
Brevard, NC 28712
Baseball V: 05/14/92

Blacque, Taurean
4207 Don Ortega Pl.
Los Angeles, CA 90008
Actor V: 03/02/93

Blades, Ruben
1234 1/2 N. Crescent Hts.
Los Angeles, CA 90046
Singer V: 03/02/93

Blaha, John E.
c/o NASA
LBJ Space Center
Houston, TX 77058
Astronaut V: 12/11/92

Blair, Betsy
11 Chalcot Gardens
Englands Lane
London, NW3 4YB England
Actress V: 04/24/92

Blair, Bonnie
1907 W. Springfield
Champaign, IL 61820
Actress V: 03/01/93

Blair, Janet
21535 Erwin St. Ste.126
Woodland Hills, CA 91367
Actress V: 03/01/93

Blair, Linda
1930 Century Park W. #403
Los Angeles, CA 90067
Actress V: 08/08/92

8033 Sunset Ave. #204
Los Angeles, CA 90046
Forwarded V: 08/08/92

Blake, Bud
c/o King Features
216 East 45th St.
New York, NY 10017
Cartoonist V: 06/06/92

Blake, Robert
11604 Dilling Street
North Hollywood, CA 91608
Actor V: 06/14/92

Blake, Stephanie
14332 Dickens St. Ste.8
Sherman Oaks, CA 91423
Actress V: 02/28/93

Blake, Whitney
P.O. Box 6088
Malibu, CA 90265
Actress V: 02/28/93

Blakely, Susan
1829 Franklin Canyon Dr.
Beverly Hills, CA 90210
Actress V: 02/28/93

Blanc, Noel
702 N. Rodeo Dr.
Beverly Hills, CA 90210
Writer V: 02/27/93

Blanchard, Nina
957 N. Cole Ave.
Los Angeles, CA 90028
Talent Agent V: 02/27/93

Blandas, George
78001 Lago Dr.
La Quinta, CA 92253
Football V: 03/17/92

Blane, Sally
1114 S. Roxbury Dr.
Los Angeles, CA 90035
Actress V: 02/26/93

Blatty, William P.
5841 Round Meadow Rd.
Woodland Hills, CA 91364
Director V: 02/26/93

Blech, Hans-Christian
c/o ZBF Agentur
Leopoldstr. 19
D-(W) 8000 Munchen 40
Germany
Actor V: 02/11/93

Bledsoe, Tempest
P.O. Box 7217
Beverly Hills, CA 90212-7217
Actress V: 02/26/93

Bleu, Bunny
c/o 5K Sales
9420 Reseda Blvd., Ste.836
Northridge, CA 91324
Adult Films V: 01/17/93

Bliss, Lucille
c/o Smurfette Society
845 Noe St. #3
San Francisco, CA 94114
Cartoon Voices V: 04/22/92

Bloch, Robert
2111 Sunset Crest Dr.
Los Angeles, CA 90046 .
Writer V: 02/25/93

Block, Hunt
2216 Vanderbuilt Ln.
Redondo Beach, CA 90272
Actor V: 02/25/93

Bloom, Brian
c/o CBS-TV
51 W. 52nd St.
New York, NY 10019
Actor V: 05/04/92

Bloom, Claire
c/o The Globe Theatre
Shaftsbury Ave.
London W1, England
Actress V: 05/22/92

Conway at 109 Jemyn St.
London SW1, England
Alternate V: 12/14/92

Bloom, Linsay
P.O. Box 2188
Hollywood, CA 90078
Actress V: 06/06/92

Bloom, Ursula
c/o Newton House
Walls Dr., Ravenglass
Cumbria, England
Actress V: 01/06/93

Bloom Agency
9200 Sunset Blvd. #710
Los Angeles, CA 90069
Talent Agency V: 02/23/93

Blount, Lisa
151 El Camino
Beverly Hills, CA 90212
Actress V: 03/29/92

3957 Albright Ave.
Los Angeles, CA 90066
Alternate V: 03/17/92

11524 Amanda Dr.
Studio City, CA 91604
Forwarded V: 04/21/92

c/o Paramount Pictures
5555 Melrose Ave., Wilder #214
Los Angeles, CA 90038
Forwarded V: 05/15/92

Blount, Mel
RR 1, Box 91
Claysville, PA 15323
Football V: 03/17/92

Bluford, Guion
NASA/LBJ Space Center
Houston, TX 77058
Astronaut V: 06/06/92

Blume, Judy
54 Riverside Dr.
New York, NY 10023
Writer V: 02/25/93

Blunt, Kelley
c/o Dallas Cowboys
One Cowboys Parkway
Irving, TX 75063-4945
Cheerleader V: 08/08/92

Blyth, Ann
P.O. Box 9754
Rancho Sante Fe, CA 92067
Actress V: 01/02/92

Bobko, Karol J.
c/o NASA LBJ Space Center
Houston, TX 77058
Astronaut V: 03/03/93

Bochco, Steven
694 Amalfi Dr.
Pacific Palisades, CA 90272
Producer V: 02/25/93

694 Amalfi Dr.
Pacific Palisades, CA 90272
Writer V: 10/10/92

Bochner, Lloyd
42 Haldeman Rd.
Santa Monica, CA 90402
Actor V: 06/14/92

Bodemann, Joe
c/o Joe Bodemann GmbH
Meinholz 1
D-(W) 3174 Meine Germany
Animal Trainer V: 03/20/93

Bodine, Brett
c/o King Racing
103 Center Lane
Huntersville, NC 28078
NASCAR Driver V: 03/02/92

Bodine, Geoff
400 N. Fairview Ave.
Spartanburg, SC 29304
NASCAR Driver V: 03/02/92

Boeing Company
Historical Archives m/s 1R-24
P.O. Box 3707
Seattle, WA 98124-2207
Archive V: 03/20/93

Boesak, Dr. Allen
P.O. Box 316
Kasselsvlei 7533
South Africa
Political Activist V: 02/12/92

Bellville South
Cape Town, South Africa
Alternate V: 04/22/92

Bogarde, Dirk
c/o London Mgmt.
235 Regent St.
London W12 7RJ, England
Actor V: 03/01/92

Bogdonovich, Peter
212 Copa de Oro Road
Los Angeles, CA 90077
Alternate V: 06/14/92

Bohay, Heidi
4304 Farmdale Ave.
Studio City, CA 91604
Actress V: 02/22/92

Bohm, Uwe
c/o ZBF Agentur
Leopoldstr. 19
D-(W) 8000 Munchen 40
Germany
Actor V: 02/11/93

Bohrer, Corinne
21110 Louella Ave.
Venice, CA 90291
Actress V: 06/06/92

Bolden Jr., Charles F.
c/o NASA
LBJ Space Center
Houston, TX 77058
Astronaut V: 06/06/92

Bolle, Frank
c/o King Features
216 E. 45th St.
New York, NY 10017
Cartoonist V: 03/11/93

Bolling, Tiffany
c/o Casares
12483 Braddock Dr.
Los Angeles, CA 90066
Actress V: 02/25/93

10653 Riverside Dr.
Toluca Lake, CA 91602
Alternate V: 03/02/92

Bologna, Joseph
613 N. Arden Drive
Beverly Hills, CA 90210
Actor V: 06/14/92

Bolton, Michael
201 W. 85th St. Ste.15A
New York, NY 10024
Singer V: 02/26/93

Bombeck, Erma
Times Mirror Square
Los Angeles, CA 90053
Humorist V: 02/16/92

4900 Main St.
Kansas City, MO 64112
Alternate V: 04/01/92

1703 Redding Rd.
Fairfield, CT 06430
L.R.U. V: 08/11/92

Bon Jovi
P.O. Box 326
Fords, NJ 08863
Musical Group V: 02/26/93

Bonarrigo, Laura
c/o ABC-TV "One Life to Live"
77 W. 66th St.
New York, NY 10033
Actress V: 04/05/93

Bond, Julian
361 Westview Drive S.W.
Atlanta, GA 30310
Politician V: 03/10/92

Bonerz, Peter
3637 Lowry Road
Los Angeles, CA 90027
Actor V: 06/14/92

Bonet, Lisa
237 S. Almont Drive.
Beverly Hills, CA 90211
Actress V: 02/26/93

6435 Balcome
Reseda, CA 91335
Alternate V: 06/06/92

c/o NBC-TV/Cosby Show
3000 W. Alameda
Burbank, CA 91523
L.R.U. V: 01/13/93

Bonner, Frank
151 El Camino
Beverly Hills, CA 90212
Actor V: 03/01/93

Bonner, Priscilla
c/o Woolfan
9400 W. Olympic Blvd. Ste.203
Beverly Hills, CA 90212-4552
Actress V: 02/27/93

Bonnett, Neil
c/o NASCAR
1811 Volusia Ave.
Daytona Beach, FL 32015
NASCAR Announcer V: 03/02/92

Bono, Chastity
4453 Stern Ave.
Sherman Oaks, CA 91423
Celebrity V: 02/26/93

9200 Sunset Blvd. #1001
Los Angeles, CA 90067
Alternate V: 01/12/92

Bono, Sonny
1700 N. Indian Dr.
Palm Springs, CA 92262
Actor V: 02/28/93

250 W. Camino
Buena Vista Park
Palm Springs, CA 92262
Alternate V: 06/19/92

Bonsall, Brian
11712 Moorpark St. Ste.204
Palm Springs, CA 92262
Actor V: 02/28/93

Booke, Sorrell
c/o Resi Inc.
205 S. Beverly Dr. Suite 205
Beverly Hills, CA 90212
Actor V: 02/01/92

P.O. Box 1105
Studio City, CA 91604
Forwarded V: 04/12/92

Boone, Debby
4334 Kester Ave.
Sherman Oaks, CA 91423
Singer V: 02/28/93

904 N. Beverly Drive
Beverly Hills, CA 90069
Alternate V: 06/11/92

c/o Resi
15315 Magnolia Blvd. Suite 208
Sherman Oaks, CA 91403-1173
Forwarded V: 06/11/92

Boone, Lesley
5206 Norwich Ave. #206
Van Nuys, CA 91411
Actress V: 02/28/93

Boone, Pat
2600 W. Olive Ste.930
Burbank, CA 91505
Actor V: 06/06/92

904 N. Beverly Drive
Beverly Hills, CA 90210
Alternate V: 06/14/92

9255 Sunset Blvd. #519
Los Angeles, CA 90069
Forwarded V: 07/06/92

Boone, Randy
14250 Califa St.
Van Nuys, CA 91401
Actor V: 02/28/93

Boosler, Elayne
11061 Wrightwood Lane
Studio City, CA 91604
Actress V: 04/14/92

Booth, Shirley
P.O. Box 103
Chatham, MA 02633
Actress V: 06/14/92

Boothe, Powers
23629 Long Valley Rd.
Hidden Hills, CA 91302
Actor V: 03/01/93

Borelli, Carla
8075 W. Third St. Ste.303
Los Angeles, CA 90048
Actress V: 03/01/93

320 E. 57th St. #12-C
New York, NY 10107
Alternate V: 01/08/92

Borge, Victor
Fieldpoint Park
Greenwich, CT 06830
Comedian V: 06/06/92

Borgman, Jim
c/o King Features
216 E. 45th St.
New York, NY 10017
Cartoonist V: 03/11/93

Borgnine, Ernest
c/o Tovern Productions
3055 Lake Glen Dr.
Beverly Hills, CA 90210
Actor V: 06/01/92

Borinstein-Oreck-Bogart
8271 Melrose Ave. #110
Los Angeles, CA 90046
Talent Agency V: 04/27/92

Borman, Frank
c/o NASA LBJ Space Center
Houston, TX 77058
Astronaut V: 03/03/93

250 Catarro Ct.
Las Cruces, NM 88005
Alternate V: 04/01/92

205 W. Boutz Rd.
Bldg. 4, Ste.4
Las Cruces, NM 88003
Alternate V: 05/04/92

c/o Eastern Airlines Inc.
Miami, FL 33148
Forwarded V: 03/04/92

Borrego, Jesse
347 N. Sweetzer
Los Angeles, CA 90048
Actor V: 03/01/93

Boryer, Lucy
2116 Ewing St.
Los Angeles, CA 90039
Actress V: 03/01/93

Bosley, Tom
c/o Universal TV
Murder She Wrote
100 Univ. City Plz., Bl.507
Universal City, CA 91608
Actor V: 03/02/92

2822 Royston Place
Beverly Hills, CA 90210
L.R.U. V: 05/01/92

Bosson, Barbara
694 Amalfi Dr.
Pacific Palisades, CA 90272
Actress V: 03/02/93

4024 Radford Ave.
Studio City, CA 91604
Alternate V: 08/16/92

c/o 20th Cent./Fox Films
P.O. Box 900
Beverly Hills, CA 90213
Forwarded V: 11/11/92

Bostick, Richard
P.O. Box 560579
Charlotte, NC 27317
NASCAR Crew V: 03/26/93

Boston Red Sox
Fenway Park
Boston, MA 02215
Team Office V: 05/15/92

Bostwick, Barry
2770 Hutton Dr.
Beverly Hills, CA 90210
Actor V: 11/11/92

11747 Moorpark #3
Studio City, CA 91604
Alternate V: 12/24/92

Bottoms, Ben
6565 Sunset Blvd. #300
Los Angeles, CA 90028
Actor V: 03/02/93

Bottoms, Sam
4719 Willowcrest Rd.
N. Hollywood, CA 91604
Actor V: 02/20/92

Bottoms, Timothy
15760 Ventura Blvd. #1730
Encino, CA 91436
Actor V: 12/23/92

532 Hot Springs Road
Santa Barbara, CA 93108
Alternate V: 06/14/92

Bow, Chuck
1811 Volusia Ave.
Daytona Beach, FL 32015
NASCAR Driver V: 03/02/92

Bowab, John
2598 Green Valley Rd.
Los Angeles, CA 90046
Director V: 02/24/93

Bower, Antoinette
c/o Brooke-Dunne-Oliver
9165 Sunset Blvd. #202
Los Angeles, CA 90069
Actress V: 04/01/92

Bowersox, Kenneth D.
c/o NASA
LBJ Space Center
Houston, TX 77058
Astronaut V: 06/06/92

Bowie, David
641 5th Ave. #22Q
New York, NY 10022
Singer V: 06/06/92

Bowman, Christopher
5653 Kester Ave.
Van Nuys, CA 91411
Actor V: 02/11/92

Boxcar Willie
26949 Chagrin Blvd.
Beachwood, OH 44122
Singer V: 11/29/92

Boxer, Barbara
307 Cannon House Office Bldg.
Washington, DC 20515
Politician V: 10/04/92

Boxleitner, Bruce
24500 John Colter Rd.
Hidden Hills, CA 91302
Actor V: 03/21/92

Boxleitner, Bruce, contd
P.O. Box 5513
Sherman Oaks, CA 91403
Alternate V: 07/03/92

151 El Camino
Beverly Hills, CA 90212
Forwarded V: 05/05/92

c/o Rogers & Cowan
10000 Santa Monica Blvd.
Los Angeles, CA 90067
Forwarded V: 03/20/92

Boyer, Erica
c/o 5K Sales
9420 Reseda Blvd., Ste.836
Northridge, CA 91324
Adult Films V: 01/17/93

Boyett, William
c/o ABC-TV/'Gen. Hosp.'
4151 Prospect Ave.
Hollywood, CA 90027
Actor V: 06/15/92

Boyle, Lara Flynn
606 N. Larchmont Bl. #309
Los Angeles, CA 90004
Actress V: 03/03/93

Boyle, Peter
40 W. 57th St.
New York, NY 10019
Actor V: 02/23/93

Boyle, Peter
c/o Robbins & Steilman
1700 Broadway
New York, NY 10019
L.R.U. V: 01/22/92

Bozworth, Brian
c/o Stone Grp. Prod. Co.
Columbia Plaza
Burbank, CA 91505
Actor V: 12/16/92

Brabham, Jack
33 Central Rd.
Worcester Park
Surrey KT4 8EG England
Race Car Driver V: 02/13/93

Bracco, Lorraine
P.O. Box 49
Palisades, NY 10964-0049
Actress V: 02/23/93

Bracken, Eddie
c/o P.O.D. Management Inc.
69 Douglas Rd.
Glen Ridge, NJ 07028
Actor V: 03/21/92

Bradbury, Ray
10265 Cheviot Dr.
Los Angeles, CA 90064
Author V: 05/15/92

Braddy, Dorie
c/o Dallas Cowboys
One Cowboys Parkway
Irving, TX 75063-4945
Cheerleader V: 08/08/92

Bradford, Greg
3752 Redwood Ave.
Los Angeles, CA 90066
Actor V: 06/10/92

Bradley, Ed
524 W. 57th St.
New York, NY 10019
Journalist V: 02/23/93

Bradley, James
1555 Riverside Dr. #4
Glendale, CA 91201
Actor V: 02/27/93

Bradley, Kathleen
The Price is Right #101
c/o Mark Goodson Prod.
5750 Wilshire Blvd.
Los Angeles, CA 90036-3697
Celebrity V: 03/27/93

Bradley, Tom
605 S. Irving Blvd.
New York, NY 90005
Politician V: 02/23/93

Bradshaw, Terry
Rt.1, Box 227
Gordonville, TX 76245
Football V: 01/12/92

P.O. Box 1607
Shreveport, LA 71165
Alternate V: 06/13/92

Terry Bradshaw Fan Club
8911 Shady Lane Dr.
Shreveport, LA 71118
Forwarded V: 10/26/92

Braeden, Eric
13723 Romany Drive
Pacific Palisades, CA 90272
Actor V: 06/14/92

c/o Young & Restless
7800 Beverly Blvd.
Beverly Hills, CA 90036
Alternate V: 06/15/92

Braga, Sonia
295 Greenwich St. #11B
New York, NY 10007-1053
Actress V: 10/26/92

210 E. 58th St.
New York, NY 10022
L.R.U. V: 01/12/93

Brand, Vance D.
c/o NASA LBJ Space Center
Houston, TX 77058
Astronaut V: 03/03/93

Brandauer, Klaus Maria
Bartensteingasse 8/9
A-1010 Vienna, Austria
Actor V: 06/06/92

Brandenstein, Daniel C.
c/o NASA LBJ Space Center
Houston, TX 77058
Astronaut V: 03/03/93

Brando, Marlon
P.O. Box 809
Beverly Hills, CA 90213
Actor V: 03/03/93

1 E. 62nd St.
New York, NY 10021
Alternate V: 12/28/92

Brandon, John
c/o Bold & Beautiful
7800 Beverly Blvd., Ste.3371
Los Angeles, CA 90036
Actor V: 06/15/92

Brandon, Michael
9320 Wilshire Blvd. #310
Beverly Hills, CA 90210
Actor V: 02/22/93

Brandt, Volker
Fasanenstr. 29
D-(W) 1000 Berlin 15
Germany
Actor V: 02/11/93

Branigan, Laura
c/o Kruteck & Leaness
509 Madison Ave.
New York, NY 10022
Singer V: 06/06/92

310 E. 65th St.
New York, NY 10021
Alternate V: 03/13/92

Braverman, Bart
524 N. Laurel Ave.
Los Angeles, CA 900482
Actor V: 02/21/93

823 S. Plymouth #10
Los Angeles, CA 90005
Alternate V: 11/11/92

Bravo Network
150 Crossways Park West
Woodbury, NY 11797
Production Company V: 11/11/92

Brazzi, Rossano
Via Giovanni Batista Martini 13
I-00100 Rome, Italy
Actor V: 02/23/93

Bregman, Martin
641 Lexington Ave.
New York, NY 10022
Producer V: 11/11/92

Bregman Productions
Universal Studios
Universal City, CA 91608
Production Company V: 03/17/92

Brennan, Eileen
P.O. Box 1777
Ojai, CA 93032
Actress V: 12/21/92

Brennan, John
c/o NBC-TV/Another World
30 Rockefeller Plaza
New York, NY 10122
Actor V: 12/06/92

Brennan, Melissa
c/o "Days"/NBC-TV
3000 W. Alameda
Burbank, CA 91523
Actress V: 12/03/92

Brenner, David
229 E. 62nd St.
New York, NY 10021
Actor V: 12/14/92

Brenner, Dori
2106 Canyon Dr.
Los Angeles, CA 90068-3609
Actress V: 02/21/93

Bresee, Bobbie
P.O. Box 1222
Hollywood, CA 90078
Actress V: 12/01/92

Bresler-Kelly-Kipperman
15760 Ventura Blvd. #1730
Encino, CA 91436
Talent Agency V: 05/13/92

Brest, Martin
831 Paseo Miramar
Pacific Palisades, CA 90272
Director V: 02/21/93

Brett, George
P.O. Box 419969
Kansas City, MO 64141
Baseball V: 12/05/92

c/o Kansas City Royals
Box 1969
Kansas City, MO 64141
Alternate V: 12/05/92

Brett, Jeremy
151 S. El Camino Dr.
Beverly Hills, CA 90212
Actor V: 12/02/92

Breuslaw, Bernard
Pinefood Film Studio
Iver Heath
Bucks. SL0 0NH, England
Actor V: 03/15/93

Brewer, Teresa
584 Prospect St.
New Haven, CT 06511
Singer V: 04/02/92

394 Pinebrook Pl.
New Rochelle, NY 10803
Alternate V: 05/13/92

Brewis Agency
12429 Laurel Terrace Dr.
Studio City, CA 91604
Talent Agency V: 06/13/92

Brialy, Jean-Claude
Theatres Boufles/Parisian
4 rue Monsigny
75002 Paris, France
Actor V: 12/14/92

Brian, Mary
4107 Troost Ave.
N. Hollywood, CA 91604
Actress V: 01/12/92

Brice, Lauren
c/o 5K Sales
9420 Reseda Blvd., Ste.836
Northridge, CA 91324
Adult Films V: 01/17/93

Brice, Pierre
c/o Olga Horstig-Primuz
78 ave. Champs-Elysees
F-75008 Paris, France
Actor V: 12/17/92

Brickell, Beth
9933 Robbins Dr. Ste.2
Beverly Hills, CA 90212
Actress V: 02/20/93

Brickman, Morrie
c/o King Features
216 East 45th St.
New York, NY 10017
Cartoonist V: 12/17/92

Bridges, Beau
9056 Santa Monica Bl.,#100
Hollywood, CA 90062
Actor V: 03/15/93

5525 N. Jed Smith Rd.
Hidden Hills, CA 91302
Alternate V: 02/20/93

8966 Sunset Blvd.
Hollywood, CA 90069
L.R.U. V: 01/02/92

Bridges, Jeff
1223 Wilshire Bl., #593
Santa Monica, CA 90403
Actor V: 01/02/92

P.O. Box 101
Valyermo, CA 93563
L.R.U. V: 01/02/92

436 Adelaide
Santa Monica, CA 90402
L.R.U. V: 01/21/93

Bridges, Lloyd
225 Loring Ave.
Los Angeles, CA 90024
Actor V: 07/02/92

Bridges, Roy D.
6510th Test Wing/CC
Edwards AFB, CA 93523-5000
Astronaut V: 12/17/92

NASA/LBJ Space Center
Houston, TX 77058
Alternate V: 03/03/93

Bridges Agency
5000 Lankershim Blvd. #7-9
N. Hollywood, CA 91601
Talent Agency V: 06/13/92

Briers, Richard
388-396 Oxford St.
London W1 9HE, England
Actor V: 12/20/92

Briggs, Joe Bob
P.O. Box 2002
Dallas, TX 75221
Film Critic V: 12/06/92

Brill, Charlie
3635 Wrightwood Dr.
Studio City, CA 91604
Actor V: 02/20/93

Brillstein Productions
9200 Sunset Blvd. #428
Los Angeles, CA 90069
Production Company V: 12/17/92

Brimley, Wilfred
c/o CAA
9320 Wilshire Blvd. Ste.310
Beverly Hills, CA 90212
Actor V: 02/20/93

Brinegar, Paul
17322 Halsey St.
Granada Hill, CA 91344
Actor V: 12/04/92

Brinkley, Christie
344 E. 59th St.
New York, NY 10022
Model V: 11/11/92

Brinkley, David
1717 DeSales St. N.W.
Washington, DC 20036-4401
Correspondant V: 02/21/93

Briscoe, Valerie
P.O. Box 21053
Long Beach, CA 90801
Athlete V: 12/14/92

Britt, Mai
P.O. Box 525
Zephyr Cove, NV 89448
Actress V: 06/14/92

Brittany, Morgan
3434 Cornell Rd.
Agoura Hills, CA 91301
Actress V: 02/21/93

10000 Santa Monica Blvd.#305
Los Angeles, CA 90067
L.R.U. V: 12/15/92

Britton, Tony
c/o Agency
388-396 Oxford St.
London W1 9HE, England
Actor V: 03/20/92

Brock, Phil
11726 San Vicente Blvd. #300
Los Angeles, CA 90049
Actor V: 12/20/92

Brodie, Kevin
4424 Moorpark Way
N. Hollywood, CA 91602
Actor V: 02/22/93

Brodie, Steve
6742 Sunnybrae Ave.
Canoga Park, CA 91306
Actor V: 03/03/93

Brody, Lane
P.O. Box 24775
Nashville, TN 37202
Singer V: 07/02/92

Brokaw, Tom
30 Rockefeller Plaza NBC-TV
New York, NY 10112
Newsman V: 04/03/92

Brolin, James
c/o August Entertainment
838 N. Fairfax Ave.
Los Angeles, CA 90046
Actor V: 01/14/93

2401 Colorado Ave. Ste.160
Santa Monica, CA 90404-3528
Actor V: 02/22/93

803 Country Club Dr.
Ojai, CA 93023
Alternate V: 11/12/92

Brolin, Josh
2401 Colorado Ave. Ste.160
Santa Monica, CA 90404-3528
Actor V: 02/22/93

Bromfield, John
1750 Whittier Ave.
Costa Mesa, CA 91344
Actor V: 11/11/92

Bronson, Charles
P.O. Box 2644
Malibu, CA 90265
Actor V: 05/05/92

8966 Sunset Blvd.
Hollywood, CA 90069
Alternate V: 03/01/92

8200 Wilshire Blvd.
Beverly Hills, CA 90212
Forwarded V: 06/14/92

121 Udine Way
Los Angeles, CA 90024
L.R.U. V: 02/02/92

Bronson, Lillian
32591 Seven Seas Dr.
Laguna Niguel, CA 92677
Actress V: 02/23/93

Brooke-Dunn-Oliver
9165 Sunset Blvd. #202
Los Angeles, CA 90069
Talent Agency V: 06/06/92

Brookins, Gary
216 East 45th St.
New York, NY 10017
Cartoonist V: 03/02/93

Brooks, Albert
3600 Longridge Ave.
Sherman Oaks, CA 91403
Actor V: 02/24/93

Brooks, Avery
20 Layne Rd.
Summerset, NJ 08873
Actor V: 02/24/93

1999 Ave. of the Stars, #2850
Los Angeles, CA 90067
Alternate V: 02/23/93

c/o Star Trek-DS9
5555 Melrose Ave.
Hollywood, CA 90036
Alternate V: 02/23/93

Brooks, Dwight
P.O. Box 102
Grass Valley, CA 95945
Director V: 06/06/92

Brooks, Garth
1109 17th Ave. S.
Nashville, TN 37212
Singer V: 05/21/92

Brooks, Mel
2301 La Mesa Dr.
Santa Monica, CA 90405
Producer V: 02/24/93

c/o Brooksfilm
P.O. Box 900
Beverly Hills, CA 90213
Alternate V: 02/22/92

10201 W. Pico Blvd.
Los Angeles, CA 90035
Forwarded V: 03/11/92

Brooks, Phyllis
P.O. Box 14
Cape Neddick, ME 03902
Actress V: 02/03/92

Brooks, Rand
440 W. Broadway
Glendale, CA 91206
Actor V: 02/10/92

Brooks, Randi
c/o Brazen
1459 Irving Ave.
Glendale, CA 91201
Actress V: 02/24/93

Brooks, Richard
Law & Order
100 Universal Plaza, Bl.G
Universal City, CA 91608
Actor V: 01/12/92

Brophy, Kevin
15010 Hamlin St.
Van Nuys, CA 91411
Actor V: 02/03/92

Brosnan, Pierce
28011 N. Parquet Place
Malibu, CA 90265
Actor V: 01/12/91

P.O. Box 9851
Glendale, CA 91206
Alternate V: 03/03/93

Brothers, Dr. Joyce
1530 Palisades Ave.
Ft. Lee, NJ 07024
Author V: 03/06/92

Broussard, Rebecca
9911 W. Pico Blvd. #PH-A
Los Angeles, CA 90035-2703
Actress V: 12/10/92

15760 Ventura Blvd. #1730
Encino, CA 91436
Alternate V: 03/03/93

Brown, Blair
434 W. 20th Ste.3
New York, NY 10011-2939
Actress V: 06/01/92

Brown, Bobby
American Baseball League
350 Park Ave.
New York, NY 10022
Baseball V: 01/12/93

Brown, Bobby
3358 Peachtree Rd. N.E.
Atlanta, GA 30326
Singer V: 02/25/93

Brown, Bryan
c/o CAA
9830 Wilshire Blvd.
Beverly Hills, CA 90212
Actor V: 03/01/93

Brown, Danny J.
P.O. Box 1531
Tampa, FL 33801
War Hero V: 03/17/93

Brown, Georg Stanford
c/o ICM
8942 Wilshir Blvd.
Beverly Hills, CA 90211
Actor V: 03/01/93

2934 1/2 N.Beverly Glen #404
Los Angeles, CA 90077
Alternate V: 06/14/92

Brown, Helen Gurley
One West 81st St. 22D
New York, NY 10024
Author V: 03/06/92

Brown, J.P.S.
1020 N. Avenida Aguila
Tucson, AZ 85748
Author V: 05/21/92

Brown, Jesse
Dept. of Veterans Affairs
810 Vermont Ave., N.W.
Washington, DC 20420
Dept. Head V: 01/31/93

Brown, Jill
c/o The Weather Channel
2600 Cumberland Parkway
Atlanta, GA 30339
Celebrity V: 04/05/93

Brown, Julie
723 Westmount Dr.
W. Hollywood, CA 90069
Actress V: 05/29/92

Brown, Kimberlin
c/o Young and the Restless
7800 Beverly Blvd.
Beverly Hills, CA 90036
Actress V: 06/15/92

Brown, Les
603 Ocean Ave. Ste.5-S
Santa Monica, CA 90405
Conductor V: 02/19/93

Brown Les
1455 Monaco
Pacific Palisades, CA 90272
Alternate V: 09/09/92

Brown, Mark N.
c/o NASA
LBJ Space Center
Houston, TX 77058
Astronaut V: 06/06/92

Brown, Peter
852 Cypress Ave.
Hermosa Beach, CA 90254
Actor V: 02/19/93

c/o Young and the Restless
7800 Beverly Blvd.
Beverly Hills, CA 90036
Alternate V: 06/15/92

3408 The Strand
Manhattan Beach, CA 90266
L.R.U. V: 06/01/92

Brown, Ronald H.
Dept. of Commerce
14th St.&Constitution Ave. N.W.
Washington, DC 20230
Politician V: 01/31/93

Brown, Ruth
600 W. 165th St., Ste.4H
New York, NY 10032
Singer V: 02/19/93

Brown, Sayer
c/o J. Halsey
24 Music Sq. W.
Nashville, TN 37203-3204
Singer V: 11/11/92

Brown Jr., Curtis L.
c/o NASA
LBJ Space Center
Houston, TX 77058
Astronaut V: 11/17/92

Browne, Chance
c/o King Features
216 E. 45th St.
New York, NY 10017
Cartoonist V: 03/11/93

Browne, Dick
c/o King Features
216 East 45th St.
New York, NY 10017
Cartoonist V: 06/03/92

Browne, Kale
c/o NBC-TV
Another World
79 Madison Ave., 5th Fl.
New York, NY 91523
Actor V: 06/15/92

Browne, Roscoe Lee
3531 Wonderview Drive
Los Angeles, CA 90068
Actor V: 06/14/92

Browner, Carol M.
Environmental Protection Agency
401 M Street, S.W.
Washington, DC 20460
Sectretary of EPA V: 01/31/93

Bruce, Carol
1361 N. Laurel Ave. #20
Los Angeles, CA 90046-4627
Actress V: 11/11/92

Bruel, Heidi
8137 Aufkirchen
Starnberger See 6-83
West Germany
Actress V: 01/02/93

Bry, Ellen
1999 Ave. of the Stars #2850
Los Angeles, CA 90067
Actress V: 03/03/93

Bryan, Dora
11 Marine Parade
Brighton
Sussex, England
Actress V: 06/12/92

Bryan, Zachery Ty
c/o Home Improvements
500 S. Buena Vista St.
Burbank, CA 91521
Actor V: 11/11/92

Bucha, Paul W.
RFD 3, Todd Rd.
Katonah, NY 10536
Medal of Honor V: 02/11/93

Buchanan, Ian
c/o ABC-TV/General Hospital
1438 N. Gower St.
Los Angeles, CA 90028
Actor V: 11/14/92

Buchanen, Jensen
c/o NBC-TV 'Another World'
30 Rockerfeller Plaza
New York, NY 10112
Actor V: 11/01/92

Buchholz, Horst
Clavdoiras
CH-7078 Lenzerheide
Switzerland
Actor V: 03/17/93

Buchli, Jim
c/o NASA
LBJ Space Center
Houston, TX 77058
Astronaut V: 06/07/92

Bucholz, Christopher
c/o Myriam Bru
80 Ave. Charles de Gaulle
F-92200 Neuilly-sur-Seine
France
Actor V: 02/11/93

Buchwald & Associates
9229 Sunset Blvd.
Los Angeles, CA 90069
Talent Agency V: 07/20/92

Buckingham, Lindsay
900 Airole Way
Los Angeles, CA 90077
Singer V: 12/12/92

Buckley, Betty
151 El Camino
Beverly Hills, CA 90210
Actress V: 08/11/92

Buckley, William F.
150 E. 35th St.
New York, NY 10016
Author V: 01/14/92

Buckner, Betty
6000 Monterey Rd. #8
Los Angeles, CA 90042
Actress V: 03/03/93

Budd, Julie
115 E. 68th St.
New York, NY 10021
Singer V: 02/02/92

Budge, Don
P.O. Box 789
Dingmans Ferry, PA 18328
Tennis V: 02/17/93

Buena Vista Co.
500 S. Buena Vista St.
Ste. 5064
Burbank, CA 91521
Fan Mail V: 12/10/92

Buffalo Bills
One Bills Dr.
Orchard Park, NY 14127
Team Offices V: 05/15/92

Buffett, Jimmy
500 Duval St., Ste.B
Key West, FL 33040-6553
Singer V: 02/17/93

80 Universal City Plaza 4th Fl
Universal City, CA 91608
Alternate V: 02/26/92

Buggs, Nicole
One Cowboys Parkway
Irving, TX 75063-4945
Cheerleader V: 08/08/92

Bujold, Genevieve
27258 Pacific Coast Hwy.
Malibu, CA 90265
Actress V: 06/21/92

Bull, John S.
c/o NASA LBJ Space Center
Houston, TX 77058
Astronaut V: 03/03/93

Bull, Richard
651 N. Wilcox, Ste.3G
Los Angeles, CA 90036
Actor V: 02/17/93

Bullock, Jim J.
6210 Temple Hill Dr.
Los Angeles, CA 90068
Actor V: 02/20/93

Bumgarner, Wayne
P.O. Box 208
Clairmont, NC 28610
NASCAR Driver V: 11/11/92

Bundy, Brooke
833 N. Martel Ave.
Los Angeles, CA 90046
Actress V: 02/16/93

Bundy, Prof. McGeorge
19 University Pl.
New York, NY 10003
Celebrity V: 05/22/92

Burbank Studios
4000 Warner Blvd.
Burbank, CA 91522
Production Company V: 03/17/93

Burford, Chris
P.O. Box 5168
Walnut Creek, CA 94596
Football V: 02/15/93

Burford, Thomas
20 Sunnyside Ave. Suite A#241
Mill Valley, CA 94941
Publisher V: 04/21/93

Burgess, Bobby
7752 Chandelle Pl.
Los Angeles, CA 90046
Actress V: 02/16/93

Burghoff, Gary
Box 33018 #315
St. Petersburg, FL 33733-8018
Actor V: 04/12/93

Burke, Alfred
219 The Plaza, 535 Kings Road
London SW10 0SZ, England
Actor V: 03/20/93

Burke, Chris
9200 Sunset Blvd. Ste.625
Los Angeles, CA 90069
Actor V: 02/16/93

Burke, Delta
c/o Wm. Morris
151 El Camino
Beverly Hills, CA 90212
Actress V: 12/10/92

1290 Inverness Dr.
Pasadena, CA 91103
Alternate V: 02/16/93

Burke, Paul
113 N. San Vicente Blvd. #202
Beverly Hills, CA 90211
Actor V: 05/22/92

Burke, Sean
c/o Hartford Whalers
1 Civic Center Dr.
Hartford, CT 06103
Hockey V: 04/05/93

Burkett Talent Agency
1700 E. Gary Ave. #113
Santa Ana, CA 92705
Talent Agency V: 07/20/92

Burkley, Dennis
5145 Costello Ave.
Sherman Oaks, CA 91403
Actor V: 02/15/93

Burnett, Carol
5750 Wilshire Blvd. #590
Los Angeles, CA 90036
Actress V: 11/11/92

7800 Beverly Blvd.
Los Angeles, CA 90036
Alternate V: 02/06/92

P.O. Box 1298
S. Pasadena, CA 91031-1298
Alternate V: 02/15/93

General Delivery
Kapalua Estates
Lahaina, HI 96761
Forwarded V: 06/19/92

Burnett, Nancy
c/o Bold & Beautiful CBS-TV
7800 Beverly Blvd.
Los Angeles, CA 90036
Actress V: 03/22/92

Burnett-Anderson, Barbara
P.O. Box 10118
Santa Fe, NM 87504-6118
Actor V: 12/12/92

Burns, George
720 N. Maple Dr.
Beverly Hills, CA 90210
Actor V: 01/03/92

Burr, Raymond
P.O. Box 678
Geyserville, CA 95441
Actor V: 03/01/93

Burrows, Darren E.
Northern Exposure
3000 Olympic Blvd., Ste.2575
Santa Monica, CA 90404
Actor V: 05/15/92

Bursch, Daniel W.
c/o NASA LBJ Space Center
Houston, TX 77058
Astronaut V: 03/03/93

Burstyn, Ellen
P.O. Box 217
Palisades, NY 10964-0217
Alternate V: 04/02/92

Burton, LeVar
c/o Star Trek-TNG Paramount
5555 Melrose Ave.
Hollywood, CA 90038
Actor V: 02/03/93

13417 Inwood Dr.
Sherman Oaks, CA 91423
Alternate V: 04/01/92

c/o Peaceful Warrior Prod.
13601 Ventura Blvd. Ste. 209
Sherman Oaks, CA 91432
Forwarded V: 02/14/92

Burton, Wendell
6526 Costello Dr.
Van Nuys, CA 91401
Actor V: 02/16/93

Burton Agency
1450 Belfast Dr.
Los Angeles, CA 90069
Talent Agency V: 11/21/92

Busey, Gary
2914 Searidge St.
Malibu, CA 90265-9518
Actor V: 01/02/92

Busey, Gary, contd
c/o Moress-Nanas-Golden
12424 Wilshire Blvd. Ste. 840
Los Angeles, CA 90025
 Alternate V: 02/12/92

Bush & Ross Talents
4942 Vineland Ave. Ste.B
N. Hollywood, CA 91601
 Talent Agency V: 02/01/93

Butcher, Susan
c/o Trail Breaker Kennel
Eureka, AK 99756
 Athelete V: 05/22/92

Buthelezi, Mangosuthu G.
Private Bag XO1, Ulundi 3838
Kwazulu, South Africa
 Politician V: 01/02/92

Butler, Dean
6220 Rodgerton Dr.
Los Angeles, CA 90068
 Actor V: 02/16/93

Buttons, Red
778 Tortuosa Way
Los Angeles, CA 90077
 Actor V: 02/22/92

Buttram, Pat
13906 Ventura Blvd. #302
Sherman Oaks, CA 91423
 Actor V: 06/13/92

Butts, Melaine
c/o Dallas Cowboys
One Cowboys Parkway
Irving, TX 75063-4945
 Cheerleader V: 08/08/92

Buzzi, Ruth
2309 Malaga Rd.
Los Angeles, CA 90068
 Actress V: 06/20/92

Byner, John
427 N. Bedford Dr.
Beverly Hills, CA 90212
 Actor V: 02/16/93

5863 Ramirez Canyon Rd.
Malibu, CA 90265
 Alternate V: 06/20/92

Byrne, David
7964 Willow Glen Rd.
Los Angeles, CA 90046
 Singer V: 02/16/93

Byrne, Gabrielle
8787 Shoreham Dr.
Los Angeles, CA 90069
 Actress V:03/09/92

Byrne, Josh
2040 Ave. of the Stars
Los Angeles, CA 90067
 Actor V: 02/17/93

Byrnes, Edd
1201 1/2 Cabrillo
Venice, CA 90291
 Actor V: 06/20/92

Byrnes, Jim
7083 Hollywood Blvd.
Hollywood, CA 90028
 Actor V: 03/23/92

Byron, Jeffrey
1419 S. Bentley Ave.
Los Angeles, CA 90025
 Actor V: 02/17/93

C

C'est La Vie Inc.
7507 Sunset Blvd. #201
Los Angeles, CA 90046
 Model/Talent Agency V: 02/28/93

C-Span
400 N. Capitol St. N.W. #650
Washington, DC 20001
 Network HQ V: 04/10/92

C.I.Inc., Talent Agency
843 N. Sycamore Ave.
Los Angeles, CA 90038
 Talent Agency V: 03/22/93

CALIFORNIA DREAMS
3000 W. Alameda Ave.
Burbank, CA 91523
 Production Company V: 03/26/93

CBN Cable Network Center
Virginia Beach, VA 23463
 Network HQ V: 03/01/93

CBS News
Film & Videotape Archive
1524 W. 57th St.
New York, NY 10019
 Archive V: 03/20/93

CBS-TV
c/o Programming
51 W. 52nd St.
New York, NY 10019
Network HQ V: 03/01/93

CBS-TV
c/o Programming
7800 Beverly Blvd.
Los Angeles, CA 90036
Alternate V: 03/01/93

CBS-TV News
524 W. 57th St.
New York, NY 10019
Studio Offices V: 12/10/92

CBS/MTM Studios
4024 Radford
Studio City, CA 91604
Production Company V: 03/17/93

CHEERS
Paramount Television
5555 Melrose Ave.
Lucille Ball Bldg. Rm. 105
Hollywood, CA 90038
TV Program V: 03/23/93

CIVIL WARS
Bochco-20th Cent./Fox
10201 W. Pico Blvd.
Los Angeles, CA 90035
Viewer Services V: 12/15/92

CLASSIC CONCENTRATION
5750 Wilshire Blvd. Ste. 475W
Los Angeles, CA 90036
TV Program V: 03/23/93

1801 Ave. of the Stars #1250
Los Angeles, CA 90067
Talent Agency V: 02/01/93

CNN
1050 Techwood Dr. NW
Atlanta, GA 30318
News Network V: 03/17/93

COLUMBO
c/o Universal TV
10201 W. Pico Blvd.
Los Angeles, CA 90035
Viewer Services V: 12/15/92

CONCENTRATION
c/o Disney Prod.
5750 Wilshire Blvd., Ste.475W
Los Angeles, CA 90036
Production Company V: 06/15/92

COSBY SHOW
Carsey Warner Co.
Kaufman Astoria Studios
34-12 36th St.
Astoria, NY 11106
TV Program V: 03/26/93

Caan, James
1435 Stone Canyon
Los Angeles, CA 90077
Actor V: 02/03/93

c/o Paramount Film Studios
5555 Melrose Ave.
Los Angeles, CA 90038
Actor V: 12/17/92

Cabana, Robert D.
c/o NASA
LBJ Space Center
Houston, TX 77058
Astronaut V: 06/20/92

Cabin Fever Entertainment
100 W. Putnam Ave.
Greenwich, CT 06830
Publicity V: 12/10/92

Cable News Network WTBS
6430 Sunset Blvd. 6th Fl.
Los Angeles, CA 90028
Production Office V: 03/17/91

Cable News WTBS
One CNN Center
P.O. Box 105366
Atlanta, GA 30348
Network HQ V: 03/01/92

Cadell, Ava
c/o Five K Sales Co.
9420 Reseda Blvd., #836
Northridge, CA 91324
Adult Films V: 03/03/93

Cady, Frank
c/o Greenvine
10100 E. 9th St. #C1005
Los Angeles, CA 90079
Actor V: 06/14/92

Caesar, Sid
1910 Loma Vista Drive
Beverly Hills, CA 90210
Comedian V: 12/14/92

Caffrey, Stephen
12338 Cantura St.
Studio City, CA 91604
Actor V: 02/17/93

Cage, Nicholas
5647 Tryon Rd.
Los Angeles, CA 90068
Actor V: 02/03/93

Caine, Michael
Rectory Farm House
North Stoke, Oxfordshire
England
Actor V: 12/20/92

388-396 Oxford St.
London W1 9HE, England
Alternate V: 03/20/93

Calder Agency
17420 Ventura Blvd. #4
Encino, CA 91316
Talent Agency V: 01/17/92

Caldwell, John
c/o King Features
216 East 45th St.
New York, NY 10017
Cartoonist V: 02/14/93

Calhoun, Rory
11532 Chiquita St.
Studio City, CA 91604
Actor V: 02/19/93

c/o Warner Bros.
4000 Warner Blvd.
Burbank, CA 91522
Forwarded V: 11/11/92

California Angeles
P.O. Box 2000
Anaheim Stadium
Anaheim, CA 92803
Team Office V: 05/15/92

Call, Brandon
5918 Van Nuys Blvd.
Van Nuys, CA 91401
Actor V: 02/20/93

Callahan, James
2125 21st St.
Santa Monica, CA 90405
Actor V: 02/19/93

342 N. Alfred St.
Los Angeles, CA 90048
Actor V: 02/19/93

Callan, Michael
9300 Wilshire Blvd. #410
Beverly Hills, CA 90212
Actor V: 03/03/93

Callan, Michael, contd
c/o Norton Styne Co.
508 N. Kings Rd., #2
Los Angeles, CA 90048
Alternate V: 07/19/92

8711 Burton Way #406
Beverly Hills, CA 90211
Forwarded V: 07/07/92

Calloway, Cab
1040 Knollwood Rd.
White Plains, NY 10019
Band Leader V: 12/03/92

Callum, John
c/o Cine-Nevada Inc.
Northern Exposure
3000 Olympic Blvd., Ste.2575
Santa Monica, CA 90404
Actor V: 05/15/92

Calvert, Phylis
c/o Argyll Lodge
Towersy, Thames
Oxon, England
Actress V: 06/20/92

Calvet, Corinne
Pacific Plaza Towers
1431 Ocean Ave., Ste.109
Santa Monica, CA 90401
Actress V: 08/08/92

Camden ITG Talent
822 S. Robertson Blvd. #200
Los Angeles, CA 90035
Talent Agency V: 12/12/92

Camel, Marvin
18331 Mansel Ave.
Redondo Beach, CA 90278
Boxer V: 12/14/92

Cameron, Candace
P.O. Box 80515
Conyers, GA 30208
Actress V: 02/15/93

Cameron, Kenneth D.
c/o NASA
LBJ Space Center
Houston, TX 77058
Astronaut V: 02/20/93

Cameron, Kirk
23548 Calabasas Rd. Ste.204
Calabasas, CA 91302
Actor V: 03/14/93

Cameron, Kirk, contd
9560 Wilshire Blvd. 5th Fl.
Beverly Hills, CA 90212
Alternate V: 03/01/93

Cameron & Associates
23548 Calabasas Rd. #204
Calabasas, CA 91302
Talent Agency V: 07/23/92

Camp, Colleen
2050 Fairburn Ave.
Los Angeles, CA 90025-5914
Actress V: 04/03/93

Campanela, Joseph
4647 Arcola Ave.
N. Hollywood, CA 91602
Actor V: 03/14/93

Campbell, Bill
21502 Velicata St.
Woodland Hills, CA 91364
Actor V: 04/17/93

Campbell, Bruce
5651 Saloma Ave.
Van Nuys, CA 91411
Actor V: 03/13/93

Campbell, Glen
5290 Exter Blvd.
Phoenix, AZ 85018
Singer V: 03/13/93

Campbell, Ken Hudson
c/o Hermans Head
500 S. Buena Vista St.
Burbank, CA 91521
Actor V: 11/11/92

Campbell, William
21502 Velicata St.
Woodland Hills, CA 91364
Actor V: 03/13/93

Canadian Broadcasting Corp.
1500 Bronson Ave. Box 8478
Ottawa, Ontario K1G 3J5 Canada
Archive V: 03/20/93

Candy, John
c/o ICM
8942 Wilshire Blvd.
Beverly Hills, CA 90211
Actor V: 03/01/93

12328 Montana
Los Angeles, CA 90049
Alternate V: 03/02/90

Candy, John, contd
11454 San Vicente Blvd.
Los Angeles, CA 90049
Alternate V: 05/14/92

1630 Mandeville Canyon Rd.
Los Angeles, CA 90049
Forwarded V: 12/11/92

Canelli, Rick
c/o Chesrown Chevrolet
7300 Broadway
Denver, CO 80221
NASCAR Driver V: 03/26/93

Caninenberg, Hans
Maria-Eich-Str. 43
D-(W) 8032 Grafelfing, Germany
Actor V: 01/19/93

Cannell, Steven J.
7083 Hollywood Blvd.
Hollywood, CA 90028
Producer V: 02/02/93

Cannell Productions
7083 Hollywood Blvd.
Hollywood, CA 90028
Production Company V: 03/17/93

Cannon, Dyan
8033 W. Sunset Blvd. Ste.254
Los Angeles, CA 90046
Actress V: 03/13/93

98 Malibu Colony Dr.
Malibu, CA 90265
L.R.U. V: 01/02/92

Cannon/Warner Bros.
4000 Warner Blvd.
Burbank, CA 91522
Publicity V: 12/10/92

Canova, Diana
8370 Wilshire Blvd. #310
Beverly Hills, CA 90211
Actress V: 03/17/93

Cantone, Vic
c/o King Features
216 E. 45th St.
New York, NY 10017
Cartoonist V: 03/11/93

Canyon, Christy
13601 Ventura Blvd. #218
Sherman Oaks, CA 91423
Adult Films V: 01/17/93

Canyon, Laurel
c/o Five K Sales Co.
9420 Reseda Blvd., #836
Northridge, CA 91324
Adult Films V: 03/03/93

Capitol Artists
6255 Sunset Blvd. 19th Fl.
Los Angeles, CA 90028
Talent Agency V: 04/27/92

Capitol Cities/ABC TV
77 W. 66th St.
New York, NY 10023
Viewer Services V: 12/10/92

Cara, Irene
8033 Sunset Blvd.
Los Angeles, CA. 90069
Actress V: 07/01/92

Carafotes, Paul
8033 Sunset Blvd. Ste.3554
Los Angeles, CA 90046
Actor V: 03/12/93

Cardiff, Jack
Lluca 4, Javea
Provence Alicante, Spain
Cinematographer V: 02/22/93

Cardinale, Claudia
Via Flaminia 17km
Rome, Italy
Actress V: 01/17/93

Career Artists Int'l.
11030 Ventura Blvd., Ste.3
Studio City, CA 91604
Talent Agency V: 04/27/92

Carelli, Rick
7300 N. Broadway
Denver, CO 80221
Race Driver V: 03/12/93

Carey, Clare
7632 Hollywood Blvd. Ste.3
Los Angeles, CA 90046
Actress V: 03/12/93

Carey, MacDonald
1543 Benedict Canyon
Beverly Hills, CA 90210
Actor V: 03/12/93

1420 N. Beachwood Dr.
Hollywood, CA 90028
L.R.U. V: 01/04/92

Carey, Maria
c/o Mottola
238 E. 67th St.
New York, NY 10021
Singer V: 03/11/93

Carey, Jr., Harry
P.O. Box 3256
Durango, CO 81302
Actor V: 01/02/92

c/o Craig Agency
8485 Melrose Place #E
Los Angeles, CA 90069
Alternate V: 06/14/92

1801 Santa Monica Rd.
Carpenteria, CA 93013
Forwarded V: 02/20/92

14159 Dickens St. #303
Sherman Oaks, CA 91423
Forwarded V: 04/14/92

Carlin, George
901 Bringham Ave.
Los Angeles, CA 90049
Actor V: 01/14/92

8033 Sunset Blvd. #1037
Los Angeles, CA 90046
Alternate V: 01/10/92

Carlisle, Belinda
3907 W. Alameda Ave. #200
Burbank, CA 91505
Singer V: 06/18/92

c/o Nigro
10100 Santa Monica Blvd. #2460
Los Angeles, CA 90067
Alternate V: 11/11/92

P.O. Box 5080
San Francisco, CA 94101
Alternate V: 03/01/92

1843 Benedict Canyon
Beverly Hills, CA 90210
Forwarded V: 07/02/92

3575 W. Cahenga Blvd. #470
Los Angeles, CA 90068
Forwarded V: 03/03/93

Carlisle, Kitty
c/o Hart
32 E. 64th St.
New York, NY 10021
Actress V: 06/14/92

Carlisle, Mary
517 N. Rodeo Dr.
Beverly Hills, CA 90210
Actress V: 04/02/92

Carmen, Julie
c/o Vestron Pictures
8800 W. Sunset Blvd. #208
Los Angeles, CA 90069-2105
Actress V: 02/28/92

Carmichael, Ian
c/o London Mgmt.
235 Regent St.
London W1, England
Actor V: 02/28/92

Carne, Judy
300 W. 12th St.
New York, NY 10014
Actress V: 03/11/93

Carnes, Kim
737 Latimer Rd.
Santa Monica, CA 90402-1015
Singer V: 02/02/92

3231 Barry Ave.
Los Angeles, CA 90066
L.R.U. V: 02/02/92

Carney, Art
143 Kingfisher Ln.
Westbrook, CT 06498
Actor V: 03/12/92

RR 20, P.O. Box 911
Westbrook, CT 06498
Alternate V: 02/01/93

Carolco Films
8800 Sunset Blvd.
Los Angeles, CA 90069
Production Company V: 03/17/91

Carolco TV
8439 Sunset Blvd.
Los Angeles, CA 90069
Production Company V: 03/17/93

Caron, Leslie
6 rue de Bellechasse
75 007 Paris, France
Actress V: 03/14/93

Caron, Leslie
c/o Fraser 5th Fl., The Chambers
Lots Rd. Chelsea Harbour
London SW10 0XF, England
Alternate V: 02/28/92

Caron, Leslie, contd
9169 Sunset Blvd.
Los Angeles, CA 90069
Forwarded V: 07/01/92

Carpenter, John
5326 Willis Ave.
Van Nuys, CA 91401
Director V: 03/10/93

3751 Avenida Del Sol
Studio City, CA 91604
Alternate V: 01/03/93

7950 Sunset Blvd.
Los Angeles, CA 90046
Forwarded V: 06/20/92

Carpenter, M. Scott
c/o NASA LBJ Space Center
Houston, TX 77058
Astronaut V: 03/03/93

Carpenter, Richard
P.O. Box 1084
Downey, CA 90240
Singer V: 02/01/92

Carr, Christina
c/o Dallas Cowboys
One Cowboys Parkway
Irving, TX 75063-4945
Cheerleader V: 08/08/92

Carr, Gerald P.
c/o NASA LBJ Space Center
Houston, TX 77058
Astronaut V: 03/03/93

Carr, Jane
c/o Arnott
6200 Mt. Angeles Dr.
Los Angeles, CA 90042
Actress V: 03/11/93

Carr, Vickie
P.O. Box 5126
Beverly Hills, CA 90210
Singer V: 01/12/92

2289 Betty Lane
Beverly Hills, CA 90210
L.R.U. V: 06/01/92

Carradine, David
9300 Wilshire Blvd. #410
Beverly Hills, CA 90212
Actor V: 03/03/93

Carradine, David, contd
3222 Benda Dr.
Los Angeles, CA 90068
 L.R.U. *V: 01/02/92*

Carradine, Robert
7453 Mulholland Dr.
Los Angeles, CA 90046
 Actor V: 03/12/93

Carrera, Barbara
15301 Ventura Blvd. #345
Sherman Oaks, CA 91403
 Actress V: 03/03/93

c/o Studio Fan Mail
1122 S. Robertson
Los Angeles, CA 90035
 Alternate V: 09/12/92

15430 Milldale Dr.
Los Angeles, CA 90077
 Alternate V: 06/15/92

3970 Overland Ave.
Culver City, CA 91230
 Forwarded V: 04/24/92

Carrere, Tia
8638 Franklin Ave.
Los Angeles, CA 90069
 Actress V: 03/13/93

c/o Paramount Pictures
5555 Melrose Ave.
Freeman Room #230
Hollywood, CA 90038
 Forwarded V: 02/19/93

Carrier, Larry
Bristol Int'l Raceway
P.O. Box 3966
Bristol, TN 37625
 NASCAR Official *V: 03/02/92*

Carrington, Laura
c/o" General Hosp."
4151 Prospect Ave.
Hollywood, CA 90027
 Actress V: 03/01/93

Carrington, Lord
32a Ovinton Sq.
London, SW3 1LR England
 Royalty V: 06/22/92

Carroll, Diahann
P.O. Box 2999
Beverly Hills, CA 90213
 Actress V: 03/13/93

Carroll, Diahann, contd
173 Riverside Dr. #11-D
New York, NY 10024
 Alternate V: 10/11/92

Carroll, Jill
c/o MGM/UA Comm.
"In the Heat of the Night"
1000 W. Washington Blvd.
Culver City, CA 90232
 Actress V: 01/07/92

Carroll, Pat
9507 Santa Monica Blvd. #221
Beverly Hills, CA 90210
 Actress V: 10/11/92

Carroll Agency
120 S. Victory Blvd. #104
Burbank, CA 91501
 Talent Agency V: 05/13/92

Carson, Johnny
6962 Wildlife
Malibu, CA 90265
 Celebrity V: 03/14/93

c/o NBC Prod.
"The Tonight Show"
3000 W. Alameda Ave.
Burbank, CA 91523
 Forwarded V: 02/21/93

Carson Productions
5300 Melrose Ave. Ste.309-E
Burbank, CA 90038
 Production Company V: 03/17/93

Carter, Dixie
151 El Camino
Beverly Hills, CA 90212
 Actress V: 03/01/93

P.O. Box 1980
Studio City, CA 91604
 Alternate V: 06/04/92

618 S. Lucerne Blvd.
Los Angeles, CA 90005
 Alternate V: 02/21/92

c/o CBS-Television City
7800 Beverly Blvd.
Los Angeles, CA 90049
 Forwarded V: 06/04/92

c/o Columbia PicturesTV/Mozark
Designing Women
Columbia Plz, Pro.Bl.8, #147
Burbank, CA 91505
 Forwarded V: 02/03/93

Carter, Dixie, contd
618 S. Lucerne Blvd.
Los Angeles, CA 90005-3704
L.R.U. *V: 02/02/92*

Carter, Don
13600 N. Kendall Dr.
Miami, FL 33186
Bowling *V: 06/12/92*

Carter, Helena
c/o Meshekoff
1655 Gilcrest Dr.
Beverly Hills, CA 90210
Actress *V: 06/06/92*

Carter, Jack
1023 Chevy Chase Dr.
Beverly Hills, CA 90210
Actor *V: 06/06/92*

Carter, Janice
603 Longboat Club Rd.
Longboat Key, FL 33548
Actress *V: 04/21/92*

Carter, Jimmy
c/o Carter Pres.Center Inc.
One Copenhill
Atlanta, GA 30307
Former President *V: 03/10/93*

1 Woodland Dr.
Plains, GA 31780
Alternate *V: 03/17/93*

Carter, John
2535 Greenvalley Rd.
Los Angeles, CA 90046
Actor *V: 06/02/92*

Carter, Lynda
21724 Ventura Blvd. Ste.195
Woodland Hills, CA 91364
Actress *V: 08/08/92*

P.O. Box 5973-215
Sherman Oaks, CA 91413
Forwarded *V: 08/08/92*

Carter, Rosalyn
1 Woodland Dr.
Plains, GA 31780
Former First Lady *V: 03/01/93*

Carter, Thomas
10958 Strathmore Dr.
Los Angeles, CA 90024
Actor *V: 02/16/93*

Carter (Cash), June
711 Summerfield Dr.
Hendersonville, TN 37075
Singer *V: 03/24/93*

Cartland, Barbara
Camfield Place
Hatfield, Herts., England
Author *V: 02/15/93*

Cartoon Art Museum
665 Third St., 5th Fl.
San Francisco, CA 94107
Museum *V: 01/02/93*

Cartwright, Angela
10143 Riverside Dr.
Toluca Lake, CA 91602
Actress *V: 07/02/92*

10112 Riverside Dr.
Toluca Lake, CA 91602
Alternate *V: 04/03/93*

Cartwright, Nancy
c/o Raw Toonage
500 S. Buena Vista St.
Burbank, CA 91521
Actress *V: 11/11/92*

Cartwright, Veronica
161 W. 15th St. #2H
New York, NY 10011
Actress *V: 06/14/92*

Caruso, Anthony
1706 Mandeville Ln.
Los Angeles, CA 90049
Actor *V: 12/14/92*

Carvey, Dana
9200 Sunset Blvd. Ste.428
Los Angeles, CA 90069
Actor *V: 01/21/92*

c/o NBC Prod./SNL
30 Rockefeller Plaza
New York, NY 10112
Forwarded *V: 01/10/93*

Casablanca Productions
8544 Sunset Blvd
Los Angeles, CA 90069
Production Company *V: 03/17/93*

Casamento, Anthony
748 Pine Ave.
W. Islip, NY 11795
Medal of Honor *V: 03/17/93*

Casares, Maria
8 Rue Asseline
Paris 75014, France
Actress V: 03/01/93

Case, Sharon
c/o General Hosp./ABC Inc.
4151 Prospect Ave.
Hollywood, CA 90027
Actress V: 03/01/93

Casella, Max
10201 W. Pico Blvd.
Los Angeles, CA 90035
Actor V: 12/15/92

Caselotti, Adriana
201 S. Larchmont Blvd.
Los Angeles, CA 90004
Actress V: 03/10/93

Casey, Collen
CBS-TV/The Young And Restless
7800 Beverly Blvd.
Los Angeles, CA 90036
Actor V: 05/04/92

Cash, Johnny
711 Summerfield Dr.
Hendersonville, TN. 37075
Musician V: 12/11/92

700 Johnny Cash Pkwy
P.O. Box 508
Hendersonville, TN 37077
Alternate V: 01/18/93

Cash, Rosalind
118 Park Pl. Ste.D
Venice, CA 90291
Singer V: 03/10/93

Cash, Rosanne
1016-17th Ave. Ste. 4
Nashville, TN 37212
Singer V: 04/21/92

1775 Broadway, 7th Fl.
New York, NY 10019
Alternate V: 06/30/92

Casper, Billy
14 Quiet Meadow Ln.
Mapleton, UT 84663
Golfer V: 12/11/92

P.O. Box 71
Springville, UT 84663
L.R.U. V: 12/12/92

Casper, John H.
NASA/LBJ Space Center
Houston, TX 77058
Astronaut V: 06/06/92

Cassel, Jean-Pierre
388-396 Oxford St.
London W1, England
Actress V: 03/10/93

Cassevettes, Nick
22722 Clarendon St.
Woodland Hills, CA 91367
Actor V: 03/09/93

Cassidy, David
1350 Ave. of the America's
New York, NY 10012
Actor V: 12/12/92

Cassidy, Jack
611 Broadway, Ste.822
New York, NY 10012
Singer V: 02/01/92

Cassidy, Joanna
463 Mesa Rd.
Santa Monica, CA 90402
Actress V: 03/09/93

12427 Sunset Blvd.
Los Angeles, CA 90049
L.R.U. V: 06/03/92

2001 S. Barrington Ave.#216
Los Angeles, CA 90025
L.R.U. V: 12/02/92

Cassidy, Shaun
8942 Wilshire Blvd.
Beverly Hills, CA 90211
Actor V: 03/09/93

Casson, Mel
c/o King Features
216 E. 45th St.
New York, NY 10017
Cartoonist V: 03/11/93

Cast, Tricia
c/o Y&R CBS-TV
7800 Beverly Blvd.
Beverly Hills, CA 90036
Actress V: 06/15/92

Castellaneta, Dan
328 Poquito Ln.
Topanga, CA 90290
Actor V: 03/09/93

Castellanos, John
c/o "Y & R"
7800 Beverly Blvd.
Beverly Hills, CA 90036
Actor V: 06/15/92

Casting Society
6565 Sunset Blvd. #306
Los Angeles, CA 90028
Production Company V: 03/17/93

Castle Rock
335 N. Maple Dr. #135
Beverly Hills, CA 90210
Production Company V: 03/17/93

Castle-Hill Talent
1101 S. Orlando
Los Angeles, CA 90035
Talent Agency V: 05/13/92

Cates, Phoebe
45 W. 67th St. Ste.27-B
New York, NY 10023
Actress V: 12/23/92

136 E. 57th St. #1001
New York, NY 10022
L.R.U. V: 08/08/92

Cates, Ronda
c/o Dallas Cowboys
One Cowboys Parkway
Irving, TX 75063-4945
Cheerleader V: 08/08/92

Catlett, Mary Jo
4375 Farmdale Ave.
North Hollywood, CA 91604
Actress V: 06/07/92

Cattrall, Kim
c/o The Gersh Agency
3232 N. Canon Dr.
Beverly Hills, CA 90210
Actress V: 10/29/92

760 N. La Cienega Blvd. #200
Los Angeles, CA 90069
Alternate V: 02/03/93

616 Lorna Lane
Los Angeles, CA 90049
Forwarded V: 07/14/92

c/o Republic Pict.
12636 Beatrice St.
Los Angeles, CA 90066
Forwarded V: 11/11/92

Caulfield, Maxwell
4036 Foothill Rd.
Carpenteria, CA 90313
Actor V: 03/08/93

Cause in Effect
4707 N. Malden
Chicago, IL 60640
Rap Music Band V: 02/04/92

Cavaleri & Associates
6605 Hollywood Blvd. #220
Hollywood, CA 90028
Talent Agency V: 06/13/92

Cavett, Dick
2200 Fletcher Ave.
Ft. Lee, NJ 07024
Celebrity V: 03/08/93

Cawelti, Michael
2239 Dwight Way
Berkeley, CA 94704
Fight Director V: 03/01/93

Celardo, John
216 East 45th St.
New York, NY 10017
Cartoonist V: 09/23/92

Celebrity Access
20 Sunnyside Ave., Ste. #A241
Mill Valley, CA 94941
Publishers V: 03/03/93

Celebrity Mail Service
932 N.Curson Ave., Ste.5
Los Angeles, CA 90046
Fan Mail V: 01/12/93

Celentano, Adriano
Viale Carso 63
I-00195 Rome, Italy
Actor V: 01/17/93

Cenker, Bob
P.O. Box 800
Princeton, NJ 08543-0800
Astronaut V: 06/12/92

Center-Film/Theatre Research
816 State St.
Madison, WI 53706
Archive V: 03/20/93

Century Home Video
2688 S. La Cienega Bl.
Los Angeles, CA 90034
Publicity V: 12/10/92

Cernan, Eugene A.
NASA/LBJ Space Center
Houston, TX 77058
Astronaut V: 03/03/93

Cey, Ron
22714 Creole Rd.
Woodland Hills, CA 91364
Baseball V: 12/31/92

Chadwick, Florence
P.O. Box 3407
La Jolla, CA 92038-3407
Swimmer V: 11/11/92

Chadwick, Florence, contd
814 Armada Terrace
San Diego, CA 92106
Alternate V: 03/08/93

Chaffee, Suzy
140 Hollister Ave.
Santa Monica, CA 90402
Celebrity V: 03/07/93

Chaio, Leroy
c/o NASA LBJ Space Center
Houston, TX 77058
Astronaut V: 03/03/93

Chakiris, George
7266 Clinton St.
Los Angeles, CA 90036
Actor V: 09/09/92

Chamberlain, Richard
10202 W. Washington Blvd.
Culver City, CA 90232
Actor V: 12/18/92

Chambers, Marilyn
4528 W. Charleston Blvd., #836
Las Vegas, NV 89102
Adult Films V: 06/01/92

c/o 5K Sales Co.
9420 Reseda Bl. #613
Northridge, CA 91324
Alternate V: 03/03/93

5627 Sepulvida Blvd. #214
Van Nuys, CA 91411
Forwarded V: 01/17/93

Champagne
P.O. Box 8595
Anaheim, CA 92812
Adult Films V: 01/17/93

Champion, Marge
Prospect Hill
Stockbridge, MA 01262
Actress V: 05/22/92

Chandler, Karen Mayo
3800 Barham Blvd. #303
Los Angeles, CA 90068
Actress V: 03/22/93

Chanel, Patrice
19216 Andmark Ave.
Carson, CA 90746
Actress V: 03/06/93

Chang-Diaz, Franklin R.
NASA/LBJ Space Center
Houston, TX 77058
Astronaut V: 06/06/92

Channing, Carol
9301 Flicker Way
Los Angeles, CA 90069
Actress V: 03/01/92

Channing, Stockard
1155 Park Ave.
New York, NY 10128-1209
Actress V: 03/06/93

8942 Wilshire Blvd.
Beverly Hills, CA 90211
Alternate V: 05/04/92

Chapin, Lauren
P.O. Box 922
Killeen, TX 76540
Actress V: 05/12/92

Chaplin, Judith
67810 Marilyn Circle
Cathedral City, CA 92234
Actress V: 03/06/93

Chaplin, Lita Grey
8440 Fountain Ave. #302
Los Angeles, CA 90069
Actress V: 06/14/92

Chapman, Philip K.
c/o NASA LBJ Space Center
Houston, TX 77058
Astronaut V: 03/03/93

Chappell, Crystal
NBC-TV/Days of Our Lives
300 W. Alameda Ave.
Burbank, CA 91523
Actress V: 01/02/93

Charisma
9420 Reseda Blvd., Ste.836
Northridge, CA 91324
Adult Films V: 01/17/93

Charisse, Cyd
10390 Wilshire Blvd. #1507
Los Angeles, CA 90024
Actress V: 01/04/92

Charles, Ray
2107 W. Washington Bl. Ste.200
Los Angeles, CA 90018
Singer V: 06/05/92

4863 Southridge Ave.
Los Angeles, CA 90008
Alternate V: 03/06/93

Charleson, Leslie
c/o General Hosp./ABC Inc.
4151 Prospect Ave.
Hollywood, CA 90027
Actress V: 03/01/93

2314 Live Oak Dr. E.
Los Angeles, CA 90068
Alternate V: 03/07/93

Charo
P.O. Box 1007
Hanalei, Kaui, HI 96714
Actress V: 03/07/93

Charter Management
8200 Wilshire Blvd. #218
Beverly Hills, CA 90211
Talent Agency V: 02/20/93

Chartoff, Melanie
c/o Abrams/Rubaloff
8075 W. 3rd St. #302
Los Angeles, CA 90048
Actress V: 11/11/92

444 S. Roxbury Dr. Ste.A
Beverly Hills, CA 90212
Alternate V: 03/08/93

Chartoff-Winkler Productions
10125 W. Washington Blvd.
Culver City, CA 90230
Production Company V: 03/17/93

Chase, Chevy
9056 Santa Monica Blvd. #100
Los Angeles, CA 90069
Actor V: 03/08/93

Chase, Chevy, contd
8436 W. 3rd St. #650
Los Angeles, CA 90048
Alternate V: 06/04/92

Chasin Agency
190 N. Canon Dr., Ste.201
Beverly Hills, CA 90210
Talent Agency V: 06/13/92

Chaves, Richard
P.O. Box 120130
Chula Vista, CA 92012
Actor V: 02/01/93

Chavez, Ceasar
c/o UFW
P.O. Box 52
Keene, CA 93531
Activist V: 05/22/92

Cheap Trick
P.O. Box 4321
Madison, WI 53711
Musical Group V: 01/22/92

Cheatham, Maree
c/o General Hosp./ABC Inc.
4151 Prospect Ave.
Hollywood, CA 90027
Actor V: 03/01/93

Cheatham, Maree
3377 Canton Ln.
Studio City, CA 91604
Alternate V: 03/08/93

Checker, Chubby
1650 Broadway Ste. 1011
New York, NY 10019
Singer V: 01/14/92

Cheech & Chong
32020 Pacific Coast Hwy.
Malibu, CA 90265
Actors V: 05/23/92

Chen, Joan
2601 Filbert St.
San Francisco, CA 94123-3215
Actress V: 03/17/93

148 S. Occidental Blvd. #204
Los Angeles, CA 90057
Actress V: 11/11/92

Cher
10960 Wilshire Blvd. #938
Los Angeles, CA 90024
Actress V: 03/03/93

Cher, contd
2727 Benedict Canyon Dr.
Beverly Hills, CA 90210
L.R.U V: 01/02/92

Cherill, Virginia
160 Pomar Lane
Montecito, CA 93108
Actress V: 06/14/92

Chicago Bears
Halas Hall
250 N. Washington Rd.
Lake Forest, IL 60045
Team Offices V: 05/15/92

Chicago Cubs
1060 W. Addison St.
Wrigley Field
Chicago, IL 06013
Team Office V: 05/15/92

Chicago Historical Society
Prints & Photographs Dept.
Clark St. at North Ave.
Chicago, IL 60614
Archive V: 03/18/93

Chicago White Sox
324 W. 35th St.
Comiskey Park
Chicago, IL 60616
Team Office V: 05/15/92

Child, Julia
103 Irving St.
Cambridge, MA 02138
Chef V: 03/09/93

Childress, Richard
c/o Childress Racing
P.O. Box 1189, Industrial Dr.
Welcome, NC 27374
NASCAR Owner V: 03/02/92

Chiles, Lois
644 San Lorenzo
Santa Monica, CA 90402
Actress V: 03/17/93

Chilton, Kevin P.
c/o NASA LBJ Space Center
Houston, TX 77058
Astronaut V: 03/03/93

Chong, Rae Dawn
32020 Pacific Coast Hwy
Malibu, CA 90265
Actress V: 02/20/93

Chong, Rae Dawn, contd
P.O. Box 181
Bearsville, NY 12409
L.R.U V: 08/17/92

Chong, Tommy
1625 Casale Rd.
Pacific Palisades, CA 90272
Actor V: 03/10/93

Christensen, Todd
991 Sunburst Ln.
Alpine, CA UT 84004-1203
Football V: 03/10/93

Christie, Julie
23 Linden Gardens
London W2, England
Actress V: 09/01/92

Christie, Lou
c/o Young
1645 E. 50th St. #10A
Chicago, IL 60615
Singer V: 05/06/92

Christie, Marsha
Warner/"Head of Class"
100 North Pass Rd.
Burbank, CA 91505
Actress V: 12/18/92

Christine, Andrew
c/o King Features
216 E. 45th St.
New York, NY 10017
Cartoonist V: 03/11/93

Christine, Virginia
12348 Rochedale Lane
Los Angeles, CA 90049
Actress V: 03/10/93

Christmas, Eric
c/o Cannell Prod.
7083 Hollywood Blvd.
Hollywood, CA 90028
Actor V: 05/15/92

Christopher, Robin
351 E. 84th St.
New York, NY 10028
Actress V: 04/23/92

Christopher, Warren
Dept. of State
2201 C St. N.W.
Washington, DC 20520
Politician V: 01/31/93

Christopher, William
P.O. Box 50698
Pasadena, CA 91105-0698
Actor V: 02/03/92

Chung, Connie
CBS/"Face to Face"
524 W. 57th St.
New York, NY 10019
Production Company V: 06/15/92

Cilton, Kevin P.
NASA/LBJ Space Center
Houston, TX 77058
Astronaut V: 06/05/92

Cincinnati Bengals
200 Riverfront Stadium
Cincinnati, OH 45202
Team Offices V: 05/15/92

Cincinnati Reds
100 Riverfront Stadium
Cincinnati, OH 45202
Team Office V: 05/15/92

Cine-Media Internat'l
P.O. Box 7005
Long Beach, CA 90807
Film Distributor V: 03/17/92

Cinefantastic
P.O. Box 270
Oak Park, IL 60303
Horror Fanzine V: 01/02/92

Cinemax
1100 Ave. of the Americas
New York, NY 10036
Network HQ V: 03/01/92

2049 Century Park. E. #1400
Los Angeles, CA 90067
Alternate V: 03/17/92

Circle Talent Associates
433 N.Camden Dr. #400
Beverly Hills, CA 90210
Talent Agency V: 06/06/92

Cisneros, Henry G.
451 7th St.,S.W.
Washington, DC 20401
Secretary of HUD V: 01/31/03

Clampett Productions
729 Seward St.
Hollywood, CA 90038
Cartoonist V: 03/17/92

Clark, Candy
5 Briarhill Rd.
Montclaire, NJ 07042
Actress V: 06/01/92

Clark, Christie
c/o Days of Our Lives
3000 W. Alemeda
Burbank, CA 91523
Actress V: 06/06/92

Clark, Dane
1680 Old Oak Rd.
Los Angeles, CA 90049
Actor V: 11/11/92

Clark, Dick
c/o Dick Clark Prod.
Super Bloopers
3003 W. Olive
Burbank, CA 91505
TV Host V: 03/03/93

Clark, Emily
c/o Dallas Cowboys
One Cowboys Parkway
Irving, TX 75063-4945
Cheerleader V: 08/08/92

Clark, Matt
9169 Sunset Blvd.
Los Angeles, CA 90069
Actor V: 11/15/92

Clark, Petula
15 Cheminbelle Fonte Coligny
Geneva, Switzerland
Singer V: 02/13/92

Clark, Ramsey
36 E. 12th St.
New York, NY 10003
Musician V: 03/05/93

Clark, Roy
c/o Roy Clark Productions
3225 S. Norwood Ave.
Tulsa, OK 74135
Actor V: 01/22/92

Clark, Susan
7943 Woodrow Wilson Dr.
Los Angeles, CA 90046
Actress V: 11/11/92

c/o Paramount Studios
5555 Melrose ave.
Los Angeles, CA 90038
Alternate V: 06/12/92

Clark, Will
San Francisco Giants
Candlestick Park
San Francisco, CA 94124
Baseball V: 11/11/92

Clark Company
2431 Hyperian Ave.
Los Angeles, CA 90027
Talent Agency V: 07/20/92

Clark Productions
c/o Dick Clark
3003 W. Olive Ave.
Burbank, CA 91505
Production Company V: 03/17/93

Clarke, Brian Patrick
c/o Bell-Phillip Prod.
Bold & Beautiful
7800 Beverly Blvd., Ste.3371
Los Angeles, CA 90036
Actor V: 06/15/92

Clarke, Brian Patrick
333 N. Kenwood St. Ste.D
Burbank, CA 91505
Alternate V: 03/05/93

Clarke, John
8350 Santa Monica Blvd. #206A
Los Angeles, CA 90069
Actor V: 11/15/92

Clarke, Julie
c/o Playboy Promotions
680 N. Lake Shore Dr.
Chicago, IL 60611
Model V: 04/05/93

Clarke Agency
2030 E. 4th, Ste.102
Santa Ana, CA 92705
Talent Agency V: 07/20/92

Clary, Robert
10001 Sundial Ln.
Beverly Hills, CA 90210
Actor V: 06/01/92

c/o Bell-Phillip Prod.
Bold & Beautiful
7800 Beverly Blvd., Ste.3371
Los Angeles, CA 90036
Alternate V: 06/15/92

Clay, Andrew (Dice)
1340 Londonderry Pl.
Los Angeles, CA 90069
Actor V: 07/08/92

Clay, Andrew (Dice), contd
163 Joralmon St., Ste. 1508
Brooklyn, NY 11201
Alternate V: 03/02/92

Clayburgh, Jill
225 McLain St.
Mt. Kisco, NY 10549
Actress V: 02/20/92

Claymation
c/o Will Vinton Prod. Inc.
1400 N.W. 22nd Ave.
Portland, OR 97210
Animators V: 04/16/92

Clayton, Jack
Herons Flight, Marlow
Bucks. SL7 2LE, England
Director V: 01/03/93

Clayton, Wendy
c/o Dallas Cowboys
One Cowboys Parkway
Irving, TX 75063-4945
Cheerleader V: 08/08/92

Cleave, Mary L.
c/o NASA
LBJ Space Center
Houston, TX 77058
Astronaut V: 06/01/92

Cleese, John
c/o RHL
8 Waterloo Place
London, SW1 England
Actor V: 06/01/92

c/o Wilkinson
24 Denmark St.
London WC2H 8NJ, England
Alternate V: 03/20/93

82 Ladbroke Road
London W11 3NU, England
Alternate V: 01/14/93

Clementi, Pierre
c/o Greek Film Centre
10 Panepistumiou Ave.
Athens 10671, Greece
Actor V: 03/14/93

Clennon, David
954 20th St., Ste.B
Santa Monica, CA 90403
Actor V: 03/05/93

Cler Talent Agency
120 S. Victory Blvd. #206
Burbank, CA 91502
Talent Agency *V: 11/21/92*

Cleveland Browns
Cleveland Stadium
Cleveland, OH 44114
Team Offices *V: 05/15/92*

Cleveland Indians
Municipal Stadium
Cleveland, OH 44114
Team Office *V: 05/15/92*

Clifford, Clark
c/o Clifford & Warnke
815 Commonwealth Ave. N.W.
Washington, DC 20006
Politician *V: 05/22/92*

Clifford, Michael R.
c/o NASA LBJ Space Center
Houston, TX 77058
Astronaut *V: 03/03/93*

Clinger, Debra
4415 Auckland Ave.
North Hollywood, CA 91602
Actress *V: 06/04/92*

Clinton, Bill
The White House
1600 Pennsylvania Ave.
Washington, DC 20515
President USA *V: 10/04/92*

1800 Center St.
Little Rock, AR 72206
Alternate *V: 03/05/93*

Clinton, Hillary Rodham
The White House
1600 Pennsylvania Ave.
Washington, DC 20515
First Lady *V: 03/03/93*

Clooney, George
11655 Laurelcrest Dr.
Studio City, CA 91604-3814
Actor *V: 03/04/93*

Close, Glenn
23 W. Main St.
Bozeman, MT 59715
Actress *V: 03/04/93*

1888 Century Park E. 14th PL.
Los Angeles, CA 90067
Forwarded *V: 06/01/92*

Close, Glenn, contd
9830 Wilshire Blvd.
Beverly Hills, CA 90212
Forwarded *V: 06/25/92*

Clower, Jerry
P.O Box 121089
Nashville, TN 37212
Comedian *V: 03/04/93*

Cluka, Scott
c/o Childress
P.O. Box 1189 Industrial Dr.
Welcome, NC 27374
Race Crew *V: 03/12/93*

Coast to Coast Talent
4942 Vineland Ave. #200
N. Hollywood, CA 91601
Talent Agency *V: 03/22/93*

Coats, Michael L.
c/o NASA LBJ Space Center
Houston, TX 77058
Astronaut *V: 03/03/93*

Cobb, Julie
4433 Bergammo Dr.
Encino, CA 91436
Actress *V: 03/04/93*

Coburn, James
3930 Hollyline Ave.
Sherman Oaks, CA 91403
Actor *V: 11/15/92*

c/o Trimark Pictures
2644 20th St.
Santa Monica CA 90405-3009
Actor *V: 01/13/93*

Cockrell, Kenneth D.
c/o NASA LBJ Space Center
Houston, TX 77058
Astronaut *V: 03/03/93*

Cody, Iron Eyes
2013 Griffith Park Blvd.
Los Angeles, CA 90039
Actor *V: 09/08/92*

Coelho, Susie
2814 Hutton Dr.
Beverly Hills, CA 90210
Actress *V: 06/01/92*

Coffin, Frederick
9301 Wilshire Blvd. #312
Beverly Hills, CA 90210
Actor *V: 02/12/93*

Coghlan, Frank
12522 Argyle Ave.
Los Alamitos, CA 90720
Actor   V: 03/04/93

Cohen, Alexander
25 W. 54th St. Ste.5F
New York, NY 10019-5411
Producer   V: 03/03/93

Cohn, Mindy
913 18th St. #2
Santa Monica, CA 90403-3209
Actress   V: 11/11/92

9606 Yoakum Dr.
Beverly Hills, CA 90210
Alternate   V: 03/03/93

Colbert, Claudette
Bellerive, St. Peter
Barbados, West Indies
Actress   V: 12/12/92

945 5th Ave.
New York, NY 10021
Alternate   V: 06/04/92

Colbert, Robert
151 Ocean Park Blvd.
Santa Monica, CA 90405
Actor   V: 03/03/93

Colcord, Webster
c/o Will Vinton Prod. Inc.
1400 N.W. 22nd Ave.
Portland, OR 97210
Animator   V: 04/16/92

Cole, Dennis
2160 Century Park E. #1712
Los Angeles, CA 90067
Actor   V: 03/03/93

Cole, George
c/o Agent
7 West Eaton Pl.
London SW1X 8LY, England
Actor   V: 06/06/92

Cole, Michael
6332 Costello Ave.
Van Nuys, CA 91401-2209
Actor   V: 03/17/92

c/o ABC-TV
General Hospital
4151 Prospect Ave.
Hollywood, CA 90027
Alternate   V: 06/15/92

Cole, Tina
2126 Cahuenga Blvd.
Los Angeles, CA 90068
Actress   V: 05/13/92

Coleman, Dabney
9200 Sunset Blvd.   Ste. 428
Los Angeles, CA 90069
Actor   V: 01/21/92

360 N. Kenter Ave.
Los Angeles, CA 90049
Alternate   V: 09/02/92

Coleman, Gary
c/o Hanson
2020 Ave. of the Stars #410
Los Angeles, CA 90067
Actor   V: 03/03/93

Coleman, Jack
7358 Woodrow Wilson Dr.
Los Angeles, CA 90046
Actor   V: 03/03/93

Colin, Margaret
366 W. 11th St., PH-C
New York, NY 10014
Actress   V: 03/04/93

Collectors Showcase
7130 S. Lewis, Ste. 210
Tulsa, OK 74136
Magazine   V: 03/03/92

Collins, Eileen M.
c/o NASA LBJ Space Center
Houston, TX 77058
Astronaut   V: 03/03/93

Collins, Gary
2751 Hutton Dr.
Beverly Hills, CA 90210
Actor   V: 06/12/92

Collins, Jackie
710 N. Foothill Rd.
Beverly Hills, CA 90210
Author   V: 05/21/92

13701 Riverside Dr. #608
Sherman Oaks, CA 91423
Alternate   V: 03/03/93

Collins, Joan
1196 Cabrillo Dr.
Beverly Hills, CA 90210
Actress   V: 07/01/92

Collins, Joan, contd
19 Eaton Pl., Flat 2
London SW1, England
Alternate V: 03/04/93

c/o Peter Charlesworth
68 Old Brompton Rd., 2nd Fl.
London SW7 3LQ, England
Forwarded V: 02/04/92

Collins, Judy
c/o Rocky Mt. Prod. Inc.
P.O. Box 1296/Cathedral Sta.
New York, NY 10025
Singer V: 04/13/92

Collins, Lewis
388-396 Oxford St.
London W1 9HE, England
Actor V: 03/20/92

Collins, Michael
c/o NASA LBJ Space Center
Houston, TX 77058
Astronaut V: 03/03/93

Collins, Phil
P.O. Box 107
London N6 5RU, England
Singer V: 05/14/92

130 W. 57th St. #6-B
New York, NY 10019
Alternate V: 03/18/93

Colomby, Scott
1425 Queens Road
Los Angeles, CA 90069
Actor V: 06/14/92

Color Me Badd
345 N. Maple Dr. Ste.205
Beverly Hills, CA 90210
Musical Group V: 03/05/93

Colours Agency
7551 Melrose Ave. #6
Los Angeles, CA 90046
Model/Talent Agency V: 02/28/93

Colter, Jessie
1117 17th Ave. S.
Nashville, TN 37212
Singer V: 06/23/92

Colton & Associates
16661 Ventura Blvd. #400
Encino, CA 91436
Talent Agency V: 01/17/92

Columbia Pictures
Columbia Plaza N. Ste.417
Burbank, CA 91505
Production Company V: 03/17/93

Columbia Pictures (TV)
"Sunset Gower Studio"
1438 N. Gower St.
Hollywood, CA 90028-8394
Viewer Services V: 11/11/92

Combs, Rodney
c/o NASCAR
1811 Volusia Ave.
Daytona Beach, FL 32015
NASCAR Driver V: 03/02/92

Comden, Betty
117 E. 95th St.
New York, NY 10128
Actress V: 03/05/93

Comedy Central
1775 Broadway
New York, NY 10019
Production Company V: 11/11/92

Commercials Unlimited
7461 Beverly Blvd. #400
Los Angeles, CA 90036
Talent Agency V: 12/12/92

Como, Perry
305 Northern Bl. #35-A
Great Neck, NY 11021
Singer V: 01/14/92

Compton, Joyce
23388 Mulholland Dr.
Woodland Hills, CA 91364
Actress V: 03/05/93

Conley, Darlene
c/o Bell-Phillip Prod.
Bold & Beautiful
7800 Beverly Blvd., Ste.3371
Los Angeles, CA 90036
Actress V: 06/15/92

Conley, Jill
P.O. Box 6487
Thousands Oaks, CA 91359-6487
Actress V: 11/11/92

10332 Christine Pl.
Chatsworth, CA 91311
L.R.U. V: 11/11/92

Conley, Joe
P.O. Box 6487
Thousand Oaks, CA 91359
Actor V: 03/30/93

Conn, Didi
14820 Valley Vista Blvd.
Sherman Oaks, CA 91403
Actress V: 06/14/92

10635 Riverside Dr.
Toluca Lake, CA 91602
L.R.U. V: 02/02/92

Connelly, Jennifer
8942 Wlishire Blvd.
Beverly Hills, CA 90211
Actress V: 03/05/93

50 Bethel St.
Cranston, RI 02920-5307
Alternate V: 11/11/92

2637 Ellendale Pl. #16
Los Angeles, CA 90007
L.R.U. V: 11/11/92

Conner, Dennis
c/o Conner Sports Inc.
720 Gateway Center Dr., Ste.E
San Diego, CA 92102
Sportsman V: 06/14/92

Conners, Mike
4810 Louise Ave.
Encino, CA 91316
Actor V: 03/17/93

Connery, Jason
219 The Plaza, 535 Kings Road
London SW10 0SZ, England
Actor V: 03/20/93

Connery, Sean
Casa Malibu, Fuente del Rodeo
Andalucia La Nueva, Spain
Actor V: 09/09/92

2220 Ave. of the Stars
Los Angeles, CA 90067
Alternate V: 03/17/93

Connick Jr., Harry
3 Hastings Sq.
Cambridge, MA 02139-4724
Singer V: 03/30/93

260 Brookline St.
Cambridge, MA 02139
Alternate V: 03/03/93

Conniff, Ray
P.O. Box 46395
Los Angeles, CA 90046
Conductor V: 04/01/93

Box 36
Encino, CA 91316
L.R.U. V: 03/03/93

Connolly, Norma
c/o General Hosp./ABC Inc.
4151 Prospect Ave.
Hollywood, CA 90027
Actress V: 03/01/93

Connor, Kenneth
Pinefood Film Studio
Iver Heath
Bucks. SL0 0NH, England
Actor V: 03/15/93

Connors, Carol
1709 Ferrari Dr.
Beverly Hills, CA 90210
Songwriter V: 06/14/92

Connors, Mike
4810 Louise Ave.
Encino, CA 91316
Actor V: 06/14/92

Conrad, Christian
15301 Ventura Blvd. #345
Sherman Oaks , CA 91403
Actor V: 03/19/93

Conrad, Paul
c/o Times/Mirror
Times Mirror Square
Los Angeles, CA 90053
Cartoonist V: 07/23/92

Conrad, Robert
21355 Pacific Coast Hwy #200
Malibu, CA 90265
Actor V: 03/19/93

8966 Sunset Blvd.
Hollywood, CA 90069
Alternate V: 04/13/92

Conrad, William
4031 Longridge Ave.
Studio City, CA 91423
Actor V: 06/01/92

Conrad Jr., Charles
McDonnell Corp./Box 516
St. Louis, MO 63166-0516
Astronaut V: 04/01/92

Conrad Jr., Charles, contd
c/o McDonnell Douglas Corp.
5301 Bolsa Ave.
Huntington Beach, CA 92647
Alternate V: 02/12/92

c/o NASA LBJ Space Center
Houston, TX 77058
Forwarded V: 03/03/93

Conroy, Kevin
9301 Wilshire Blvd. #312
Beverly Hills, CA 90210-5410
Actor V: 03/19/93

Conte, John
75600 Beryl Dr.
Indian Wells, CA 92260
Actor V: 01/24/93

Contemporary Artists
1427 3rd. St. Promenade #205
Santa Monica, CA 90401
Talent Agency V: 07/23/92

Conti, Tom
c/o Markham
Julian House, 4 Windmill St.
London W1, England
Actor V: 03/20/92

Converse, Peggy
1900 Ave. of the Stars #2270
Los Angeles, CA 90067
Actress V: 11/11/92

2525 Briarcrest Rd.
Beverly Hills, CA 90210
Actress V: 01/24/93

Conway, Gary
2035 Mandeville Canyon
Los Angeles, CA 90049
Actor V: 06/14/92

Conway, Tim
P.O. Box 17047
Encino, CA 91416-7047
Actor V: 01/12/92

425 S. Beverly Dr.
Beverly Hills, CA 91316
Alternate V: 03/23/92

Conwell, Carolyn
c/o Young and the Restless
7800 Beverly Blvd.
Beverly Hills, CA 90036
Actress V: 06/15/92

Cook, Barry
c/o Sabco Racing
5901 Orr Rd.
Charlotte, NC 28213
NASCAR Crew V: 03/26/93

Cook, Peter
24 Perrine Walks
London NW3, England
Alternate V: 06/14/92

Cook, Robin
22 Prince Albert Rd.
London NW1 7ST, England
Author V: 06/05/92

Cook, Jr., Elisha
P.O. Box 335
Bishop, CA 93514
Actor V: 06/14/92

Cooke, Alistair
Nassau Point
Cutchogue, NY 11935
Author V: 09/04/92

Cooke, Peter
10 Soho Sq.
London W1, England
Actor V: 02/25/93

Coolidge, Rita
9200 Sunset Blvd. #706
Los Angeles, CA 90069
Singer V: 03/03/93

Cooper, Alice
8033 Sunset Blvd. Suite 745
Los Angeles, CA 90046
Singer V: 03/02/92

4135 E. Kiem Dr.
Paradise Valley, AZ 85253
Alternate V: 09/03/92

Cooper, Jackie
9621 Royalton Dr.
Beverly Hills, CA 90210
Actor V: 02/01/93

Cooper, Jeanne
c/o Y & R, 7800 Beverly Blvd.
Beverly Hills, CA 90036
Actress V: 06/15/92

Cooper Jr., L. Gordon
c/o NASA LBJ Space Center
Houston, TX 77058
Astronaut V: 03/03/93

Cope, Derrike
4428 Taggart Creek Rd.
Suite 107, Rm.313
Charlotte, NC 28208
Race Driver V: 03/12/93

Cope, Dick
9201 Garrison Rd.
Charlotte, NC 28208
NASCAR Driver V: 03/02/92

Copperfield, David
11777 San Vicente Blvd. #601
Los Angeles, CA 90049
Magician V: 03/17/92

15456 Ventura Blvd. #300
Sherman Oaks, CA 91403
L.R.U. V: 01/10/92

Coppola, Francis Ford
916 Kearny St.
San Francisco, CA 94133
Director V: 02/01/93

Coppola, Sofia
6747 Milner Rd.
Los Angeles, CA 90068
Actress V: 02/14/93

781 5th Ave.
New York, NY 10022
Alternate V: 02/19/93

Coralie Jr. Agency
4789 Vineland, Ste.100
N. Hollywood, CA 91602
Talent Agency V: 04/27/92

Corbet, Glenn
15010 Ventura Blvd. #219
Sherman Oaks, CA 91403
Actor V: 02/20/93

Corbett, John
Northern Exposure
3000 Olympic Blvd., Ste.2575
Santa Monica, CA 90404
Actor V: 05/15/92

Corbett, Michael
c/o CBS-TV/Young & Restless
7800 Beverly Blvd.
Los Angeles, CA 90036
Actor V: 06/02/92

Corbin, Barry
4529 Tyrone Ave.
Sherman Oaks, CA 91403
Actor V: 03/19/93

Corbin, Barry, contd
Northern Exposure
3000 Olympic Blvd., Ste.2575
Santa Monica, CA 90404
Alternate V: 05/15/92

Corby, Ellen
9026 Harratt St.
Los Angeles, CA 90069
Actress V: 06/01/92

Corea, Chic
2635 Griffith Park Blvd.
Los Angeles, CA 90039
Musician V: 05/14/92

Corley, Pat
c/o Warner Bros. Television
Murphy Brown
4000 Warner Blvd.
Burbank, CA 91522
Actor V: 03/02/92

Cornell, Lydia
321 S. Beverly Dr., Ste.M
Beverly Hills, CA 90212
Actress V: 07/14/92

Corri, Adrienne
66 Berkeley House
Hay Hill
London W1, England
Actress V: 11/11/92

Corriganville
c/o Don Bradley
P.O. Box 3688
Simi Valley, CA 93093
Movie Ranch V: 12/12/92

Corsaut, Aneta
4312 Agnes Ave.
Studio City, CA 91604
Actress V: 06/16/92

Cort, Bud
606 Larchmont Blvd. #309
Los Angeles, CA 90004
Actor V: 02/11/92

2749 Lyric Ave.
Los Angeles, CA 90027
Alternate V: 06/14/92

Cortez, Stacy
c/o ABC-TV General Hospital
4151 Prospect Ave.
Los Angeles, CA 90027
Actress V: 04/05/93

Cosby, Bill
c/o William Morris
151 El Camino Dr.
Beverly Hills, CA 90212
Actor V: 01/17/93

P.O. Box 69646
Los Angeles, CA 90069
Alternate V: 03/03/93

Cosden Enterprises
7135 Hollywood Blvd., PH#2
Los Angeles, CA 90046
Talent Agency V: 04/27/92

Cossell, Howard
150 E. 69th St.
New York, NY 90027
Sportscaster V: 06/14/92

Costa, Mary
321 Barton Ave.
Palm Beach, FL 33480
Singer V: 06/14/92

Costner, Kevin
1888 Century Park East #1400
Los Angeles, CA 90067
Actor V: 12/14/92

1820 Fairmont Ave.
La Canada, CA 91011
Alternate V: 05/20/92

136 E. 57th St. #100
New York, NY 10023
Alternate V: 01/12/92

P.O. Box 275
Montrose, CA 91021
Alternate V: 03/03/93

c/o Dances With Wolves
TIG Productions
650 N. Bronson, Ste.211
Los Angeles, CA 90004
Forwarded V: 03/30/92

c/o T.I.G. Prod./Warner
4000 Warner Blvd.
Burbank, CA 91522
Forwarded V: 12/16/92

P.O. Box 772
La Canada, CA 91011
L.R.U. V: 05/12/92

Cotten, Joseph
10445 Wilshire Blvd. #201
Los Angeles, CA 94002-4606
Actor V: 03/19/93

Cotton, Joseph, contd
1993 Mesa Dr.
Palm Springs, CA 92264
L.R.U. V: 11/15/92

Coulier, David
c/o Funniest People
4151 Prospect Ave., Prod.Bldg.
Hollywood, CA 90078
Actor V: 12/19/92

259 20th St.
Santa Monica, CA 90401
Alternate V: 04/06/93

c/o Lorimar
Full House
3970 Overland Ave.
Culver City, CA 90230
Alternate V: 12/18/92

Court, Hazel
c/o Taylor
1111 San Vicente Blvd.
Santa Monica, CA 90402
Actress V: 06/14/92

Cousins, Robin
27307 Highway 189
Blue Jay, CA 92317
Skater V: 12/12/92

Coustau, Jacques
930 W. 21st St.
Norfolk, VA 23517
Explorer V: 11/11/92

Cousy, Bob
427 Salisbury St.
Worcester, MA 01609
Basketball V: 05/05/92

Covey, Richard O.
c/o NASA LBJ Space Center
Houston, TX 77058
Astronaut V: 03/03/93

Cowper, Nicola
c/o Brunskill Management
169 Queens Gate, Ste. A8
London SW7 5EH, England
Actress V: 02/04/93

Cox, Courtney
9016 Wilshire Blvd. #500
Beverly Hills, CA 90211
Actress V: 06/01/92

Cox, Jimmy
P.O. Box 85619
Mt. Lemmon, AZ 85619
Actor V: 12/12/92

Cox, Ronnie
c/o ICM
8942 Wilshire Blvd.
Beverly Hills, CA 90211
Actor V: 02/21/92

20th Cent./Fox TV
10201 W. Pico Ave.
Los Angeles, CA 90035
L.R.U. V: 02/21/92

Cox Talent Agency
6362 Hollywood Blvd. #219
Hollywood, CA 90028
Talent Agency V: 05/13/92

Coyote, Peter
c/o Smith
121 N. San Vincente Blvd.
Beverly Hills, CA 90211
Actor V: 05/02/92

c/o Judy Banevicius
3425 Knox Pl.
Bronx, NY 10467
Alternate V: 06/06/92

Craig, Michael
c/o Chatto & Linnit, Ltd.
Coventry St.
London W1 England
Actor V: 03/09/93

Craig, Yvonne
c/o Champagne Towers
Batmail
1221 Ocean Ave. #202
Santa Monica, CA 90401
Actress V: 06/01/92

Craig Agency
8485 Melrose Place, Ste.E
Los Angeles, CA 90069
Talent Agency V: 05/13/92

Crampton, Barbara
c/o Young and the Restless
7800 Beverly Blvd.
Beverly Hills, CA 90036
Actress V: 06/15/92

6314 Orange Ave.
Los Angeles, CA 90069
Alternate V: 03/12/93

Crampton, Bruce
7107 Spanky Ranch Dr.
Dallas, TX 75248-1531
Golfer V: 05/04/92

Crane, Cheryl
1271 Ozeta Terrace
Los Angeles, CA 90069
Actress V: 01/24/93

Crane, Matt
c/o NBC-TV
Another World
79 Madison Ave., 5th Fl.
New York, NY 91523
Actor V: 06/15/92

Craven, Gemma
41 Hazelbury Rd.
London SW6, England
Actress V: 01/24/93

Craven, Wes
2015 Navy St.
Santa Monica, CA 90402
Director V: 03/04/92

c/o Alive Films
8271 Melrose Ave.
Los Angeles, CA 90046
L.R.U. V: 02/28/92

10000 W. Washington, Ste.3011
Culver City, CA 90232
Production Company V: 03/17/92

Crawford, Christina
18653 Ventura Blvd. #143
Tarzana, CA 91356
Author V: 07/03/92

c/o Koontz
3530 Pine Valley Dr.
Sarasota, FL 34239
Alternate V: 01/20/93

Crawford, Cindy
c/o Elite
111 E. 22nd St.
New York, NY 10010
Model V: 11/15/92

345 N. Maple Dr., #183
Beverly Hills, CA 90210
Alternate V: 11/11/92

Crawford, Johnny
2440 El Contento Dr.
Los Angeles, CA 90068
Actor V: 02/20/93

Crawford, Michael
7605 Santa Monica Blvd., #644
W. Hollywood, CA 90046
Actor V: 01/12/92

c/o The Globe Theatre
Shaftsbury Ave.
London W1, England
Alternate V: 03/03/93

Crawford, Randy
911 Park St. S.W.
Grand Rapids, MI 49504
Cartoonist V: 03/01/91

1169 Chicago Dr.
Wyoming, MI 49509
Forwarded V: 03/01/91

Crawford, William J.
Box 4
Palmer Lake, CO 80133
Medal of Honor V: 02/06/93

Creative Artists Agency
9830 Wilshire Blvd.
Beverly Hills, CA 90212
Talent Agency V: 06/13/92

Crenna, Richard
3951 Valley Meadow Rd.
Encino, CA 91436
Actor V: 02/22/92

Crenshaw, Ben
1811 W. 35th St.
Austin, TX 78703
Golf V: 06/02/92

2905 San Gabriel, #213
Austin, TX 78705
Alternate V: 11/11/92

Crenshaw, George
c/o King Features
216 East 45th St.
New York, NY 10017
Cartoonist V: 06/04/92

Crews, John R.
1324 SW 54th St.
Oklahoma, OK 73119
Medal of Honor V: 01/14/92

Cribbins, Bernard
c/o Salmon
59 Frith St.
London W1V 5TA, England
Actor V: 01/17/93

Crippen, Robert L.
c/o NASA LBJ Space Center
Houston, TX 77058
Astronaut V: 03/03/93

Crisp, Quentin
46 E. 3rd St.
New York, NY 10003
Author V: 06/02/92

Cristal, Linda
9129 Hazen Dr.
Beverly Hills, CA 90210
Actress V: 02/20/92

Croft, Annabel
233 Regent St.
London W1R 7DB, England
Actress V: 07/03/92

Cromer, Tandra
c/o Dallas Cowboys
One Cowboys Parkway
Irving, TX 75063-4945
Cheerleader V: 08/08/92

Cronyn, Hume
63-23 Carlton St.
Rego Park, NY 11374
Actor V: 03/10/93

Crosby, Cathy Lee
1223 Wilshire Blvd. #404
Santa Monica, CA 90403-5400
Actress V: 03/19/93

329 N. Wetherly Dr.
Beverly Hills, CA 90210
L.R.U. V: 01/02/92

Crosby, Denise
c/o Edwards
1005 N. Crescent Heights Blvd.
Los Angeles, CA 90046
Actress V: 06/14/92

c/o Star Trek-TNG Paramount
5555 Melrose Ave.
Hollywood, CA 90038
Forwarded V: 07/02/92

232 N. Canon Dr.
Beverly Hills, CA 90210
L.R.U. V: 02/28/92

130 W.42nd St., Ste.1804
New York, NY 10036
L.R.U. V: 10/04/92

Crosby, Katherine
P.O. Box 85
Genda, NV 89411
Actress V: 01/24/93

Crosby, Kathryn
400 S. Burnside Ave. #12H
Los Angeles, CA 90036
Actress V: 02/20/92

Crosby, Lucinda
c/o Coast to Coast
12307-C Ventura Blvd.
Studio City, CA 91604
Actress V: 11/15/92

Crosby, Mary
6454 Gentry Ave.
N. Hollywood, CA 91606
Actress V: 07/01/92

2875 Barrymore Dr.
Malibu, CA 90265
Forwarded V: 07/01/92

Crosby, Norm
1400 Londonderry
Los Angeles, CA 90069
Actor V: 07/01/92

9200 Sunset Blvd. #428
Los Angeles, CA 90069
Alternate V: 01/21/92

Cross, Ben
29 Burlington Gardens
London W4, England
Alternate V: 06/14/92

Cross, Natalie
c/o Dallas Cowboys
One Cowboys Parkway
Irving, TX 75063-4945
Cheerleader V: 08/08/92

Crossfield, A. Scott
12100 Thoroughbred Rd.
Herndon, VA 22071
Test Pilot V: 04/01/93

Cruise, Tom
1888 Century Park E. #1400
Los Angeles, CA 90067
Actor V: 03/03/93

14775 Ventura Blvd. #1-710
Sherman Oaks, CA 91403
Alternate V: 02/26/93

Cruise, Tom, contd
5555 Melrose Ave.
Los Angeles, CA 90038
Actor V: 12/17/92

Crystal, Billy
860 Chautauqua Blvd.
Pacific Palisades, CA 90272
Actor V: 11/11/92

Culbertson Jr., Frank L.
NASA/LBJ Space Center
Houston, TX 77058
Astronaut V: 04/02/93

Culkin, Kieran
510 E. 87th St.
New York, NY 10128
Actor V: 02/11/93

Culkin, Macaulay
8942 Wilshire Blvd.
Beverly Hills, CA 90211
Actor V: 06/14/92

40 W. 57th St.
New York, NY 10019
Alternate V: 03/19/93

Cullum, Mark
c/o King Features
216 E. 45th St.
New York, NY 10017
Cartoonist V: 03/11/93

Cumber Attractions Agency
6363 Sunset Blvd. #807
Hollywood, CA 90028
Talent Agency V: 06/13/92

Cummings, Quinn
121 N. San Vicente Blvd.
Beverly Hills, CA 90211
Actor V: 08/15/92

Cunningham, Walter
NASA/LBJ Space Center
Houston, TX 77058
Astronaut V: 03/03/93

Cunningham-Escott-Dipene
261 S. Robertson Blvd.
Beverly Hills, CA 90211
Talent Agency V: 06/06/92

Cuomo, Mario
Sate of New York
Executive Chamber
Albany, NY 12224
Politician V: 11/11/92

Currie, Cherie
6512 Corbin Ave.
Reseda, CA 91335
Actress V: 01/24/93

Curry, Anne
9113 Sunset Blvd.
Los Angeles, CA 90069
Actress V: 11/15/92

Curry, Tim
3 Lord Napier Pl.
London W6, England
Actor V: 03/12/93

2401 Wild Oak Dr.
Los Angeles, CA 90068
Actor V: 03/06/93

Curtis, Jamie Lee
1242 S. Camden Dr.
Los Angeles, CA 90035
Actress V: 05/03/92

1625 Summit Ridge Dr.
Beverly Hills, CA 90210
L.R.U. V: 06/01/92

Curtis, Keene
6363 Ivarene
Los Angeles, CA 90068
Actor V: 02/20/92

Curtis, Robin
c/o ABC-TV
General Hospital
4151 Prospect Ave.
Hollywood, CA 90027
Actress V: 06/15/92

Curtis, Todd
c/o Young and the Restless
7800 Beverly Blvd.
Beverly Hills, CA 90036
Actor V: 06/15/92

Curtis, Tony
P.O. Box 15577
Honolulu, HI 96830-5577
Actor V: 04/21/92

P.O. Box 540
Beverly Hills, CA 90213
Forwarded V: 04/19/92

Cusack, Cyril
41 Burlington Lane, Chiswick
London N4, England
Actor V: 03/13/93

Cusack, John
838 Sheridan
Evanston, IL 60202
Actor V: 11/23/92

Cushing, Peter
c/o John Redway
16 Berners St.
London W1, England
Actor V: 03/10/93

c/o Redway
Seasalter
Whitstable, Kent, England
Alternate V: 05/13/93

Cutter, Lise
1423 Nadeau Dr.
Los Angeles, CA 90019
Actress V: 01/24/93

Cyrus, Billy Ray
818 18th Ave. South
Nashville, TN 37203
Singer V: 03/06/93

818 18th Ave. S.
Nashville, TN 37203
Forwarded V: 03/26/93

D

D'Abo, Maryam
c/o STE Agency
9301 Wilshire Blvd. #312
Beverly Hills, CA 90210
Actress V: 06/01/92

7495 Mulholland Dr.
Los Angeles, CA 90046
Alternate V: 08/09/82

9320 Wilshire Blvd. 3rd Fl.
Beverly Hills, CA 90212
Forwarded V: 03/30/93

D'Abo, Olivia
1440 S. Sepulveda Blvd.
Los Angeles, CA 90025
Actress V: 12/11/92

335 N. Maple Drive #360
Beverly Hills, CA 90210
Alternate V: 03/03/93

D'Angelo, Beverly
8033 Sunset Blvd. #247
Los Angeles, CA 90046-2427
Actress V: 01/25/93

D'Angelo, Beverly, contd
151 El Camino Dr.
Beverly Hills, CA 90212
L.R.U. *V: 08/08/92*

DANGEROUS CURVES
11811 W. Olympic Blvd.
Los Angeles, CA 90064
Production Company *V: 03/18/93*

DANIELLE STEEL TV MOVIES
330 Bob Hope Dr.
Burbank, DA 91523
Production Company *V: 03/23/93*

DARK JUSTICE
Lorimar/"Dark Justice"
4000 Warner Blvd., Bl.137
Burbank, CA 91522
Production Company *V: 05/15/92*

DAYS OF OUR LIVES
Columbia Pictures TV
c/o NBC Burbank
3000 W. Alameda Ave.
Burbank, CA 91523
Production Company *V: 03/26/93*

DEAR JOHN
Paramount Pictures
5555 Melrose Ave.
Clara Bow Bldg., 2nd Fl.
Hollywood, CA 90038
Production Company *V: 03/26/93*

DESIGNING WOMEN
Mozark Prod.
4000 Warner Blvd.
Producers Build. 8, Rm. 143
Burbank, CA 91505
Production Company *V: 03/15/93*

DH Talent Agency
917 N. Larrabee #29
Los Angeles, CA 90069
Talent Agency *V: 02/01/93*

DISNEY
Walt Disney Prod.
500 S. Buena Vista St.
Burbank, CA 91521
Production Company *V: 03/26/93*

DISNEY'S RAW TOONAGE
Walt Disney Company
500 South Buena Vista ATTN: Fan Mail
Burbank, CA 91521
Production Company *V: 03/18/93*

DISNEY'S LITTLE MERMAID
Walt Disney Co.
500 South Buena Vista
Burbank, CA 91521
Production Company *V: 03/18/93*

DOCTOR DEAN
NBC 3000 W. Alameda Ave.
Burbank, CA 91523
Production Company *V: 03/26/93*

DOOGIE HOWSER, M.D.
c/o Steven Bochco Prods.
Doogie Howser, M.D.
10201 W. Pico Blvd.
Los Angeles, CA 90035
Production Company *V: 12/15/92*

DOUBLE UP
DIC Enterprises
3601 W. Olive Ave.
Burbank, CA 91505
Production Company *V: 03/26/93*

DR. QUINN, MEDICINE WOMAN
CBS Entertainment
4024 Radford Ave.
Build. 1, Rm.115
Studio City, CA 91604
Production Company *V: 03/14/93*

DaFoe, Willem
33 Wooster St. #200
New York, NY 10013
Actor *V: 03/17/91*

1888 Century Park E. #1400
Los Angeles, CA 90067
Alternate *V: 07/21/92*

Dade/Schultz Associates
11846 Ventura Blvd.
Studio City, CA 91604
Talent Agency *V: 03/13/93*

Dahl, Arlene
P.O. Box 116
Sparkhill, NY 10976
Actress *V: 01/22/92*

Dailey, Bill
133 Park Ave. S.W.
Albuquerque, NM 87104
Actor *V: 05/20/92*

5245 E. Coldwater Canyon
Van Nuys, CA 91401
Forwarded *V: 02/01/92*

Dalley, Irene
c/o NBC-TV
Another World
79 Madison Ave., 5th Fl.
New York, NY 91523
Actress V: 06/15/92

Daily, Janet
c/o Janbill Ltd.-SR#4
Box 2197
Branson, MO 65616
Author V: 06/05/92

Dalai Lama
Thekchen Choling, McLeod Gundi
Kangra Distr., Himachal
Pradesh, India
Religious Leader V: 03/17/93

Dale, Jim
26 Pembridge Villa's
London, W11 England
Actor V: 01/11/93

c/o Hutton Mgmt.
200 Fulham Rd.
London SW10, England
Alternate V: 02/28/92

Daley, Tyne
2934 1/2 Beverly Glen Cir.#404
Bel Aire, CA 90077
Alternate V: 05/04/92

Dallas Cowboys
Cowboys Center
One Cowboys Parkway
Irving, TX 75063-4727
Team Offices V: 05/15/92

Dallas Cowboys Cheerleaders
Cowboys Center
One Cowboys Parkway
Irving, TX 75063-4945
Cheerleaders V: 08/08/92

Dallenbach, Wally
P.O. Box 1089
Liberty, NC 27298
NASCAR Driver V: 03/02/92

Dallesandro, Joe
711 N. Formosa
Los Angeles, CA 90046
Actor V: 03/17/93

c/o Cannell Prod.
7083 Hollywood Blvd.
Hollywood, CA 90028
Alternate V: 05/15/92

Dallis, Dr. Nick
c/o King Features
216 East 45th St.
New York, NY 10017
Cartoonist V: 05/02/92

Dalton, Timothy
Third Floor, Suite 315
15 Golden Square
London, W1 England
Actor V: 06/01/92

Daltry, Roger
5 Milner Place
London, W1 England
Actor V: 10/18/93

Daly, Timothy
c/o Grub Street Prod.
Wings
5555 Melrose Av./Wilder #101
Hollywood, CA 90038
Actor V: 01/07/93

Daly, Tyne
2934 1/2 N. Beverly Glen Cir.#404
Los Angeles, CA 90077
Actress V: 01/24/93

Damian, Michael
c/o Young and the Restless
7800 Beverly Blvd.
Beverly Hills, CA 90036
Actor V: 06/15/92

Damon, Stuart
c/o General Hosp./ABC Inc.
4151 Prospect Ave.
Hollywood, CA 90027
Actor V: 03/01/92

367 N. Van Ness
Los Angeles, CA 90004
Actor V: 06/15/92

Dana, Bill
P.O. Box 1792
Santa Monica, CA 90406
Actor V: 09/08/92

5965 Peacock Ridge Rd. #563
Rancho Palos Verdes, CA 90274
Alternate V: 04/06/93

Dance, Charles
c/o Caroline Dawson Assoc.
Apt. 20, 47 Courtfield Rd.
London SW7 4DB, England
Actor V: 05/03/92

Dance, Charles, contd
31 Kings Rd.
London SW3 4RP England
Alternate V: 06/12/92

Dandridge, Ray
P.O. Box 61139
Palm Bay, FL 32906
Baseball V: 07/01/92

Dangerfield, Rodney
1118 1st. Ave.
New York, NY 10022
Actor V: 03/21/92

530 E. 76th St.
New York, NY 10021
Comedian V: 04/06/93

Paper Clip Productions
1888 Century Park E.
Los Angeles, CA 90067
Forwarded V: 06/22/92

Daniel, Faith
c/o CBS This Morning
51 W. 52nd St.
New York, NY 10019
Celebrity V: 03/19/93

Daniels, William
12805 Hortense St.
Studio City, CA 91604
Actor V: 11/12/92

Danner, Blythe
304 21st St.
Santa Monica, CA 90402
Actress V: 03/02/92

Danning, Sybil
3575 Cahuenga Blvd. West #200
Los Angeles, CA 90068
Actress V: 02/20/93

8578 Walnut Dr.
Los Angeles, CA 90046
L.R.U. V: 01/08/92

9300 Wilshire Blvd. #410
Beverly Hills, CA 90212
L.R.U. V: 07/01/92

Dano, Linda
Another World/NBC-TV
30 Rockefeller Plaza
New York, NY 10020
Actress V: 06/06/92

Dano, Linda, contd
NBC-TV/Another World
79 Madison Ave., 5th Fl.
New York, NY 91523
Alternate V: 06/15/92

Dano, Royal
517 20th St.
Santa Monica, CA 90402
Actor V: 03/02/92

Danson, Ted
c/o Paramount
Cheers
5555 Melrose Ave./Ball RM105
Hollywood, CA 90038
Actor V: 01/07/92

31504 Victoria Pointe Rd.
Malibu, CA 90265
Actor V: 04/06/93

Danyel
631 Las Vegas Blvd. S.
Las Vegas, NV 89101
Adult Films V: 01/17/93

Danza, Tony
19722 Trull Brook Dr.
Tarzana, CA 91356
Actor V: 03/06/93

Dare, Barbara
P.O. Box 11826
Marina del Rey, CA 90295
Adult Films V: 01/17/93

Darkow, John
c/o King Features
216 E. 45th St.
New York, NY 10017
Cartoonist V: 03/11/93

Darling, Jean
294 S. Circular Rd.
Dublin, 8 Ireland
Actress V: 06/06/92

Darling, Joan
33533 Shoreline Dr.
Laguna Niguel, CA 92677
Director V: 06/06/92

Darren, James
c/o Chasin
190 Canyon Dr.
Beverly Hills, CA 90210
Actor V: 01/17/92

Darren, James, contd
P.O. Box 1088
Beverly Hills, CA 90213
Alternate V: 06/15/92

Darrien, Racquel
2899 Agoura Rd. #266
Westlake Village, CA 91361
Adult Films V: 01/17/93

Darrow, Henry
9169 Sunset Blvd.
Los Angeles, CA 90069
Actor V: 01/02/93

Davalos, Elyssa
c/o Paramount TV
MacGyver
5555 Melrose Ave.
Los Angeles, CA 90038
Actress V: 12/07/92

Davalos, Richard
1958 Vestal Ave.
Los Angeles, CA 90026
Actor V: 06/15/92

Davenport, Jim
1016 Hewitt Dr.
San Carlos, CA 94070
Baseball V: 12/10/92

Davenport, Nigel
c/o Leading Artists
60 Saint James St.
London SW1, England
Actor V: 04/02/93

2 Conduit St.
London W1, England
Alternate V: 02/28/93

David, Hal
5253 Lankershim Blvd.
N. Hollywood, CA 91601
Lyricist V: 06/16/92

Davidson, Doug
c/o Young & Restless CBS-TV
7800 Beverly Blvd.
Los Angeles, CA 90036
Actor V: 03/02/92

Davidson, Eileen
620 Vallombrosa Dr.
Pasadena, CA 91107
Actress V: 01/24/93

Davidson, John
21243 Ventura Blvd. Ste.101
Woodland Hills, CA 91364
Actor V: 03/02/92

1567 Spinnaker Dr.
P.O. Box 213/189
Ventura Harbor, CA 93001
Alternate V: 01/22/92

5219 Alhambra Dr.
Woodland Hills, CA 91364-2017
Forwarded V: 04/21/92

Davidson, Peter
1924 Euclid St.
Santa Monica, CA 90404
Musician V: 06/26/92

Davies, John Rhys
4 Court Lodge, 48 Slone Square
London SW 1, ENGLAND
Actor V: 01/17/93

Davis, Altovis
279 S. Beverly Dr. #1006
Beverly Hills, CA 90212
Actress V: 01/24/93

Davis, Ann B.
P.O. Box 5825
Denver, CO 80217
Actress V: 04/01/92

1427 Beaver Rd.
Ambridge, PA 15003
Alternate V: 03/19/03

Davis, Billy
P.O. Box 7905
Beverly Hills, CA 90212
Singer V: 06/15/92

Davis, Eric
c/ Klasy/Csupo
1258 N. Highland Ave.
Hollywood, CA 90038
Cartoonist V: 02/04/93

Davis, Eric
c/o Los Angeles Dodgers
Dodger Stadium
1000 Elysian Park Ave.
Los Angeles, CA 90012
Baseball V: 04/05/93

Davis, Glenn
47-650 Eisenhower Dr.
La Quinta, CA 92253
Football V: 04/03/92

Davis, Jeff
c/o NASCAR
1811 Volusia Ave.
Daytona Beach, FL 32015
NASCAR Driver V: 03/26/93

Davis, Judy
c/o Colin Friels
129 Bourke St.
Woollomooloo, Sydney
NSW 2011, Australia
Actress V: 03/02/93

c/o Prince of Wales Theatre
Coventry St.
London W1, England
Alternate V: 02/28/92

Davis, Mac
759 Nimes Place Rd.
Los Angeles, CA 90077
Actor V: 06/15/92

Davis, N. Jan
c/o NASA
LBJ Space Center
Houston, TX 77058
Astronaut V: 06/06/92

Davis, Ossie
c/o Emmalyn II Prod. Co.
P.O. Box 1318
New Rochelle, NY 10802
Actor V: 06/15/92

c/o Mozark Prod./CBS-MTM
Evening Shade
4024 Radford Ave., Bl.5, Rm.104
Studio City, CA 91604
Forwarded V: 05/15/92

Davis, Sammy L.
RR22 Box 80A
Flat Rock, IL 62427
Medal of Honor V: 02/01/93

Davis, Skeeter
508 Seward Rd.
Brentwood, TN 37027
Singer V: 04/20/93

Davison, Bruce
P.O. Box 57593
Sherman Oaks, CA 91403
Actor V: 04/06/93

Davison, Peter
Eagle House, 109 Jermyn St.
London SW1 6HB, England
Actor V: 01/17/93

Dawber, Pam
4000 Warner Blvd.
Burbank, CA 91522
Actress V: 03/01/92

9738 Arby Dr.
Beverly Hills, CA 90210
Alternate V: 03/01/93

Dawn, Sabrina
c/o 5K Sales
9420 Reseda Blvd., Ste.836
Northridge, CA 91324
Adult Films V: 01/17/93

Dawson, Richard
1117 Angelo Dr.
Beverly Hills, CA 90210
Actor V: 03/21/92

Day, Doris
P.O. Box 223163
Carmel, CA 93922
Actress V: 03/21/92

P.O. Box 8509
Universal City, CA 91608
Alternate V: 03/30/93

Day, Laraine
c/o Grilikhes
10313 Lauriston Ave.
Los Angeles, CA 90025-6010
Actress V: 05/12/92

463 S. Elm Dr.
Beverly Hills, CA 90212
L.R.U. V: 07/03/92

Day, Lynda
10310 Riverside Dr.
North Hollywood, CA 91602-2457
Actress V: 05/13/92

Day-Lewis, Daniel
c/o Alister Reid
65 Connaught St.
London W 2, ENGLAND
Actor V: 01/17/93

Dayne, Taylor
6 W. 57th St.
New York, NY 10019
Actor V: 04/20/92

2288 Jerusalem Ave. N.
Bellmore, NY 11710
Actor V: 04/06/93

De Becker, Gavin
11684 Ventura Blvd. #440
Studio City, CA 91604
Security Consultant V: 03/03/93

De Carlo, Yvonne
4 Martine Ave. #501
White Plains, NY 10606
Actress V: 03/03/93

1665 N. Bronson Ave. #914
Los Angeles, CA 90028
L.R.U. V: 12/15/92

De Cordova, Fred
1875 Carla Ridge
Beverly Hills, CA 90210
Producer V: 02/21/92

3000 W. Alemeda Ave.
Burbank, CA 91523
Alternate V: 05/16/92

De Haven, Gloria
73 Devonshire Rd.
Cedar Grove, NJ 07009
Actress V: 03/15/93

De Havilland, Olivia
3 Rue Benouville
Paris, 751116 France
Actress V: 06/02/92

Boite Postale 156-16
Paris Cedex 16, 75764 France
Forwarded V: 07/01/92

De Laurentis, Dino
8670 Wilshire Blvd.
Beverly Hills, CA 90211
Producer V: 03/18/93

De Luise, Dom
1186 Corsica Dr.
Pacific Palasides, CA 90272
Actor V: 04/16/93

De Luise, Peter
10201 W. Pico Blvd.
Los Angeles, CA 90056
Actor V: 02/20/92

5632 Van Nuys Blvd. Ste.286
Van Nuys, CA 91401
Alternate V: 05/14/92

c/o Wm. Morris
151 S. El Camino Dr.
Beverly Hills, CA 90212
Forwarded V: 11/11/92

De Mornay, Rebecca
c/o JPM
760 N. La Cienega Blvd. #200
Los Angeles, CA 90069
Actress V: 03/03/93

9830 Wilshire Blvd.
Beverly Hills, CA 90212
L.R.U. V: 01/02/92

De Noire, Mauvias
c/o Five K Sales Co.
9420 Reseda Blvd., #836
Northridge, CA 91324
Adult Films V: 03/03/93

De Witt, Joyce
1121 N. Olive Dr.
Los Angeles, CA 90069-2723
Actress V: 08/07/92

DeCamp, Rosemary
317 Camino De Los Colinas
Rendondo Beach, CA 90277
Actress V: 05/25/92

DeCarlo, Yvonne
P.O. Box 374
Los Olivos, CA 93441
Actress V: 04/11/92

200 E. 89th St. #9C
New York, NY 10128
L.R.U. V: 10/04/92

DeFore, Don
2496 Mandeville Canyon Dr.
Los Angeles, CA 90049
Actor V: 04/14/92

DeHaven, Gloria
1427 3rd St. Promenade, Ste.205
Santa Monica, CA 90401-2358
Actress V: 03/30/93

c/o Contemporary Artists
132 Lasky Dr.
Beverly Hills, CA 90212
Actress V: 10/04/92

DeMornay, Rebecca
760 N. La Cienega Blvd.
Los Angeles, CA 90069
Actress V: 03/19/93

DeNiro, Robert
c/o Yohalem Gillman
477 Madison Ave. 9th Fl.
New York, NY 10022
Actor V: 07/01/92

DeNiro, Robert, contd
375 Greenwich St.
New York, NY 10013
Alternate V: 03/17/93

1501 Broadway #2600
New York, NY 10036
Alternate V: 05/13/92

DeVell, Alexis
P.O. Box 480005
Denver, CO 80248
Adult Films V: 02/13/93

Dean, Eddie
32161 Sailview Ln.
Westlake Village, CA 91360
Actor V: 02/19/92

P.O. Box 3688
Simi Valley, CA 93093
Alternate V: 12/12/92

Dee, Frances
Rt. 3, Box 375
Camarillo, CA 93010
Actress V: 05/01/92

Dee, Ruby
P.O. Box 1318
New York, NY 10802
Singer V: 05/15/92

44 Cortland Ave.
New Rochelle, NY 10801
Alternate V: 01/24/93

Dee, Sandra
10780 Santa Monica Blvd. #280
Los Angeles, CA 90025
Actress V: 04/01/92

10351 Santa Monica Blvd. #211
Los Angeles, CA 90025
Alternate V: 05/15/92

Dees, Rick
6255 Sunset Blvd.
Los Angeles, CA 90028
Personality V: 03/01/93

Del Rio, Vanessa
163 Joralemon St. Suite 1544
New York, NY 11201
Actress V: 06/06/92

Delancie, John
1313 Brunswick Ave.
S. Pasadena, CA 91030
Actor V: 04/02/92

Delaney, Delvene
c/o Showcast/Ste. 4
5 Alexander St., P.O.Box 951
Crows Nest 2065, Austrailia
Actress V: 07/03/92

Delaney, Kim
4724 Poe Ave.
Woodland Hills, CA 91364-4656
Actress V: 03/19/93

Delany, Dana
2521 6th St.
Santa Monica, CA 90405
Actress V: 01/19/93

9200 Sunset Blvd.   Ste. 428
Los Angeles, CA 90069
Alternate V: 01/21/92

165 W. 46th St. #710
New York, NY 10036
Forwarded V: 01/18/92

21 Ozone Ave. #30
Venice, CA 90291
L.R.U. V: 08/08/92

Dell, Myrna
12958 Valleyheart Dr.
Studio City, CA 91604
Actress V: 01/24/93

Delon, Alain
c/o Adel Productions
4 rue Chambiges 3rd Fl.
F-75008 Paris, France
Actor V: 01/17/93

Delora, Jennifer
c/o Scwartz/Clay/Rose
8228 Sunset Blvd. #212
Los Angeles, CA 90046
Actress V: 04/16/93

Demento, Dr.
c/o KMET
5746 Sunset Blvd.
Los Angeles, CA 90028
Personality V: 03/05/93

Demme, Jonathan
9000 Sunset Blvd. #1115
Los Angeles, CA 90069
L.R.U. V: 07/06/92

Dench, Judith
60 Saint James St.
London SW1, England
Actress V: 03/12/93

Deneuve, Catherine
40 Rue Francois
Paris 75008, France
Actress V: 03/02/93

76 Rue Bonaparte
Paris 75016, France
Alternate V: 03/01/93

Denham, Maurice
c/o Agent
Flat 2, 44 Brunswich Gardens
London W8, England
Actor V: 04/05/93

Dennehy, Brian
121 N. San Vicente Blvd.
Beverly Hills, CA 90211
Actor V: 11/11/92

Dennison, Michael
c/o Agency
388 Oxford St.
London W1, England
Actor V: 02/28/92

Denton, Christa
6212 Banner Ave.
Los Angeles, CA 90038
Actress V: 11/10/92

Denver, Bob
P.O. Box 196
Bearsville, NY 12409-0196
Actor V: 05/14/92

c/o USPO
Main Branch
Princeton, W. VA 24740
Alternate V: 01/02/92

P.O. Box 426
Pacific Palisades, CA
L.R.U. V: 12/12/92

Denver, John
P.O. Box 1587
Aspen, CO 81612
Singer V: 01/12/92

Denver Broncos
5700 Logan St.
Denver, CO 80216
Team Offices V: 05/15/92

Depardieu, Gerard
c/ DD Productions
10 ave. George-V
F-75008 Paris, FRANCE
Actor V: 01/17/93

Depardieu, Gerard, contd
4 Place de la Chapele
Bougival, France
Alternate V: 06/15/92

Depp, Johnny
722 Copeland Ct. #3
Santa Monica, CA 90405-4445
Actor V: 02/03/92

Derek, Bo
3275 Monticiello
Santa Ynez, CA 93460
Actress V: 06/01/92

3625 Roblar Rd.
Santa Ynez, CA 93460
Alternate V: 06/01/92

c/o Nu Image
110 N. Doheny
Beverly Hills, CA 90211
Forwarded V: 01/20/93

Derek, John
3275 Monticiello
Santa Ynez, CA 93460
Actor V: 06/01/92

3625 Roblar Rd.
Santa Ynez, CA 93460
Alternate V: 06/01/92

Dern, Bruce
23430 Malibu Colony Dr.
Malibu, CA 90265
Actor V: 01/28/93

P.O. Box 691093
Los Angeles, CA 90069
L.R.U. V: 01/02/93

Dern, Laura
c/o Judy Thomas Management
9243 1/2 Doheny Rd.
Los Angeles, CA 90069
Actress V: 05/21/92

23430 Malibu Colony
Malibu, CA 90265
Alternate V: 05/25/92

760 N. La Cienega Blvd.
Los Angeles, CA 90069
Alternate V: 10/04/92

c/o ICM
8942 Wilshire Blvd.
Beverly Hills, CA 90069
Forwarded V: 03/03/93

Derr, Richard
8965 Cynthia St.
Los Angeles, CA 90069
Actor V: 01/15/92

Derrick, Coleman
c/o New Jersey Nets
Meadowlands Arena
E. Rutherford, NJ 07073
Basketball V: 04/05/93

Desiderio, Robert
3960 Laurel Canyon #280
Studio City, CA 91604
Actor V: 03/03/93

Detmers, Maruschka
c/o Myriam Bru
80 ave. Charles-de-Gaulle
F-92200 Neuilly s/s, France
Actress V: 01/17/93

Detroit Lions
1200 Featherstone Rd.
Pontiac, MI 48057
Team Offices V: 05/15/92

Detroit Tigers
Tiger Stadium
Detroit, MI 48218
Team Office V: 05/15/92

Deutsch, Patti
9255 Sunset Blvd. #603
Los Angeles, CA 90069
Actress V: 01/24/93

Devane, William
11511 Decente Dr.
Studio City, CA 91604
Actor V: 01/24/93

15027 Valley Vista Blvd.
Sherman Oaks, CA 91403
Alternate V: 03/18/92

Devito, Danny
2424 Nottingham Dr.
Los Angeles, CA 90027
Actor V: 03/18/93

P.O. Box 27365
Los Angeles, CA 90027
L.R.U. V: 08/08/92

Devon, Richard
5727 Canoga Park
Woodland Hills, CA 91367
Actor V: 03/30/93

Devroe Agency
3365 Cahuenga Blvd.
Los Angeles, CA 90068
Talent Agency V: 11/21/92

Dewitt, Joyce
101 Ocean Ave. #L-4
Santa Monica, CA 90402
Actress V: 03/18/93

Dey, Susan
c/o William Morris
151 El Camino Dr.
Beverly Hills, CA 90212
Actress V: 03/20/92

Di Preta, Tony
c/o King Features
216 East 45th St.
New York, NY 10017
Cartoonist V: 01/04/93

Dial, Nikki
9056 Santa Monica Blvd. #204
W. Hollywood, CA 90069
Adult Films V: 02/13/93

Diamond, Debi
2554 Lincoln Blvd. #240
Marina del Rey, CA 90292
Adult Films V: 02/13/93

Diamond, Neil
P.O. Box 3357
Los Angeles, CA 90028
Singer V: 03/03/93

Diamond Artists
215 N. Barrington Ave.
Los Angeles, CA 90049
Talent Agency V: 03/22/93

Diamont, Don
c/o CBS-TV/Young&Restless
7800 Beverly Blvd.
Los Angeles, CA 90036
Actor V: 01/21/92

Diana, Princess
St. James Palace
London SW1A 1BS, England
Princess of Wales V: 02/14/93

Dicenzo, George
Stone Hollow Farm
Rt. 1, Box 728
Pipersville, PA 18947
Actor V: 01/12/93

Dick, Douglas
604 Gretna Green Way
Los Angeles, CA 90049
Actor V: 05/13/92

Dick & Dee Dee
9227 Nichols St.
Bellflower, CA 90706
Singers V: 05/14/92

Dickerson, Eddie
c/o Penske
6 Knob Hill Rd.
Mooresville, NC 28256
Race Crew V: 03/12/93

Dickinson, Angie
c/o Dorothy Howe
1524 Walgrove Ave.
Mar Vista, CA 90066
Actress V: 10/04/92

9580 Lime Orchard Rd.
Beverly Hills, CA 90210
Forwarded V: 10/04/92

2121 Ave. of the Stars #410
Los Angeles, CA 90067
L.R.U. V: 07/01/92

Dickinson, Sandra
c/o Howes & Prior
66 Berkeley House, Hay Hill
London W1X 7LH, England
Actress V: 02/04/93

Diddley, Bo
200 W. 57th St. #907
New York, NY 10019
Singer V: 05/14/92

3697 Andreas Hill Dr. #A
Palm Springs, CA 92262
Alternate V: 12/14/92

P.O. Box 474
Archer, FL 32618
L.R.U. V: 08/08/92

Die Prinzen
Postfach 26
D-(O) 7027 Leipzig, Germany
Musical Group V: 01/17/93

Diller, Phyllis
c/o Phildil Prod. Ltd.
230 Park Ave.
New York, NY 10017
Actress V: 06/23/92

Diller, Phyllis
163 S. Rockingham Rd.
Los Angeles, CA 90049
Alternate V: 05/13/92

Dillman, Bradford
770 Hot Springs
Santa Barbara, CA 93103
Actor V: 05/12/92

Dillon, Matt
49 W. 9th St.
New York, NY 10010
Actor V: 06/15/92

c/o American Playhouse
1776 Broadway
New York, NY 10019
Forwarded V: 03/14/93

Dillon, Melinda
c/o Artists Reps
The Allstars
3949 Rambla Orienta
Malibu, CA 90265
Production Company V: 06/15/92

Dion
c/o Di Mucci
2639 NW 42nd St.
Boca Ratan, FL 33434
Singer V: 02/15/93

Dion, Colleen
c/o Bell-Phillip Prod.
Bold & Beautiful
7800 Beverly Blvd., Ste.3371
Los Angeles, CA 90036
Actress V: 06/15/92

Directors Guild
7920 Sunset Blvd.
Los Angeles, CA 90046
Guild Office V: 01/12/92

Discovery Channel
7700 Wisconsin Ave.
Bethesda, MD 20814-3522
Network HQ V: 03/01/92

Disney, Roy E.
500 S. Buena Vista St.
Burbank, CA 91521
Producer V: 03/03/93

Disney Channel
3800 W. Alameda Ave.
Burbank, CA 91505
Network HQ V: 03/01/93

Disney Channel, contd
4111 W. Alameda
Burbank, CA 91605
 Alternate V: 03/01/93

500 S. Buena Vista St.#5064
Burbank, CA 91521
 Viewer Services V: 12/12/92

Disney Company Archives
c/o Dave Smith
500 S. Buena Vista St.
Burbank, CA 91521
 Disney Expert V: 03/10/93

Disney Imagineering
1401 Flower St.
Glendale, CA 91201
 Production Company V: 03/17/93

Disney Productions Ltd.
European Offices
31-32 Soho Sq.
London W1, England
 Company HQ V: 03/01/93

Dixon, Donna
c/o Dan Akroyd
9200 Sunset Blvd. #428
Los Angeles, CA 90069
 Actress V: 02/18/92

7708 Woodrow Wilson Ave.
Los Angeles, CA 90046
 Alternate V: 04/16/92

11288 Ventura Blvd. #371
Studio City, CA 91604
 Forwarded V: 01/19/93

Dixon, Ivan
3432 N. Marengo Ave.
Altadena, CA 91001
 Actor V: 05/17/92

Dobson, Kevin
c/o Freeman
8961 Sunset Blvd.
Los Angeles, CA 90069
 Actor V: 01/17/92

11930 Iredell St.
Studio City, CA 91604
 Forwarded V: 05/14/92

Dodson, Jack
870 N. Vine St.
Los Angeles, CA 90038
 Actor V: 02/23/92

Doherty, Shannen
P.O. Box 900
Beverly Hills, CA 90213
 Actress V: 05/15/92

1654 N. Doherty Dr.
Los Angeles, CA 90069
 Alternate V: 02/03/92

1011 1/2 Carol Dr.
Los Angeles, CA 90069
 Alternate V: 03/30/93

4735 Sepulveda Blvd. Apt.413
Sherman Oaks, CA 91403-5424
 Forwarded V: 03/30/93

Dohm, Gaby
Trogerstr. 17
D-(W) 8000 Munchen 80
Germany
 Actress V: 02/23/93

Dolan, Don
c/o General Hosp./ABC Inc.
4151 Prospect Ave.
Hollywood, CA 90027
 Actor V: 03/01/92

Dolby, Ray
c/o Dolby Labs.
100 Potraro Ave.
San Francisco, CA 94103-4813
 Inventor V: 04/16/93

Dolenz, Ami
6058 St. Clair Ave.
N. Hollywood, CA 91606
 Actress V: 01/19/93

c/o General Hosp./ABC
4151 Prospect Ave.
Hollywood, CA 90027
 Alternate V: 03/01/92

c/o ABC-TV/General Hospital
1438 N. Gower St.
Los Angeles, CA 90028
 Forwarded V: 01/17/92

Dolenz, Mickey
2921 W. Alameda Ave.
Burbank, CA 91505
 Actor V: 06/12/92

c/o Agent
8A Brunswick Gardens
London W8, England
 Forwarded V: 03/09/93

Domino, Fats
5525 Marais St.
New Orleans, LA 70117
Singer V: 05/14/92

Donahue, Elinor
4525 Lemp Ave.
N. Hollywood, CA 91602
Actress V: 02/28/92

Donahue, Phil
30 Rockefeller Plaza Suite 827
New York, NY 10112
TV Host V: 02/17/92

Donaldson, Sam
c/o ABC News
Prime Time Live
1926 Broadway
New York, NY 10023
Correspondent V: 12/07/92

Donlavey, Junie
5011 Midlothian Turnpike
Richmond, VA 23224
NASCAR Driver V: 03/02/92

Donner, Robert
3828 Glenridge Dr.
Sherman Oaks, CA 91423
Actor V: 05/29/92

Donner Productions
c/o Richard Donner
4000 Warner Blvd. Bldg. 102
Burbank, CA 91522
Production Company V: 03/17/92

Donoghue, Mary Agnes
427 Alta Ave.
Santa Monica, CA 90402
Actress V: 01/24/93

Donohoe, Amanda
c/o Gores/Fields Agency
10100 Santa Monica Blvd. #700
Los Angeles, CA 90067
Actress V: 03/30/93

c/o Studio Fan Mail
1122 S. Robertson Blvd.
Los Angeles, CA 90035
Forwarded V: 03/30/93

Donovan
P.O. Box 472
London SW7 2QB, England
Singer V: 10/10/92

Donovan, Art
1512 Jeffers Rd.
Baltimore, MD 21204
Football V: 03/17/92

Doohan, James
P.O. Box 1100
Burbank, CA 91507
Actor V: 11/11/92

Doran, Ann
1610 N. Orange Grove
Los Angeles, CA 90046
Actress V: 06/15/92

Dorn, Michael
c/o Star Trek-TNG Paramount
5555 Melrose Ave.
Hollywood, CA 90038
Actor V: 04/19/92

3751 Multiview Dr.
Los Angeles, CA 90068
Alternate V: 01/12/93

Dorsey, Reginald T.
9000 Sunset Blvd.
Los Angeles, CA 90069
Actor V: 04/16/92

Dotter, Bobby
Rt.8, Box 530-P
Raleigh, NC 27603-3634
Race Driver V: 03/12/93

Doucette, John
P.O. Box 252
Cabazon, CA 92230
Actor V: 01/12/92

Douglas, Donna
P.O. Box 49455
Los Angeles, CA 90049
Actress V: 03/02/92

Douglas, James
2525 Oakstone Dr. Ste.C
Columbus, OH 43231
Boxer V: 07/06/92

Douglas, Jerry
Y & R/CBS-TV
7800 Beverly Blvd.
Los Angeles, CA 90036
Actor V: 01/06/92

Douglas, Kirk
141 El Camino Dr.
Beverly Hills, CA 90212
Actor V: 03/22/92

Douglas, Kirk, contd
805 N. Rexford
Beverly Hills, CA 90210
 Alternate V: 07/25/92

Douglas, Michael
936 Hot Springs Rd.
Montecito, CA 93108
 Actor V: 03/16/92

P.O. Box 49054
Los Angeles, CA 90049-9054
 Alternate V: 03/14/92

P.O. Box 540148
Orlando, FL 32854-0148
 Forwarded V: 04/22/92

Dourif, Brad
213 1/2 S. Arnaz Dr.
Beverly Hills, CA 90211
 Actor V: 04/06/93

Dove, Billie
P.O. Box 5005
Rancho Mirage, CA 92270
 Actress V: 01/24/93

Down, Lesley-Anne
6509 Wandermere Rd.
Malibu, CA 90265
 Actress V: 10/15/92

Downery, Jr., Robert
1494 N. Kings Rd.
Los Angeles, CA 90069
 Actor V: 04/06/93

Downs, Hugh
c/o ABC News
20/20
1926 Broadway
New York, NY 10023
 Correspondent V: 12/07/92

Downs, Johnny
812 San Luis Rey Ave.
Coronado, CA 92118
 Celebrity V: 02/02/92

Doyle, David
4731 Noeline Ave.
Encino, CA 91316
 Actor V: 06/15/92

Doyle, Jerry
c/o Henderson/Hogan
247 S. Beverly Dr., #102
Beverly Hills, CA 90210
 Actor V: 02/23/93

Drake, Ellen
c/o 20th Century Fox TV
L.A. Law
P.O. Box 900
Beverly Hills, CA 90213
 Actress V: 01/12/92

Drake, Frances
1511 Summit Ridge Dr.
Beverly hills, Ca 90210
 Actress V: 06/15/92

Drake, Kelly
c/o Dallas Cowboys
One Cowboys Parkway
Irving, TX 75063-4945
 Cheerleader V: 08/08/92

Drake, Larry
1122 S. Robertson Blvd.
Los Angeles, CA 90035
 Actor V: 04/01/92

2293 Bronson Hill Dr.
Los Angeles, CA 90068
 Actor V: 04/06/93

c/o 20th Century Fox TV
L.A. Law
P.O. Box 900
Beverly Hills, CA 90213
 Alternate V: 01/12/92

Drake, Stan
c/o King Features
216 East 45th St.
New York, NY 10017
 Cartoonist V: 05/13/92

Dravecky, Dave
P.O. Box 3505
Boardman, OH 44513
 Celebrity V: 05/14/92

Dream So Real
P.O. Box 8061
Athens, GA 30603
 Musical Group V: 04/20/92

Drescher, Fran
c/o Rich
2400 Whitman Pl.
Los Angeles, CA 90068
 Actress V: 03/03/93

Drew, Stacie
c/o Dallas Cowboys
One Cowboys Parkway
Irving, TX 75063-4945
 Cheerleader V: 08/08/92

Dreyfuss, Richard
2809 Nichols Canyon Rd.
Los Angeles, CA 90046
Actor V: 02/28/92

Dru, Joanne
c/o Janie Jackson
1455 Carla Ridge Dr.
Beverly Hills, CA 90210
Actress V: 06/01/92

Drury, James
12755 Mill Ridge Ste. 622
Cypress, TX 77429
Actor V: 04/05/92

Dryer, Fred
c/o Stephen J. Cannell Prod.
7083 Hollywood Blvd.
Hollywood, CA 90028
Actor V: 02/21/93

9834 Wanda Park Dr.
Beverly Hills, CA 90210
L.R.U. V: 07/07/92

c/o William Morris
151 El Camino Dr.
Beverly Hills, CA 90212
L.R.U. V: 01/02/92

Dubbins, Don
15010 Ventura Blvd. #219
Sherman Oaks, CA 91403
Actor V: 11/11/92

Dubois, Ja'Net
c/o Amsel
6310 San Vicente Blvd. #407
Los Angeles, CA 90048
Actress V: 06/15/92

405 W. Ivy St. #204
Glendale, CA 91204
Actress V: 01/24/93

Dubuc, Nicole
c/o Universal Television
Major Dad
100 Univ. City Plz., Bl.426-2E
Universal City, CA 91608
Actress V: 03/02/92

Duffy, Brian
c/o NASA
LBJ Space Center
Houston, TX 77058
Astronaut V: 01/31/93

Duffy, Brian
c/o King Features
216 E. 45th St.
New York, NY 10017
Cartoonist V: 03/11/93

Duffy, Julia
c/o Gores-Fields
10100 Santa Monica Blvd. #700
Los Angeles, CA 90067
Actress V: 06/15/92

Duffy, Patrick
c/o Writers & Artists
11726 San Vicente Blvd.
Los Angeles, CA 90049
Actor V: 01/17/92

P.O. Box D
Tarzana, CA 91356
Alternate V: 04/06/93

c/o ABC-TV/Step by Step
4151 Prospect Ave.
Los Angeles, CA 90027
Forwarded V: 12/16/92

Dugan, Dennis
1755 Old Ranch Road
Los Angeles, CA 90049
Actor V: 03/12/92

Dukakas, Olympia
222 Upper Monutain Road
Montclair, NJ 07043
Actress V: 02/20/92

Duke, Patty
326 N. Forest Dr.
Coeur d'Alene, ID 83814-2163
Actress V: 03/14/93

Duke Jr., Charles M.
280 Lakeview
New Braunfels, TX 78130
Astronaut V: 03/17/93

P.O. Box 310345
New Braunfels, TX 78131-0345
Alternate V: 05/14/92

c/o NASA
LBJ Space Center
Houston, TX 77058
Forwarded V: 01/19/93

Dukes, David
328 S. Beverly Dr.
Beverly Hills, CA 90212
Actor V: 04/04/92

Dukes, David, contd
255 S. Lorraine Blvd.
Los Angeles, CA 90004
 Actor V: 04/05/93

Dullea, Keir
6 Dogwood Lane
Westport, CT 06880
 Actor V: 02/16/92

c/o Mitosky
151 Central Park S.
New York, NY 10019
 Actor V: 03/17/93

Dumas, Jerry
c/o King Features
216 East 45th St.
New York, NY 10017
 Cartoonist V: 06/01/92

Dumont, Sky
c/o General Hosp./ABC
4151 Prospect Ave.
Hollywood, CA 90027
 Actor V: 03/01/92

Dunagin, Ralph
c/o King Features
216 East 45th St.
New York, NY 10017
 Cartoonist V: 07/26/92

Dunaway, Faye
c/o Fox Broadcasting
P.O. Box 900
Beverly Hills, CA 90213
 Actress V: 12/10/92

9056 Santa Monica Blvd. #100
Hollywood, CA 90069
 Alternate V: 03/15/93

1435 Linda Crest Dr.
Beverly Hills, CA 90210
 Alternate V: 03/19/93

c/o New Line Cinema
116 N. Robertson Blvd.
Los Angeles, CA 90048
 Alternate V: 01/23/93

300 Central Park W.
New York, NY 10024
 Alternate V: 10/04/92

15147 Mulholland Dr.
Los Angeles, CA 90077
 L.R.U. V: 07/01/92

Dunbar, Bonnie J.
c/o NASA
LBJ Space Center
Houston, TX 77058
 Astronaut V: 01/19/93

Duncan, Carmen
c/o NBC-TV
Another World
79 Madison Ave., 5th Fl.
New York, NY 91523
 Actress V: 06/15/92

Dunn, Bob
c/o King Features
216 East 45th St.
New York, NY 10017
 Cartoonist V: 03/19/93

Dunn, Nora
c/o NBC Prod.
Saturday Night Live
30 Rockefeller Plaza
New York, NY 10112
 Actress V: 01/10/93

Dunne, Griffin
40 W. 12th St.
New York, NY 10011
 Actor V: 03/12/93

Dunne, Holly
c/o Ten Ten
1010 16th Ave. S.
Nashville, TN 37212
 Actress V: 02/03/92

Durbin, Deanna
B.P. 767
75123 Paris, Cedex 03 France
 Actress V: 03/15/93

c/o Agent
10 Rue du Vivier
78640 Neauphle-le-Chateau
Yvelines, France
 L.R.U. V: 02/01/93

Durkin Artists Agency
12229 Ventura Blvd. #202
Studio City, CA 91604
 Talent Agency V: 01/17/92

Durning, Charles
c/o Mozark Prod./CBS-MTM
Evening Shade
4024 Radford Ave., Bl.5, Rm.104
Studio City, CA 91604
 Actor V: 05/15/92

Durning, Charles, contd
10590 Wilshire Blvd. #506
Los Angeles, CA 90024
Alternate V: 03/17/93

Durrell, Michael
c/o Viacom Prod.
Matlock
100 Universal City Plaza
Bl. 448
Universal City, CA 91608
Actor V: 12/01/92

Durst, Will
c/o Just For Laughs
22 Miller Ave.
Mill Valley, CA 94941
Comedian V: 02/01/93

Dusay, Debra
9000 Sunset Blvd. #1200
Los Angeles, CA 90069
Actress V: 03/03/93

Dusay, Marj
6310 San Vicente Blvd. #407
Los Angeles, CA 90048
Actress V: 03/03/93

Dussalt, Nancy
12211 Iredell St.
Studio City, CA 91604
Actress V: 01/24/93

P.O. Box 279
New York, NY 10017
L.R.U. V: 01/02/92

Dusty
c/o 5K Sales
9420 Reseda Blvd., Ste.836
Northridge, CA 91324
Adult Films V: 01/17/93

Duvall, Robert
257 W. 86th St.
New York, NY 10021
Actor V: 04/16/92

c/o Wizan/Black Films
Warner Bros. Ltd.
4000 Warner Blvd.
Burbank, CA 91522
Forwarded V: 01/29/93

Duvall, Shelley
c/o Think Entertainment
12725 Ventura Blvd. Ste. J
Studio City, CA 91604
Actress V: 02/11/93

Duvall, Shelley, contd
4151 Prospect Ave.
Los Angeles, CA 90027
Forwarded V: 05/14/92

13280 Valley Vista
Sherman Oaks, CA 91423
L.R.U. V: 01/02/92

Dylan, Bob
P.O. Box 264
New York, NY 10003
Singer V: 01/19/92

P.O. Box 870 Cooper Station
New York, NY 10276
Alternate V: 08/01/92

Dysart, Richard
c/o 20th Century Fox TV
L.A. Law
P.O. Box 900
Beverly Hills, CA 90213
Actor V: 01/12/92

654 Copeland Ct.
Santa Monica, CA 90405
Actor V: 04/06/93

c/o Writers & Artists
11726 San Vicente Blvd.
Los Angeles, CA 90049
Alternate V: 01/17/92

Dzundza, George
c/o Law & Order
100 Universal City Plaza, Bl.G
Universal City, CA 91608
Actor V: 01/12/92

E

EERIE, INDIANA
Cosgrove-Meurer Prod.
4024 Radford Ave. #3
Studio City, CA 91644
Production Company V: 03/26/93

EMPTY NEST
Witt, Thomas, Harris Prod.
846 N. Cahuenga Blvd.
Hollywood, CA 90038
Production Company V: 03/26/93

EQUAL JUSTICE
c/o Orion
1888 Century Park East
Los Angeles, CA 90067
Production Company V: 12/18/92

ESPN
9665 Wilshire Blvd. #800
Beverly Hills, CA 90210
 Production Company V: 03/17/93

ESPN Plaza
935 Middle St.
Bristol, CT 06010
 Alternate V: 03/01/93

EVENING SHADE
c/o Mozark Prod./CBS-MTM
4024 Radford Ave., Bl.5, Rm.104
Studio City, CA 91604
 Production Company V: 05/15/92

Eakes, Bobbie
c/o Bell/Bold & Beautiful
7800 Beverly Blvd., Ste.3371
Los Angeles, CA 90036
 Actor V: 06/15/92

Earles, H. Clay
Martinsville Speedway
P.O. Box 3311
Martinsville, VA 24115
 NASCAR Official V: 03/02/92

Earnhardt, Dale
c/o Childress Racing
P.O. Box 1189, Industrial Dr.
Welcome, NC 27374
 NASCAR Driver V: 03/02/92

Earnhardt, Dale
Rt. 8, Box 463
Mooresville, NC 28115
 Alternate V: 03/01/92

Easterbrook, Leslie
17352 Sunset Blvd. #401
Pacific Palisades, Ca 90272
 Actress V: 02/18/93

Easton, Sheena
c/o Wasserman
5954 Wilkinson Ave.
N. Hollywood, CA 91069
 Singer V: 02/01/92

Eastwood, Clint
c/o Malpaso
1900 Ave. of the Stars
Los Angeles, CA 90067
 Director V: 04/14/92

P.O. Box 4366
Carmel, CA 93921
 Alternate V: 03/18/93

Eastwood, Clint, contd
4000 Warner Blvd. #16
Burbank, CA 91522
 Forwarded V: 03/19/93

Ebersole, Christine
c/o Wm. Morris
151 El Camino
Beverly Hills, CA 90212
 Actress V: 12/19/92

c/o Hart
1244 11th St., Ste.A
Santa Monica, CA 90401
 Alternate V: 01/24/93

Ebsen, Buddy
605 Via Horquilla
Palos Verdes Estates, CA 90274
 Actor V: 12/14/92

P.O. Box 33 Suite 407
Long Beach, CA 90801
 L.R.U. V: 01/05/92

Eckersley, Dennis
263 Morse Rd.
Sudbury, MA 01778
 Baseball V: 12/10/92

Eckhardt, Fritz
Bochlinstr. 34/35
A-1020 Wien, Austria
 Actor V: 02/23/93

Eddington, Paul
c/o ICM
388-396 Oxford St.
London W1N 9HE, England
 Actor V: 01/17/93

Edelman, Herb
c/o Witt/Thomas
Golden Palace
846 N. Cahuenga Blvd.
Hollywood, CA 90038
 Actor V: 01/17/92

Eden, Barbara
P.O. Box 57593
Sherman Oaks, CA 91403
 Actress V: 01/14/92

c/o Eicholtz
9816 Denbigh
Beverly Hills, CA 90210
 Actress V: 03/19/93

1332 N. Ulster St.
Allentown, PA 18103
 Alternate V: 01/21/92

P.O. Box 5556
Sherman Oaks, CA 91403
Forwarded V: 12/10/92

Edney, Beattie
c/o Equity
8 Harley St.
London, W1N 2AB, England
Actress V: 01/03/92

Edson, Hilary
NBC-TV/Another World
79 Madison Ave., 5th Fl.
New York, NY 91523
Actress V: 06/15/92

Edwards, Anthony
8820 Lookout Mtn.
Los Angeles, CA 90046
Actor V: 03/21/92

Edwards, Blake
9336 W. Washington Blvd.
Culver City, CA 90230
Director V: 03/03/92

1888 Century Park E. # 1616
Los Angeles, CA 90067
Forwarded V: 03/03/92

Edwards, Douglas
4183 Boca Pointe Dr.
Sarasota, FL 34238
Celebrity V: 01/02/92

Edwards, Gail
2321 21st St.
Santa Monica, CA 90405
Actress V: 02/23/93

Edwards, Stephanie
533 18th St.
Santa Monica, CA 90402
Actress V: 02/23/93

Efendi Talent Agency
6525 Sunset Blvd. #207
Los Angeles, CA 90028
Talent Agency V: 12/12/92

Egger, Samantha
15430 Mulholland Dr.
Los Angeles, CA 90024
Actress V: 08/08/92

Eggert, Nicole
20591 Queens Park
Huntington Beach, CA 92646
Actress V: 02/23/93

Eikenberry, Jill
c/o 20th Century Fox TV
L.A. Law
P.O. Box 900
Beverly Hills, CA 90213
Actress V: 01/12/92

2183 Mandeville Canyon Rd.
Los Angeles, CA 90049
Alternate V: 02/23/93

c/o STE
211 S. Beverly Dr.
Beverly Hills, CA 90212
L.R.U. V: 01/02/92

Eilbacher, Cindy
11051 Ophir Dr.
Los Angeles, CA 90024
Actress V: 03/19/93

Einstein, Bob
c/o Super Dave Osborn
8955 Beverly Blvd.
Los Angeles, CA 90048
Producer V: 01/23/92

Eisman, Hy
c/o King Features
216 East 45th St.
New York, NY 10017
Cartoonist V: 04/13/92

Eisner, Michael D.
500 S. Buena Vista
Burbank, CA 91521
Executive V: 06/15/92

Ekland, Brit
1744 N. Doheny Dr.
Los Angeles, CA 90232-1108
Actress V: 03/02/92

16830 Ventura Blvd. #501
Encino, CA 91436-1717
Alternate V: 01/02/92

El Fadil, Saddig
c/o Star Trek-DS9
5555 Melrose Ave.
Hollywood, CA 90036
Alternate V: 02/23/93

Elam, Jack
P.O. Box 5718
Santa Barbara, CA 93150
Actor V: 04/14/92

Elcar, Dana
c/o Paramount/MacGyver
5555 Melrose Ave.
Los Angeles, CA 90038
Actor V: 12/07/92

c/o Artists
10000 Santa Monica Blvd #305
Los Angeles, CA 90067
Actress V: 06/15/92

Eleniak, Erika
1999 Ave. of the Stars #2850
Los Angeles, CA 90067
Actress V: 02/23/93

Elizondo, Hector
151 El Camino
Beverly Hills, CA 90212
Actor V: 02/03/92

Ellerby, Linda
c/o King Features
216 E. 45th St.
New York, NY 10017
Writer V: 03/11/93

17 St. Lukes Pl.
New York, NY 10014
Writer V: 02/23/93

Elliot, Denholm
c/o London Mgmt.
235 Regent St.
London W1, England
Actor V: 02/28/92

Elliot, Jane
c/o General Hosp./ABC Inc.
4151 Prospect Ave.
Hollywood, CA 90027
Actress V: 03/01/92

606 N. Larchmont Blvd. #309
Los Angeles, CA 90046
Alternate V: 03/03/93

Elliott, Bill
c/o Johnson & Assoc.
Rt.2, Box 162
Rhonda, NC 28670
NASCAR Driver V: 03/02/92

Elliott, Denholm
c/o The Garrick Club
Garrick St.
London WC2, England
Actor V: 01/17/93

Elliott, Sam
33050 Pacific Coast Hwy.
Malibu, CA 90265
Actor V: 06/15/92

Ellis, Janet
c/o Arlington Ent.
1/3 Charlotte St.
London W1P 1HD, England
Actress V: 02/04/93

Ellis Talent Group
6025 Sepulveda Blvd. #201
Van Nuys, CA 91411
Talent Agency V: 07/23/92

Elrod, Jack
c/o King Features
216 East 45th St.
New York, NY 10017
Cartoonist V: 03/24/92

Elvira
c/o Cassandra Peterson
P.O. Box 38246
Hollywood, CA 90038
TV Personality V: 03/01/92

Ely, Ron
4161 Mariposa Dr.
Santa Barbara, CA 93110-2437
Actor V: 03/19/93

Emberg, Kelly
1608 N. Poinsettia
Manhattan Beach, CA 90266
Actress V: 02/23/93

Emerald Artists
6565 Sunset Blvd. #310
Hollywood, CA 90068
Talent Agency V: 04/27/92

Emmerich, Roland
c/o Centopolis Films
1818 Outpost Drive
Los Angeles, CA 90068
Director V: 01/17/93

Encore
4643 S. Ulster St., #300
Denver, CO 80237
Cable TV Station V: 11/11/92

England, Anthony W.
c/o NASA LBJ Space Center
Houston, TX 77058
Astronaut V: 03/03/93

Engle, Georgia
350 W. 57th St. Ste.10E
New York, NY 10019
Actress V: 07/21/92

Engle, Joe H.
c/o NASA LBJ Space Center
Houston, TX 77058
Astronaut V: 03/03/93

Englund, Robert
2451 Horseshoe Canyon Rd.
Los Angeles, CA 90046
Actress V: 01/02/92

Entertainment Network
11111 Santa Monica Blvd. #1210
Los Angeles, CA 90025
Production Company V: 03/17/92

Entertainment Weekly
1675 Broadway
New York, NY 10019
Publishers V: 03/01/92

Eplin, Tom
c/o NBC-TV
Another World
79 Madison Ave., 5th Fl.
New York, NY 91523
Actor V: 06/15/92

Epperson, Brenda
c/o Young and the Restless
7800 Beverly Blvd.
Beverly Hills, CA 90036
Actress V: 06/15/92

Epstein-Wycoff & Assoc.
280 S. Beverly Dr. #400
Beverly Hills, CA 90212
Talent Agency V: 04/27/92

Erdman, Richard
5655 Greenbush Ave.
Van Nuys, CA 91401-4517
Actor V: 05/29/92

Erskine, Carl
6214 S. Madison Ave.
Anderson, IN 46013
Baseball V: 05/14/92

Ertl, Martina
Ertlhofe 17
D-(W) 8172 Lenggries, Germany
Athlete V: 03/13/93

Espy, Mike
Dept. of Agriculture
14th St. and Independence Ave. S.W.
Washington, DC 20250
Secretary of Agriculture V: 01/31/93

Estefan, Gloria
6205 SW 40th St.
Miami, FL 33155
Singer V: 04/03/92

c/o Rubenstein Assoc.
1345 6th Ave. Ste.3100
New York, NY 10105
Alternate V: 03/17/92

8390 S.W. 4th St.
Miami, FL 33144
L.R.U. V: 07/02/92

Estevez, Emilio
120 S. Victory Blvd. Suite 104
Burbank, CA 91502
Actor V: 02/01/92

320 Kearney #8
Santa Fe, NM 87501
Alternate V: 03/12/92

31709 Sea Level Dr.
Malibu, CA 90265
Alternate V: 02/22/92

4024 Radford Ave. Bldg.3
Studio City, CA 91604
Forwarded V: 12/18/92

Estevez, Ramon
837 Ocean Ave. #101
Santa Monica, CA 90402
Actor V: 01/20/92

Estrada, Eric
3768 Eureka Dr.
Studio City, CA 91604
Actor V: 03/19/93

Eurythmics
Box 245
London N8 9AG, England
Musical Group V: 04/16/92

Evans, Andrea
310 W. 72nd St. #7G
New York, NY 10023
Actress V: 08/30/92

c/o Stone Manners
8091 Selma Ave.
Los Angeles, CA 90046
Alternate V: 03/03/93

Evans, Carl T.
c/o CBS/Guiding Light
51 W. 52nd St.
New York, NY 10019
Actor V: 01/17/92

Evans, Dale
15650 Seneca Rd.
Victorville, CA 92392
Actress V: 03/10/92

Evans, Gene
1583 Church St.
Ventura, CA 93001
Actor V: 04/05/92

Evans, George
c/o King Features
216 East 45th St.
New York, NY 10017
Cartoonist V: 06/26/92

Evans, Greg
c/o King Features
216 East 45th St.
New York, NY 10017
Cartoonist V: 02/13/92

Evans, Josh
1032 N. Beverly Dr.
Beverly Hills, CA 90210
Actor V: 03/17/93

Evans, Judi
20955 Warner Center Ln.
Woodland Hills, CA 91367
Actress V: 02/23/93

Evans, Linda
c/o ICM
8942 Wilshire Blvd.
Beverly Hills, CA 90211
Actress V: 03/30/93

1041 N. Formosa
Los Angeles, CA 90046
Alternate V: 03/24/92

167 S. Canon Dr.
Beverly Hills, CA 90212
Alternate V: 12/08/92

9115 Hazen Dr.
Beverly Hills, CA 90270
L.R.U. V: 05/29/92

Evans, Mariel
5825 Resedee Blvd. #324
Tarzana, CA 91356
Actress V: 12/19/92

Evans, Mary Beth
106 N. Grand Ave.
Pasadena, CA 91103
Actress V: 02/23/93

Evans, Michael
c/o Y&R/7800 Beverly Blvd.
Beverly Hills, CA 90036
Actor V: 06/15/92

Everett, Chad
19901 Northridge Rd.
Chatsworth, CA 91311
Actor V: 03/21/92

Everly, Don & Phil
10414 Camarillo St.
North Hollywood, CA 91602
Singers V: 06/15/92

Everson, Cory
7324 Reseda Blvd. Ste.208
Reseda, CA 91335
Ms. Olympia V: 03/03/92

Evert, Chris
7100 W. Camino Real, Ste.203
Boca Raton, FL 33433
Tennis V: 05/11/92

500 N.E. 25 St.
Wilton Manors, FL 33305-1135
Alternate V: 02/20/92

5400 Champion Blvd.
Boca Raton, FL 33496
Forwarded V: 02/20/92

Ewell, Tom
53 Aspin Way
Rolling Hills Estates, CA 90274
Actor V: 03/17/93

F

F.P.A.
4051 Radford Ave. Ste.A
Studio City, CA 91604
Talent Agency V: 05/13/92

FBI-UNTOLD STORIES
100 Universal Plaza #447
Universal City, CA 91608
Production Company V: 03/19/93

4024 Radford Ave.
Studio City, CA 91604
Alternate V: 12/15/92

FIEVEL'S AMERICAN TAILS
Universal Cartoon Studios
100 Universal City Plz.
Building 507, Suite 4G
Universal City, CA 91608
Production Company V: 03/18/93

FIFTH CORNER
New World TV
1440 S. Sepulveda Blvd.
Los Angeles, CA 90025
Production Company V: 03/26/93

FINAL APPEAL
Cosgrove-Meurer Prod.
4303 W. Verdugo Ave.
Burbank, CA 91505
Production Company V: 03/26/93

FLESH-N-BLOOD
Paramount
5555 Melrose Ave.
Hollywood, CA 91608
Production Company V: 03/26/93

FOREVER KNIGHT
Tri-Star Television
7 Curity Avenue, 2nd Fl.
Toronto, Ontario, Canada M4Y 1W5
Production Company V: 03/18/93

FORTY EIGHT HOURS
c/o CBS Broadcast Center
48 Hours
524 W. 57th St.
New York, NY 10019
Production Company V: 06/15/91

FRANNIE'S TURN
The Carsey-Werner Co.
4024 Radford Ave.
Build. 3
Studio City, CA 91604
Production Company V: 03/15/93

FRESH PRINCE OF BEL AIR
NBC Prod.
330 Bob Hope Dr.
Burbank, CA 91523
Production Company V: 03/26/93

FUNNIEST HOME VIDEOS
c/o Vin Di Bona Prods.
America's Funniest Video
P.O. Box 4333
Los Angeles, CA 90078
Production Company V: 12/15/92

FUNNIEST PEOPLE
c/o Vin Di Bona Prods.
America's Funniest People
4151 Prospect Ave., Prod.Bldg.
Hollywood, CA 90078
Production Company V: 12/19/92

Fabares, Shelley
Box 6010 - #85
Sherman Oaks, CA 91413
Actress V: 04/03/92

c/o Universal TV
Coach
100 Universal Plaza, Bung. 78
Universal City, CA 91608
Alternate V: 12/18/92

Fabian, Ava
c/o Playboy Ent.
8560 Sunset Blvd.
Los Angeles, CA 90069
Playmate V: 11/11/92

Fabian, John M.
c/o NASA LBJ Space Center
Houston, TX 77058
Astronaut V: 03/03/93

Fabray, Nanette
14360 Sunset Blvd.
Pacific Palisades, CA 90272
Actress V: 02/12/92

Face To Face
c/o CBS/Connie Chung
524 W. 57th St.
New York, NY 10019
Production Company V: 06/15/92

Faces International
45 W. 45th St., PH
New York, NY 10036
Publication V: 04/19/93

Faces International
10537 Santa Monica Blvd.
Los Angeles, CA 90025
Alternate V: 04/19/93

Faherty, Tim
c/o King Features
216 E. 45th St.
New York, NY 10017
Cartoonist V: 03/11/93

Fahey, Jeff
250 N. Robertson Blvd. #518
Beverly Hills, CA 90211
Actor V: 03/28/93

Fairbanks Jr., Douglas
The Vicarage
448 N. Lake Way
Palm Beach, FL 33480
Actor V: 04/01/93

575 Park Ave. #608
New York, NY 10021
L.R.U. V: 01/04/92

Fairchild, Morgan
3480 Blair Dr.
Los Angeles, CA 90068-1412
Actress V: 07/23/92

3321 Dixie Canyon Lane
Beverly Hills, CA 90210
L.R.U. V: 01/02/92

Falana, Lola
P.O. Box 50369
Henderson, NV 89106-0369
Singer V: 04/23/92

Falk, Lee
c/o King Features
216 East 45th St.
New York, NY 10017
Cartoonist V: 05/21/92

Falk, Peter
1004 N. Roxbury Dr.
Beverly Hills, CA 90210
Actor V: 09/23/92

Producers 8 Suite 209
Columbia Plaza
Burbank, CA 91505
Alternate V: 04/15/92

Falkenburg, Jinx
10 Shelter Rock Rd.
Manhasset, NY 11030
Model V: 06/16/92

Fallon
c/o 5K Sales
9420 Reseda Blvd., Ste.836
Northridge, CA 91324
Adult Films V: 01/17/93

Falwell, Jerry
P.O. Box 190
Forrest, VA 24551
Evangelist V: 03/13/92

Old Time Gospel Hour
Lynchburg, VA 24514
Alternate V: 02/21/92

Falwell, Jerry, contd
P.O. Box 1111
Lynchburg, VA 24505
Forwarded V: 04/13/92

Family Channel
1000 Centerville Turnpike
Virginia Beach, VA 23463
Production Company V: 01/12/92

Family Feud
c/o Goodson Prod.
Family Feud
5750 Wilshire Blvd. #475 W
Los Angeles, CA 90036
Production Company V: 06/15/92

Faracy, Stephanie
8765 Lookout Mtn. Rd.
Los Angeles, CA 90046
Actress V: 02/23/93

Farentino, Debra
20521 Roca Chica Dr.
Malibu, CA 90265-5333
Actress V: 08/08/92

586 Lorna Lane
Los Angeles, CA 90049
L.R.U. V: 08/08/92

Farentino, James
1340 Londonderry Pl.
Los Angeles, CA 90069
Actor V: 03/17/93

Farina, Dennis
8457 Melrose Pl. #200
Los Angeles, CA 90069
Actor V: 01/10/92

6922 Hollywood Blvd.
Los Angeles, CA 90028
Alternate V: 03/21/92

Farnsworth, Richard
c/o Diamond D Ranch
Box 123
Lincoln, NM 88338-0123
Actor V: 01/07/92

3219 Ellington Dr.
Hollywood, CA 90068
L.R.U. V: 01/14/92

Farr, Jamie
99 Buckskin Rd.
Bell Canyon
Canoga Park, CA 91307
Actor V: 03/21/93

Farr, Jamie, contd
53 Ranchero, Bell Canyon
Canoga Park, CA 91307
Alternate V: 01/20/93

Farrel, Tommy
5225 Riverton Ave.
N. Hollywood, CA 91601
Actor V: 12/12/92

Farrell, Cirroc
c/o 20th Cent. Artists
14724 Ventura Blvd. 5th Fl.
Sherman Oaks, CA 91403
Actor V: 02/23/93

Farrell, Mike
P.O. Box 5961-85
Sherman Oaks, CA 91413-5961
Actor V: 05/02/92

P.O. Box 6010-826
Sherman Oaks, CA 91413
Alternate V: 06/15/92

Farrell, Terry
c/o Metro. Talent Agency
9320 Wilshire Blvd. 3rd Fl.
Beverly Hills, CA 90212
Actress V: 02/23/93

c/o Star Trek-DS9
5555 Melrose Ave.
Hollywood, CA 90036
Alternate V: 02/23/93

Farrell, Tommy
5225 Riverton Ave.
N. Hollywood, CA 91601
Actor V: 01/06/93

Farrell Talent Agency
18261 San Fernando Mission Blvd.
Northridge, CA 91326
Talent Agency V: 06/13/92

Farrow, Mia
135 Central Park West
New York, NY 10023
Actress V: 12/12/92

950 Fifth Ave.
New York, NY 10021
L.R.U. V: 07/01/92

Fashion-L.A. Agency
6533 Hollywood Blvd. #400
Los Angeles, CA 90028
Talent Agency V: 06/06/92

Faustino, David
1320 N. Maple St.
Burbank, CA 91505
Actor V: 03/03/93

Favored Artists Agency
8150 Beverly Blvd. #201
Los Angeles, CA 90048
Talent Agency V: 06/13/92

Fawcett, Farrah
3130 Antelo Rd.
Los Angeles, CA 90024
Actress V: 01/07/92

328 S. Beverly Dr. #A
Beverly Hills, CA 90212
Alternate V: 04/02/92

1888 Century Park E. Su.1400
Los Angeles, CA 90067
Forwarded V: 02/18/92

Faye, Alice
49400 JFK Trail
Palm Desert, CA 92260
Actress V: 02/12/92

Feather, Leonard
13833 Riverside Dr.
Sherman Oaks, CA 91423
Author V: 02/17/92

Feinstein, Diane
30 Presidio Terr.
San Francisco, CA 94118
Politician V: 03/14/93

Feinstein, Michael
1800 N. Argyle #408
Hollywood, CA 90028
Singer V: 10/11/92

P.O. Box 6342
Orange, CA 92613
Alternate V: 06/14/92

Felber Agency
2126 Cahuenga Blvd.
Los Angeles, CA 90068
Talent Agency V: 07/20/92

Feld, Fritz
12348 Rochedale Ln.
Los Angeles, CA 90049
Actor V: 03/14/92

Feldman/Gold Agency
19301 Ventura Blvd., Ste.202
Tarzana, CA 91356
Talent Agency V: 03/13/93

Feldon, Barbara
14 E. 74th St.
New York, NY 10021
Actress V: 06/12/92

8899 Beverly Blvd.
Beverly Hills, CA 90212
Alternate V: 01/11/92

Creative Artists Agency
9830 Wilshire Blvd.
Beverly Hills, CA 90212
Alternate V: 03/12/92

Fell, Norman
113 N. San Vicente Blvd. #202
Beverly Hills, CA 90211
Actor V: 01/20/93

Feller, Bob
c/o Ro-An-Fel Inc.
Box 170
Novelty, OH 44072
Baseball V: 04/16/92

Fellini, Federico
Via Margutta 141a
I-00110 Rome, Italy
Director V: 01/17/93

Fellows, Edith
2016 1/2 Vista Del Mar
Los Angeles, CA 90068
Actress V: 06/15/92

Fenn, Sherilyn
8033 W. Sunset Blvd. #4054
Los Angeles, CA 90048
Actress V: 08/12/92

Fenneman, George
13214 Moorpark St. #206
Sherman Oaks, CA 91423
Personality V: 02/19/92

Ferdin, Pamelyn
c/o Vlasak
727 Esplinade #203
Redondo, Beach, CA 90277
Actress V: 04/01/93

Ferrare, Christina
1280 Stone Canyon Rd.
Los Angeles, CA 90077
Actress V: 01/23/93

Ferraro, Geraldine
22 Deepdene Rd.
Forest Hills, NY 11375
Politician V: 05/22/92

Ferratti, Rebecca
7461 Beverly Blvd. #400
Los Angeles, CA 90036
Actress V: 03/03/93

Ferrell, Conchata
1347 N. Seward St.
Los Angeles, CA 90028
Actor V: 05/13/92

Ferreol, Andrea
c/o Artmedia
10 Ave. George-V
F-75008 Paris, France
Actress V: 02/11/93

Ferrer, Mel
6590 Camino Carreta
Carpenteria, CA 93013
Actor V: 03/17/92

Ferrigno, Lou
621 17th St.
Santa Monica, CA 90402
Body Builder V: 03/07/92

Field, Sally
12307 7th Helena Dr.
Los Angeles, CA 90049
Actress V: 08/25/92

825 S. Barrington Ave. #204
Los Angeles, CA 90049
Alternate V: 01/04/93

8436 W. 3rd St. #650
Beverly Hills, CA 90211
Alternate V: 06/01/92

Field, Shirley Ann
68 St James St.
London SW1, England
Actress V: 02/28/92

4260 Arcola Ave.
Toluca Lake, CA 91602
Alternate V: 04/01/93

Fields, Holly
3800 Barham Blvd.
Los Angeles, CA 90068
Actress V: 02/14/93

Fields, Holly, contd
9301 Wilshire Blvd. #312
Beverly Hills, CA 90210
L.R.U. *V: 06/01/92*

Fields Talent Agency
3325 Wilshire Blvd. #749
Los Angeles, CA 90010
Talent Agency *V: 03/29/93*

Fierstein, Harvey
15 Hawthorne Rd.
Ridgefield, CT 06877
Actor *V: 03/19/93*

Film Artists Associates
7080 Hollywood Blvd. #704
Hollywood, CA 90028
Talent Agency *V: 03/29/93*

Film Arts Foundation
Videotape Library
346 9th St. 2nd Fl.
San Francisco, CA 94103
Archive *V: 03/14/93*

Fimple, Dennis
6736 Laurel Canyon Blvd. #369
N. Hollywood, CA 91606
Actor *V: 01/03/92*

Financial News Network
6701 Center Dr. W.
W. Los Angeles, CA 90045
Production Company *V: 03/17/92*

Finch, Jon
135 New Kings Rd.
London SW6 4SL, England
Actor *V: 03/03/93*

Fine, Jeanna
9420 Reseda Blvd., #836
Northridge, CA 91324
Adult Films *V: 03/03/93*

P.O. Box 93128
Hollywood, CA 90093
Alternate *V: 02/13/93*

Finlay, Frank
55 Park Lane
London W1, England
Actor *V: 04/14/93*

Finneran, Kike
c/o Warner/Night Court
4000 Warner Blvd., Office 12A
Burbank, CA 91521
Actor *V: 01/12/92*

Finney, Albert
39 Seymour Walk
London, SW10 England
Actor *V: 02/23/93*

25 Dover St.
London W1, England
Alternate *V: 02/18/93*

388 Oxford St.
London W1 England
Alternate *V: 01/19/93*

Fiorentino, Linda
9200 Sunset Blvd. PH25
Los Angeles, CA 90069
Actress *V: 03/01/92*

First Artists Agency
10000 Riverside Dr. #6
Toluca Lake, CA 91602
Talent Agency *V: 03/17/93*

Firth, Peter
c/o Froggert Mgmt.
4 Windmill St.
London W1, England
Actor *V: 02/28/92*

Fischer, Helmut
Kaiserplatz 5
D-(W) 8000 Munchen 40
Germany
Actor *V: 02/23/93*

Fish, Nancy
ABC-TV/General Hospital
4151 Prospect Ave.
Hollywood, CA 90027
Actress *V: 06/15/92*

Fisher, Anna L.
c/o NASA
LBJ Space Center
Houston, TX 77058
Astronaut *V: 01/19/92*

Fisher, Carrie
c/o Kaufman
1201 Alta Loma Rd.
W. Hollywood, CA 90069
Actress *V: 03/03/93*

9555 Oak Pass Rd.
Beverly Hills, CA 90210
Alternate *V: 06/15/92*

8966 Sunset Blvd.
Hollywood, CA 90069
Forwarded *V: 09/08/92*

Fisher, Eddie
1000 N. Point St. #1802
San Francisco, CA 94109
Singer V: 03/19/93

Fisher, Gail
1150 S. Hayworth Ave.
Los Angeles, CA 90035
Actress V: 04/01/93

Fisher, William F.
c/o NASA LBJ Space Center
Houston, TX 77058
Astronaut V: 03/03/93

Fitzgerald, Ella
908 Whittier
Beverly Hills, CA 90210
Singer   V: 01/04/93

Fitzgerald, Geraldine
50 E. 79th St.
New York, NY 10021
Actress V: 04/01/93

Fitzgerald, Kathleen
c/o Young and the Restless
7800 Beverly Blvd.
Beverly Hills, CA 90036
Actress V: 06/15/92

Flack, Roberta
c/o Dakota Hotel
1 W. 72nd St.
New York, NY 10023
Singer   V: 06/15/92

Flagg, Fannie
1520 Willina Ln.
Montecito, CA 93108
Actress V: 04/12/92

Flame
c/o Five K Sales Co.
9420 Reseda Blvd., #836
Northridge, CA 91324
Adult Films V: 03/03/93

Flanagan, Markus
c/o Nurses
500 S. Buena Vista St.
Burbank, CA 91521
Actor V: 11/11/92

Flanders, Ed
c/o Artists Agency
10000 Santa Monica Blvd.
Los Angeles, CA 90067
Actor V: 03/17/92

Flannery, Susan
c/o CBS-TV/Bold & Beautiful
7800 Beverly Blvd., Ste.3371
Los Angeles, CA 90036
Actress V: 12/19/92

Flash Cadillac
c/o Music Hall Records
885 O'Farrell St.
San Francisco, CA 94109
50's Music Band V: 02/01/92

Flavin, Jennifer
7271 Angela Ave.
Canoga Park, 91307
Actress V: 04/22/92

Fleetwood, Mick
29169 Heathercliffe #574
Malibu, CA 90265
Singer V: 03/19/93

7200 Birdview
Malibu, CA 90265
L.R.U. V: 01/02/92

Fleming, Rhonda
c/o Mann
2129 Century Woods Way
Los Angeles, CA 90067
Actress V: 01/15/93

8831 Sunset Blvd.
Los Angeles, CA 90069
L.R.U. V: 07/03/92

Flemming, Peggy
P.O. Box 173
Los Gatos, CA 95030
Olympian V: 03/12/92

Fletcher, Louise
1520 Camden Ave. #105
Los Angeles, CA 90025
Actress V: 03/02/92

Fleury, Theoren
c/o Calgary Flames
P.O Box 1540
Calgary, Alberta T2P 3B9
Canada
Hockey V: 04/05/93

Flick East West Talents
9057-A Nemo St.
W. Hollywood, CA 90069
Talent Agency V: 03/20/93

Flippin, Lucy Lee
1753 Canfield Ave.
Los Angeles, CA 90035
Actress V: 04/01/93

Flock, Tim
Charlotte Motor Speedway
P.O. Box 600
Concord, NC 28026-0600
NASCAR Driver V: 03/02/92

Flood, Curt
4139 Cloverdale Ave.
Los Angeles, CA 90008
Baseball Player V: 06/15/92

Flores, Tom
c/o Seattle Seahawks
11220 N.E. 53rd St.
Kirkland, WA 98033
Football V: 12/10/92

Flores, Yvette
c/o Dallas Cowboys
One Cowboys Parkway
Irving, TX 75063-4945
Cheerleader V: 08/08/92

Floyd, Ray
1 Erieview Plaza Ste. 1300
Cleveland, OH 44114
Golf V: 01/20/92

Flynn, Barbara
c/o Markham & Froggatt
Julian House, 4 Windmill St.
London W1, England
Actress V: 02/04/93

Foale, C. Michael
NASA/LBJ Space Center
Houston, TX 77058
Astronaut V: 01/31/92

Foch, Nina
P.O. Box 1884
Beverly Hills, CA 90213
Author V: 01/10/92

Fogelberg, Dan
Mt. Bird Ranch
P.O. Box 824
Pagosa Springs, CO 81147
Singer V: 02/16/93

Foley, Ellen
Warner/Night Court
4000 Warner Blvd., Office 12A
Burbank, CA 91521
Actress V: 01/03/92

Folger, Franklin
c/o King Features
216 East 45th St.
New York, NY 10017
Cartoonist V: 03/27/93

Fonda, Bridget
Indian Hill Ranch
Livingston, MT 59047
Actress V: 05/01/92

611 S. Burnside Ave. #303
Los Angeles, CA 90036
Alternate V: 02/02/92

9560 Wilshire Blvd. #500 c/o UTA
Beverly Hills, CA 90212
Alternate V: 03/19/93

Fonda, Jane
914 Montana #200
Santa Monica, CA 90402
Actress V: 01/20/92

c/o Fonda Films Inc.
P.O. Box 1198
Santa Monica, CA 90406
Alternate V: 01/02/92

P.O. Box 491355
Los Angeles, CA 90049-1355
L.R.U. V: 07/01/92

Fonda, Peter
Indian Hill Ranch
Rt. 38
Livingston, MT 59047
Actor V: 03/19/93

c/o Hatch Entertainment
10880 Wilshire Blvd.#911
Los Angeles, CA 90024
Alternate V: 06/14/92

Fong, Kam
9430 W. Washington Blvd. #5
Culver City CA 90230
Actor V: 02/20/93

Fontaine, Joan
Villa Fontana
229 A Lower Walden RD.
Carmel Highlands, CA 93923
Actress V: 03/01/92

P.O. Box 222600
Carmel, CA 93922
Alternate V: 01/20/92

Fontaine Agency
1720 N. La Brea Ave.
Hollywood, CA 90046
Talent Agency V: 03/29/93

Football Hall of Fame
2121 George Hallas Dr., NW
Canton, OH 44708
Sports Museum V: 03/17/92

Foray, June
c/o Donovan
22745 Erwin St.
Woodland Hills, CA 91367
Actress V: 06/02/92

Forbes, Bryan
The Bookshop
Virginia Water
Surry, England
Writer/Actor V: 03/10/93

Ford, Betty
40365 Sand Dune Rd.
Rancho Mirage, CA 92270
Former First Lady V: 06/05/92

Ford, Constance
c/o NBC-TV
Another World
79 Madison Ave., 5th Fl.
New York, NY 91523
Actress V: 06/15/92

Ford, Faith
9200 Sunset Blvd. #710
Los Angeles, CA 90069
Actress V: 04/20/92

c/o Warner Bros. Television
Murphy Brown
4000 Warner Blvd.
Burbank, CA 91522
Forwarded V: 03/02/92

Ford, Gerald
P.O. Box 927
Rancho Mirage, CA 92270
Former President V: 04/20/92

40365 Sand Dune Road
Rancho Mirage, CA 92270
Alternate V: 03/17/92

Ford, Harrison
3555 N. Moose Wilson Rd.
Jackson Hole, WY 83001
Actor V: 02/11/93

Ford, Harrison, contd
7101 Woodrow Wilson Dr.
Los Angeles, CA 90068
Alternate V: 01/12/92

655 MacCullock Dr.
Los Angeles, CA 90049
Alternate V: 05/13/92

P.O. Box 49344
Los Angeles, CA 90049-0344
Forwarded V: 02/20/92

P.O. Box 5617
Beverly Hills, CA 90210
L.R.U. V: 01/02/92

Ford Model Agency
344 E. 59th St.
New York, NY 10022
Talent Agency V: 12/10/92

Foreman, Deborah
1341 Ocean Ave. Ste.213
Santa Monica, CA 90401
Actress V: 04/01/92

Foreman, George
7639 Pine Oak Dr.
Humble, TX 77397-1438
Actor V: 01/15/93

2202 Lone Oak
Houston, TX 77093
Alternate V: 05/22/92

Formesa, Fern
5018 N. 61st Ave.
Glendale, AZ 85301
Actress V: 01/21/92

Forrest, Frederic
4121 Wilshire Blvd.
Los Angeles, CA 90010
Actor V: 03/17/92

Forrest, Helen
1870 Caminito del Cielo
Glendale, CA 91208
Singer V: 04/01/93

Forrest, Sally
1125 Angelo Dr.
Beverly Hills, CA 90210
Actress V: 02/03/92

Forslund, Constance
8942 Wilshire Blvd.
Beverly Hills, CA 90211
Actress V: 03/21/92

Forslund, Constance, contd
1717 N. Highland Ave. #414
Los Angeles, CA 90028
 Forwarded V: 04/13/92

Forsyth, David
c/o NBC-TV
Another World
79 Madison Ave., 5th Fl.
New York, NY 91523
 Actor V: 06/15/92

Forsythe, John
c/o Charter Mgmt.
9000 Sunset Blvd.
Los Angeles, CA 90069
 Actor V: 03/17/92

14215 Sunset Blvd.
Pacific Palisades, CA 90272
 Alternate V: 04/06/93

Forte, Fabian
6671 Sunset Blvd. #1502
Hollywood, CA 90028
 Singer V: 01/21/93

Foster, Jim
Daytona Int'l Speedway
P.O. Box 2801
Daytona Beach, FL 32115-2801
 NASCAR Official V: 03/02/92

Foster, Jodie
10960 Wilshire Blvd.#1428
Los Angeles, CA 90024
 Actress V: 05/11/92

c/o ICM
8942 Wilshire Blvd.
Beverly Hills, CA 90211
 Alternate V: 01/21/93

P.O. Box 846
Woodland Hills, CA 91367
 L.R.U. V: 12/08/92

Foster, Susanna
11255 W. Morrison St. Ste.F
N. Hollywood, CA 91601
 Actress V: 04/01/93

Fox, Edward
c/o Leading Artists
60 Saint James St.
London W1, England
 Actor V: 07/14/92

Fox, James
49 Murry Rd., Wimbeldon
London SW19 4PF, England
 Actor V: 11/03/92

Fox, Michael
c/o Bell-Phillip Prod.
Bold & Beautiful
7800 Beverly Blvd., Ste.3371
Los Angeles, CA 90036
 Actor V: 06/15/92

Fox, Michael J.
12828 Victory Blvd. #344
N. Hollywood, CA 91606
 Actor V: 02/22/92

3960 Laurel Canyon
Studio City, CA 91604
 Alternate V: 02/01/92

c/o Touchstone Films
500 S. Buena Vista St.
Burbank, CA 91521
 Forwarded V: 01/14/93

Fox, Samantha
P.O. Box 33
Huntingdon, PE18 7PJ
England
 Actress V: 11/22/92

c/o RCA
1133 Ave. of the Americas
New York, NY 10019
 Alternate V: 06/14/92

11 Mt Pleasant Villa
London W1 England
 Alternate V: 03/19/93

Fox TV
P.O. Box 900
Beverly Hills, CA 90213
 Viewer Services V: 03/01/92

c/o Viewer Services
205 E. 67th St.
New York, NY 10021
 Alternate V: 02/27/93

c/o Viewer Services
5746 Sunset Blvd.
Hollywood, CA 90028
 Alternate V: 03/17/92

Fox Talent Agency
4655 Kingswell #203
Los Angeles, CA 90027
 Talent Agency V: 03/17/93

Foxworth, Robert
1230 Benedict Canyon Dr.
Beverly Hills, CA 90210
Actor V: 02/10/92

c/o ICM
8942 Wilshire Blvd.
Beverly Hills, CA 90211
L.R.U. V: 01/02/92

Foxxx, Leanna
c/o Five K Sales Co.
9420 Reseda Blvd., #836
Northridge, CA 91324
Adult Films V: 03/03/93

Foyt, A. J.
6415 Toledo St.
Houston, TX 77008
Race Driver V: 02/20/92

Frakes, Jonathan
c/o Star Trek TNG Paramount
5555 Melrose Ave.
Hollywood, CA 90038
Actor V: 03/04/93

Frakes, Jonathan
5062 Calvin Ave.
Tarzana, CA 91356
Alternate V: 05/13/92

Frampton, Peter
2669 Lamar Rd.
Los Angeles, CA 90068
Musician V: 03/19/93

Franciosa, Tony
567 Tigertail Rd.
Los Angeles, CA 90024
Actor V: 06/15/92

Francis, Anne
P.O. Box 5417
Santa Barbara, CA 93103
Actress V: 06/01/92

Francis, Arlene
Ritz Towers/59th & Park Ave.
New York, NY 10021
Actress V: 01/20/92

112 Central Park S.
New York, NY 10019
Alternate V: 01/14/93

Francis, Connie
11 Pompton
Verona, NJ 07044
Singer V: 03/19/93

Francis, Connie, contd
1975 Howard Ave.
Pottsville, PA 17901
L.R.U. V: 01/05/92

Francis, Genie
c/o Jonathan Frakes
211 S. Beverly Dr. #201
Beverly Hills, CA 90212
Actress V: 03/24/92

5062 Calvin Ave.
Tarzana, CA 91356
Alternate V: 04/03/92

Franciscus, James
12549 Addison St.
North Hollywood, CA 91607
Actor V: 06/15/92

Frank, Charles
900 Chapea Rd.
Pasadena, CA 91107
Actor V: 06/15/92

Frank, Clinton
28 Bridlewood Rd.
Northbrook, IL 60062
Football V: 02/17/93

Frank, Joanna
c/o 20th Century Fox TV
L.A. Law
P.O. Box 900
Beverly Hills, CA 90213
Actress V: 01/12/93

Frank, Phil
c/o SF Chronicle/Features
901 Mission St.
San Francisco, CA 94103
Cartoonist V: 05/11/92

Franklin, Aretha
P.O. Box 12137
Birmingham, MI 48012
Singer V: 04/12/92

Franklyn, Sabina
c/o Michael Ladkin
2A Warwick Place N.
London SW1V 1QW, England
Actress V: 02/04/92

Franks, Randall
P.O. Box 30451
Chamblee, GA 30366
Actor V: 01/02/92

Franks, Randall, contd
30 Rockerfeller Plaza
New York, NY 10112
L.R.U. *V: 03/30/92*

Frann, Mary
250 N. Robertson Blvd. #518
Beverly Hills, CA 90211
Actress *V: 03/19/93*

2790 Hutton Dr.
Beverly Hills, CA 90210
L.R.U. *V: 03/03/92*

Franz, Arthur
32960 Pacific Coast Hwy
Malibu, CA 90265
Actor *V: 03/01/92*

Franz, Dennis
11805 Bellagio Rd.
Los Angeles, CA 90049
Actor *V: 04/06/93*

Franz, Doreen
32960 Pacific Coast Hwy
Malibu, CA 90265
Actress *V: 03/01/92*

Fratianne, Linda
18214 Septo St.
Northridge, CA 91324
Actress *V: 06/15/92*

Frazer, Liz
42/43 Grafton House
2/3 Golden Square
London W1, England
Actress *V: 05/28/92*

Frazier, Joe
2917 N. Broad St.
Philadelphia, PA 19132
Boxer *V: 03/21/92*

Frazier, Shannon
c/o Dallas Cowboys
One Cowboys Parkway
Irving, TX 75063-9932
Cheerleader *V: 02/22/92*

Fredericks, Fred
216 East 45th St.
New York, NY 10017
Cartoonist *V: 07/16/92*

Freeman, Kathleen
6247 Orion Ave.
Van Nuys, CA 91406
Actress *V: 04/16/92*

Freeman, Kathleen, contd
c/o ABC-TV
General Hospital
4151 Prospect Ave.
Hollywood, CA 90027
Alternate *V: 06/15/92*

Freeman, Mona
608 N. Alpine Dr.
Beverly Hills, CA 90210
Actress *V: 06/15/92*

Freeman, Morgan
c/o Wm. Morris
151 El Camino
Beverly Hills, CA 90210
Actor *V: 05/25/92*

340 E. 87th St. #1A
New York, NY 10128-4835
Alternate *V: 03/19/93*

Freeman & Sutton
8967 Sunset Blvd.
Los Angeles, CA 90069
Talent Agency *V: 02/23/93*

Frehm, Walter
c/o King Features
216 East 45th St.
New York, NY 10017
Cartoonist *V: 04/12/93*

French, Leigh
1850 N. Vista
Los Angeles, CA 90046
Actress *V: 04/01/93*

Frewer, Matt
5007 Roma Dt.
Marina del Rey, CA 90292
Actor *V: 03/17/93*

Fricke, Janie
P.O. Box 798
Lancaster, TX 75146
Singer *V: 01/06/92*

Fricke, Paul
c/o Tru Studios/Troll Comics
4520 N. Monitor
Chicago, IL 60630
Artist *V: 07/30/92*

Fricker, Brenda
c/o Casualty/BBC-TV
Whitehead Rd.
Bristol, Avon, England
Actress *V: 01/03/92*

Frid, Jonathan
157 E. 18th St. #5J
New York, NY 10003
Actor V: 03/22/93

Frischman, Dan
c/o Warner Brothers TV
Head of the Class
100 North Pass Rd.
Burbank, CA 91505
Actor V: 12/18/92

Fritz, Harold A.
225 Meade Ave.
Ft. Leavenworth, KS 66027
Medal of Honor V: 01/19/92

Froman, David
c/o Viacom Prod.
Matlock
100 Universal City Plaza, Bl. 448
Universal City, CA 91608
Actor 01/12/93

Frontiere, Georgia
2327 W. Lincoln Ave.
Anaheim, CA 92801
Football Executive V: 06/15/92

Frost, Terry
1005 Toluca Lake Ave.
Toluca Lake, CA 91602
Actor V: 01/21/92

Frosyth, Rosemary
1591 Benedict Canyon Rd.
Beverly Hills, CA 90210
Actress V: 04/01/93

Frye, Soleil Moon
P.O. Box 5164
Glendale, CA 91201
Actress V: 01/27/93

Fullerton, Charles G.
c/o Ames Research
P.O. Box 273
Edwards AFB, CA 93523
Astronaut V: 03/17/93

c/o NASA LBJ Space Center
Houston, TX 77058
Forwarded V: 03/03/93

Fullerton, Fiona
235 Regent St.
London W1, England
Actress V: 11/22/92

Fulton, Eileen
301 W. 57th St.
New York, NY 10019
Actress V: 01/27/93

Fundacion Luiz Munoz Marin
Apartado 2367
San Juan, Puerto Rico 00936
Archive V: 03/20/93

Funicello, Annette
16102 Sandy Lane
Encino, CA 91436
Actress V: 06/15/92

Funt, Allen
2359 Nichols Canyon Rd.
Los Angeles, CA 90046
TV Celebrity V: 01/07/92

Furst, Stephen
c/o Artists Agency
10000 Santa Monica Blvd.
Los Angeles, CA 90067
Actor V: 03/17/92

G

GARFIELD AND FRIENDS
United Media Licensing
200 Park Ave. ATTN: Chris Sela
New York, NY 10166
Production Company V: 03/18/93

GENERAL HOSPITAL
c/o ABC-TV
4151 Prospect Ave.
Hollywood, CA 90027
Production Company V: 06/15/92

GOING TO EXTREMES
c/o Lorimar
300 S. Lorimar Plaza
Burbank, CA 91505
Production Company V: 03/19/93

GOLDEN GIRLS
Witt, Thomas, Harris Prod.
846 N. Cahuenga Blvd., Bldg.G
Hollywood, CA 90038
Production Company V: 03/26/93

GOLDEN PALACE
c/o Witt/Thomas
846 N. Cahuenga Blvd.
Los Angeles, CA 90038
Production Company V: 01/17/92

GOOD MORNING AMERICA
c/o ABC News
147 Columbus Ave.
New York, NY 10023
Production Company V: 03/19/93

GROWING PAINS
c/o Warner Brothers TV
Growing Pains
4000 Warner Blvd.
Burbank, CA, 91522
Production Company V: 12/18/92

GUIDING LIGHT
c/o New York Production Center
222 E. 44th St.
New York, NY 10017
Production Company V: 03/18/93

Gabb, Peter
c/o MGM/UA Comm.
In the Heat of the Night
1000 W. Washington Blvd.
Culver City, CA 90232
Actor V: 01/07/92

Gabor, Eva
100 Delfern Dr.
Los Angeles, CA 90024
Actress V: 03/12/92

Gabor, Zsa Zsa
1001 Belair Rd.
Los Angeles, CA 90077
Actress V: 02/11/92

Gabriel, Peter
P.O. Box 35
Bath, Avon, England
Singer V: 02/01/92

Gailforce Management
81-83 Walton St.
London SW3 2HP, England
Alternate V: 01/21/93

Gabrielle, Monique
4520 Van Nuys Blvd. #538
Sherman Oaks, CA 91403
Actress V: 11/16/92

P.O. Box 2682
Malibu, CA 90265
L.R.U. V: 06/02/92

Gage Group
c/o The Gage Group
9255 Sunset Blvd., #515
Los Angeles, CA 90069
Talent Agency V: 02/23/93

Gagnier, Holly
ABC-TV/One Life to Live
1330 Ave. of the Americas
New York, NY 10019
Actress V: 03/02/92

Gail, Max
29451 Bluewater Rd.
Malibu, CA 90265
Actor V: 07/03/92

Gaines, Boyd
9220 Sunset Blvd.
Los Angeles, CA 90044
Actor V: 03/03/92

Gallagher
12164 Emelita St.
N. Hollywood, CA 91607
Comedian V: 10/04/92

Gallagher, Megan
442 Landfair Ave.
Los Angeles, CA 90024
Actress V: 01/27/93

Gallagher, Peter
c/o Agency
40 W. 57th St.
New York, NY 10019
Actor V: 08/17/92

Gallardo, Silvana
4270 Camilla Ave.
Studio City, CA 91604
Actress V: 01/27/93

Gallego, Gina
c/o Bailey
6550 Murietta Ave.
Van Nuys, CA 91401
Actress V: 01/27/93

Galliand, Richard
c/o Columbia/Mozark
Designing Women
Columbia Plaza, Prod.Bl.8, #147
Burbank, CA 91505
Actor V: 02/03/93

Gallison, Joe
c/o NBC-TV/Days Of Our Lives
3000 W. Alameda Ave.
Burbank, CA 91523
Actor V: 01/13/92

Gallo, Ernest & Julio
600 Yosemite Blvd.
Modesto, CA 95354
Wine Masters V: 02/01/92

Gam, Rita
180 W. 58th St. #8B
New York, NY 10022
Actress V: 03/23/93

Gamble, Ed
c/o King Features
216 E. 45th St.
New York, NY 10017
Cartoonist V: 03/11/93

Gammon, James
8350 Santa Monica Blvd. #206A
Los Angeles, CA 90069
Actor V: 12/18/92

c/o Cunningham-Escott-Dipene
261 S. Roberson Blvd.
Beverly Hills, CA 90211
Alternate V: 03/20/93

c/o R. Barr
P.O. Box 69590
Los Angeles, CA 90069
Forwarded V: 06/15/92

Garagiola, Joe
6221 E. Huntress Dr.
Paradise Valley, AZ 85253
Baseball V: 06/15/92

Garber, Terri
c/o NBC-TV, 'Santa Barbara'
3000 W. Alameda Ave.
Burbank, CA 91523
Actress V: 01/21/93

Garcia, Andy
4519 Varna Ave.
Sherman Oaks, CA 91423
Actor V: 03/23/93

Gardner, Dale A.
c/o NASA
LBJ Space Center
Houston, TX 77058
Astronaut V: 01/19/93

Gardner, Guy S.
c/o NASA LBJ Space Center
Houston, TX 77058
Astronaut V: 03/03/93

Gardner, Randy
8730 Sunset Blvd. 6th Fl.
Los Angeles, CA 90069
Ice Skater V: 01/02/93

Gardner, Randy, contd
4640 Glencoe Ave. #6
Marina del Rey, CA 90292
Alternate V: 06/15/92

Garland, Beverly
8014 Briar Summit Dr.
Los Angeles, CA 90046
Actress V: 04/12/92

Garner, James
33 Oakmont Dr.
Los Angeles, CA 90049
Actor V: 02/22/92

Garner, Phil
c/o Brewers
201 S. 46th St.
Milwaukee, WI 53214
Baseball Manager V: 01/21/93

Garr, Teri
9200 Sunset Blvd. #428
Los Angeles, CA 90069
Actress V: 03/23/93

c/o PMK
1776 Broadway 8th Fl.
New York, NY 10019
Alternate V: 03/30/93

1462 Rising Glen
Los Angeles, CA 90069
L.R.U. V: 11/11/92

Garrett, Betty
3231 Oakdell Rd.
Studio City, CA 91604
Actress V: 01/11/92

Garrett, Joy
11552 Hesby St.
N. Hollywood, CA 91601
Actress V: 01/27/93

Garrett, Steve L.
3221 20th St. Studio C-1
San Francisco, CA 94110
Sci-fi Artist V: 11/11/92

Garrett Agency
6525 Sunset Blvd. 5th Fl.
Los Angeles, CA 90028
Talent Agency V: 03/17/93

Garrick Intl. Agency
8831 Sunset Blvd. #402
Los Angeles, CA 90069
Talent Agency V: 03/16/93

Garriott, Owen
c/o NASA
LBJ Space Center
Houston, TX 77058
Astronaut V: 01/19/92

Garrison, David
c/o Fox TV
10201 W. Pico Blvd.
Los Angeles, CA 90035
Actor V: 01/12/92

Garson, Greer
3232 McKinney Ave. Ste.1210
Dallas, TX 75204-2429
Actress V: 03/30/93

Garver, Kathy
c/o Travis
170 Woodbridge
Hillsborough, CA 94010
Actress V: 03/23/93

Garvey, Cynthia
3516 Malibu Country Dr.
Malibu, CA 90265
TV Personality V: 03/23/93

Gascoine, Jill
c/o Marina Martin
6A Danbury St.
London N1 8JU, England
Actress V: 02/04/93

Gavin, John
2415 Century Hill
Los Angeles, CA 90067
Actor V: 06/15/92

Gayheart, Rebecca
c/o 'Loving'
77 W. 66th St.
New York, NY 10023
Actress V: 11/11/92

Gayle, Crystal
51 Music Square East
Nashville, TN 37203
Singer V: 04/18/92

Gaylord, Scott
1451 Depen
Lakewood, CO 80214
Race Driver V: 03/12/93

Gaynor, Mitzi
c/o Jack Bean Enterprises
9200 Sunset Blvd. Pent.#7
Los Angeles, CA 90069
Actress V: 03/14/92

Gaynor, Mitzi, contd
610 N. Arden Dr.
Beverly Hills, CA 90210
L.R.U. V: 07/06/92

Gazzara, Ben
1080 Madison Ave.
New York, NY 10028
Actor V: 03/23/93

Geary, Anthony
7010 Pacific View Dr.
Los Angeles, CA 90068
Actor V: 01/12/92

c/o ABC-TV
General Hospital
4151 Prospect Ave.
Hollywood, CA 90027
Alternate V: 06/15/92

Geary, Cynthia
c/o Cine-Nevada Inc.
Northern Exposure
3000 Olympic Blvd., Ste.2575
Santa Monica, CA 90404
Actress V: 05/15/92

Geddes Agency
8457 Melrose Pl. #200
Los Angeles, CA 90069
Talent Agency V: 03/29/93

Geeson, Judy
c/o Agent
D'Arblay St.
London W1V 3FD, England
Actress V: 03/18/93

c/o M.L.R.
200 Fulham Rd.
London SW10, England
Alternate V: 02/28/92

Geffen Records
9130 Sunset Blvd.
Los Angeles, CA 90019
Studio HQ V: 03/10/92

Gehesse, Bryan
c/o CBS-TV/Bold&Beautiful
7800 Beverly Blvd.
Los Angeles, CA 90036
Actor V: 01/21/92

Gelbart, Larry
807 N. Alpine Dr.
Beverly Hills, CA 90210
Producer V: 03/10/93

Geldof, Bob
Davington Priory
Faversham, Kent England
Singer V: 03/23/93

Gelff Assoc.
16133 Ventura Blvd. #700
Encino, CA 91436
Talent Agency V: 03/17/93

Gelman, Jacob
c/o Universal Television
100 Universal City Plaza 422-2
Universal City, CA 91608
Actor V: 05/15/92

Gemar, Charles D.
c/o NASA
LBJ Space Center
Houston, TX 77058
Astronaut V: 01/31/93

Genesis
P.O. Box 107
London N6 5RU, England
Musical Group V: 05/14/92

c/o Hit & Run Music
25 Ives St.
London SW3, England
Alternate V: 02/11/93

George, Phyllis
Cave Hill Ln., Box 4308
Lexington, KY 40511
Actress V: 04/05/92

George, Susan
P.O. Box 428
Maidenhead
Berkshire, 5L6 4EW England
Actress V: 12/09/92

235 Regent St.
London W1, England
Alternate V: 11/22/92

George, Wally
14155 Magnolia Blvd. #127
Sherman Oaks, CA 91423
Commentator V: 02/12/92

P.O. Box 787
Los Angeles, CA 90028
Alternate V: 02/01/92

Gerard, Gil
P.O. Box 4218
N. Hollywood, CA 91607
Actor V: 07/01/92

Gerard, Gil, contd
32 Hurricaine St.
Marina del Rey, CA 90292
Alternate V: 04/06/93

10000 Santa Monica Blvd. #305
Los Angeles, CA 90067
Forwarded V: 02/01/92

Gere, Ashlyn
c/o Five K Sales Co.
9420 Reseda Blvd., #836
Northridge, CA 91324
Adult Films V: 03/03/93

Gerler-Stevens & Assoc.
3349 Cahuenga Blvd. #2
Los Angeles, CA 90068
Talent Agency V: 03/29/93

Gersh Agency
232 N. Canon Dr.
Beverly Hills, CA 90210
Talent Agency V: 03/29/93

Gertz, Jami
151 S. El Camino Dr.
Beverly Hills, CA 90212
Actress V: 06/01/92

1440 Veteran Ave. #352
Los Angeles, CA 90024
L.R.U. V: 05/29/92

Getty, Estelle
68-85 218th St.
Bayside, NY 11364
Actress V: 02/20/92

c/o Witt/Thomas/Harris
Golden Palace
846 N. Cahuenga Blvd., Bl. G
Hollywood, CA 90038
Forwarded V: 01/17/93

1140 N. Alta Loma #105
Los Angeles, CA 90069
L.R.U. V: 01/02/92

Ghostley, Alice
3800 Reklaw Dr.
N. Hollywood, CA 91604
Actress V: 03/30/92

Giannini, Giancarlo
c/o Squillante
Via Della Guiliana, 101
Rome, Italy
Actor V: 02/28/92

Gibbons, Leeza
207 N. Oakhurst Dr.
Beverly Hills, CA 90210-4411
Actress V: 12/18/92

1760 N. Courtney Ave.
Los Angeles, CA 90046
Alternate V: 08/15/92

Gibbs, Joe
c/o Gibbs Racing
5301 Harris Blvd.
Charlotte, NC 28269
NASCAR Owner V: 03/02/92

Gibbs, Marla
2323 W. Martin Luther King Jr.
Los Angeles, CA 90008
Actress V: 02/16/92

Gibson, Debbie
375 N. Broadway
Jericho, NY 11753
Singer V: 11/22/92

1684 Sterling Ave.
Merrick, NY 11566
Alternate V: 01/12/92

P.O. Box 489
Merrick, NY 11566
Alternate V: 03/23/93

Gibson, Edward G.
c/o NASA LBJ Space Center
Houston, TX 77058
Astronaut V: 03/03/93

Gibson, Mel
P.O. Box 4307
Hollywood, CA 90078
Actor V: 12/12/92

P.O. Box 478
King Cross, NSW 2011
Australia
Alternate V: 04/01/92

129 Bourke St.
Woolloomooloo, NSW 2011
Australia
Forwarded V: 07/08/92

23333 Palm Canyon Dr.
Malibu, CA 90265
Forwarded V: 12/18/92

P.O. Box 2156
Santa Monica, CA 90406-2156
Alternate V: 10/04/92

Gibson, Robert L.
c/o NASA LBJ Space Center
Houston, TX 77058
Astronaut V: 03/03/93

Gielgud, John
South Pavillion
Wotton Underwood, Bucks.
Aylesbury HP18, England
Actor V: 05/01/92

Giella, Joe
c/o King Features
216 E. 45th St.
New York, NY 10017
Cartoonist V: 03/11/93

Gifford, Frances
940 E. Colorado Blvd. #306
Pasadena, CA 91106
Actor V: 03/23/93

Gifford, Frank
10 Bird Lane
Rye, NY 10580
Football V: 04/12/92

Gifford, Kathie Lee
c/o Live
7 Lincoln Sq., 5th Fl.
New York, Ny 10023
Celebrity V: 03/30/92

c/o Buena Vista TV
500 Park Ave.
New York, NY 10022
Alternate V: 04/22/92

625 Madison Ave. #1200
New York, NY 10022
Forwarded V: 03/23/93

Giftos, Elaine
10351 Santa Monica Blvd. #211
Los Angeles, CA 90025
Actress V: 10/10/92

Gilbert, Lewis
Clement House/99 Aldwych
London WC2B 4JY, England
Actor V: 02/28/92

Gilbert, Melissa
3960 Laurel Canyon Blvd. #370
Studio City, CA 91604
Actress V: 02/12/92

337 W. St.
New York, NY 10014
Alternate V: 02/12/92

Gilbert, Melissa, contd
151 El Camino
Beverly Hills, CA 90212
Forwarded V: 12/18/92

Gilbert, Sara
16254 High Valley Dr.
Encino, CA 91346
Actress V: 03/15/93

c/o Carsey-Werner
Roseanne
4024 Radford Ave.
Studio City, CA 91604
Alternate V: 12/07/92

Giles, Nancy
433 Shirle Pl. #4
Beverly Hills, CA 90210
Actress V: 01/27/93

Giles, Sandra
3500 W. Olive #1400
Burbank, CA 91505
Actress V: 01/27/93

Gilla Roos
9744 Wilshire Blvd. #203
Beverly Hills, CA 90212
Talent Agency V: 03/29/93

Gillard, Starr
6525 Sunset Blvd. #303
Hollywood, CA 90028
Actress V: 01/21/93

Gillatt, John
c/o King Features
216 E. 45th St.
New York, NY 10017
Cartoonist V: 03/11/93

Gilley, Mickey
c/o Interest Inc.
P.O. Box 1242
Pasadena, TX 77501
Singer V: 03/26/93

Gilliam, Terry
The Old Hall
South Grove
Highgate, London N6 England
Actor V: 03/23/93

Gilliland, Butch
c/o Anaheim Racing
313 N. Anaheim Blvd.
Anaheim, CA 92805
Race Driver V: 03/12/93

Gillis, Ann
Oostsatiestraat 187
2550 Kontich, Belgium
Actress V: 01/27/93

Gillman, Sid
2968 Playa Rd.
Carlsbad, CA 92009
Football V: 03/17/92

Gilly Talent Agency
8721 Sunset Blvd. #103
Los Angeles, CA 90069
Talent Agency V: 03/28/93

Ginsberg, Allen
c/o City Lights
261 Columbus Ave.
San Francisco, CA 94133
Poet V: 02/11/93

Ginty, Robert
P.O. Box 5248
Whittier, CA 90607
Actro V: 03/12/92

c/o ABC
1313 N. Vine St.
Hollywood, CA 90028
Forwarded V: 01/16/92

Gipsy Kings
B.P. 38
F-13633 Arles Cedex, France
Music Group V: 01/17/93

Giradot, Annie
c/o Editions Laffont
6 Place Saint-Sulpice
75002 Paris, France
Actress V: 12/14/92

Gish, Lillian
430 E. 57th St.
New York, NY 10022
Actress V: 06/01/92

Givens, Robin
885 3rd Ave. #2900
New York, NY 10022-4834
Actress V: 12/16/92

8818 Thrasher Ave.
Los Angeles, CA 90069
Alternate V: 01/27/93

Glaser, Paul Michael
317 Georgina Ave.
Santa Monica, CA 90402
Actor V: 06/15/92

Glaser, Paul Michael, contd
c/o Interscope Commun.
10900 Wilshire Blvd. #1400
Los Angeles, CA 90024
Alternate V: 03/14/93

Gleason, Paul
1999 Ave. of the Stars #2850
Los Angeles, CA 90067
Actor V: 01/21/93

Glenn, John
503 Hart Senate Office Bldg.
Washington, DC 20510
Astronaut V: 11/25/92

c/o NASA LBJ Space Center
Houston, TX 77058
Alternate V: 03/03/93

Glenn, Scott
126 E. De Vargas St. #1902
Santa Fe, NM 87501
Actor V: 03/04/92

690 Gonzales
Santa Fe, NM 87504
Alternate V: 03/04/92

Gless, Sharon
c/o CAA
9830 Wilshire Blvd.
Beverly Hills, CA 90212
Actress V: 01/21/93

4709 Teesdale Ave.
Studio City, CA 91604-1117
Alternate V: 07/01/92

106 Pocono Park
Wilkes-Barre, PA 18702
L.R.U. V: 07/01/92

Global Pictures
4774 Melrose Ave.
Hollywood, CA 90029
Distributor V: 03/17/92

Glover, Brian
c/o DeWolfe
Manfield House
376-378 The Strand
London WC2R 0LR, England
Actor V: 03/17/93

Glover, Crispin
1811 Whitley #1400
Los Angeles, CA 90028
Actor V: 03/17/92

Glover, Danny
41 Sutter St. #1648
San Francisco, CA 94104-4903
Actor V: 07/24/92

P.O. Box 590237
San Francisco, CA 94159
L.R.U. V: 03/03/93

Glover, John
8942 Wilshire Blvd.
Beverly Hills, CA 90211
Actor V: 06/15/92

Glover, John
2417 Micheltorena St.
Los Angeles, CA 90039
Actor V: 04/06/93

Godunov, Alexander
8787 Shoreham Rd. #1001
Los Angeles, CA 90069
Actor V: 02/03/92

Godwin, Linda M.
c/o NASA
LBJ Space Center
Houston, TX 77058
Astronaut V: 01/19/93

Gold, Missy
c/o Gold Agency
3500 W. Olive Ste.1400
Burbank, CA 91505
Actress V: 03/02/93

937 N. Vista St.
Los Angeles, CA 90046
Forwarded V: 12/15/92

Gold, Tracy
c/o Gold Agency
3500 W. Olive Ste.1400
Burbank, CA 91505
Actress V: 03/02/93

12631 Addison St.
N. Hollywood, CA 91607
Alternate V: 03/23/93

c/o Warner Bros. TV
Growing Pains
4000 Warner Blvd.
Burbank, CA 91522
Forwarded V: 12/03/92

Gold & Associates
3500 W. Olive, Ste.1400
Burbank, CA 91505
Talent Agency V: 03/17/93

Goldberg, Whoopi
33021 Pacific Coast Hwy.
Malibu, CA 90265
Actress V: 03/23/93

5555 Melrose Ave. Wilder 114
Los Angeles, CA 90038
Alternate V: 06/01/92

c/o Addis/Wexler
955 Carrillo Dr. 3rd Fl.
Los Angeles, CA 90048
Alternate V: 03/17/92

8730 Sunset blvd. #PH-W
Los Angeles, CA 90069
L.R.U. V: 07/03/92

2212 McKinley
Berkley, CA 94703
L.R.U. V: 06/01/92

Goldblum, Jeff
8033 Sunset Blvd. #367
Los Angeles, CA 90046
Actor V: 03/23/93

8225 Hollywood Blvd.
Los Angeles, CA 90069-1611
L.R.U. V: 01/02/92

Goldhor, David
Eagle Eye
4019 Tujunga Ave.
Studio City, CA 91604
Director V: 01/21/93

Goldin, Ricky Paull
c/o NBC-TV
Another World
79 Madison Ave., 5th Fl.
New York, NY 91523
Actor V: 06/15/92

Goldoni, Lelia
15459 Wyandotte St.
Van Nuys, CA 91405
Actress V: 02/15/93

Goldrup, Ray
2383 Broderick
West Jordan, UT 84084
Writer V: 12/18/92

Goldsmith, Paul
1148 Vivian Ln.
Munster, IN 46321
NASCAR Driver V: 03/02/92

Goldwyn Co.(Samuel)
10203 Santa Monica Blvd. #500
Los Angeles, CA 90067
Production Company V: 03/17/92

Golonka, Arlene
1835 Pandora Ave. #3
Los Angeles, CA 90025
Actress V: 04/21/92

Gonshaw, Francesca
c/o Greg Mellard
12 D'Arblay St., 2nd Fl.
London W1V 3FP, England
Actress V: 02/04/92

c/o GMM
Canonbury House
Canonbury Sq.
London N1 2NQ, England
Alternate V: 07/07/92

Goodall, Caroline
c/o James Sharkey
15 Golden Square, 3rd Fl. Ste.
London W1RV 3AG, England
Actress V: 02/04/92

Goodfriend, Lynda
c/o Cohen & Luckenbache
740 N. La Brea Ave.
Los Angeles, CA 90038-3339
Actress V: 03/21/92

Goodman, Dody
10144 Culver Blvd. #21
Culver City, CA 90232-3146
Actress V: 01/02/92

Goodman, John
5180 Louise Ave.
Encino, CA 91316-2532
Actor V: 11/11/92

c/o Carsey-Werner/CBS-MTM
Roseanne
4024 Radford Ave.
Studio City, CA 91604
Alternate V: 03/02/92

2412 Jupitor Dr.
Los Angeles, CA 90046
L.R.U. V: 06/21/92

Goodson Productions
c/o Mark Goodson
5757 Wilshire Blvd. #5750
Los Angeles, CA 90036
Production Company V: 03/17/92

Goranson, Lecy
c/o Carsey-Werner/CBS-MTM
Roseanne
4024 Radford Ave.
Studio City, CA 91604
Actress   V: 12/07/92

Gordon, Cecil
c/o Childress
P.O. Box 1189 Industrial Dr.
Welcome, NC 27374
Race Crew   V: 03/12/93

Gordon, Don
2095 Linda Flora Rd.
Los Angeles, CA 90077
Actor   V: 06/16/92

Gordon, Gale
P.O. Box 179
Borrego Springs, CA 92004
Actor   V: 05/15/92

Gordon, Hannah
c/o Hutton Mgmt.
200 Fulham Rd.
London SW10 9PN, England
Actress   V: 02/04/92

Gordon, Jeff
c/o Hendrick Motor Sports
5325 Stowe Lane, P.O. Box 9
Harrisburg, NC 28075
NASCAR Driver   V: 03/02/92

Gordon Jr., Richard F.
c/o Astro Sciences Corp.
6151 W. Century Blvd.
P.O. Box 45005
Los Angeles, CA 90045
Astronaut   V: 03/17/92

c/o NASA LBJ Space Center
Houston, TX 77058
Forwarded   V: 03/03/93

Gore, Al
Old Executive Office Bldg.
Washington, DC 20500
Vice-Pres. USA   V: 10/04/92

The Admiral House
34th & Massachuttes Ave.
Washington, DC 20005
Alternate   V: 02/23/93

Gore, Lesley
141 Vernon Ave.
Patterson, NJ 07503
Singer   V: 03/03/92

Gore, Lesley, contd
170 E. 77th St. #2-A
New York, NY 10021-1912
Singer   V: 02/15/93

Gore, Tipper
Executive Office Bldg.
Washington, DC 20501
Wife of V.P.   V: 10/04/92

The Admiral House
34th & Massachuttes Ave.
Washington, DC 20005
Alternate   V: 02/23/93

Gores/Fields Agency
10100 Santa Monica Blvd. #700
Los Angeles, CA 90067
Talent Agency   V: 03/16/93

Gorfaine Schwartz Roberts
3301 Barham Blvd. #201
Los Angeles, Ca 90068
Talent Agency   V: 03/20/93

Goring, Marius
c/o Film Rights
483 Southbank House
Black Prince Rd.
London SE1 7SJ, England
Actor   V: 12/14/92

Gorme, Eydie
Stage 2 Productions
P.O. Box 5140
Beverly Hills, CA 90210
Actress   V: 03/07/92

Gorrell, Bob
c/o King Features
216 East 45th St.
New York, NY 10017
Cartoonist   V: 02/13/93

Gorshin, Frank
75 S. Morningside Dr.
Westport, CT 06880
Actor   V: 03/17/93

Gossett, Jr., Lou
P.O. Box 6187
Malibu, CA 90265
Actor   V: 01/21/93

5916 Bonsall Dr.
Malibu, CA 90265
Alternate   V: 02/02/93

Gottschalk, Thomas
c/o Soll & Haben
Frankfurter Ring 105a
D-(W) 8000 Munchen 40, Germany
Actor V: 01/17/93

Alte Lansberger Str. 2
D-(W) 8084 Inning, Germany
Alternate V: 03/20/93

Gough, Michael
c/o Peters
The Chambers, 5th Fl.
Chelsea Harbour, Lots Rd.
London SW10 0XF, England
Actor V: 03/17/93

Gould, Elliott
9903 Santa Monica Blvd. #301
Beverly Hills, CA 90212-1671
Actor V: 11/27/92

c/o Together We Stand CBS-TV
7800 Beverly Blvd.
Los Angeles, CA 90038
Alternate V: 01/15/92

Gould, Harold
8942 Wilshire Blvd.
Beverly Hills, CA 90211
Actor V: 12/14/92

Gould, Morton
c/o Amer. Soc. of Composers
One Lincoln Place
New York, NY 10023
Composer V: 01/11/92

Goulet, Robert
c/o Backstage Intl.
P.O. Box 20000
Las Vegas, NV 89112
Actor V: 04/01/92

3110 Monte Rosa Ave.
Las Vegas, NV 89102
Alternate V: 01/12/92

c/o Backstage International
1201 Wilshire Blvd. #101
Los Angeles, CA 90025
Forwarded V: 11/11/92

Grabe, Ronald J.
c/o NASA
LBJ Space Center
Houston, TX 77058
Astronaut V: 01/31/93

Grace, Bud
c/o King Features
216 East 45th St.
New York, NY 10017
Cartoonist V: 03/14/93

Graceland Estates
3734 Elvis Presley Blvd.
Memphis, TN 38116
Presley Home V: 10/19/92

Grady, Don
3575 W. Cahuenga Blvd. #320
Los Angeles, CA 90068
Actor V: 03/02/92

4537 Simpson Ave.
N. Hollywood, CA 91607
Alternate V: 03/17/93

Grady, Wayne
8619 French Oak Dr.
Orlando, FL 32811
Golfer V: 02/04/92

Graf, Steffi
6831 Bruel
Bei Manheim, W. Germany
Tennis V: 03/02/93

Graf, Steffi
The Polo Club of B.R.
5400 Champion Blvd
Boca Raton, FL 33496
Alternate V: 01/17/93

Graff, Ilene
11455 Sunshine Terrace
Studio City, CA 91604
Actress V: 02/15/93

Grahn, Nancy
4910 Agnes Ave.
N. Hollywood, CA 91607
Actress V: 02/15/93

Grahn, Nancy Lee
NBC Studio 11/ Santa Barbara
3000 West Alameda Ave.
Burbank, CA 91523
Actress V: 12/12/92

Grammer, Kelsey
c/o Paramount
Cheers
5555 Melrose Ave./Ball RM105
Hollywood, CA 90038
Actor V: 01/07/92

Grandy, Fred
5904 Mt. Eagel Dr. #1118
Alexandria, VA 22303
Actor V: 03/17/93

Granger, Farley
18 West 72nd St. #25
New York, NY 10023
Actor V: 02/22/92

Granger, Stewart
17331 Tramonto Dr. #1
Pacific Palisades, CA 90272
Actor V: 02/19/93

c/o Craig Agency
8484 Melrose Pl. #E
Los Angeles, CA 90069
Alternate V: 04/22/92

Grant, Amy
Reverston Farm, Moran Rd.
Franklin, TN 37064
Singer V: 09/06/92

P.O. Box 50701
Nashville, TN 37205
Alternate V: 06/01/92

Grant, Deborah
c/o Larry Dalzall
17 Broad Court, Ste. 12
London WC2B 5QN, England
Actress V: 03/06/93

Grant, Faye
322 W. 20th St.
New York, NY 10011
Actress V: 02/15/93

Grant, Gogi
10323 Almayo #202
Los Angeles, CA 90064
Singer V: 02/15/93

Grant, Harry
c/o Jackson Racing
P.O. Box 726
Arden, NC 28705
NASCAR Driver V: 03/02/92

Grant, Mickie
250 W. 94th St. #6-G
New York, NY 10025
Actress V: 01/12/93

Grappelli, Stephane
223 1/2 E. 48th St.
New York, NY 10017-1538
Violinist V: 12/18/92

Grateful Dead
P.O. Box 1073-C
San Rafael, CA 94915
Musical Group V: 03/03/93

6 W. 57th St.
New York, NY 10019
Forwarded V: 02/01/92

Graveline, Duane E.
c/o NASA LBJ Space Center
Houston, TX 77058
Astronaut V: 03/03/93

Graves, Peter
660 E. Channel Rd.
Santa Monica, CA 90402
Actor V: 02/21/92

Graves, Teresa
3437 W. 78th Pl.
Los Angeles, CA 90043
Actress V: 01/20/93

Gray, Billy
19612 Grandview Dr.
Topanga Canyon, CA 90290
Actor V: 01/15/92

Gray, Charles
c/o London Management
235-241 Regent St.
London, W1A 2JI England
Actor V: 07/17/92

Gray, Coleen
1432 N. Kemwood St.
Burbank, CA 91505
Actress V: 02/15/93

Gray, Dulcie
388 Oxford St.
London W1, England
Actress V: 02/28/92

Gray, Erin
10921 Alta View Dr.
Studio City, CA 91604
Actress V: 02/21/92

c/o Silver Spoons, NBC
3000 W. Alemeda
Burbank, CA 91523
Alternate V: 04/12/92

c/o Hissong & Co., Inc.
1438 N. Gower St.
Courtyard Suite 41/ Box 13
Hollywood, CA 90028
Alternate V: 01/02/92

Gray, Linda
P.O. Box 5064
Sherman Oaks, CA 91403
Actress V: 11/11/92

15659 Knokavn Dr.
Canyon City, CA 91351
Alternate V: 02/21/92

c/o UTA
9560 Wilshire Blvd. 5th Fl.
Beverly Hills, CA 90212
Forwarded V: 01/21/93

P.O. Box 4399
N. Hollywood, CA 91607
L.R.U. V: 01/02/92

Gray/Goodman
211 S. Beverly Dr. Ste. 100
Beverly Hills, CA 90212
Talent Agency V: 03/25/93

Grayson, Kathryn
2009 La Mesa Dr.
Encino, CA 91316
Actress V: 01/05/92

Green, Hubert
P.O. Box 71, Bay Point
Panama City, FL 32407
Golfer V: 02/04/92

Green, Lynda Mason
c/o Grosso-Jacobson
Night Heat
767 Third Ave.
New York, NY 10017
Actress V: 03/02/92

Green Bay Packers
1265 Lombardi Ave.
Green Bay, WI 54303
Team Offices V: 05/15/92

Greene, David
c/o CAA
1888 Century Park E.
Los Angeles, CA 90067
Actor V: 02/28/92

142 Adelaide Dr.
Santa Monica, CA 90402
Alternate V: 03/14/93

Greene, Michele
2281 Holly Dr.
Los Angeles, CA 90068
Actress V: 03/08/93

Greene, Michele, contd
c/o 20th Century Fox TV
L.A. Law
P.O. Box 900
Beverly Hills, CA 90213
Forwarded V: 01/12/92

Greenwood, L.C.
329 S. Dallas Ave.
Pittsburg, PA 15235
Football V: 05/11/92

Greer, Brodie
5840 Shirley Ave.
Tarzana, CA 91356
Actor V: 03/03/93

Greer, Jane
966 Moraga Dr.
Los Angeles, CA 90049
Actress V: 04/18/92

Greer, R.W. (Dabbs)
P.O. Box 322
Pasadena, CA 91102
Actor V: 01/04/92

284 S. Madison #102
Pasadena, CA 91101
Alternate V: 04/05/93

P.O. Box 34
Anderson, MO 64831
Alternate V: 12/13/92

Gregg, Julie
8091 1/2 Melrose Ave. #3
Los Angeles, CA 90046
Actress V: 12/18/92

Gregory, Frederick D.
c/o NASA LBJ Space Center
Houston, TX 77058
Astronaut V: 03/03/93

Gregory, James
55 Cathedral Rock Dr. #33
Sedona, AZ 85336
Actor V: 03/01/92

Gregory, James Michael
c/o Young and the Restless
7800 Beverly Blvd.
Beverly Hills, CA 90036
Actor V: 06/15/92

Gregory, Mary
1350 N. Highland Ave. #24
Los Angeles, CA 90028
Actress V: 12/18/92

Gregory, Stephen
c/o Y & R
7800 Beverly Blvd.
Beverly Hills, CA 90036
Actor V: 06/15/92

Gregory, William G.
c/o NASA LBJ Space Center
Houston, TX 77058
Astronaut V: 03/03/93

Gretsky, Wayne
c/o LA Kings
P.O. Box 10
Inglewood, CA 90306
Hockey V: 03/07/92

Grey, Jennifer
c/o CAA
9830 Wilshire Blvd.
Beverly Hills, CA 90212
Actress V: 01/21/93

Grey, Virginia
15101 Magnolia Blvd. #54
Sherman Oaks, CA 91403
Actress V: 03/23/93

Grieco, Richard
15263 Mulholland Dr.
Los Angeles, CA 90077
Actor V: 03/09/93

c/o Fox Broadcasting Co.
P.O. Box 900
Beverly Hills, CA 90213
Forwarded V: 11/07/92

Griem, Helmut
Klugstr. 36
D-(W) 8000 Munchen 19
Germany
Actor V: 02/11/93

Grier, Pam
Agency for Performing Arts
9000 Sunset Blvd. 12th Fl.
Los Angeles, CA 90069
Actress V: 01/16/93

Grier, Rosey
1977 S. Vermont Ave. Ste. 200
Los Angeles, CA 90007
Actor V: 04/13/92

3005 South Grand Ave.
Los Angeles, CA 90007
Alternate V: 04/12/92

Grier, Rosey, contd
11656 Montana Ave. Ste.430
Sherman Oaks, CA 91403
Forwarded V: 07/13/92

Griese, Bob
3250 Mary St.
Miami, FL 33133
Football V: 06/20/92

Griffith, Andy
P.O. Box 1968
Manteo, NC 27954-1768
Actor V: 05/11/92

c/o Viacom Prod.
Matlock
100 Universal City Plaza, Bl. 448
Universal City, CA 91608
Alternate V: 12/01/92

c/o Link Inc.
4445 Cartwright Ave. #110
N. Hollywood, CA 91602
L.R.U. V: 06/01/92

Griffith, Bill
c/o King Features
216 East 45th St.
New York, NY 10017
Cartoonist V: 02/19/93

Griffith, James
P.O. Box 351
Avila Beach, CA 93424
Actor V: 07/01/92

Griffith, Ken
c/o Agency
388 Oxford St.
London W1, England
Actor V: 02/28/92

Griffith, Melanie
3930 Legion Ln.
Los Angeles, CA 90039-1425
Actress V: 05/18/92

8340-F DeLongpre
Los Angeles CA 90069
Alternate V: 03/25/92

9555 Heather Rd.
Beverly Hills, CA 90210
Alternate V: 03/13/93

c/o Tippi Hedren
6867 Soldad Canyon
Acton, CA 93510
L.R.U. V: 06/01/92

Griffith-Joyner, Florence
11444 W. Olympic, 10th Fl.
Los Angeles, CA 90064
Olympian V: 02/03/92

Griffiths, Ken
c/o Agency
388 Oxford St.
London W1 9HE, England
Actor V: 01/02/92

Grimes, Gary
10637 Burbank Blvd.
N. Hollywood, CA 91601
Actor V: 03/17/93

Grissom, Steve
c/o NASCAR
1811 Volusia Ave.
Daytona Beach, FL 32015
NASCAR Driver V: 03/02/92

Grizzard, Lewis
c/o King Features
216 E. 45th St.
New York, NY 10017
Humorist V: 03/11/93

Groat, Dick
320 Beech St.
Pittsburgh, PA 15218
Baseball V: 04/18/92

Grodin, Charles
9560 Wilshire Blvd. #500
Beverly Hills, CA 90212
Actor V: 04/05/93

Groening, Matt
c/o Acme Features Syndicate
2219 Main St. #E
Santa Monica, CA 90405
Cartoonist V: 11/22/92

c/o The Simpsons
10201 W. Pico Blvd.
Los Angeles, CA 90035
Alternate V: 05/02/92

Groom, Sam
140 Riverside Dr. #16-0
New York, NY 10024
Actor V: 04/06/93

Grout, James
c/o Crouch & Salmon
59 Frith St.
London W1V 5TA, England
Actor V: 03/17/92

Groza, Lou
906 Terminal Tower Bldg.
Cleveland, OH 44113
Football V: 03/17/92

Gruner, Wolfgang
Westendallee 57
D-(W) 1000 Berlin 19
Germany
Actor V: 01/19/93

Guardino, Harry
c/o PM Entertainment Group
16780 Shoenborn St.
Sepulveda, CA 91343
Actor V: 01/23/93

Guest, Cornelia
2411 Briarcrest Rd.
Beverly Hills, CA 90210-1819
Actress V: 04/18/92

Guest, Lance
2269 La Granada Dr.
Los Angeles, CA 90068-2723
Actor V: 02/18/92

Guilbert, Ann
5750 Wilshire Blvd. Ste.512
Los Angeles, CA 90036
Actress V: 04/18/92

Guillaume, Robert
3853 Longridge Ave.
Sherman Oaks, CA 91403
Forwarded V: 02/01/82

Guiness, Alec
c/o London Mgmt.
235-241 Regent St.
London W1A 2JT, England
Actor V: 03/17/93

Kettlebrook Meadows
Steep Marsh
Petersfield, Hamps., England
Alternate V: 05/01/92

Guisewite, Cathy
4900 Main St.
Kansas City, MO 64112
Cartoonist V: 06/16/92

Gulliver, Dorothy
28792 Lajos Ln.
Valley Center, CA 92082
Actress V: 04/18/92

Gunthor, Werner
Rue de Chateau 25
CH-2520 La Neuveville
Switzerland
Skiing V: 01/19/93

Gurney, Tom
c/o Will Vinton Prod. Inc.
1400 N.W. 22nd Ave.
Portland, OR 97210
Animator V: 04/16/92

Gutensohn, Katherin
Oberfeldweg 12
D-(W) 8203 Oberaudorf
Germany
Skiing V: 02/11/93

Guthrie, Arlo
The Farm
Washington, MA 01223
Singer V: 03/12/92

c/o Rising Son Records
Blunderton Pike
Washington, MA 01223
Alternate V: 02/18/92

c/o Rolling Blunder Review
P.O. Box 657
Housatonic, MA 01236-0657
Alternate V: 03/30/93

Gutierrez, Sidney M.
c/o NASA
LBJ Space Center
Houston, TX 77058
Astronaut V: 01/31/93

Guttenberg, Steve
8444 Wilshire Blvd. Ste. 500
Beverly Hills, CA 90211-3217
Actor V: 01/03/92

Guy, Jasmine
Pantich
21243 Ventura Blvd. #101
Woodland Hills, CA 91364-2109
Actress V: 03/23/93

c/o Carsey-Warner Co.
A Different World
P.O.Box 1-701
14755 Ventura Bl
Sherman Oaks, CA 91403
Forwarded V: 01/07/93

c/o NBC TV
3000 W. Alamenda Ave.
Burbank, CA 91523
Forwarded V: 11/11/92

Guyton, Pamela
c/o Dallas Cowboys
One Cowboys Parkway
Irving, TX 75063-4945
Cheerleader V: 08/08/92

Gwynne, Anne
4350 Colfax, #2
Studio City, CA 91604
Actress V: 04/18/92

H

HAT SQUAD
Stephen J. Cannell Prod.
7083 Hollywood Blvd.
Los Angeles, CA 90028
Production Company V: 03/15/93

HBO & HBO Pictures
1100 6th Ave.
New York, NY 10036
Publicity V: 11/12/92

HEARTS AFIRE
Mozark Prod.
4024 Radford Ave.
Build. 5, Rm. 104
Studio City, CA 91604
Production Company V: 03/14/93

HERE AND NOW
NBC Prod.
c/o Kaufman-Astoria Studios
34-12 36th St.
Astoria, NY 11106
Production Company V: 03/26/93

HOMEFRONT
c/o Lorimar
300 S. Lorimar Plaza
Burbank, CA 91505
Production Company V: 03/19/93

HOME IMPROVEMENT
5065 Fan Mail
500 S. Buena Vista St.
Burbank, CA 91521
Production Company V: 03/19/93

HOMEFIRES
Paltrow Group
Pier 62, 3rd. Fl.
West 23rd and Hudson
New York, NY 10001
Production Company V: 03/26/93

HOT COUNTRY NIGHTS
Dick Clark Prod.
3003 W. Olive Ave.
Burbank, CA 91505
Production Company V: 03/26/93

Hack, Shelley
209 12th St.
Santa Monica, CA 90402
Actress V: 05/02/92

Hackett, Buddy
800 N. Whittier Dr.
Beverly Hills, CA 90210
Actor V: 01/18/92

485 Fifth Ave. #1000
New York, NY 10019
Alternate V: 03/17/92

Hackman, Gene
8500 Wilshire Blvd. #801
Beverly Hills, CA 90211
Actor V: 07/03/92

Haddix, Harvey
2105 Cheviot Hills Dr.
Springfield, OH 45505
Baseball V: 05/14/92

Hadley, Brett
c/o Young and the Restless
7800 Beverly Blvd.
Beverly Hills, CA 90036
Actor V: 06/15/92

Hagan, Molly
c/o Hermans Head
500 S. Buena Vista St.
Burbank, CA 91521
Actress V: 11/11/92

Hagar, Sammy
31740 Broad Beach Rd.
Malibu, CA 90265
Musician V: 03/18/93

Hagen, Uta
c/o Kroll
390 W. End Ave.
New York, NY 10024
Actress V: 03/03/93

Haggard, Merle
P.O. Box 536
Palo Cedro, CA 96073
Singer V: 06/30/92

Hagman, Larry
23730 Malibu Colony Rd.
Malibu, CA 90265
Actor V: 03/30/92

Hahn, Jesica
P.O. Box 54927
Phoenix, AZ 85078
Personality V: 03/06/92

999 N. Doheny Dr. #601
Los Angeles, CA 90069
Actress V: 03/23/93

Haig Jr., Alexander
1340 Chain Bridge Rd.
McLean, VA 22101
Soldier V: 03/19/92

1155 15th St. N.W. Suite 800
Washington, DC 20005
Alternate V: 02/11/92

Haim, Corey
3960 Laurel Canyon Blvd. #384
Studio City, CA 91604-3709
Actress V: 03/15/93

Haise Jr., Fred W.
c/o NASA LBJ Space Center
Houston, TX 77058
Astronaut V: 03/03/93

Haje, Khrystyne
3509 Blair Dr.
Los Angeles, CA 90068
Actress V: 02/27/92

P.O. Box 8750
Universal Ciry, CA 91608
Alternate V: 01/23/93

Hale, Barbara
P.O. Box 1980
N. Hollywood, CA 91614
Actress V: 03/03/93

Hall, Anthony Michael
65 Roosevelt Ave.
Valley Stream, NY 11581
Actor V: 05/01/92

9255 Sunset Blvd. #710
Beverly Hills, CA 90069
L.R.U. V: 05/29/92

Hall, Arsenio
5746 Sunset Blvd.
Hollywood, CA 90028
Celebrity V: 03/01/93

Hall, Arsenio, contd
c/o Arsenio Hall Show
5555 Melrose Ave.
Hollywood, CA 90038
Alternate V: 01/12/92

Hall, Deidre
9023 Norma Pl.
Los Angeles, CA 90069
Actress V: 01/02/92

Hall, Fawn
8339 Chapel Lake Ct.
Annandale, VA 22003
Celebrity V: 04/18/92

Hall, Huntz
12512 Chandler Blvd. #307
N. Hollywood, CA 91607
Actor V: 03/23/93

Hall, Lois
1368 Benedict Canyon Dr.
Beverly Hills, 90210-2020
Actress V: 01/22/92

Hall, Monty
519 N. Arder Dr.
Beverly Hills, CA 90210
Celebrity V: 07/14/92

Hall, Ruth
422 Alandale
Los Angeles, CA 90036
Actress V: 04/18/92

Hall, Tom T.
P.O. Box 1246
Franklin, TN 37065-1246
Actor V: 01/13/92

P.O. Box 121089
Nashville, TN 37212
Alternate V: 01/11/92

Hall & Oates
130 W. 57th St.
New York, NY 10019
Singer V: 02/12/92

c/o Arista Records
6 W. 57th St.
New York, NY 10019
Forwarded V: 02/18/92

Hallstromn, Holly
The Price is Right #101
5750 Wilshire Blvd.
Los Angeles, CA 90036-3697
Celebrity V: 03/27/93

Halop, Florence
c/o Warner Bros. TV
Night Court
4000 Warner Blvd., Office 12A
Burbank, CA 91521
Actress V: 01/03/93

Halsell Jr., James D.
c/o NASA LBJ Space Center
Houston, TX 77058
Astronaut V: 03/03/93

Ham, Jack
409 Broad ST.
Sewiddey, PA 15143
Football V: 05/07/92

Hamel, Veronica
9000 Sunset Blvd. #1200
Los Angeles, CA 90069
Actress V: 01/11/92

4024 Radford Ave.
Studio City, CA 91604
Alternate V: 10/10/92

129 N. Woodburn Dr.
Los Angeles, CA 90049
Forwarded V: 04/18/92

Hamill, Dorothy
c/o Marco Ent.
1 Erieview Plaza #1000
Cleveland, OH 44114-1715
Olympian V: 03/03/93

2331 Century Hill
Los Angeles, CA 90067
Alternate V: 05/16/92

Hamill, Mark
20358 Big Rock Rd.
Malibu, CA 90265
Actor V: 01/12/92

P.O. Box 526177
Salt Lake City, UT 84152-6177
Alternate V: 05/19/92

P.O. Box 124
Malibu, CA 90264
Alternate V: 03/15/93

c/o APA
9000 Sunset Blvd.
Los Angeles, CA 90069
Forwarded V: 01/12/92

217 Central Park W. Ste.1E
New York, NY 10024
Forwarded V: 05/15/92

Hamilton, Bobby
c/o Tristar Racing
Rt.2, Box 1-C
Flat Rock, NC 28792
NASCAR Driver V: 03/02/92

Hamilton, Carrie
2114 Ridgemont Dr.
Los Angeles, CA 90046
Actress V: 06/16/92

Hamilton, George
9141 Burton Way #3
Beverly Hills, CA 90210-4932
Actor V: 01/22/92

Hamilton, Linda
c/o Wm. Morris
151 El Camino
Beverly Hills, CA 90210
Actress V: 07/02/92

8957 Norma Pl.
Los Angeles, CA 90069
Alternate V: 01/21/93

721 Via de la Paz
Pacific Palisades, CA 90272
Alternate V: 07/18/92

Hamilton, Scott
1 Erieview Plaza #1000
Cleveland, OH 90038
Olympian V: 03/03/93

Hamlin, Harry
c/o William Morris
151 El Camino Dr.
Beverly Hills, CA 90212
Actor V: 03/17/92

P.O. Box 25578
Los Angeles, CA 90025
Actor V: 04/06/93

c/o 20th Century Fox TV
L.A. Law
P.O. Box 900
Beverly Hills, CA 90213
Alternate V: 01/12/92

Hamlisch, Marvin
970 Park Ave. 5th Fl. #65
New York, NY 10028
Composer V: 02/19/92

Hammer
80 Swan Way #130
Oakland, CA 94621
Rapper V: 01/02/92

Hammond, Jeff
c/o Darwal Inc.
6780 Hudsdeth Rd.
Harrisburg, NC 28705
NASCAR Crew V: 03/02/92

Hammond Jr., L. Blaine
c/o NASA
LBJ Space Center
Houston, TX 77058
Astronaut V: 01/31/93

Han, Maggie
9200 Sunset Blvd. #710
Los Angeles, CA 90069
Actress V: 11/02/92

c/o Curry Up Prod. Inc.
549 Carrall St. 4th Fl.as
Vancouver, BC, Canada V6B 2J8
Alternate V: 03/02/92

c/o ABC-TV
1330 Ave. of the Americas
New York, NY 10019
Forwarded V: 03/02/92

Hancock, Herbie
1680 N. Vine St.
Hollywood, CA 90028
Composer V: 09/03/92

1250 N. Doheny
Los Angeles, CA 90069
Alternate V: 03/17/93

1250 N. Doheny Dr.
Los Angeles, CA 90069
Alternate V: 03/20/92

Hanks, Tom
c/o Walt Disney Pictures
500 S. Buena Vista St.
Burbank, CA 91521
Actor V: 01/21/92

P.O. Box 49032
Los Angeles, CA 90049-0032
Forwarded V: 09/17/92

c/o Creative Artists Agency
1888 Century Park E. Ste.1400
Los Angeles, CA 90067
Forwarded V: 12/16/92

Hanna-Barbera
3400 Cahuenga Blvd.
Hollywood, CA 90068
Animators V: 03/03/93

Hannah, Daryl
8306 Wilshire Blvd. #535
Beverly Hills, CA 90212
Actress V: 06/01/92

c/o Columbia Pictures
Columbia Plz., Prod. Bl.8 Ste.153
Burbank, CA 91505
Forwarded V: 01/17/92

Harbaugh, Gregory J.
c/o NASA
LBJ Space Center
Houston, TX 77058
Astronaut V: 01/31/93

Hardison, Kadeem
324 N. Brighton St.
Burbank, CA 91506
Actor V: 04/05/93

Hardy, Robert
c/o Chatto
Prince of Wales Theatre
Coventry St.
London W1V 7FE, England
Actor V: 03/17/92

Harewood, Dorian
1865 Hill Dr.
Los Angeles, CA 90041
Actress V: 04/06/93

Hargity, Mariska
9274 Warbler Way
Los Angeles, CA 90069
Actress V: 03/23/93

Harlem Globetrotters
15301 Ventura Blvd. Suite 430
Sherman Oaks, CA 91403
Basketball Stars V: 04/10/92

Harmon, Mark
2236 Encinitas Blvd. #A
Encinitas, CA 92024-4353
Actor V: 03/23/93

c/o NBC-TV/Reasonable Doubt
3000 W. Alemeda Ave.
Burbank, CA 91523
Alternate V: 12/16/92

Harper, Heck
13647 Gaffney #17
Oregon City, OR 97045
Personality V: 01/13/92

Harper, Ron
c/o Los Angeles Clippers
3939 Figueroa
Los Angeles, CA 90037
Basketball V: 11/01/92

Harper, Tess
2271 Berry Lane
Beverly Hills, CA 90210
Actress V: 05/15/92

Harper, Valerie
616 N. Maple Dr.
Beverly Hills, CA 90210
Alternate V: 06/16/92

Harrelson, Woody
c/o Paramount/Cheers
5555 Melrose Ave.
Hollywood, CA 90038
Actor V: 01/02/92

Harrington, Pat
c/o Bash
20 W. 64th St.
New York, NY 10023
Actor V: 01/09/92

Harrington, Robert
2609 Woodsdade Ave.
Kannapolic, NC 28127
NASCAR Driver V: 11/11/92

Harris, Barbara
823 W. Montrose 1 Fl.
Chicago, IL 60613-1431
Actress V: 03/13/93

Harris, Bill
201 N. Robertson Blvd. #A
Beverly Hills, CA 90211
Critic V: 03/01/92

c/o Showtime
10900 Wilshire Blvd.
Los Angeles, CA 90024
Alternate V: 02/12/92

Harris, Cynthia
c/o 20th Century Fox TV
L.A. Law
P.O. Box 900
Beverly Hills, CA 90213
Actress V: 01/12/92

Harris, Ed
1427 N. Poinsettia Pl. #303
Los Angeles, CA 90046
Actor V: 03/26/93

Harris, Emmylou
P.O. Box 2689
Danbury, CT 06813-2689
Singer V: 10/17/92

P.O. Box 1481
Murfreesboro, TN 37133
L.R.U. V: 06/01/92

Harris, Franco
400 W. North Ave.
Pittsburgh, PA 15212
Football V: 03/25/93

Complex-D
800 Vinial St.
Pittsburgh, PA 15212
Alternate V: 12/10/92

Harris, Jay
c/o King Features
216 East 45th St.
New York, NY 10017
Cartoonist V: 03/12/93

Harris, Jonathan
16830 Marmeduke Pl.
Encino, CA 91316
Actor V: 04/15/92

Harris, Julie
132 Barn Hill Rd.
W. Chatham, MA 02669
Actress V: 03/01/92

Youngs Farm Rd.
W. Chatham, MA 02669
Alternate V: 12/05/92

Harris, Mel
P.O. Box 5617
Beverly Hills, CA 90210
Actress V: 12/14/92

Harris, Neil Patrick
c/o Booh Schut
11350 Ventura Blvd. #206
Studio City, CA 91604
Actor V: 03/26/93

c/o Steven Bochco Prods.
Doogie Howser, M.D.
10201 W. Pico Blvd.
Los Angeles, CA 90035
Forwarded V: 12/15/92

Harris, Richard
502 Park Ave.
New York, NY 10022
Actor V: 03/26/93

Harris Jr., Bernard A.
c/o NASA LBJ Space Center
Houston, TX 77058
Astronaut V: 03/03/93

Harris Jr., Glenn Walker
c/o ABC-TV
General Hospital
4151 Prospect Ave.
Hollywood, CA 90027
Actor V: 06/15/92

Harrison, Gregory
8966 Sunset Blvd.
Hollywood, CA 90069
Actor V: 02/12/92

Harrison, Jenilee
3800 Barham Blvd.#303
Los Angeles, CA 90068
Actress V: 02/02/92

Harrison, Kathleen
91 Regent St.
London W1, England
Actress V: 03/01/93

Harrison, Linda
211 N. Main St. Ste.-A
Berlin, CA 21811
Actress V: 04/18/92

Harrison, Mark
c/o Young and the Restless
7800 Beverly Blvd. #3305
Beverly Hills, CA 90036
Actor V: 06/15/92

Harrison, Noel
5-11 Mortimer St.
London W1, England
Actor V: 02/03/92

Harrison, Schea
c/o Bell-Phillip Prod.
Bold & Beautiful
7800 Beverly Blvd., Ste.3371
Los Angeles, CA 90036
Actress V: 06/15/92

Harrold, Kathryn
10390 Santa Monica Blvd. #300
Los Angeles, CA 90025
Actress V: 06/01/92

Harry, Debbie
1775 Broadway #700
New York, NY 10019
Singer V: 05/11/92

Harry, Debbie, contd
c/o Creative Artists Agency
9830 Wilshire Blvd.
Beverly Hills, CA 90212
Forwarded V: 07/23/92

425 W. 21st St.
New York, NY 10011
Forwarded V: 12/07/92

600 3rd Ave.
New York, NY 10016
L.R.U. V: 06/01/92

Hart
200 N. Robertson Blvd. #219
Beverly Hills, CA 90211
Talent Agency V: 03/26/93

Hart, David
c/o MGM/UA Comm.
In the Heat of the Night
1000 W. Washington Blvd.
Culver City, CA 90232
Actor V: 01/07/92

Hart, Gary
370-17th St. Suite 4700
P.O. Box 185
Denver, CO 80201-0185
Senator V: 06/01/92

1748 High St.
Denver, CO 80201
Forwarded V: 03/11/92

Hart, Jim
c/o AD Southern Illinois U.
Carondale, IL 62901
Football V: 05/09/92

Hart, Johnny
c/o King Features
216 East 45th St.
New York, NY 10017
Cartoonist V: 03/10/92

1703 Kaiser St.
Irvine, CA 92714
Alternate V: 03/02/92

c/o Creators Synd. Inc.
1554 S. Sepulveda Blvd.
Los Angeles, CA 90025
L.R.U. V: 01/02/92

Hart, Mary
c/o Entertainment Tonight
5555 Melrose Ave.
Hollywood, CA 90038
Celebrity V: 04/10/92

Hart, Mary, contd
150 S. El Camino Dr. #303
Beverly Hills, CA 90212
Alternate V: 01/21/93

Hart, Terry J.
c/o NASA LBJ Space Center
Houston, TX 77058
Astronaut V: 03/03/93

Hart, Veronica
c/o 5K Sales
9420 Reseda Blvd., Ste.836
Northridge, CA 91324
Adult Films V: 01/17/93

Harter-Manning-Woo
201 N. Robertson Blvd. #D
Beverly hills, CA 90211
Talent Agency V: 03/17/93

Hartley, Mariette
14755 Ventura Blvd. #839
Sherman Oaks, CA 91403
Actress V: 03/30/93

9744 Wilshire Blvd.
Beverly Hills, CA 90212
Alternate V: 03/22/92

c/o Agency
10100 Santa Monica Blvd. #2460
Los Angeles, CA 90067
Forwarded V: 06/15/92

c/o GTG Ent./Culver Studios
9336 W. Washington Blvd.
Culver City, CA 90232
L.R.U. V: 06/01/92

Hartley, Nina
1442-A Walnut St. #242
Berkeley, CA 94709
Actress V: 05/11/92

c/o 5K Sales
9420 Reseda Blvd. #836
Northridge, CA 91324
Alternate V: 02/13/93

Hartman, Dan
3 E. 54th St. #1400
New York, NY 100221
Singer V: 03/03/93

Hartman, Lisa
8037 Sunset Blvd. #2641
Los Angeles, CA 90046
Actress V: 03/13/93

Hartman, Lisa, contd
304 Broom Way
Los Angeles, CA 90049
L.R.U. *V: 07/01/92*

Hartman, Phil
c/o NBC Prod.
Saturday Night Live
30 Rockefeller Plaza
New York, NY 10112
Actor *V: 01/10/92*

Hartsfield, Hank
c/o NASA
LBJ Space Center
Houston, TX 77058
Astronaut *V: 01/19/93*

Harvey, Paul
1035 Park Ave.
River Forrest, IL 60305
Humorist *V: 03/13/92*

Haskell, Peter
19924 Acre St.
Northridge, CA 91324
Actor *V: 06/16/92*

Haskell, Susan
ABC-TV/One Life to Live
77 W. 66th St.
New York, NY 10023
Actress *V: 12/24/92*

Haskett, Gene
MI Int'l Speedway
12626 U.S. 12
Brooklyn, MI 49230
NASCAR Official *V: 03/02/92*

Hassett, Marilyn
8485 Brier Dr.
Los Angeles, CA 90046
Actress *V: 03/26/93*

Hasslehoff, David
4310 Sutton Pl.
Van Nuys, CA 91403
Actor *V: 03/17/92*

c/o Fritz Dorazil
Schmidgasse 9/1/13
A-2320 Schwechat, Austria
Alternate *V: 03/17/92*

Hatfield, Hurd
c/o Ballinterry House
Rathcormac
County Cork, Ireland
Actor *V: 03/12/92*

Hauer, Rutger
c/o Wm. Morris
151 El Camino Dr.
Beverly Hills, CA 90212
Actor *V: 03/06/93*

8966 Sunset Blvd.
Hollywood, CA 90069
L.R.U. *V: 03/03/93*

Hauff, Volker
Winston Churchill-Str. la
D-(W) 5300 Bonn
Germany
Politician *V: 02/01/93*

Hauk, Frederick H.
c/o NASA LBJ Space Center
Houston, TX 77058
Astronaut *V: 03/03/93*

Hauser, Fay
c/o Young and the Restless
7800 Beverly Blvd.
Beverly Hills, CA 90036
Actress *V: 06/15/92*

Hauser, Wings
7473 Mulholland Dr.
Los Angeles, CA 90046
Actor *V: 01/24/92*

Hausl, Regina
Jettenburg 49
D-(W) 8230 Schneizlreuth
Germany
Skier *V: 02/01/93*

Haussmann, Ezard
c/o Agentur Mattes
Mertzstr. 14
D-(W) 8000 Munchen 80
Germany
Actor *V: 02/23/93*

Haver, June
485 Halvern Dr.
Los Angeles, CA 90049
Actress *V: 05/01/92*

Haves, Nigel
c/o Whitehall
125 Gloucester Rd.
London SW7 4TE, England
Actor *V: 03/17/93*

c/o BBC TV Center
Woodlane
London W12 7RJ, England
Alternate *V: 03/01/93*

Havoc, June
405 Old Long Rd.
Stamford, CT 06903
Actress V: 04/18/92

Hawaii Public Television
2350 Dole St.
P.O. Box 23284
Honolulu, HI 96822
Archive V: 01/15/93

Hawkins, Hersey
c/o Philadelphia 76ers
P.O. Box 25040
Philadelphia, PA 19147
Basketball V: 11/17/92

Hawley, Steven A.
c/o NASA LBJ Space Center
Houston, TX 77058
Astronaut V: 03/03/93

Hawn, Goldie
9830 Wilshire Blvd.
Beverly Hills, CA 90212
Actress V: 01/21/93

2029 Century Park E. #300
Los Angeles, CA 90067-2904
Alternate V: 05/18/92

8966 Sunset Blvd.
Hollywood, CA 90069
L.R.U. V: 10/10/92

1849 Sawtelle Blvd. #500
Los Angeles, CA 90025
L.R.U. V: 06/01/92

Hawthorne, Nigel
c/o McReddie
91 Regent St.
London W1R 7TB, England
Actor V: 03/17/93

Hay, Robert
1122 S. Robertson Blvd.
Los Angeles, CA 90035
Actor V: 06/22/92

Hayden, Melissa
c/o Guiding Light/CBS
222 E. 44th St.
New York, NY 10017
Actress V: 06/01/92

Hayden, Nora
156 E. 61st ST.
New York, NY 10021
Actress V: 03/13/93

Hayes, Peter Lind
3538 Pueblo Way
Las Vegas, NV 89109
Actor V: 11/10/92

Haynes, Marques
2442 W. Skelly Dr.
Tulsa, OK 74107
Harlem Globetrotter V: 01/12/92

Headly, Glenne
c/o ICM
8942 Wilshire Blvd.
Beverly Hills, CA 90211
Actress V: 12/14/92

Healy, Mary
3538 Pueblo Way
Las Vegas, NV 89109
Actress V: 11/10/92

Heard, John
853 7th Ave., #9-A
New York, NY 10019
Actor V: 08/22/92

23215 Mariposa de Oro
Malibu, CA 90265
Alternate V: 01/21/92

347 W. 84th St. #5
New York, NY 10004
Alternate V: 12/14/92

Hearns, Tommy
19260 Britton Dr.
Detroit, MI 48223
Boxer V: 12/11/92

Heart
1202 E. Pike St., Suite 767
Seattle, WA 98122
Musical Group V: 12/12/92

P.O. Box 77505
San Francisco, CA 94107-0505
Alternate V: 01/15/92

219 First Ave. N. Suite 333
Seattle, WA 98109
L.R.U. V: 10/10/92

Heche, Anne
c/o Another World
30 Rockefeller Plaza
New York, NY 10020
Actress V: 01/12/92

Heche, Anne, contd
c/o NBC-TV
Another World
79 Madison Ave., 5th Fl.
New York, NY 91523
Alternate V: 06/15/92

Heckart, Eileen
135 Comstock Hill Rd.
New Canaan, CT 06840
Actress V: 03/18/92

Hect, Gina
c/o Herskowitz
5930 Foothill Dr.
Los Angeles, CA 90068
Actress V: 04/18/92

Hedison, David
2940 Trudy Dr.
Beverly Hills, CA 90210
Actor V: 03/26/93

Hedren, Tippi
1006 Fallen Leaf Rd.
Arcadia, CA 91006
Actress V: 05/18/92

6867 Soledad Canyon Rd.
Acton, CA 93510
Forwarded V: 06/01/92

c/o Bell-Phillip Prod.
Bold & Beautiful
7800 Beverly Blvd., Ste.3371
Los Angeles, CA 90036
Forwarded V: 06/15/92

Hedrick, Larry
P.O. Box 749
Statesville, NC 28677
Race Driver V: 03/12/93

Heesters, Nicole
c/o ZBF Agentur
Leopoldstr. 19
D-(W) 8000 Munchen 40
Germany
Actress V: 02/11/93

Hefner, Hugh
10236 Charing Cross Rd.
Los Angeles, CA 90024
Executive V: 05/05/92

Heinz, Eggert
Hainstr.
D-(O) 8806 Oybin, Germany
Politician V: 03/20/93

Helgenberger, Margaret
816 N. Stanley
Los Angeles, CA 90046
Actress V: 03/13/93

Helm, Susan J.
c/o NASA LBJ Space Center
Houston, TX 77058
Astronaut V: 03/03/93

Helmond, Katherine
P.O. Box 10029
Beverly Hills, CA 90213
Actress V: 03/04/92

155 El Camino
Beverly Hills, CA 90212
Alternate V: 01/12/92

2035 Davies Way
Los Angeles, CA 90046
Forwarded V: 03/26/93

Helmsley, Leona
36 Central Park Lane South
New York, NY 10019
Businesswoman V: 03/03/93

Helton, Mike
Tallapega Speedway
P.O. Box 777
Tallapega, AL 35160
NASCAR Official V: 03/02/92

Hemingway, Margot
P.O. Box 2249
Sun Valley, ID 83340
Actress V: 12/12/92

9454 Wilshire Blvd. #PH
Beverly Hills, CA 90212
Alternate V: 03/24/93

Hemingway, Mariel
P.O. Box 2249
Sun Valley, ID 83340
Actress V: 12/12/92

Hemmings, David
60 Saint James St.
London SW1, England
Director V: 03/01/92

c/o Michael Whitehall
135 Gloucester Rd.
London SW7, England
Alternate V: 02/28/92

Hemphill, Shirley
539 Trona Ave.
West Covina, CA 91790
Actress V: 06/16/92

Hemsley, Sherman
1907 Jewitt Dr.
Los Angeles, CA 90046
Actor V: 01/04/92

8033 Sunset Blvd. #193
Los Angeles, CA 90046
Alternate V: 03/02/92

c/o Dinosaurs
500 S. Buena Vista St.
Burbank, CA 91521
Forwarded V: 11/11/92

Henderson, Don
c/o AIM
5 Denmark St.
London WC2H 8LP, England
Actor V: 03/17/93

Henderson, Florence
c/o FHB Prod.
P.O. Box 11295
Marina Del Rey, CA 90295
Actress V: 01/12/92

Henderson, Kelo
c/o Rimrock Video
P.O. Box 5003
Apache Junction, AZ 85278
Actor V: 12/12/92

Henderson/Hogan Agency
c/o Henderson/Hogan
247 S. Beverly Dr., #102
Beverly Hills, CA 90210
Talent Agency V: 02/23/93

Hendler, Lauri
4034 Stone Canyon Ave.
Sherman Oaks, CA 91403
Actress V: 06/23/92

Henize, Karl
c/o NASA
LBJ Space Center
Houston, TX 77058
Astronaut V: 01/19/92

Henley, Don
345 N. Maple St. #235
Beverly Hills, CA 90210
Singer V: 01/21/93

Henner, Marilu
151 S. El Camino Dr.
Beverly Hills, CA 90212
Actress V: 01/21/93

c/o Mozark Prod./CBS-MTM
Evening Shade
4024 Radford Ave., Bl.5, Rm.104
Studio City, CA 91604
Forwarded V: 05/15/92

Henning, Linda Kaye
4231 Warner Blvd.
Burbank, CA 91505
Actress V: 06/23/92

Hennings, Linda
8831 Sunset Blvd. Ste.304
Los Angeles, CA 90069
Actress V: 04/01/92

Henricks, Terence T.
c/o NASA
LBJ Space Center
Houston, TX 77058
Astronaut V: 01/31/92

Henriksen, Lance
9540 Dale Ave.
Sunland, CA 91040
Actor V: 03/26/93

c/o Stone Grp. Prod. Co.
Columbia Plaza
Burbank, CA 91505
Forwarded V: 12/16/92

Henry, Gloria
11846 Ventura Blvd. #100
Studio City, CA 91604
Actress V: 01/21/93

Hensley, Jimmy
c/o Yarborough Racing
9617 Dixie River Rd.
Charlotte, NC 28270
NASCAR Driver V: 03/02/92

Hensley, Pamela
9526 Dalegrove Dr.
Beverly Hills, CA 90210
Actress V: 03/13/93

Henson and Assoc.
c/o Jim Henson Prod.
Tower Bldg., 28th Fl.
3900 Alameda
Burbank, CA 91595
Production Company V: 06/15/92

Hepburn, Katherine
244 E. 49th St.
New York, NY 10017
Actress *V: 07/01/92*

Hera Agency
3575 Cahuenga Blvd. W. 2nd Fl.
Los Angeles, CA 90068
Talent Agency *V: 03/24/93*

Herman, Pee Wee
P.O. Box 19070
Encino, CA 91416-9070
Actor *V: 02/12/92*

12725 Ventura Blvd. #H
Studio City, CA 91604
Alternate *V: 03/14/93*

855 S. Citrus Ave.
Los Angeles, CA 90036
Forwarded *V: 03/13/92*

Herring, Lynn
3500 W. Olive Ave. #1400
Burbank, CA 91505
Actress *V: 03/01/93*

c/o ABC-TV/General Hospital
1438 N. Gower St.
Los Angeles, CA 90028
Alternate *V: 01/17/92*

c/o ABC-TV
General Hospital
4151 Prospect Ave.
Hollywood, CA 90027
Forwarded *V: 06/15/92*

Herring, Rufus G.
P.O. Box 128
Roseboro, NC 28382
Medal of Honor *V: 02/04/93*

Herriot, James
c/o James Alfred Wight
23 Kirkgate, Thirsk
North Yorkshire, England
Author *V: 03/22/93*

Hershey, Barbara
9830 Wilshire Blvd.
Beverly Hills, CA 90212
Actress *V: 03/30/93*

Hertford, Chelsea
Universal TV/Major Dad
100 Universal Plz., Bl.426-2E
Universal City, CA 91608
Actress *V: 03/02/92*

Hervey, Jason
c/o New World TV
The Wonder Years
1440 S. Sepulveda Blvd.
Los Angeles, CA 90025
Actor *V: 12/11/92*

Hervey/Grimes Agency
14200 Ventura Blvd. #108
Sherman Oaks, CA 91413
Talent Agency *V: 03/24/93*

Hesseman, Howard
7146 La Presa Dr.
Hollywood, CA 90068
Actor *V: 02/13/92*

Heston, Charlton
2859 Coldwater Canyon Dr.
Beverly Hills, CA 90068
Actor *V: 03/04/92*

Heywood, Anne
9966 Liebe Dr.
Beverly Hills, CA 90210
Actress *V: 02/19/92*

Hickman, Dwayne
c/o J. Roberts Hickman
812 16th St. #1
Santa Monica, CA 90403
Actor *V: 01/04/92*

Hicks, Catherine
2801 N. Keystone St.
Burbank, CA 91504
Actress *V: 03/26/93*

9973 Durant Dr. #2
Beverly Hills, CA 90212
L.R.U. *V: 06/01/92*

Hicks, Dan
P.O. Box 5481
Mill Valley, CA 94942
Songwriter *V: 06/01/92*

Hieb, Richard J.
c/o NASA
LBJ Space Center
Houston, TX 77058
Astronaut *V: 01/31/92*

Higgins, Joel
5261 Cleon Ave.
N. Hollywood, CA 91601
Actor *V: 04/01/92*

Higgins, Joel, contd
246 16th St.
Santa Monica, CA 90402-2216
Alternate V: 09/18/92

Hildegarde
230 E. 48th St.
New York, NY 10017
Singer V: 04/27/92

Hill, Dana
c/o Goetz
848 Lincoln Blvd.
Santa Monica, CA 90403
Actress V: 03/26/93

c/o Goof Troop
500 S. Buena Vista St.
Burbank, CA 91521
Forwarded V: 11/11/92

Hill, Steven
18 Jill Lane
Monsey, NY 10952
Actor V: 12/14/92

Hill, Terrance
P.O. Box 818
Stockbridge, MA 01262
Actor V: 03/10/92

c/o T. Hill Productions
1 Fifth Ave.
New York, NY 10003
Alternate V: 04/11/92

Hillary, Sir Edmond
New Zealand High Commissioner
25 Golf Links
New Delhi, 110003 India
Politician V: 03/01/92

New Zealand High Commissioner
228A Remuera Rd.
Auckland, SE2 New Zealand
Alternate V: 01/11/92

Hillerman, John
10390 Santa Monica Blvd. #310
Los Angeles, CA 90025
Actor V: 03/17/92

7102 La Presa Dr.
Los Angeles, CA 90068
Alternate V: 03/26/93

Hillin, Bobby
5011 Midlothian Turnpike
Richmond, VA 23224
NASCAR Driver V: 02/27/93

Hilmers, David C.
NASA/LBJ Space Center
Houston, TX 77058
Astronaut V: 01/31/92

Hinckle, Robert
P.O. Box 368
Tujunga, CA 91043
Actor V: 11/11/92

Hindman, Earl
c/o Home Improvements
500 S. Buena Vista St.
Burbank, CA 91521
Actor V: 11/11/92

Hines, Gregory
377 W. 11th St. #PH
New York, NY 10014
Actor V: 08/10/92

Hingle, Pat
41 Viola Rd.
Suffern, NY 10901
Actor V: 06/16/92

Hinterseer, Ernst
Hahnenkammstr.
A-6370 Kitzbuhel, Austria
Skiing V: 01/19/93

Hirschfield, Al
122 E. 95th St.
New York, NY 10028
Caricaturist V: 03/14/93

Hirsh, Elroy
1440 Monroe St.
Madison, WI 53711
Football V: 03/17/92

Hitch, David M.
c/o King Features
216 E. 45th St.
New York, NY 10017
Cartoonist V: 03/11/93

Hobart, Rose
23388 Mulholland Dr.
Woodland Hills, CA 91364
Actress V: 03/13/93

Hodge, Patricia
c/o Agency
388-396 Oxford St.
London W1 9HE, England
Actress V: 03/06/93

Hodge, Stephanie
c/o Nurses
500 S. Buena Vista St.
Burbank, CA 91521
Actress V: 11/11/92

Hodges, Craig
c/o Chicago Bulls
980 Michigan Ave.
Chicago, IL 60611
Basketball V: 04/05/93

Hodges, Joy
P.O. Box 254
Katonah, NY, 10536
Actress V: 03/13/93

Hodgins, Dick
c/o King Features
216 East 45th St.
New York, NY 10017
Cartoonist V: 02/14/92

Hoest, Bill
P.O. Box 4203
New York, NY 10017
Cartoonist V: 01/19/92

Hoffman, Alice
3 Hurlbut St.
Cambridge, MA 02138-1603
Writer V: 11/11/92

Hoffman, Dustin
75 Rockefeller Pl. Ste.1104
New York, NY 10019
Actor V: 04/23/92

315 E. 65th St.
New York, NY 10021
Forwarded V: 03/12/92

Hoffman, Jeffrey A.
c/o NASA LBJ Space Center
Houston, TX 77058
Astronaut V: 03/03/93

Hoffmann, Cecile
c/o 20th Century Fox TV
L.A. Law
P.O. Box 900
Beverly Hills, CA 90213
Actress V: 01/12/92

Hoffs, Susanna
c/o Bangles
1106 Marine St.
Venice, CA 90291
Singer V: 09/09/92

Hoffs, Susanna, contd
9720 Wilshire Blvd.#400
Beverly Hills, CA 90212
Alternate V: 03/01/93

Hofmann, Peter
Schonrueth
D-(W) 8584 Kemnath
Germany
Singer V: 02/11/93

Hubschstr. 8
D-(W) 8580 Bayreuth
Germany
Alternate V: 02/11/93

Hogan, Ben
2911 W. Pafford St.
Ft. Worth, TX 76110
Golf V: 01/14/92

P.O. Box 11276
Ft. Worth, TX 76110
Alternate V: 02/04/92

Hogan, Hulk
1055 Summer St.
P.O. Box 3859
Stamford, CT 06905
Wrestler V: 02/15/92

4505 Morella Ave.
N. Hollywood, CA 91607
Alternate V: 01/29/93

19350 Business Center Dr.
Northridge, CA 91324
Forwarded V: 03/17/92

10901 Winnetka Ave.
Chatsworth, CA 91311
Alternate V: 01/29/93

Hogan, Paul
7 Parr Ave., N. Curl Curl
NSW 2099, Australia
Actor V: 02/01/93

18 Marshall Crescent
Beacon Hill
2100 NSW, Australia
Forwarded V: 04/14/92

65 Lavender St.
N. Sydney, NSW 2060, Australia
Forwarded V: 03/17/92

Hogestyn, Drake
9255 Sunset Blvd. #515
Los Angeles, CA 90069
Actor V: 03/20/93

Holbrook, Anna
c/o NBC-TV
Another World
79 Madison Ave., 5th Fl.
New York, NY 91523
Actress V: 06/15/92

Holbrook, Bill
c/o King Features
216 East 45th St.
New York, NY 10017
Cartoonist V: 03/13/93

1321 Weatherstone Way
Atlanta, GA 30324
Alternate V: 04/12/93

Holbrook, Hal
15301 Ventura Blvd. #301
Beverly Hills, CA 90212
Actor V: 03/01/93

c/o Mozark/CBS-MTM
Evening Shade
4024 Radford Ave., Bl.5, Rm.104
Studio City, CA 91604
Forwarded V: 05/15/92

Holden, Rebecca
P.O. Box 23504
Nashville, TN 37202
Actress V: 03/21/92

Holland, Deidre
c/o Five K Sales Co.
9420 Reseda Blvd., #836
Northridge, CA 91324
Adult Films V: 03/03/93

Holley, Lee
c/o King Features
216 East 45th St.
New York, NY 10017
Cartoonist V: 04/21/92

Holliday, Fred
11300 W. Olympic Blvd.
W. Los Angeles, CA 90064
Actor V: 03/30/93

Holliday, Kene
Viacom/Matlock
100 Universal Plz.,Bl448
Universal City, CA 91608
Actor V: 12/01/92

Holliday, Polly
888 7th Ave. Ste.2500
New York, NY 10106
Actress V: 06/23/92

Holliman, Earl
P.O. Box 1969
Studio City, CA 91604
Actor V: 02/21/92

1219 Bellingham Ave.
Studio City, CA 91604
Forwarded V: 01/21/92

Holly, Lauren
c/o ABC-TV/All My Children
1330 Ave. of the Americas
New York, NY 10019
Actress V: 03/21/92

Hollywood Chamber
6255 Sunset Blvd. #911
Hollywood, CA 90028
Organization V: 03/17/92

Hollywood Foreign Press
292 S. La Cienega Blvd. #316
Beverly Hills, CA 90211
Production Company V: 03/17/92

Hollywood Radio & TV Society
5315 Laurel Canyon Blvd. #202
N. Hollywood, CA 91607
Production Company V: 03/17/92

Hollywood Reporter
P.O. Box 1431
Hollywood, CA 90099-4927
Newspaper HQ V: 03/10/92

Hollywood Stuntman's Assn.
1043 Rafael Dr.
Arcadia, CA 91006
Production Company V: 03/17/92

Holm, Celeste
88 Central Park W.
New York, NY 10023
Actress V: 01/15/92

Holm, Ian
60 ST James St. Suite 1205
London SW1, England
Actor V: 04/23/93

Holmes, Larry
413 Northampton St.
Easton, PA 18042
Boxer V: 01/09/93

Holmquest, Donald L.
c/o NASA LBJ Space Center
Houston, TX 77058
Astronaut V: 03/03/93

Holt, Georgia
12341 Hesby St.
N. Hollywood, CA 91607
Actress V: 06/23/92

Holt, Hans
Weyrg. #5
1030 Wien, Austria
Actor V: 01/19/93

Holt, Jennifer
Apartado Postal 170
Cuernevaca, Morel, Mexico
Actress V: 03/12/93

Holtz, Jurgen
Bornemannstr. 18
D-(W) 6000 Frankfurt/Main
Germany
Actor V: 02/01/93

Home Box Office (HBO)
2049 Century Park. E. #1400
Los Angeles, CA 90067
Production Company V: 03/17/92

Honeymoon Suite
P.O. Box 70/Station C
Queen St. W.
Toronto, Ont., Canada M6J 3M7
Musical Group V: 01/14/92

Hong, James
8235 Santa Monica Blvd. #309
Los Angeles, CA 90046
Actor V: 04/03/92

Hood, George
c/o Will Vinton Prod. Inc.
1400 N.W. 22nd Ave.
Portland, OR 97210
Editor V: 07/06/92

Hooks, Jan
c/o Columbia Pictures TV
Designing Women
Columbia Plaza, Prod.Bl.8
#147
Burbank, CA 91505
Actress V: 12/16/93

Hope, Bob
10346 Moorpark St.
N. Hollywood, CA 91602
Actor V: 04/12/92

9021 Melrose Ave. Ste.#308
Los Angeles, CA 90038
Alternate V: 04/12/92

Hope, Bob, contd
3808 Riverside Dr.
Burbank, CA 91505
Forwarded V: 01/12/92

Hopkins, Anthony
388 Oxford St.
London W1, England
Actor V: 01/16/92

c/o Lantz Office
9255 Sunset Blvd. Ste. 505
Los Angeles, CA 90069
Alternate V: 03/01/92

7 High Park Rd.
Kew, Surrey
Richmond, TW9 3BL England
Alternate V: 03/26/93

c/o ICM
8942 Wilshire Blvd.
Beverly Hills, CA 90211
Forwarded V: 03/01/92

Hopkins, Bo
6628 Ethel Ave.
N. Hollywood, CA 91606
Actor V: 01/12/92

Hopper, Dennis
330 Indiana Ave.
Venice, CA 90291
Actor V: 04/02/92

Hordern, Michael
c/o Flat 7, Rectory Chambers
Old Church St.
London SW3, England
Actor V: 01/18/93

Hordern, Michael
c/o Thames Television Ltd.
306-316 Euston Rd.
London NW1 3BB, England
Alternate V: 03/22/93

388-396 Oxford St.
London W1 9HE, England
Forwarded V: 03/17/93

Horkheimer, Jack
3280 South Miami Ave.
Miami, FL 33129
Astronomer V: 03/25/92

Horn, Paul
c/o Global Records
180 E. Napa St.
Sonoma, CA 95476
Musician V: 02/01/92

Hornaday, Linda
36554 Sierra Hwy.
Palmdale, CA 93550
Race Driver V: 03/12/93

Hornaday, Ron
36554 Sierra Hwy.
Palmdale, CA 93550
Race Driver V: 03/12/93

Horne, Lena
1564 Broadway
New York, NY 10036
Singer V: 03/21/92

23 E. 74th St.
New York, NY 10021
Singer V: 06/23/92

5950 Canoga Ave. #200
Woodland Hills, CA 91367
Alternate V: 01/19/92

2005 Massachusetts Ave. N.W.
Lower Level
Washington, DC 20036
Forwarded V: 03/03/92

Horse, Michael
3151 Cahuenga Blvd. W. #310
Los Angeles, CA 90068
Actor V: 03/15/92

Horsey, David
c/o King Features
216 E. 45th St.
New York, NY 10017
Cartoonist V: 03/11/93

Horsley, Lee
P.O. Box 456
Gypsum, CO 81637
Actor V: 02/12/92

10202 W. Washington Blvd.
Culver City, CA 90232
Alternate V: 02/12/92

1941 Cummings Dr.
Los Angeles, CA 90027
Alternate V: 05/14/92

Horst, Frank
c/o Buro fur Promotion
Cansteinerstr. 20
D-(W) 4800 Biefeld
Germany
Actor V: 02/11/93

Horton, Jimmy
c/o NASCAR
1811 Volusia Ave.
Daytona Beach, FL 32015
NASCAR Driver V: 03/02/92

Horton, Michael
c/o Universal Television
"Murder She Wrote"
100 Univ. City Plz., Bldg.507
Culver City, CA 90232
Actor V: 03/02/92

Horton, Peter
222 Adelaide Dr.
Santa Monica, CA 90402
Actor V: 04/06/93

Horton, Robert
c/o The Studio
5317 Andasol Ave.
Encino, CA 91316
Actor V: 12/12/92

Horwitz, Dominique
c/o ZBF Agentur
Jenfelder Allee 80
D-(W) 2000 Hamburg 70
Germany
Actress V: 02/01/93

Hoskins, Bob
c/o Hope & Lyne
5 Milner Pl.
London, N1 England
Actor V: 10/12/92

40 Belmont Rd.
Exeter, Devon, England
Alternate V: 04/07/93

c/o Hutton Management
200 Fulham Rd.
London SW10 9PN, England
Alternate V: 01/17/93

Hossack, Allison
c/o NBC-TV
"Another World"
79 Madison Ave., 5th Fl.
New York, NY 91523
Actress V: 06/15/92

Housley, Phil
c/o Winnipeg Jets
15-1430 Maroons Rd.
Winnipeg, Manitoba, R3G 0L5
Hockey V: 11/09/92

Houston, Cissy
2160 N. Central Rd.
Ft. Lee, NJ 07024-7547
Singer V: 06/23/92

Houston, Thelma
4296 Mt. Vernon Dr.
Los Angeles, CA 90008
Singer V: 06/16/92

Houston, Tommy
c/o NASCAR
1811 Volusia Ave.
Daytona Beach, FL 32015
NASCAR Driver V: 03/02/92

Houston, Whitney
2160 N. Central Rd.
Fort Lee, NJ 07024-7547
Singer V: 05/18/92

8942 Beverly Blvd.
Beverly hills, CA 90212
Alternate V: 06/23/92

c/o William Morris Agency
151 El Camino Dr.
Beverly Hills, CA 90210
Alternate V: 12/17/92

140 Sylvan Ave. 3rd Fl.
Englewood Cliffs, NJ 07632
L.R.U. V: 03/02/92

Houston Astros
P.O. Box 288
The Astrodome
Houston, TX 77001
Team Office V: 05/15/92

Houston Oilers
6910 Fannin St.
Houston, TX 77030
Team Offices V: 05/15/92

Howard, Frankie
18 Queen Ann St.
London SW3, England
Actor V: 02/13/92

Howard, Greg
c/o King Features
216 East 45th St.
New York, NY 10017
Cartoonist V: 03/12/92

Howard, Ken
59 E. 54th St. #22
New York, NY 10022
Actor V: 06/16/92

Howard, Ron
1925 Century Park East #2300
c/o Imagine Films Ent.
Los Angeles, CA 90067
Actor/Producer V: 03/14/93

Howard, Susan
c/o Kohner
9169 Sunset Blvd.
Los Angeles, CA 90069
Actress V: 11/26/92

Howard Talent West
12229 Ventura Blvd. #201
Studio City, CA 91604
Talent Agency V: 03/29/93

Howell, C. Thomas
926 N. La Jolla Ave.
Los Angeles, CA 90046
Actor V: 04/05/93

Howland, Beth
255 Amalfi Dr.
Santa Monica, CA 90402
Actress V: 01/13/92

Hoy, Linda
c/o New World TV
"The Wonder Years"
1440 S. Sepulveda Blvd.
Los Angeles, CA 90025
Actress V: 12/11/92

Hubbard, Elizabeth
c/o "As The World Turns"
530 W. 57th St.
New York, NY 10019
Actress V: 01/12/92

Hubbard, Freddie
c/o Tooper
211 Thompson St.
New York, NY 10012
Jazz Musician V: 02/01/92

Hubert, Janet
c/o NBC Prod.
"Fresh Prince of Bel Air"
330 Bob Hope Dr.
Burbank, CA 91523
Actress V: 01/09/92

Hughes, Barnard
1244 11th St. #A
Santa Monica, CA 90401
Actor V: 01/02/92

Hughes, Barnard, contd
c/o Sunset Gower Studios
1238 N. Gower St.
Hollywood, CA 90038
Alternate *V: 01/02/92*

c/o Blossom
500 S. Buena Vista St.
Burbank, CA 91521
Forwarded *V: 11/11/92*

Hughes, Finola
4334 S. Belaire
Flintridge, CA 91001
Actress *V: 03/26/93*

4334 S. Belaire
Flintridge, CA 91011
Actress *V: 03/17/93*

c/o ABC TV-General Hospital
1438 N. Gower St.
Los Angeles, CA 90028
Alternate *V: 04/02/92*

c/o ABC-TV
General Hospital
4151 Prospect Ave.
Hollywood, CA 90027
Forwarded *V: 06/15/92*

Hughes, Kathleen
c/o Atkins & Assoc.
303 S. Crescent Hts. Blvd.
Los Angeles, CA 90048
Actress *V: 03/08/93*

8818 Rising Glen Pl.
Los Angeles, CA 90069
Alternate *V: 03/26/93*

Human Studies Film Archives
Smithsonian Institution
Room E307
National Museum of Natural History
Washington, DC 20560
Archive *V: 03/20/93*

Hunnicut, Gayle
174 Regents Park Rd.
London, NW1 England
Actor *V: 02/21/93*

Hunt, Bonnie
c/o Carsey-Warner/Grand
4024 Radford Ave., Bldg. 3
Studio City, CA 91604
Actress *V: 01/07/92*

Hunt, Garth
c/o Agency
388-396 Oxford St.
London W1 9HE, England
Actor *V: 07/03/92*

Hunt, Helen
9350 Wilshire Blvd. #324
Beverly Hills, CA 90212
Actress *V: 02/01/93*

Hunt, Marsha
13131 Magnolia Blvd.
Van Nuys, CA 91403
Actress *V: 06/23/92*

Hunter, Holly
41 Sutter St. #1649
San Francisco, CA 94104
Actress *V: 02/01/93*

c/o Kohner
9169 Sunset Blvd.
Sherman Oaks, CA 91403
L.R.U. *V: 06/01/92*

Hunter, Holly
10390 Santa Monica Bl.#250
Los Angeles, CA 90025
L.R.U. *V: 12/02/92*

Hunter, Kim
42 Commerce St.
New York, NY 10014
Actress *V: 07/02/92*

Hunter, Rachel
391 N. Carolwood Dr.
Los Angeles, CA 90077
Actress *V: 06/23/92*

Hunter, Tab
P.O. Box 1084
La Tierra Nueva
Santa Fe, NM 87501
Actor *V: 03/15/93*

Huntley, Leslie
8484 Wilshire Blvd. #530
Beverly Hills, CA 90211
Actress *V: 02/11/93*

Huppert, Isabelle
c/o Artmedia Varieties
40 Rue Francois
Paris 75008, France
Actress *V: 02/28/92*

Hurrelson, Woody
c/o Paramount
Cheers
5555 Melrose Ave./Ball RM105
Hollywood, CA 90038
 Actor V: 01/07/92

Hurt, John
Ascott-Under Wy'Wd
Oxfordshire, England
 Actor V: 01/12/92

c/o Agent
23 Black Lane
London NW2, England
 Alternate V: 02/17/93

Hurt, Mary Beth
1619 Broadway, #900
New York, NY 10019
 Actress V: 03/26/93

Hurt, William
8942 Wilshire Blvd.
Beverly Hills, CA 90211
 Actor V: 07/26/92

Rt. 1, Box 251 A
Palisades, NY 10964
 Alternate V: 03/26/93

c/o Wm. Morris
151 El Camino
Beverly Hills, CA 90212
 Forwarded V: 12/16/92

Hurwitz Associates
427 N. Canon Dr. #215
Beverly Hills, CA 90210
 Talent Agency V: 03/29/93

Husain, Jory
c/o Warner Brothers TV
Head of the Class
100 North Pass Rd.
Burbank, CA 91505
 Actor V: 12/18/92

Hussey, Olivia
c/o Wm. Morris Agency
147 Wardour St.
London W1, England
 Actress V: 02/27/92

Hussey, Ruth
3361 Don Pablo Dr.
Carlsbad, CA 92008
 Actress V: 02/01/92

Huston, Anjelica
c/o ICM
40 W. 57th St.
New York, NY 10019
 Actress V: 03/30/93

2771 Hutton Dr.
Beverly Hills, CA 90210
 Alternate V: 03/26/93

Hutchins, Wil
3461 Waverly Dr. #108
Los Angeles, CA 90027
 Actor V: 03/03/92

Hutchinson, Fiona
ABC-TV/One Life to Live
1330 Ave. of the Americas
New York, NY 10019
 Actress V: 02/01/92

c/o One Life To Live
77 W. 66th St.
New York, NY 10023-6298
 Alternate V: 01/12/92

Hutton, Betty
Harrison Ave.
Newport, RI 02840
 Actress V: 06/23/92

Hutton, Lauren
54 Bond St.
New York, NY 10012
 Actress V: 12/14/92

124 Waverly Pl.
New York, NY 10011
 Alternate V: 04/20/92

Hutton, Timothy
P.O. Box 9078
Van Nuys, CA 91409
 Actor V: 03/02/92

9255 Sunset Blvd. #910
Los Angeles, CA 90069
 Alternate V: 02/13/92

52 W. 82nd St.
New York, NY 10020
 Forwarded V: 05/15/92

Hyatt, Missy
c/o WCW/Turner Broad.
One CNN Center, Box 105366
Atlanta, GA 30348-5366
 Celebrity V: 03/26/93

Hyde, Harry
P.O. Box 291
Harrisburg, NC 28075
NASCAR Driver *V: 11/11/92*

Hyer, Martha
c/o Wallis
4100 W. Alameda Ave. #204
Toluca Lake, CA 91602
Actress *V: 06/23/92*

100 Universal City Plaza
Universal City, CA 91608
L.R.U. *V: 01/02/92*

I

I'LL FLY AWAY
Lorimar
3000 W. Olympic Blvd.
Suite 1540, Bldg. 2
Santa Monica, CA 90404
Production Company *V: 03/26/93*

IN THE HEAT OF THE NIGHT
Silverman-Bartlett Prod.
9211 Hazelbrand Rd.
Covington, GA 30209
Production Company *V: 03/14/93*

Iaccoca, Lee
c/o Chrysler Corp.
12000 Chrysler Dr.
Highland Park, MI 48288-1919
Executive *V: 10/10/92*

Ian, Janis
629 S. Lucerne Blvd.
Los Angeles, CA 90020
Singer *V: 12/15/92*

Idle, Eric
68-A Delancy St.
London, NW1 England
Actor *V: 03/26/93*

Idol, Billy
8209 Melrose Ave.
Los Angeles, CA 90046-6832
Singer *V: 10/10/92*

200 W. 57th St. Ste. 1403
New York, NY 10019
Alternate *V: 01/21/92*

7267 Outpost Cove
Los Angeles, CA 90068
Alternate *V: 01/12/92*

Idol, Billy, contd
P.O. Box 4843
San Francisco, CA 94101
Forwarded *V: 01/21/92*

c/o AuCoin
645 Madison Ave.
New York, NY 10022
Forwarded *V: 03/24/92*

Iglesias, Julio
5 Indian Creek Dr.
Miami, FL 33154
Singer *V: 03/15/93*

Image
c/o SF Chronicle
925 Mission St.
San Francisco, CA 94103
Magazine *V: 03/03/93*

In Marin Magazine
640 Mission Ave.
San Rafael, CA 94901
Magazine *V: 03/03/93*

Indianapolis Colts
P.O. Box 24100
Indianapolis, IN 4624-0100
Team Offices *V: 03/03/93*

Ingram, James
867 Muirfield Rd.
Los Angeles, CA 90005
Singer *V: 02/02/92*

Inman, John
c/o W. & J. Theatrical Ent.
51a Oakwood Rd.
London NW11 6RJ, England
Actor *V: 03/21/92*

Innovative Agency
1999 Ave. of the Stars #2850
Los Angeles, CA 90067
Artists *V: 03/03/93*

Innovative Artists Talent
c/o Innovative Artists
1999 Ave. of the Stars, #2850
Los Angeles, CA 90067
Talent Agency *V: 02/23/93*

Inside Collector
P.O. Box 98
Elmont Branch
Elmont, New York 11003
Magazine *V: 03/03/93*

Int'l Contemporary Artists
19301 Ventura Blvd. #203
Tarzana, CA 91356
Talent Agency V: 03/17/93

Int'l Creative Mgmt.
8942 Wilshire Blvd.
Beverly Hills, CA 90211
Talent Agency V: 03/29/93

c/o ICM
40 W. 57th St.
New York, NY 10019
Alternate V: 03/30/93

Int'l Fashion Library
110 E. 9th St., Ste. C602
Los Angeles, CA 90079
Archive V: 03/20/93

Int'l Museum of Photography
at George Eastman House
Department of Film
900 East Ave.
Rochester, NY 14607
Archive V: 03/20/93

Int'l Press Assn.
P.O. Box 8560
Universal City, 91608
Production Company V: 03/17/93

Int'l Stunt Assn.
3518 Cahuenga Blvd. W. #300
Hollywood, CA 90068
Production Company V: 03/17/93

Int'l Talent Agency
1124 W. Angelino Ave. #M
Burbank, CA 91506
Talent Agency V: 03/29/93

Interface Model Management
12023 1/2 Ventura Blvd. #1
Studio City, CA 91604
Model/Talent Agency V: 03/29/93

Ireland, Kathy
c/o Sterling/Winters
1900 Av. of the Stars, #739
Los Angeles, CA 90067
Actress V: 11/11/92

c/o Elite
111 E. 22nd St.
New York, NY 10010
Alternate V: 03/03/93

Ireland, Kathy, contd
9000 Sunset Blvd. 12th Fl.
Los Angeles, CA 90069
Forwarded V: 03/20/93

Irons, Jeremy
194 Old Brompton St.
London SW5, England
Actor V: 03/03/92

Irvan, Ernie
c/o McClure Racing
Rt.10, Box 780
Abington, VA 24210
NASCAR Driver V: 03/02/92

Irving, Amy
c/o Wm. Morris
151 El Camino
Beverly Hills, CA 90212
Actress V: 02/25/92

11693 San Vicente Blvd. #335
Los Angeles, CA 90049-5000
Alternate V: 04/06/93

1515 Amalfi Dr.
Pacific Palisades, CA 90272
L.R.U. V: 07/01/92

Irwin, James B.
P.O. Box 1387
Colorado Springs, CO 80901
Astronaut V: 04/01/93

Irwin, Tom
9350 Wilshire Blvd. #324
Beverly Hills, CA 90212
Actor V: 03/01/93

It Model Management
941 N. Mansfield #C
Los Angeles, CA 90038
Talent Agency V: 03/29/93

Ito, Robert
c/o Diamond Artists Ltd.
9200 Sunset Blvd. #909
Los Angeles, CA 90069
Actor V: 03/19/92

Ives, Burl
2084 Oakes Ave.
Anacortes, WA 98221
Singer V: 01/02/92

Ivins, Marsha S.
NASA/LBJ Space Center
Houston, TX 77058
Astronaut V: 03/03/93

J

Jackee
8649 Metz Pl
Los Angeles, CA 90069
Actress V: 03/26/93

Jackson, Alan
P.O. Box 121945
Nashville, TN 37212
Singer V: 03/30/93

Jackson, Anne
90 Riverside Dr.
New York, NY 10024
Actress V: 03/03/93

Jackson, Glenda
51 Harvey Rd.
Blackheath
London SE3, England
Actress V: 03/03/93

59 Firth St.
London W1, England
Alternate V: 01/19/92

Jackson, Gordon
388 Oxford St.
London W1, England
Actor V: 02/10/93

Jackson, Jesse
6845 S. Constance
Chicago, IL 60649
Activist V: 07/03/92

30 W. Washington St. #300
Chicago, IL 60602
Alternate V: 07/16/92

400 T St. NW
Washington, DC 20515
Alternate V: 03/18/93

930 E. 50th St.
Chicago, IL 60615
Forwarded V: 04/18/92

Jackson, Kate
1628 Marlay Dr.
Los Angeles, CA 90069
Actress V: 03/26/93

Jackson, Latoya
301 Park Ave., #1970
New York, NY 10022
Singer V: 03/23/93

Jackson, Mary Anne
c/o Kovner
1242 Alessandro Dr.
Newbury Park, CA 91320
Actress V: 06/23/92

Jackson, Michael
Sycamore Valley Ranch
Zacca Landeras
Santa Ynez, CA 93460
Singer V: 07/01/92

10960 Wilshire Blvd.
Los Angeles, CA 90024
Alternate V: 01/02/92

P.O. Box 933024
Los Angeles, CA 90093-9113
Forwarded V: 05/10/92

Jackson, Reggie
2449 Fort Union Blvd. #11-A
Islip, NY 11751
Baseball V: 02/01/92

Jackson, Victoria
P.O. Box 781
Fulton, CA 65251
Actress V: 01/10/92

c/o NBC/SNL
30 Rockefeller Plaza
New York, NY 10112
Forwarded V: 01/10/92

Jackson, Wanda
P.O. Box 7007
Oklahoma City, OK 73153
Singer V: 06/01/92

Jacobi, Derek
388 Oxford St.
London, W1 England
Actor V: 01/19/93

Jacobi, Lou
240 Central Park South
New York, NY 10019
Actor V: 03/14/93

Jacobs, Rachael
c/o Warner/Growing Pains
4000 Warner Blvd.
Burbank, CA 91522
Actress V: 12/03/92

Jaeckel, Richard
P.O. Box 1818
Santa Monica, CA 90406
Actor V: 06/16/92

Jagger, Mick
2 Munro Terrace
London SW10 0DL, England
Alternate V: 03/16/93

James, Clifton
95 Buttonwood Dr.
Dix Hills, NY 11746
Actor V: 09/03/92

James, Etta
P.O. Box 5025
Gardena, CA 90249
Singer V: 06/16/92

James, John
7310 Mulholland Dr.
Los Angeles, CA 90046
Actor V: 06/16/92

Jameson, Louise
c/o Jeremy Conway
8 Cavendish Place
London W1M 9DJ, England
Actress V: 03/12/93

Jamieson, Patrick
P.O. Box 2315
Sarasota, FL 34230
Author V: 02/02/93

Jan & Dean
215 Portland Circle #3507
Huntington Beach, CA 92648
Singers V: 05/29/92

6310 Rodgerton Dr.
Los Angeles, CA 90068
L.R.U. V: 05/29/92

Janis, Conrad
300 N. Swall Dr. #251
Beverly Hills, CA 90210
Actor V: 06/16/92

Jarre, Maurice
27011 Sea Vista Dr.
Malibu, CA 90265
Composer V: 03/15/92

Jarreau, Al
9034 Sunset Blvd. #250
Los Angeles, CA 90069
Singer V: 03/01/93

Jarrett, Dale
c/o Gibbs Racing
5301 Harris Blvd.
Charlotte, NC 28269
NASCAR Driver V: 03/02/92

Jarrett, Ned
c/o NASCAR
1811 Volusia Ave.
Daytona Beach, FL 32015
NASCAR Driver V: 03/02/92

Jay Talent Agency
6269 Selma Ave. #15
Hollywood, CA 90028
Talent Agency V: 03/16/93

Jean, Gloria
6625 Variel Ave.
Canoga Park, CA 91306
Actress V: 03/02/92

20309 Leadwell St.
Canoga Park, CA 91303
Alternate V: 05/22/92

Jeavons, Colin
c/o Stone
25 Whitehall
London SW1A 2BS, England
Actor V: 03/17/92

Jeffreys, Anne
121 S. Bently Ave.
Los Angeles, CA 90049
Actress V: 01/15/92

Jeffries, Lionel
c/o Agency
388 Oxford St.
London W1, England
Director V: 03/03/93

c/o Redway & Assoc.
16 Berners St.
London W1P 3DD, England
Alternate V: 03/17/92

c/o Thames Television Ltd.
306-316 Euston Rd.
London NW1 3BB, England
Forwarded V: 03/22/92

Jemison, Mae C.
c/o NASA
LBJ Space Center
Houston, TX 77058
Astronaut V: 03/03/93

Jenkins, Daniel
c/o Michael Bloom Ltd.
9200 Sunset Blvd. #710
Los Angeles, CA 90069
Actor V: 03/20/93

Jenner, Bruce
P.O. Box 665
Malibu, CA 90265
Actor V: 07/01/92

24536 Vantage Point Terr.
Malibu, CA 90265-4722
Actor V: 07/01/92

Jennings, Doug
7807 Evening Star Lane
Tallahasse, FL 32312
Baseball V: 12/10/92

Jennings, Waylon
c/o Waylons Pony Express
P.O. Box 121556
Nashville, TN 37212
Singer V: 02/19/92

Jennings & Associates
28035 Dorothy Dr. #210A
Agoura, CA 91301
Talent Agency V: 03/29/93

Jens, Salome
9400 Readcrest Dr.
Beverly Hills, CA 90210
Actress V: 03/12/93

Jergens, Adele
c/o Langan
32108 Village #32
Camarillo, CA 93010
Actress V: 05/22/92

Jernigan, Preea
c/o Dallas Cowboys
One Cowboys Parkway
Irving, TX 75063-4945
Cheerleader V: 08/08/92

Jernigan, Tamara E.
c/o NASA
LBJ Space Center
Houston, TX 77058
Astronaut V: 01/19/93

Jessup, Brian
c/o Columbia Pictures TV
Baby Talk
1438 N. Gower Blvd.
Los Angeles, CA 90028
Actor V: 12/15/92

Jessup, Paul
c/o Columbia/Baby Talk
1438 N. Gower Blvd.
Los Angeles, CA 90028
Actor V: 12/15/92

Jett, Joan
c/o Laguna
750 Shore Rd.
Long Beach, L.I., NY 11561
Singer V: 01/11/92

250 W. 57th St. Ste.613
New York, NY 10107
Alternate V: 05/29/92

P.O. Box 600
Long Beach, NY 11561
Alternate V: 05/10/92

Jillian, Ann
4241 Woodcliff Rd.
Sherman Oaks, CA 91403
Actress V: 11/15/92

Jobe, Emmett
Phoenix Int'l Raceway
P.O. Box 13088
Phoenix, AZ 85002
NASCAR Official V: 03/02/92

Joel, Billy
200 W. 57th St. #308
New York, NY 10019
Singer V: 04/27/92

128 Central Park South
New York, NY 10019
Alternate V: 03/18/93

375 N. Broadway Ste.208
Jerico, NY 11753
L.R.U. V: 01/02/92

Johan, Zita
P.O. Box 302
W. Nyack, NY 10994
Actress V: 05/22/92

John, Elton
c/o J. Reid Enterprises Ltd.
Singles House England
32 Galena Rd.
London W6 0LT, England
Singer V: 02/03/93

125 Kensington
High St.
London, W8 55N, England
Alternate V: 01/03/92

John E. Allen
116 North Ave.
Park Ridge, NJ 07656
Archive V: 02/18/93

Johncock, Gordon
1042 Becker Rd.
Hastings, MI 49053
Race Driver V: 02/18/92

2239 W. Windrose Dr.
Phoenix, AZ 85029
Alternate V: 03/01/92

Johns, Glynis
555 Fifth Ave.
New York, NY 10017
Actress V: 03/01/92

Johns, Mervyn
42 Hazelbury Rd.
London SW6, England
Actor V: 03/01/92

Johnson, Addison
c/o King Features
216 East 45th St.
New York, NY 10017
Cartoonist V: 02/28/93

Johnson, Anne-Marie
c/o MGM/UA Comm.
In the Heat of the Night
1000 W. Washington Blvd.
Culver City, CA 90232
Actress V: 01/07/92

Johnson, Arte
2725 Bottlebrush Dr.
Los Angeles, CA 90026
Actor V: 02/01/92

c/o ABC-TV
General Hospital
4151 Prospect Ave.
Hollywood, CA 90027
Alternate V: 06/15/92

Johnson, Ben
c/o Mesa Ent.
2466 Leisure World
Mesa, AZ 85206
Actor V: 04/05/93

c/o Gerler-Stevens
3349 Cahuenga Blvd., W. Ste.1
Los Angeles, CA 90068
Alternate V: 01/02/92

31509 Germain Lane
Westlake Village, CA 91361
L.R.U. V: 01/02/92

Johnson, Don
144 S. Beverly Dr.
Beverly Hills, CA 90212
Actor V: 02/21/92

9555 Heather Rd.
Beverly Hills, CA 90210
Alternate V: 04/06/93

c/o Mike Belson
50 Beverly Dr.
Beverly Hills, CA 90212
L.R.U. V: 01/02/92

Johnson, Earvin Magic
Beverly Estates
13100 Mulholland Dr.
Beverly Hills, CA 90210
Basketball V: 02/11/93

Johnson, Frank
c/o King Features
216 East 45th St.
New York, NY 10017
Cartoonist V: 01/19/93

Johnson, Junior
c/o Johnson & Assoc.
Rt.2, Box 161A & 162
Rhonda, NC 28670
NASCAR Owner V: 03/02/92

Johnson, Lynn-Holly
2109 Broadway #13-1597
New York, NY 10023
Actress V: 06/01/92

Johnson, Russell
c/o Jones Agency
117 S. Main St.
Seattle, WA 98109
Actor V: 03/26/93

Jones, Carrie
c/o 5K Sales
9420 Reseda Blvd., Ste.836
Northridge, CA 91324
Adult Films V: 01/17/93

Jones, Christine
ABC-TV/One Life to Live
1330 Ave. of the Americas
New York, NY 10019
Actress V: 01/13/92

Jones, Chuck
P.O. Box Box 2319
Costa Mesa, CA 92628
Cartoonist V: 03/15/93

Jones, Davy
P.O. Box 400
Beavertown, PA 17813
Actor V: 02/03/92

21 Elm Rd.
Fareham, Hants., England
Forwarded V: 02/03/93

Jones, Dean
5055 Casa Dr.
Tarzana, CA 91356
Actor V: 04/06/93

Jones, George
48 Music Sq. East
Nashville, TN 37203
Singer V: 03/30/93

Jones, Grace
P.O. Box 82
Great Neck, NY 11021
Actress V: 03/14/92

166 Bank St.
New York, NY 10014
Alternate V: 03/26/93

Jones, Henry
12221 Tweed Ln.
Los Angeles, CA 90049
Actor V: 03/01/92

Jones, James Earl
c/o S. Aron
10 E. 40th St.
New York, NY 10016
Actor V: 08/13/92

Jones, Jennifer
c/o Dallas Cowboys
One Cowboys Parkway
Irving, TX 75063-4945
Cheerleader V: 08/08/92

Jones, Jenny
454 N. Columbus Dr.
Chicago, IL 60611
Celebrity V: 03/30/93

Jones, Kara
c/o Dallas Cowboys
One Cowboys Parkway
Irving, TX 75063-4945
Cheerleader V: 08/08/92

Jones, L.Q.
2144 N. Cahuenga Blvd.
Hollywood, CA 90068
Director V: 03/21/92

Jones, Parnelli
20555 Earl St.
Torrance, CA 90503
Race Driver V: 02/02/92

Jones, Quincy
P.O.Box 11509
Burbank, CA 91510
Composer V: 03/01/93

Jones, Renee
c/o 20th Century/L.A. Law
P.O. Box 900
Bevery Hills, CA 90213
Actress V: 02/03/92

Jones, Sam J.
151 El Camino
Beverly Hills, CA 90210
Actor V: 05/10/92

Jones, Shirley
701 N. Oakhurst Dr.
Beverly Hills, CA 90210
Actress V: 03/02/93

Jones, Thomas D.
c/o NASA/LBJ Space Center
Houston, TX 77058
Astronaut V: 03/03/93

Jones, Tom
151 El Camino
Beverly Hills, CA 90212
Singer V: 03/02/93

363 Copa de Oro Rd.
Los Angeles, CA 90077
Forwarded V: 03/22/93

Jones, Tommy Lee
P.O. Box 966
San Saba, TX 76877
Actor V: 05/10/92

Jong, Erica
121 Davis Hill Rd.
Weston, CT 06883
Author V: 05/22/92

Jordan, Alex
8424-A Santa Monica Blvd. #587
W. Hollywood, CA 90069
Adult Films V: 02/13/93

Jordan, Barbara
c/o Baker Hostetler, #1100
1050 Connecticut Ave. N.W.
Washinton, DC 20036
Politician V: 11/11/92

Jordan, Lee Roy
2425 Burbank
Dallas, TX 75235
Football V: 05/14/92

Jordan, Michael
c/o Chicago Bulls
980 N. Michigan Ave., Ste.1600
Chicago, IL 60611
Basketball V: 01/12/93

Jordan, Richard
3704 Carbon Canyon
Malibu, CA 90265
Actor V: 07/06/92

9350 Wilshire Blvd. #324
Beverly Hills, CA 90212
Alternate V: 03/01/93

Jordan, Will
435 W. 57th St. Suite 10F
New York, NY 10019
Personality V: 12/12/92

Jorgensen, J. 'Spider'
8267 Kirkwood Court
Cucamonga, CA 91730
Baseball V: 01/02/92

Joseph-Heldfond-Rix
1717 N. Hignland Ave. #414
Los Angeles, CA 90026
Talent Agency V: 03/17/93

Joseph/Knight
1680 N. Vine St. #726
Hollywood, CA 90028
Talent Agency V: 03/29/93

Jourdan, Louis
1139 Maybrook Dr.
Beverly Hills, CA 90210
Actor V: 04/02/92

Jovi, Bon
240 Central Park S.
New York, NY 10019
Musical Group V: 09/08/92

Joyce, Elaine
724 N. Roxbury Dr.
Beverly Hills, CA 90210
Actress V: 03/14/93

Joyner-Kersee, Jackie
c/o JJK Assoc.
3466 Bridge Land Dr. #105
Bridgeton, MO 63044
Athlete V: 03/20/93

Judd, Naomi and Wynnona
P.O. Box 17325
Nashville, TN 37217-0325
Singers V: 06/01/92

Judd, Naomi and Wyonna
P.O. Box 17087
Nashville, TN 37217
Forwarded V: 03/13/93

Julia, Raul
200 W. 54th St. #7G
New York, NY 10019
Actor V: 03/26/93

Jump, Gordon
1631 Hillcrest Ave.
Glendale, CA 91202
Actor V: 06/16/92

Jurasik, Peter
c/o MTM Prod.
4024 Radford Ave.
Studio City, CA 91604
Actor V: 03/27/92

c/o Innovative Artists
1999 Ave. of the Stars, #2850
Los Angeles, CA 90067
Alternate V: 02/23/93

969 1/2 Manzanita St.
Los Angeles, CA 90029
Forwarded V: 03/27/92

Jurgensen, Sonny
c/o Office
P.O. Box 53
Mt. Vernon, VA 22121
Football V: 12/11/92

Just For Laughs
22 Miller Ave.
Mill Valley, CA 94941
Comedy Newspaper V: 03/26/93

Justice, Charles "Choo Choo"
P.O. Box 819
Cherryville, NC 28021
Football V: 05/14/92

K

KIDS IN THE HALL
25 St. Nicholas St., 4th Fl.
Toronto, Ontario, Canada M4Y 1W5
Production Company V: 03/18/93

Kahana's Stunt School
21828 Lassen #E
Chatsworth, CA 91311
School Office V: 03/17/93

Kahn, Madeline
975 Park Ave. #9-A
New York, NY 10028
Actress V: 05/02/92

Kanaly, Steve
3611 Longridge Ave.
Sherman Oaks, CA 91423
Actor V: 07/14/92

Kane, Bob
P.O. Box 1099
Forestville, NY 95436
Cartoonist V: 07/03/92

Kane, Carol
1416 N. Hayvenhurst Dr. #1C
Los Angeles, CA 90046
Actress V: 03/26/93

2400 Broadway St. #100
Santa Monica, CA 90404
L.R.U. V: 06/01/92

Kansas City Chiefs
One Arrowhead Dr.
Kansas City, MO 64129
Team Offices V: 05/15/92

Kansas City Royals
P.O. Box 1969
Royals Stadium
Kansas City, MO 64141
Team Office V: 05/15/92

Kanter, Hal
15941 Woodvale Rd.
Encino, CA 91316
Producer V: 04/13/92

Kantner, China
P.O. Box 69
Mill Valley, CA 94942
MTV Commentator V: 06/18/92

Kaplan, Gabriel
9551 Hidden Valley Rd.
Beverly Hills, CA 90210
Actor V: 06/16/92

Kaplan Agency
1800 N. Highland Ave. #405
Los Angeles, CA 90028
Talent Agency V: 03/29/93

Kaplan-Stahler Agency
8383 Wilshire Blvd. #923
Beverly Hills, CA 90211
Talent Agency V: 03/29/93

Kapture, Mitzi
c/o Shapiro
1503 Ventura Bl. #345
Sherman Oaks, CA 91403
Actress V: 11/11/92

Karg/Weissenbach
329 N. Wetherly Dr. Ste. 101
Beverly Hills, CA 90211
Talent Agency V: 03/29/93

Karn, Richard
c/o Home Improvements
500 S. Buena Vista St.
Burbank, CA 91521
Actor V: 11/11/92

Karras, Alex
7943 Woodrow Wilson Dr.
Los Angeles, CA 90046
Actor V: 05/21/92

Kasdan, Lawrence
c/o UTA
9560 Wilshire Blvd. 5th Fl.
Beverly Hills, CA 90212
Writer V: 03/01/93

Kasem, Casey
138 N. Mapleton Dr.
Los Angeles, CA 90077
Personality V: 05/10/92

Kasem, Jean
138 N. Mapleton Dr.
Los Angeles, CA 90077
Actress V: 05/10/92

Katsulas, Andreas
c/o Innovative Artists
1999 Ave. of the Stars, #2850
Los Angeles, CA 90067
Actor V: 02/23/93

Katt, William
25218 Malibu Rd.
Malibu, CA 90265
Actor V: 03/02/92

15301 Ventura Blvd. #345
Sherman Oaks, CA 91403
Alternate V: 03/01/93

Kaukonen, Jorma
611 Broadway, Ste.822
New York, NY 10012
 Singer V: 02/01/92

Kavner, Julie
25154 Malibu Rd. #2
Malibu, CA 90265
 Actress V: 03/26/93

Kay, Dianne
1559 Palisades Dr.
Pacific Palisades, CA 90077
 Actress V: 05/22/92

Kaye, Caren
12700 Ventura Blvd. #350
Studio City, CA 91604
 Actress V: 03/01/93

Kaye, Darwood
9318 Scotmont Dr.
Tujunga, CA 91042
 Actor V: 11/10/92

Kazan, Elia
174 E. 95th St.
New York, NY 10128-2511
 Director V: 05/22/92

Kazer, Beau
c/o Young and the Restless
7800 Beverly Blvd.
Beverly Hills, CA 90036
 Actor V: 06/15/92

Keach Jr., Stacy
151 El Camino
Beverly Hills, CA 90212
 Actor V: 09/09/92

27425 Winding Way
Malibu, CA 90265
 Alternate V: 03/03/93

8966 Sunset Blvd.
Hollywood, CA 90069
 Forwarded V: 04/07/92

Keach Sr., Stacey
3969 Longridge Ave.
Sherman Oaks, CA 91423
 Actor V: 03/26/93

Keanan, Staci
c/o ABC-TV Step by Step
2040 Ave. of the Stars
Los Angels, CA 90067
 Actress V: 05/22/92

Keane, Bill
c/o King Features
216 East 45th St.
New York, NY 10017
 Cartoonist V: 03/04/93

Keane, Diane
23 Primrose Hill
Charleton Mackrell
Nr.Someton, Summerset, England
 Actress V: 02/21/93

Keating, Charles
c/o NBC-TV
Another World
79 Madison Ave., 5th Fl.
New York, NY 91523
 Actor V: 06/15/92

Keaton, Diane
2255 Verde Oak Dr.
Los Angeles, CA 90068
 Actress V: 05/11/92

Keaton, Michael
826 Napoli
Pacific Palisades, CA 90272
 Actor V: 05/02/92

Keefe, Mike
c/o King Features
216 East 45th St.
New York, NY 10017
 Cartoonist V: 02/21/93

Keel, Howard
15252 Longbow Dr.
Sherman Oaks, CA 91403
 Actor V: 07/02/92

Keeler, Ruby
71029 Early Times Rd.
Rancho Mirage, CA 92270
 Actress V: 02/11/92

Keenen, Mary Jo
c/o Nurses
500 S. Buena Vista St.
Burbank, CA 91521
 Actress V: 11/11/92

Keeshan, Bob
40 W. 57th St.
New York, NY 10019
 Captain Kangaroo V: 03/01/92

Keisha
P.O. Box 49715
Los Angeles, CA 90049
 Adult Films V: 02/13/93

Keitel, Harvey
P.O. Box 49
Palisades, NY 10964
Actor V: 03/26/93

Keith, Brian
23449 Malibu Canyon Rd.
Malibu, CA 90265
Actor V: 03/01/93

Keith, David
Chateau Marmot
8221 Sunset Blvd.
Los Angeles, CA 90069
Actor V: 05/14/92

Keith, Penelope
c/o London Mgmt.
235-241 Regent St.
London W1A 2JT, England
Actress V: 03/17/93

Keller, Marthe
Lamonstrasse 9
8 Munich, 80 W. Germany
Actress V: 03/15/93

Keller, Mary Page
151 El Camino
Beverly Hills, CA 90212
Actress V: 09/18/92

c/o Leone
5303 Doon Way
Anacortes, WA 98221-2913
Alternate V: 05/22/92

Kellerman, Sally
7944 Woodrow Wilson
Los Angeles, CA 90046
Actress V: 12/12/92

Kelley, De Forrest
15463 Greenleaf St.
Sherman Oaks, CA 91403
Actor V: 04/20/92

c/o Sue Keenan
8717 S. La Cienega Blvd. #29
Inglewood, CA 90301
Alternate V: 03/01/92

Kelley, Kitty
3927 Highwood Ct. N.W.
Washington, DC 20007-2132
Author V: 05/29/92

666 Fifth Ave.
New York, NY 10103
Forwarded V: 07/03/92

Kelley, Kitty, contd
3037 Dunbarton Ave. N.W.
Washington, DC 20007
L.R.U. V: 05/29/92

Kelley, Shiela
624 S. Dunsmuir Ave. #204
Los Angeles, CA 90036
Actress V: 03/13/93

Kelly, Gene
725 N. Rodeo Dr.
Beverly Hills, CA 90210
Actor V: 04/23/92

904 N. Bedford Dr.
Beverly Hills, CA 90210
L.R.U. V: 01/02/92

Kelly, Moira
c/o Kaplan
501 N. Spalding Ave. #5
Los Angeles, CA 90036
Actress V: 04/17/93

Kelly, Paula
c/o Warner Bros. TV
Night Court
4000 Warner Blvd., Office 12A
Burbank, CA 91521
Actress V: 01/03/92

Kelly, Roz
5614 Lemp Ave.
N. Hollywood, CA 91601-1754
Actress V: 05/22/92

Kelman/Arletta Agency
7813 Sunset Blvd.
Los Angeles, CA 90046
Talent Agency V: 03/15/93

Kelsey, Linda
1116 S. Alvera St.
Los Angeles, CA 90035
Actress V: 02/22/92

Kelso, Susan
c/o King Features
216 E. 45th St.
New York, NY 10017
Cartoonist V: 03/11/93

Kemmerling, Warren
6736 Laurel Canyon Blvd. #306
N. Hollywood, CA 91601
Actor V: 05/10/92

Kemp, Jeromy
c/o Marina Martin
6A, Danbury St.
London N1 8JJ, England
Actor V: 02/28/92

Kemp, Sally
c/o Dade&Schultz
11846 Ventura Blvd. #100
Studio City, CA 91604-2620
Actress V: 05/10/92

Kendall, Felicity
c/o Chatto
Prince of Wales Theatre
Coventry St.
London W1V 7FE, England
Actress V: 03/06/93

c/o The Globe Theatre
Shaftsbury Ave.
London W1, England
Alternate V: 03/14/93

Kennedy, George
1900 Ave. of the Stars #2270
Los Angeles, CA 90067
Actor V: 04/01/92

Kennedy, I.F.
RR 2
Cumberland, Ont.
Canada K0A 1SO
War Hero V: 03/24/92

Kennedy, Jayne
151 El Camino
Beverly Hills, CA 90212
Actress V: 03/01/92

Kennedy, Patricia
3971 W. Sixth St., Box #191
Los Angeles, CA 90020
Adult Films V: 02/13/93

c/o 5K Sales
9420 Reseda Blvd., Ste.836
Northridge, CA 91324
Alternate V: 01/17/93

Kennedy, Ted
U.S. Senate Bldg.
Washington, DC 20510
Politician V: 03/10/92

Kennedy Jr., John
1040 5th Ave.
New York, NY 10028
Attorney V: 03/14/93

Kennedy Jr., Robert F.
78 N. Broadway
White Plains, NY 10603
Politician V: 02/17/93

Kenny G
21940 Lamplighter Ln.
Malibu, CA 90265
Entertainer V: 03/26/93

Kensit, Patsy
50 Lissom St.
Unit 1B
London NW1 5DF, England
Actress V: 03/26/93

Kent, Jean
c/o London Mgmt.
235 Regent St.
London W1, England
Actress V: 03/12/92

Kepler, Shell
c/o General Hosp./ABC Inc.
4151 Prospect Ave.
Hollywood, CA 90027
Actress V: 03/01/92

c/o ABC TV-General Hospital
1438 N. Gower St.
Los Angeles, CA 90028
Alternate V: 03/17/92

Kercheval, Ken
P.O. Box 1350
Los Angeles, CA 90078
Actor V: 12/19/92

Kern & Associates
7080 Hollywood Blvd. #1009
Los Angeles, CA 90028
Talent Agency V: 03/02/93

Kerns, Joanna
151 El Camino
Beverly Hills, CA 90212
Actress V: 03/30/93

P.O. Box 56302
Sherman Oaks, CA 90048
Alternate V: 11/11/92

178 N. Carmelina
Los Angeles, CA 90046
L.R.U. V: 12/02/92

Kerns, Sandra
620 Resolano Dr.
Pacific Palisades, CA 90272
Actress V: 05/22/92

Kerr, Deborah
7250 Klosters
Grisons, Switzerland
Actress V: 03/03/93

Viertel, Los Montaros
E-29600 Marbella
Malaga, Spain
Alternate V: 03/02/93

Kerwin, Brian
8428 Melrose Pl. #C
Los Angeles, CA 90069
Actor V: 01/02/92

Kerwin, Joseph P.
c/o NASA LBJ Space Center
Houston, TX 77058
Astronaut V: 03/03/93

Kerwin Agency
1605 N. Cahuenga Blvd. #1009
Los Angeles, CA 90028
Talent Agency V: 03/29/93

Ketcham, Hank
P.O. Box 800
Pebble Beach, CA 90210
Cartoonist V: 05/16/92

512 Pierce St.
Monterey, CA 93940
Alternate V: 05/10/92

78 Rue du Rhone
1204 Geneva
Switzerland
Alternate V: 05/10/92

c/o King Features
216 East 45th St.
New York, NY 10017
Forwarded V: 02/21/93

Kettle, Roger
c/o King Features
216 E. 45th St.
New York, NY 10017
Cartoonist V: 03/11/93

Key, Ted
c/o King Features
216 East 45th St.
New York, NY 10017
Cartoonist V: 03/13/93

1694 Glenhardie Rd.
Wayne, PA 19087
Alternate V: 05/14/92

Key/Fox Pictures
P.O. Box 900
Beverly Hills, CA 90213
Publicity V: 12/15/92

Keyes, Evelyn
c/o Shaw
999 N. Doheny Dr., Ste.506
Los Angeles, CA 90069
Actress V: 05/22/92

1155 N. La Cienega Blvd. #909
Los Angeles, CA 90069
L.R.U. V: 03/03/93

Kidman, Nicole
c/o Odin Productions
4400 Coldwater Canyon Ave. #220
Studio City, CA 91604
Actress V: 03/30/93

Kiel, Richard
500 Grand Ave.
S. Pasadena, CA 91030
Actor V: 04/05/93

6736 Laurel Canyon #302
N. Hollywood, CA 91606
L.R.U. V: 01/02/92

c/o New Generation Ent.
P.O. Box 750
Bathlake, CA 93604
L.R.U. V: 01/02/92

Kilby, Jack
6600 LBJ Freeway Suite 4155
Dallas, TX 75240-6507
Invented Microchip V: 02/01/92

7723 Midbury
Dallas, TX 75230
Forwarded V: 02/10/92

Kiley, Richard
c/o Cosgrove-Meurer Prod.
4303 W. Verdugo Ave.
Burbank, CA 91505
Actor V: 01/09/92

Killebrew, Harmon
P.O. Box 14550
Scottsdale, AZ 85267
Baseball V: 11/26/92

Kilmer, Val
Rt.4, Box 23
Santa Fe, NM 87501
Actor V: 02/02/92

Kilmer, Val, contd
P.O. Box 362
Tesuque, NM 87574
Alternate V: 03/26/93

c/o Starr
350 Park Ave.
New York, NY 10022
Alternate V: 11/16/92

Kimball, Ward
8910 Ardendale Ave.
San Gabriel, CA 91775
Animator V: 03/20/93

Kimbrough, Charles
c/o Warner TV
Murphy Brown
4000 Warner Blvd.
Burbank, CA 91522
Actor V: 03/02/92

Kincaid, Aron
261 S. Robertson Blvd.
Beverly Hills, CA 90211
Actor V: 01/02/92

Kincaid, Aron
13111 Ventura Blvd. #204
Studio City, CA 91604
Forwarded V: 01/02/92

Kind, Diana
8871 Burton Way #303
Los Angeles, CA 90048
Actress V: 05/22/92

Kind, Roslyn
8871 Burton Way #303
Los Angeles, CA 90048
Actress V: 05/22/92

King, Alan
888 7th Ave. #3800
New York, NY 10106
Actor V: 01/05/93

King, Andrea
c/o Willis
1225 Sunset Plaza #3
Los Angeles, CA 90069
Actress V: 05/22/92

King, Ben E.
1301 Princeton Rd.
Teaneck, NJ 07666
Singer V: 05/10/92

King, Ben E., contd
c/o Smiling Clown Music
P.O. Box 1097
Teaneck, NJ 07666
Alternate V: 11/11/92

King, Billie Jean
101 W. 79th St.
New York, NY 10024
Tennis V: 05/22/92

King, Carole
P.O. Box 7308
Carmel, CA 93921
Singer V: 02/01/92

King, Mabel
7100 Teesdale Ave.
N. Hollywood, 91605
Actress V: 04/27/92

King, Perry
3647 Wrightwood Dr.
Studio City, CA 91604
Actor V: 04/01/93

King, Stephen
P.O. Box 1186
Bangor, ME 04401
Author V: 02/12/93

49 Florida Ave.
Bangor, ME 04401
Alternate V: 03/06/93

King, Tony
1333 N. Sweetzer #2G
Los Angeles, CA 90046
Actor V: 06/16/92

King Features
216 East 45th St.
New York, NY 10017
Cartoon Syndicate V: 01/19/93

King World Entertainment
12400 Wilshire Blvd. #1200
Los Angeles, CA 90025
Film Distributor V: 03/17/93

Kings X Band
P.O. Box 968
Katy, TX 77491
Musical Group V: 01/22/92

Kingsley, Ben
c/o Agency
388-396 Oxford St.
London W1, England
Actor V: 04/01/92

Kingsley, Ben, contd
New Penworth House
Stratford Upon Avon
Warwickshire OV3 7QX, England
Alternate V: 03/17/92

Kinkade, Amelia
c/o Young and the Restless
7800 Beverly Blvd.
Beverly Hills, CA 90036
Actress V: 06/15/92

Kinskey, Leonid
11652 Huston St.
North Hollywood, CA 91604
Actor V: 06/15/92

Kinski, Natassja
11 W. 81st St.
New York, NY 10024
Actress V: 03/18/93

Kirchenbauer, Bill
4850 Riverton Ave.
N. Hollywood, CA 91607
Actor V: 04/01/93

Kirk, Phyllis
125 Sunset Plaza Dr. #1
Los Angeles, CA 90069
Actress V: 04/27/92

Kirk, Tommy
833 S. Beacon Ave.
Los Angeles, CA 90017
Actor V: 06/16/91

Kirkland, Sally
292 S. La Cienga Blvd. #315
Beverly Hills, CA 90211
Actress V: 03/22/93

1930 Ocean Ave. #11
Santa Monica, CA 90405
L.R.U. V: 06/01/92

Kirkpatrick, Jeane
6812 Granby St.
Bethesda, MD 20817
Diplomat V: 04/20/92

Kiser, Terry
c/o Warner Bros. TV
Night Court
4000 Warner Blvd., Office 12A
Burbank, CA 91521
Actor V: 01/12/92

Kissinger, Henry
c/o Strategic Study
1800 K St. NW Ste.#1021
Washington, DC 20006
Politician V: 03/02/93

c/o Kissinger Assoc. Inc.
350 Park Ave.
New York, NY 10022-6022
Alternate V: 04/01/92

c/o River House
435 E. 52nd St.
New York, NY 10022
Forwarded V: 03/17/93

Kitaen, Tawny
c/o Agency
151 El Camino
Beverly Hills, CA 90212
Actress V: 02/12/92

9255 Doheny Rd. Ste.2501
Los Angeles, CA 90069
L.R.U. V: 02/18/92

Kitt, Eartha
c/o Agency
40 W. 57th St.
New York, NY 10019
Actress V: 11/11/92

Kjar Agency
10653 Riverside Dr.
Toluca Lake, CA 91602
Talent Agency V: 03/05/93

Klasky/Csupo Prod.
1258 N. Highland Ave.
Hollywood, CA 90038
Cartoonist V: 02/04/92

Klein, Calvin
205 W. 39th St.
New York, NY 10018
Designer V: 01/16/92

55 Central Park West. #19F
New York, NY 10023
L.R.U. V: 12/15/92

Klein, Robert
c/o Conversation Co.
Edgehill Sleepy Hollow Rd.
Briarcliff Manor, NY 10510
Actor V: 04/02/92

c/o Conversation Co.
70 Middleneck Rd. #7
Great Neck, NY 11021
Alternate V: 07/02/92

Klemperer, Werner
44 W. 62nd St. 10th Fl.
New York. NY 10023
Actor V: 03/27/93

1229 Horn Ave.
Los Angeles, CA 90069
Alternate V: 03/21/92

Kline, Richard
14322 Mulholland Dr.
Los Angeles, CA 90077
Actor V: 04/01/93

Klous, Pat
18096 Karen Dr.
Encino, CA 91316
Actress V: 04/27/92

Klugman, Jack
22548 Pacific Coast Hwy. #110
Malibu, CA 90265
Actor V: 03/19/93

Knapp, Charles
c/o Schwartz
8749 Sunset Blvd.
Los Angeles, CA 90069
Actor V: 03/01/93

Knef, Hildegard
c/o Agentur Lentz
Holbeinstr. 4
D-(W) 8000 Munchen 80, Germany
Singer V: 01/17/93

Maria-Theresia-Str.
800 Munchen-Bogenhausen
Germany
Alternate V: 04/27/92

Knight, Edmond
9 Cork St.
London W1X 1PD, England
Actor V: 02/01/93

Knight, Esmond
52 Cranmere Ct.
London SW3, England
Actor V: 03/01/93

Knight, Holly
1585 Stone Canyon Rd.
Los Angeles, CA 90077
Actress V: 04/27/92

Knight, Shirley
P.O. Box 69405
Los Angeles, CA 90069
Actress V: 01/02/92

Knight, Summer
c/o Five K Sales Co.
9420 Reseda Blvd., #836
Northridge, CA 91324
Adult Films V: 03/03/93

Knight-Pulliam, Keisha
P.O. Box 866
Teaneck, NJ 07666
Actress V: 04/27/92

Knittel, Luise Rainer
Vico-Morcotte 6911
Switzerland
Actress V: 01/19/92

Knokem, Heinz
Ahornweg 7
D-4505 Bad Ibure, Germany
Knights Cross V: 03/17/92

Knotts, Don
1854 S. Beverly Glen #402
Los Angeles, CA 90025
Actor V: 05/22/92

Knox, Alexander
388 Oxford St.
London W1, England
Actor V: 02/13/93

8 Harley St.
London W1N 2AB, England
Alternate V: 05/20/92

Knox, Elyse
c/o Harmon
320 N. Gunston
Los Angeles, CA 90049
Actress V: 04/27/92

Kober, Jeff
151 El Camino
Beverly Hills, CA 90212
Actor V: 09/18/92

Koch, Howard
5555 Melrose Ave. Ste.3000
Los Angeles, CA 90038-3197
Producer V: 01/20/92

Koch Talent Agency
1783 Westwood Blvd.
Los Angeles, CA 90024
Talent Agency V: 03/26/93

Koenig, Walter
P.O. Box 4395
N. Hollywoods, CA 91607
Actor V: 04/12/92

Koenig, Walter, contd
Kohner Inc.
9169 Sunset Blvd.
Los Angeles, CA 90069
Talent Agency V: 02/14/93

Koontz, Dean R.
P.O. Box 5686
Orange, CA 92613-5686
Author V: 03/02/93

Kopell, Bernie
19413 Olivos Dr.
Tarzana, CA 91356
Actor V: 06/16/92

Kopins, Karen
10989 Bluffside Dr.
Studio City, CA 91604-4400
Actress V: 04/27/92

Koppel, Ted
c/o ABC-TV/Nightline
1717 DeSales St. NW
Washington, DC 20036
Correspondant V: 03/19/93

Korman, Harvey
1136 Stradella Rd.
Los Angeles, CA 90049
Actor V: 06/16/92

Korot, Alla
c/o NBC-TV
Another World
79 Madison Ave., 5th Fl.
New York, NY 91523
Actress V: 06/15/92

Koshiroe, Matsumoto
c/o Kabukiza Theatre
12 15-4 Ginza
Chuoku, Tokyo 104 Japan
Kabuki Actor V: 03/20/93

Koslow, Lauren
c/o Bell-Phillip Prod.
Bold & Beautiful
7800 Beverly Blvd., Ste.3371
Los Angeles, CA 90036
Actress V: 06/15/92

Koslow-Schillace, Zach
c/o Bell-Phillip Prod.
Bold & Beautiful
7800 Beverly Blvd., Ste.3371
Los Angeles, CA 90036
Actor V: 06/15/92

Kotzky, Alex
c/o King Features
216 East 45th St.
New York, NY 10017
Cartoonist V: 02/16/92

Koury, Rex
5370 Happy Pines Dr.
Foresthill, CA 95631
Songwriter V: 09/18/92

Kove, Martin
2150 Sunset crest Dr.
Los Angeles, CA 90046
Actor V: 09/18/92

8705 Wonderland Park
Los Angeles, CA 90046
Alternate V: 04/06/93

c/o The Agency
10351 Santa Monica Blvd.
Los Angeles, CA 90025
Alternate V: 03/17/92

Kozack, Harley Jane
8730 Sunset Blvd. #480
Los Angeles, CA 90069
Actress V: 04/27/92

Kozlowski, Linda
1472 Rising Glen Rd.
Los Angeles, CA 90069
Actress V: 06/13/92

Krabbe, Katrin
Am Oberbach 10
D-(0) 2000 Neubrandenburg
Germany
Athlete V: 02/01/93

Kramer, Stanley
12386 Ridge Circle
Los Angeles, CA 90049
Director V: 02/11/93

c/o Columbia Pictures
Columbia Plaza
Burbank, CA 91505
Forwarded V: 01/05/92

Kramer, Stepfanie
c/o William Morris
151 El Camino Dr.
Beverly Hills, CA 90212
Actress V: 03/20/93

8455 Beverly Blvd. #505
Los Angeles, CA 90048-3416
Alternate V: 04/27/92

Krebbs, John
c/o Diamond Ridge
3232 Amoruso Way
Amoruso, CA 95747
Race Driver V: 03/12/93

Krofft, Sid & Marty
1040 N. Las Palmas Ave.
Hollywood, CA 90038
Puppeteers V: 01/12/92

7710 Woodrow Wilson Dr.
Los Angeles, CA 90046
L.R.U. V: 05/20/92

Krueger, Kirsten
c/o Dallas Cowboys
One Cowboys Parkway
Irving, TX 75063-4045
Cheerleader V: 08/08/92

Kruger, Pit
Geleitstr. 10
D-(W) 6000 Frankfurter/Main
70 Germany
Actor V: 01/17/93

Kruglov & Associates
7060 Hollywood Blvd. #1220
Los Angeles, CA 90028
Talent Agency V: 03/17/93

Kubrick, Stanley
P.O. Box 123
Borehamwood, Herts, England
Director V: 03/20/93

Kulwicki, Alan
c/o Kulwicki Racing
6007 Victory Lane
Harrisburg, NC 28075
NASCAR Driver V: 03/02/92

Kumagai, Denice
c/o Warner Bros. TV
Night Court
4000 Warner Blvd., Office 12A
Burbank, CA 91521
Actress V: 01/12/92

Kupcinet, Kari
c/o CBS TV
7800 Beverly Blvd.
Los Angeles, CA 90036
Actress V: 11/11/92

Kurosawa, Akira
Seijo 2-21-6, Setagaja-ku
Tokyo 157, Japan
Director V: 03/17/93

Kuter, Kay E.
5331 Denny Ave.
N. Hollywood, CA 91601
Actor V: 02/17/92

Kwan, Nancy
Contemporary Artists
132 Lasky Dr.
Beverly Hills, CA 90212
Actress V: 04/02/92

4154 Woodman Ave.
Sherman Oaks, CA 91403
Alternate V: 03/27/93

Kwouk, Burt
235-241 Regent St.
London W1A 2JT, England
Actor V: 03/17/93

Kyle, Rote
1175 York Ave.
New York, NY 10021
Football V: 05/14/92

L

L.A. Artists Talent Agency
2566 Overland Ave. #550
Los Angeles, CA 90064
Talent Agency V: 03/04/93

L.A. LAW
20th Century Fox TV
P.O. Box 900
Bldg. 89, Room 3037
Beverly Hills, CA 90213
Production Comapny V: 03/26/93

L.A. Models
8335 Sunset Blvd.
Los Angeles, CA 90069
Model/Talent Agency V: 03/29/93

L.A. Press Club
480 Riverside Dr.
Burbank, CA 91506
Production Company V: 03/17/93

L.A. Sports Talent Agency
2121 Ave. of the Stars 6th Fl.
Los Angeles, CA 90067
Talent Agency V: 03/13/93

L.A. Talent
8335 Sunset Blvd.
Los Angeles, CA 90069
Talent Agency V: 03/29/93

LATE NIGHT

NBC/David Letterman
30 Rockefeller Plaza
New York, NY 10112
Production Company V: 03/26/93

LATER WITH BOB COSTAS

NBC Productions
888 7th Ave., 30th Fl.
New York, NY 10106
Production Company V: 03/26/93

LAW & ORDER

c/o Witt/Thomas
Law & Order
100 Universal City Plaza, Bl.G
Universal City, CA 91608
Production Company V: 01/12/92

Wolf Films
In assoc w/Universal
Universal City, CA 91608
Alternate V: 03/26/93

LET'S MAKE A DEAL

c/o Disney Prod.
Monte Hall
Bungalow 2
Lake Buena Vista, FL 32830
Production Company V: 06/15/92

LOCAL HEROES

Paramount
5555 Melrose Ave.
Bow Building, Room 115
Los Angeles, CA 90038
Production Company V: 03/23/93

LOVE AND WAR

Shukovsky/English Ent.
4024 Radford Ave.
Administration Build., Ste. 330
Studio City, CA 91604
Production Company V: 03/14/93

LW 1 Inc.,

8383 Wilshire Blvd. #649
Beverly Hills, CA 90211
Talent Agency V: 03/19/93

La Rue, Lash

P.O. Box 2484
Sanford, NC 27330
Actor V: 02/15/92

7052 Quail Hill Rd.
Charlotte, NC 28210
Alternate V: 03/12/92

LaLanne, Jack

c/o Befit Ent.
P.O. Box 1249
Burbank, CA 91507-1249
Fitness Expert V: 01/17/92

c/o Befit Ent.
P.O. Box 1023
San Louis Obispo, CA 93406
Alternate V: 05/10/92

LaRue, Bobbie

c/o Dallas Cowboys
One Cowboys Parkway
Irving, TX 75063-4945
Cheerleader V: 08/08/92

Labonte, Terry

c/o Davis Racing
11 N. Robbins St.
Thomasville, NC 27360
NASCAR Driver V: 03/02/92

Lacamara, Carlos

c/o Nurses
500 S. Buena Vista St.
Burbank, CA 91521
Actor V: 11/11/92

Lacey, Ronald

c/o Edwards
275 Kennington Rd.
London SE1 6BY, England
Actor V: 03/17/93

Ladd, Cheryl

P.O. Box 1329
Santa Ynez, CA 93460-1329
Actress V: 03/02/92

9051 Oriole Way
Los Angeles, CA 90069
L.R.U. V: 01/21/92

Ladd, Diane

c/o Gladys M. Hart
1244 11th St. #A
Santa Monica, CA 90401
Actress V: 11/11/92

12214 Viewcrest Rd.
Studio City, CA 91604
Alternate V: 03/01/93

Lafontaine, Pat

c/o Buffalo Sabres
Memorial Aud
Buffalo, NY 14202
Hockey V: 11/20/92

Lahti, Christine
927 Berkeley St.
Santa Monica, CA 90403-2307
Actress V: 03/02/92

Laine, Cleo
c/o International Artistes
235 Regent St. Mezz. Fl.
London, W1R 8AX, England
Singer V: 03/20/92

Old Rectory, Wavendon
Milton Keys MK17 8LT, England
Alternate V: 03/02/92

Laine, Frankie
14322 Califa
Van Nuys, CA 91401
Singer V: 05/22/92

Lakin, Christine
c/o ABC-TV Step by Step
2040 Ave. of the Stars
Los Angeles, CA 90067
Actress V: 04/27/92

Lamarr, Hedy
568 Orange Dr. #47
Altamonte Springs, FL 32701
Actress V: 03/27/93

Lamas, Lorenzo
c/o Casa Cleon
5261 Cleon Ave.
N. Hollywood, CA 91601
Actor V: 08/15/92

6100 Wilshire Blvd. #400
Beverly Hills, CA 90211
Alternate V: 05/04/92

230 Park Ave., 5th Fl.
New York, NY 10169
Alternate V: 05/04/92

641 S. Mariposa Dr.
Burbank, CA 91506
Alternate V: 03/27/93

7800 Beverly Blvd.
Los Angeles, CA 90036
Forwarded V: 03/10/92

2419 Burbank Blvd.
Woodland Hills, CA 91367
L.R.U. V: 01/02/92

Lamour, Dorothy
5309 Goodland Ave.
N. Hollywood, CA 91607
Actress V: 04/04/92

Lamparski, Richard
924-D Garden St.
Santa Barbara, CA 93101
Author V: 03/27/93

Lampton, Dr. Michael
Space Science Lab/UC Berkley
Berkley, CA 94720
Astronaut V: 04/16/92

NASA/LBJ Space Center
Houston, TX 77058
Alternate V: 01/19/92

Lancaster, Burt
P.O. Box 67-B-38
Los Angeles, CA 90067
Actor V: 03/27/93

2220 Ave. of the Stars #1805
Los Angeles, CA 90067
Alternate V: 04/20/92

8966 Sunset Blvd.
Los Angeles, CA 90069
L.R.U. V: 01/02/92

Landau, Martin
7455 Palo Vista Dr.
Los Angeles, CA 90046
Actor V: 03/19/93

Lander, David
7009 W. Senalda Rd.
Los Angeles, CA 90069
Actor V: 06/16/92

Landers, Ann
435 N. Michigan Ave.
Chicago, IL 60611
Columnist V: 01/14/92

401 Wabash Ave.
Chicago, IL 60611
Forwarded V: 01/23/92

Landers, Audrey
1913 N. Beverly Dr.
Beverly Hills, CA 90210
Actress V: 06/16/92

Landers, Judy
1913 N. Beverly Dr.
Beverly Hills, CA 90210
Actress V: 04/16/92

c/o Niedenfuer
9849 Denbigh
Beverly Hills, CA 90210
Alternate V: 04/27/92

Landis, John
7920 Sunset Blvd. 6th Fl.
Los Angeles, CA 90046
Director V: 03/01/93

Lando, Brian
c/o Columbia/Mozark
Designing Women
Columbia Plaza, Prod.Bl.8, #147
Burbank, CA 91505
Forwarded V: 02/03

Landsburg, Valerie
22745 Chamera Lane
Los Angeles, CA 90290
Actress V: 04/27/92

Lane, Abbe
444 N. Faring Rd.
Los Angeles, CA 90077
Actress V: 05/16/92

Lane, Cleo
Old Rectory
Wavedon
Mil Key MK17 8LT, England
Singer V: 02/10/93

Lane, Dick
18100 Meyers
Detroit, MI 48235
Football V: 01/09/92

Lane, Frankie
352 San Gregorio St.
San Diego, CA 91106
Singer V: 01/09/92

Lane, Priscilla
Howards Grove
Derry, NH 03038
Actress V: 03/02/92

RR1, North Shore Rd.
Derry, NH 03038
Alternate V: 04/27/92

Lane Talent Agency
13455 Ventura Blvd. #214
Sherman Oaks, CA 91423
Talent Agency V: 03/04/93

Lang, June
c/o Morgan
12756 Kahlenberg Lane
N. Hollywood, CA 91607
Actress V: 04/27/92

Lang, Katherine Kelly
317 S. Carmelina Ave.
Los Angeles, Ca 90049
Actress V: 03/02/92

c/o CBS-TV/Bold & Beautiful
7800 Beverly Blvd., Ste.3371
Los Angeles, CA 90036
Forwarded V: 12/19/92

Langdon, Sue Ane
24115 Long Valley Rd.
Hidden Hills, CA 91302
Actress V: 10/10/92

c/o ABC-TV
General Hospital
4151 Prospect Ave.
Hollywood, CA 90027
Alternate V: 06/15/92

Lange, Heinz
12 Ferdinand-Strucker Strasse
D-5060 Berg., Gladbach 1
(Bensberg) Germany
Actor V: 02/05/92

Lange, Hope
c/o Hollerith
803 Bramble Way
Los Angeles, CA 90049
Actress V: 02/13/92

320 Skyeway
Los Angeles, CA 90049
L.R.U. V: 07/03/92

Lange, Jessica
9830 Wilshire Blvd.
Beverly Hills, CA 90212
Actress V: 03/01/93

1720 Kaweah Dr.
Pasadena, CA 91105
Alternate V: 03/15/92

Langella, Frank
1999 Ave. of the Stars, #2850
Los Angeles, CA 90067
Actor V: 02/18/93

Langenkamp, Heather
1999 Ave. of the Stars #2850
Los Angeles, CA 90067
Actress V: 10/10/92

Langford, Frances
P.O. Box 96
Jensen Beach, FL 33457
Singer V: 02/01/92

Langley, Elmo
c/o Nascar
1811 Volusia Ave.
Daytona Beach, FL 32015
Race Driver *V: 03/12/93*

Lanier, Monique
c/o Warner Bros. TV
Life Goes On
4000 Warner Blvd.
Burbank, CA 91522
Actress *V: 12/18/92*

Lansbury, Angela
7800 Beverly Blvd.
Los Angeles, CA 90036
Actress *V: 01/04/92*

635 N. Bonhill Rd.
Los Angeles, CA 90049-2301
Alternate *V: 05/13/92*

c/o Universal Television
"Murder She Wrote"
100 Univ. City Plz., Bldg.507
Universal City, CA 91608
Forwarded *V: 03/02/92*

Lantz, Walter
6311 Romaine St.
Hollywood, CA 90038
Cartoonist *V: 01/05/92*

4444 Lakeside Dr. #310
Burbank, CA 91505
Alternate *V: 03/02/92*

Lantz Office
888 Seventh Ave. #2500
New York, NY 10106
Talent Agency *V: 03/20/93*

Larroquette, John
P.O. Box 6303
Malibu, CA 90264
Actor *V: 04/01/92*

c/o Warner Bros. TV
"Night Court"
4000 Warner Blvd., Office 12A
Burbank, CA 91521
Alternate *V: 01/12/92*

Larsen, Don
17090 Copper Hill
Morgan Hill, CA 95037
Baseball *V: 03/12/92*

Larson, Jack
449 Skyewiay Rd. N.
Los Angeles, CA 90049
Actor *V: 02/22/92*

c/o Skyewiay Prod.
9336 W. Washington Blvd.
Culver City, CA 90230
Alternate *V: 01/21/92*

Larson, Wolf
10600 Holman Ave. #1
Los Angeles, CA 90024
Celebrity *V: 05/10/92*

Larue, Florence
4300 Louise Ave.
Encino, CA 91316
Actress *V: 04/27/92*

Larue, Lash
9145 Hinson Dr.
Matthews, NC 28105
Actor *V: 03/27/93*

Lasorda, Tommy
1000 Elysian Park Ave.
Los Angeles, CA 90012
Baseball *V: 02/21/92*

Lasser, Louise
200 E. 71st St. #20C
New York, NY 10021
Actress *V: 05/20/92*

Lasswell, Fred
c/o King Features
216 East 45th St.
New York, NY 10017
Cartoonist *V: 04/23/92*

Lau, Lawrence
c/o NBC-TV/Another World
30 Rockefeller Plaza
New York, NY 10122
Actor *V: 01/21/92*

Lauder, Estee
767 5th Ave.
New York, NY 10153
Executive *V: 03/01/93*

Lauer, Andrew
c/o Gersch
232 N. Canon Dr.
Beverly Hills, CA 90210
Actor *V: 11/26/92*

Laughlin, Tom
20933 Big Rock Dr.
Malibu, CA 90265
Actor V: 03/27/93

Lauper, Cyndi
853 7th Ave. #9-D
New York, NY 10019
Singer V: 03/01/92

c/o Premier Talent
3 E. 54th St.
New York, NY 10022
Alternate V: 04/01/92

Lauria, Dan
1420 N. Alta Vista
Los Angeles, CA 90046
Actor V: 02/02/92

c/o New World TV
The Wonder Years
1440 S. Sepulveda Blvd.
Los Angeles, CA 90025
Forwarded V: 12/11/92

Laurie, Piper
907 12th St. #4
Santa Monica, CA 90403
Actress V: 02/02/92

c/o Wizan/Black Films
Warner Bros. Ltd.
4000 Warner Blvd.
Burbank, CA 91522
Forwarded V: 01/20/93

Lavi, Daliah
Postfach 300 348
5000 Koln 30, Germany
Actress V: 07/01/92

Lavin, Linda
4000 Warner Blvd.
Burbank, CA 91522
Actress V: 03/17/92

20781 Big Rock Rd.
Malibu, CA 90265
Alternate V: 06/20/92

27 E. 87th St.
New York, NY 10128
L.R.U. V: 12/12/92

Law, John Philip
1339 Miller Dr.
Los Angeles, CA 90069
Actor V: 03/02/92

Lawless, Rick
c/o Hermans Head
500 S. Buena Vista St.
Burbank, CA 91521
Actor V: 11/11/92

Lawley Jr., William R.
3547 Dalraida Ct.
Montgomery, AL 36109
Medal of Honor V: 02/01/92

Lawrence, Carol
P.O. Box 1895
Studio City, CA 91604-0895
Actress V: 02/13/92

12337 Ridge Circle
Los Angeles, CA 90049
Alternate V: 04/27/92

c/o ABC-TV
General Hospital
4151 Prospect Ave.
Hollywood, CA 90027
Alternate V: 06/15/92

Lawrence, Danny
c/o Childress
P.O. Box 1189 Industrial Dr.
Welcome, NC 27374
Race Crew V: 03/12/93

Lawrence, Elizabeth
c/o ABC-TV/All My Children
101 W. 67th St.
New York, NY 10023
Actress V: 01/17/92

Lawrence, Joey
c/o Blossom
500 S. Buena Vista St.
Burbank, CA 91521
Actor V: 11/11/92

Lawrence, Marc
14016 Bora Bora Way #19
Marina Del Rey, CA 90291
Actor V: 06/16/92

Lawrence, Steve
Stage 2 Productions
P.O. Box 5140
Beverly Hills, CA 90210
Actor V: 03/07/92

Lawrence, Vickie
6000 Lido Ln.
Long Beach, CA 90803
Actress V: 01/04/92

5855 Naples Plaza #217
Long Beach, CA 90803
L.R.U. V: 07/01/92

Lawrence Agency
3575 Cahuenga Blvd. West. #125
Los Angeles, CA 90068
Talent Agency V: 04/15/93

Lawson, Twiggy
c/o Shulman
4 St. George's House
15 Hanover Square
London W1R 9AJ, England
Actress/Model V: 03/06/93

1920 Los Encinos Ave.
Glendale, CA 91203
L.R.U. V: 12/01/92

Laye, Evelyn
109 Jermyn St.
London SW1, England
Actress V: 03/01/92

Lazenby, George
30066 Longview Ave.
Jupiter Hills, CA 93533
Actor V: 07/20/93

1127 21st St. #2
Santa Monica, CA 90402
Alternate V: 03/27/93

Le Beau, Becky
505 S. Beverly Dr. Ste 973
Beverly Hills, CA 90212
Actress V: 03/26/93

Le Blanc, Christian
c/o MGM/UA Comm.
In the Heat of the Night
1000 W. Washington Blvd.
Culver City, CA 90232
Actor V: 01/07/92

Le Brock, Kelly
P.O. Box 727
Los Olivos, CA 93441-0727
Actress V: 02/21/92

Le Doux, Harold
c/o King Features
216 East 45th St.
New York, NY 10017
Cartoonist V: 04/19/92

Le Grand, Michel
c/o Nat Shapiro
157 W. 57th St.
New York, NY 10019
Composer V: 01/04/92

Le Mat, Paul
1100 N. Alta Loma #805
Los Angeles, CA 90069
Actor V: 04/06/93

Le Roy, Gloria
3500 W. Olive Ave. #1400
Burbank, CA 91505
Actress V: 06/01/92

LeGuin, Ursula K.
c/o Virginia Kidd
Box 278
Milford, PA 18337
Writer V: 03/20/93

LeHane, Denis
c/o Totten Prod.
19548 Vose St.
Reseda, CA 91335
Actor V: 01/02/92

LeHane, Denis
c/o Whitaker Agency
12725 Ventura Bl., Ste.F
Studio City, CA 91604
Actor V: 11/11/92

LeMat, Paul
160 Alta Loma Rd. #805
W. Hollywood, CA 90069
Actor V: 05/10/92

LeRoy, Jennifer
c/o Playboy Promotions
8560 Sunset Blvd.
Los Angeles, CA 90069
Model V: 01/30/93

Leach, Robin
875 3rd Ave. #1800
New York, NY 10022
Celebrity V: 03/02/92

Leachman, Cloris
13127 Boca de Canyon Ln.
Los Angeles, CA 90049
Actress V: 06/01/92

Lear, Norman
1999 Ave. of the Stars #500
Los Angeles, CA 90067
Producer V: 03/01/93

Learned, Michael
8966 Sunset Blvd.
Hollywood, CA 90069
Actress V: 01/11/92

145 Central Park W.
New York, NY 10023
L.R.U. V: 06/01/92

Leary, Timothy
10106 Sunbrook
Beverly Hills, CA 90210
60's Guru V: 09/02/92

Lederer, Francis
23134 Sherman Way
Canoga Park, CA 91307
Actor V: 06/16/92

P.O. Box 32
Canoga Park, CA 91305
Actor V: 04/06/93

Lee, Anna
c/o Andy Ronson
868 W. Knoll Dr.
Los Angeles, CA 90069
Actress V: 03/02/92

c/o Nathan
1240 N. Doheny
Los Angeles, CA 90069
Alternate V: 04/27/92

c/o General Hosp./ABC Inc.
4151 Prospect Ave.
Hollywood, CA 90027
Alternate V: 03/01/92

1240 N. Doheny Dr.
Los Angeles, CA 90069
Forwarded V: 01/29/92

c/o Genral Hospital ABC-TV
1438 N. Gower
Los Angeles, CA 90028
L.R.U. V: 06/01/92

Lee, Brenda
2174 Carson St.
Nashville, TN 37210
Singer V: 05/10/92

2174 Carson St.
Nashville, TN 37210
Singer V: 04/27/92

Lee, Christopher
9000 Sunset Blvd. #315
Beverly Hills, CA 90210
Actor V: 01/15/92

Lee, Christopher, contd
151 S. El Camino Dr.
Beverly Hills, CA 90212
L.R.U. V: 01/02/92

Lee, Gordon Porky
950 W. 103rd Pl. #202D
Denver, CO 80221
Actor V: 04/15/92

Lee, Hyapatia
15127 Califa St.
Van Nuys, CA 91314
Actress V: 02/23/93

P.O. Box 1924
Indianapolis, IN 46206
Alternate V: 02/13/93

c/o 5K Sales
9420 Reseda Blvd. #836
Northridge, CA 91325
Forwarded V: 02/13/93

P.O. Box 39437
Rochester, NY 14064
L.R.U. V: 07/01/92

Lee, Mark C.
c/o NASA
LBJ Space Center
Houston, TX 77058
Astronaut V: 01/31/93

Lee, Michele
c/o Michele Lee Prod.
11355 W. Olympic Blvd., Ste.500
Los Angeles, CA 90064
Actress V: 11/01/92

830 Birchwood Dr.
Los Angeles, CA 90024
Alternate V: 01/10/92

c/o Pierosh
114 Magnolia Dr.
Levittown, PA 19054
Forwarded V: 03/30/93

c/o CBS-TV Knots Landing
7800 Beverly Blvd.
Los Angeles, CA 90036
Forwarded V: 04/05/93

Lee, Peggy
11404 Bellagio Rd.
Los Angeles, CA 90049
Singer/Actress V: 01/07/92

Lee, Ricky
c/o KY Headhunters
192 Ridge Crest Drive
Goodlettsville, TN 37072
Celebrity V: 03/26/93

Lee, Ruta
2623 Laurel Canyon Rd.
Los Angeles, CA 90046
Actress V: 01/25/92

Lee, Spike
c/o Forty Acres & A Mule
124 DeKalb Ave.
Brooklyn, NY 11217
Director V: 02/13/92

Lee, Stan
c/o King Features
216 East 45th St.
New York, NY 10017
Cartoonist V: 03/10/93

c/o Marvel Comics
387 Park Ave. South
New York, NY 10016
Alternate V: 02/12/92

Lee, Tommy
4970 Summit View Dr.
Westlake Village, CA 91362
Actor V: 04/06/93

Lee & Associates
8235 Santa Monica Blvd. #202
Los Angeles, CA 90046
Talent Agency V: 03/29/93

Leestma, David C.
c/o NASA
LBJ Space Center
Houston, TX 77058
Astronaut V: 01/31/92

Lehman, Edie
c/o General Hosp./ABC Inc.
4151 Prospect Ave.
Hollywood, CA 90027
Actress V: 03/01/92

Leigh, Janet
1625 Summit Ridge Dr.
Beverly Hills, CA 90210
Actress V: 05/22/92

Leigh, Jennifer Jason
335 N. Maple Dr. #254
Beverly Hills, CA 90210
Actress V: 03/01/93

Leigh, Jennifer Jason, contd
2400 Whitman Place
Los Angeles, CA 90068
Alternate V: 01/21/92

Leisure, David
c/o Empty Nest
500 S. Buena Vista St.
Burbank, CA 91521
Actor V: 11/11/92

Lemke, Cheryl
c/o The Weather Channel
2600 Cumberland Prky.
Atlanta, GA 30339
Commentator V: 01/27/93

Lemmon, Jack
c/o Jalem Prod.
141 El Camino Dr., Ste.201
Beverly Hills, CA 90212
Actor V: 02/12/92

Lenard, Mark
845 Via de la Paz Ste.A234
Pacific Palisades, CA 90272
Actor V: 03/10/92

1742 Palisades Dr.
Pacific Palisades, CA 90272
L.R.U. V: 02/25/93

Lennie, Angus
c/o Jean Drysdale
15 Pembroke Gardens
London W8, England
Actor V: 02/17/93

Lennon Sisters
944 Harding Ave.
Venice, CA 90291
Singers V: 03/02/92

P.O. Box 1492
Birmingham, NY 13902
Alternate V: 03/02/92

3230 Corinth Ave.
Los Angeles, CA 90006
Forwarded V: 03/02/92

Lennox, Annie
P.O. Box 245
London N8 9OG, England
Singer V: 05/16/92

Leno, Jay
1151 Tower Dr.
Beverly Hills, CA 90210
Comedian V: 05/15/92

Leno, Jay, contd
c/o General Mngmt. Grp.
9000 Sunset Blvd. #400
Los Angeles, CA 90069
Alternate V: 02/12/92

c/o NBC Prod.
'The Tonight Show'
3000 W. Alameda Ave.
Burbank, CA 91523
Forwarded V: 01/10/92

Lenoir, William
c/o NASA
LBJ Space Center
Houston, TX 77058
Astronaut V: 01/19/92

Lenz, Kay
c/o Gage Group
9255 Sunset Blvd.
Los Angeles, CA 90069
Actress V: 02/10/92

5930 Manola Way
Los Angeles, CA 90068
Alternate V: 04/21/92

Leonard, Lu
12245 Chandler Blvd. #302
N. Hollywood, CA 91607
Actress V: 04/27/92

Leonard, Sugar Ray
13916 King George Way
Upper Marlboro, MD 20772-5950
Boxing V: 03/30/93

Leslie, Joan
c/o Caldwell
2228 N. Catalena St.
Los Angeles, CA 90027
Actress V: 04/21/92

Lester, Tom
P.O. Box 1854
Beverly Hills, CA 90213
Actor V: 05/23/92

Letterman, David
c/o CBS-Ed Sullivan Theatre
1697 Broadway
New York, NY 10019
Celebrity V: 03/19/93

c/o CBS-TV
7800 Beverly Blvd.
Los Angeles, CA 90036
Alternate V: 11/26/92

Leverington, Shelby
11325 Morrison St. #211
N. Hollywood, CA 91607
Actress V: 04/27/92

Levin, Ira
c/o HOA
40 E. 49th St.
New York, NY 10017
Author V: 02/18/92

Levin Agency
9255 Sunset Blvd. #401
W. Hollywood, CA 90069
Talent Agency V: 03/17/93

Lewis, Al
575 Main St. #203
Roosevelt Island, NY 10044
Actor V: 01/02/92

14755 Hartsook St.
Van Nuys, CA 91403
L.R.U. V: 01/02/92

Lewis, Carl
P.O. Box 57-1990
Houston, TX 77257-1990
Personality V: 05/10/92

Lewis, Daniel Day
151 El Camino Dr.
Beverly Hills, CA 90210
Actor V: 12/17/92

65 Connaught St.
London W2, England
Alternate V: 03/04/92

c/o Julian Belfrage
60 St. James St.
London SW1, England
Forwarded V: 06/16/92

Lewis, Huey
P.O. Box 819
Mill Valley, CA 94942
Singer V: 03/30/92

Lewis, Jerry
1701 Waldman Ave.
Las Vegas, NV 89102
Actor V: 01/02/92

Lewis, Jerry Lee
c/o Kerrie Enterprise
P.O. Box 84
Nesbit, MS 38651
Singer V: 02/12/92

Lewis, Jerry Lee, contd
P.O. Box 3864
Memphis, TN 38103
 Alternate V: 02/13/92

Lewis, Joe
c/o Precision Prod.
Hwy.16, P.O. Box 569
Denver, NC 28037
 Race Transport V: 03/12/93

Lewis, Monica
c/o Lang
606 Mountain Dr.
Beverly Hills, CA 90210
 Singer V: 05/13/92

Lewis, Shari
603 N. Alta Dr.
Beverly Hills, CA 90210
 Ventriloquist V: 01/21/92

Lewis, Tony
c/o LA & HA Enterprises
19528 Ventura Blvd. Ste.289
Tarzana, CA 91356
 Writer V: 03/10/92

**Library of Congress
Washington, DC 20540**
 Archive V: 03/20/93

Lichtman Company
12456 Ventura Blvd., Ste.1
Studio City, CA 91604
 Talent Agency V: 03/17/93

Liddy, G. Gordon
9909 E. Joshoa Tree Ln.
Scottsdale, AZ 85253
 Actor V: 06/14/92

9113 Sunset Blvd.
Los Angeles, CA 90069
 L.R.U. V: 07/01/92

Life In Hell Cartoon Co.
2219 Main St., #E
Santa Monica, CA 90405
 Cartoonist V: 01/13/92

Lifetime Network
36-12 35th Ave.
Astoria, NY 11106
 Network HQ V: 03/01/93

10880 Wilshire Blvd. #2010
Los Angeles, CA 90024
 Alternate V: 03/17/93

Light, Judith
3960 Laurel Canyon Blvd. #280
Studio City, CA 91604
 Actress V: 05/16/92

3410 Wrightview Dr.
Studio City, CA 91604
 Alternate V: 01/27/92

1122 S. Robertson Blvd.
Los Angeles, CA 90035
 Alternate V: 04/21/92

c/o Who's the Boss
1438 N. Gower Blvd.
Los Angeles, CA 90028
 Forwarded V: 12/01/92

Light Agency
6404 Wilshire Blvd. Ste.900
Los Angeles, CA 90048
 Talent Agency V: 02/12/92

Light Company
1148 4th St., Ste. 900
Santa Monica, CA 90403
 Talent Agency V: 01/26/93

Lightfoot, Gordon
1365 Yong St. #207
Toronto, Ontario, Canada
 Singer V: 01/28/92

Lillie, Beatrice
Peel Fold, Mill Lane
Henley-on-Thames, Oxon.
England
 Actress V: 01/03/93

Lim, Pik-Sen
c/o OCA
34 Grafton Terr.
London, NW5 4HY England
 Actress V: 03/01/93

Lincoln, Lar Park
10390 Santa Monica Blvd. #300
Los Angeles, CA 90025
 Actor V: 03/27/93

Lind, Don L.
NASA LBJ/Space Center
Houston, TX 77058
 Astronaut V: 03/03/93

Lind, Will
P.O. Box 1189
Industrial Dr.
Welcome, NC 27374
 NASCAR Crew V: 03/26/93

Linden, Hal
c/o Tush Mgmt./119 W. 57th St.
New York, NY 10019
Actor V: 01/18/92

151 El Camino Dr.
Beverly Hills, CA 90212
Alternate V: 02/01/92

Lindenberg, Udo
Hotel Intercontiental
Fontane 10
D-(W) 2000 Hamburg 36, Germany
Singer V: 01/17/93

Linder, Kate
1801 Ave. of the Stars #1250
Los Angeles, CA 90067
Actress V: 03/01/93

c/o Y&R
7800 Beverly Blvd.
Beverly Hills, CA 90036
Forwarded V: 06/15/92

Lindfors, Vivica
172 E. 95th St.
New York, NY 10028
Actress V: 05/02/92

Lindner & Associates
2049 Century Park E. #2717
Los Angeles, CA 90067
Talent Agency V: 01/24/93

Lindsay, Shona
28 Berkeley Square
London W1X 6HD, England
Actress V: 03/06/92

Lindsey, Charlotte
c/o Dallas Cowboys
One Cowboys Parkway
Irving, TX 75063-4945
Cheerleader V: 08/08/92

Lindsey, George
3225 S. Norwood
Tulsa, OK 74135
Actor V: 03/12/92

Linkletter, Art
1100 Belair Rd.
Los Angeles, CA 90077
Celebrity V: 03/02/92

Linn, Teri Ann
4267 Marina City Dr., #312
Marina del Rey, CA 90292
Actress V: 01/15/93

Linn, Teri Ann, contd
c/o CBS-TV/Bold & Beautiful
7800 Beverly Blvd., Ste.3371
Los Angeles, CA 90036
Alternate V: 12/19/92

Linn-Baker, Mark
c/o Lorimar
"Perfect Strangers"
3970 Overland Ave.
Culver City, CA 90230
Actor V: 12/15/92

Linton, Betty
525 N. Palm Dr.
Beverly Hills, CA 90210
Actress V: 03/10/92

Linville, Joanne
3148 Fryman Rd.
Studio City, CA 91604
Actress V: 06/17/92

Lipscomb, Dennis
c/o Cannell Prod.
7083 Hollywood Blvd.
Hollywood, CA 90028
Actor V: 05/15/92

c/o MGM/UA Comm.
In the Heat of the Night
1000 W. Washington Blvd.
Culver City, CA 90232
Forwarded V: 01/07/92

Lipton, Peggy
15250 Ventura Blvd. Ste.900
Sherman Oaks, CA 91403
Actress V: 01/28/92

Lisa, Mona
8860 Corbin, #185
Northridge, CA 91324
Adult Films V: 02/13/93

Lister, Moira
c/o Richard Stone
18 York Bldg.
London WC2N 6JU, England
Actress V: 01/23/93

Lithgow, John
1888 Century Park E. #1400
Los Angeles, CA 90067
Actor V: 02/01/92

1319 Warnall Ave.
Los Angeles, CA 90024
Alternate V: 02/01/92

Little, Rich
24800 Pacific Coast Hwy.
Malibu, CA 90265
Actor V: 04/20/92

21822 Pacific Coast Hwy.
Malibu, CA 90265
L.R.U. V: 01/02/92

Little, Tawny
4151 Prospect Ave.
Los Angeles, CA 90027
Actress V: 04/13/92

Littler, Gene
P.O. Box 1949
Rancho Santa Fe, CA 92067
Golf V: 01/14/92

Live Home Video
15400 Sherman Way
P.O. Box 10124
Van Nuys, CA 91410-0124
Production Company V: 12/12/92

Lively, Robyn
9200 Sunset Blvd. #625
Los Angeles, CA 90069
Perfomer V: 02/04/92

Livingston, Barry
11310 Blix St.
N. Hollywood, CA 91602
Actor V: 09/09/92

Livingston, Stanley
P.O. Box 1782
Studio City, CA 91604
Actor V: 09/09/92

Lizer, Karl
12312 Gorham Ave.
Los Angeles, CA 90049-5206
Actress V: 11/11/92

c/o Viacom Prod.
Matlock
100 Universal City Plaza Bl. 448
Universal City, CA 91608
Actress V: 01/02/93

8543 Walnut Dr.
Los Angeles, CA 90046
L.R.U. V: 11/11/92

Llewellyn, Desmond
Linkwell, Old Town
Bexhill On Sea
E. Sussex TN40 2HA, England
Actor V: 10/11/92

Llewellyn, Doug
c/o The Peoples Court
1717 N. Highland Ave.
Hollywood, CA 90028
Actor V: 11/01/92

Llewellyn, John A.
c/o NASA LBJ Space Center
Houston, TX 77058
Astronaut V: 03/03/93

Lloyd, Christopher
c/o Managemint
P.O. Box 491246
Los Angeles, CA 90049
Actor V: 04/01/93

c/o Warner Bros.
4000 Warner Blvd.
Burbank, CA 91522
Alternate V: 03/14/93

Lloyd, Kathleen
Equal Justice
1888 Century Park East
Los Angeles, CA 90067
Actress V: 12/18/92

Lloyd, Norman
1813 Old Ranch Rd.
Los Angeles, CA 90049
Actor V: 01/18/92

Lloyd Bloom
1440 S. Sepulveda Blvd. #110
Los Angeles, CA 90025
Talent Agency V: 03/20/93

Location Update
6922 Hollywood Blvd. Ste.612
Hollywood, CA 90028
Magazine V: 03/03/92

Locke, Sondra
P.O. Box 69865
Los Angeles, CA 90069
Actress V: 04/18/92

9869 Santa Monica Blvd. #207
Beverly Hills, CA 90212
Actress V: 05/15/92

6955 La Presa Dr.
Los Angeles, CA 90068
L.R.U. V: 12/02/92

Lockhart, Anne
28245 Driver Ave.
Agoura Hills, CA 91301
Actress V: 04/27/92

Lockhart, June
404 San Vicente Blvd. #208
Santa Monica, CA 90402
Actress V: 05/05/92

9021 Melrose Ave. #207
Los Angeles, CA 90069
Alternate V: 11/01/92

151 S. El Camino Dr.
Beverly Hills, CA 90212
Forwarded V: 01/16/92

Locklear, Heather
10350 Wilshire Blvd. #502
Los Angeles, CA 90024
Actress V: 03/01/93

4970 Summit View Dr.
Westlake Village, CA 91362
Alternate V: 02/19/92

4415 Westchester Dr.
Woodland Hills, CA 91364
Forwarded V: 04/18/92

3208 Cahuenga Blvd., W.
P.O. Box 124
Los Angeles, CA 90068
Forwarded V: 03/12/92

8942 Wilshire Blvd.
Beverly Hills, CA 90211
Forwarded V: 03/20/92

Lockyer, Gary
P.O. Box 141
Hayward, CA 94541
Senator V: 01/21/92

Loft Agency
9713 Santa Monica Blvd. #201
Beverly Hills, CA 90210
Talent Agency V: 01/24/93

Lofton, Cirroc
c/o Star Trek-DS9
5555 Melrose Ave.
Hollywood, CA 90036
Alternate V: 02/23/93

Logan, Johnny
c/o MSM, Postfach 61 04 63
D-(W) 6000 Franfurt/Main 61
Germany
Singer V: 02/23/93

Loggia, Robert
1718 Angelo Dr.
Beverly Hills, CA 90210
Actor V: 03/21/92

Loggia, Robert, contd
31228 Bailard Rd. #1
Malibu, CA 90265
Forwarded V: 06/13/92

Lollobrigida, Gina
Via Appia Antica 223
Rome, 1-00178 Italy
Actress V: 03/10/92

Lom, Hebert
c/o Morris Agency
147 Wardour St.
London, W1V 3DF England
Actor V: 03/12/92

London, Bobby
c/o King Features
216 East 45th St.
New York, NY 10017
Cartoonist V: 02/16/92

London, Julie
16074 Royal Oak Rd.
Encino, CA 91316
Actress V: 02/12/92

London, Lisa
1680 N. Vine St. #203
Hollywood, CA 90028
Actress V: 03/26/93

London, Nicole
P.O. Box 442
Sunland, CA 91040-0442
Adult Films V: 03/11/93

Lone, John
1341 Ocean Ave. #104
Santa Monica, CA 90401
Actor V: 03/27/93

Long, Glen
Sears Point Int'l Raceway
Hwys. 37 & 121
Sonoma, CA 95476
NASCAR Official V: 03/02/92

Long, John
c/o King Features
216 East 45th St.
New York, NY 10017
Cartoonist V: 06/02/92

Long, Shelley
c/o CAA
9830 Wilshire Blvd.
Beverly Hills, CA 90212
Actress V: 03/01/93

Long, Shelley, contd
c/o Willam Morris
151 El Camino Dr.
Beverly Hills, CA 90212
Alternate V: 03/20/92

c/o Paramount
"Cheers"
5555 Melrose Ave./Ball RM105
Hollywood, CA 90038
Forwarded V: 01/07/92

905 Napoli Way
Beverly Hills, CA 90211
L.R.U. V: 01/02/92

Lopat, Ed
99 Oak Trail Rd.
Hillsdale, NJ 07205
Baseball V: 05/14/92

Lopez, Dan
77 N. Ellsworth Ave.
San Mateo, CA 94401
Cartoonist V: 03/12/92

Lopez, Trini
1139 Abrigo Rd.
Palm Springs, CA 92262
Actor V: 01/16/92

Lord, Jack
4999 Kahala Ave.
Honolulu, HI 96816
Actor V: 08/23/92

Lord, Marjorie
1110 Maytor Pl.
Beverly Hills, CA 90210
Actress V: 05/13/92

Lords, Tracy
3349 Cahuenga Blvd. W. Ste.2B
Los Angeles, CA 90068
Actress V: 03/12/92

c/o Kuzma
22845 Epsilon St.
Woodland Hills, CA 91364
L.R.U. V: 02/01/92

Loren, Sophia
6 Rue Charles Bonnet
Geneva, Switzerland
Actress V: 02/01/92

c/o La Concordia Ranch
1151 Hidden Valley Rd.
Thousand Oaks, CA 91361
Alternate V: 03/10/92

Loren, Sophia, contd
Via di Villa Ada 10
I-00199 Rome, Italy
Forwarded V: 01/17/93

Loren, Trinity
c/o Five K Sales Co.
9420 Reseda Blvd., #836
Northridge, CA 91324
Adult Films V: 03/03/93

Lorenzan, Fred
c/o ReMax
575-2 W. St. Charles Rd.
Elmhurst, IL 60126
NASCAR Driver V: 03/02/92

Lorimar Telepictures
10202 W. Washington Blvd.
Culver City, CA 90232
Production Company V: 03/17/92

300 S. Lorimar Plaza
Burbank, CA 91505
Alternate V: 03/19/93

Loring, Gloria
14755 Ventura Ste. 744
Sherman Oaks, CA 91423
Actress V: 01/02/92

14746 Valley Vista Blvd.
Sherman Oaks, CA 91423
Alternate V: 01/02/92

Loring, Lisa
11130 Huston St. #6
W. Hollywood, CA 91601
Actress V: 11/11/92

Loring, Lynn
2641 Nichols Canyon
Los Angeles, CA 90046
Actress V: 11/21/92

506 N. Camden Dr.
Beverly Hills, CA 90210
Actress V: 04/27/92

Lorrin, Mick
P.O. Box 15394
N. Hollywood, CA 91615
Adult Films V: 03/11/93

Los Angeles Dodgers
1000 Elysian Park Ave.
Dodger Stadium
Los Angeles, CA 90012
Team Office V: 05/15/92

Los Angeles Raiders
332 Center St.
El Segundo, CA 90245
Team Offices V: 05/15/92

Los Angeles Rams
2327 W. Lincoln Ave.
Anaheim, CA 92801
Team Offices V: 05/15/92

Los Lobos
P.O.Box 1304
Burbank, CA 91507
Musical Group V: 02/01/92

Loudon, Dorothy
101 Central Park W.
New York, NY 10023
Actress V: 04/27/92

Louganis, Greg
P.O. Box 4068
Malibu, CA 90265
Olympiad V: 10/11/92

Loughlin, Lori
c/o Studio Fan Mail
1122 S. Robertson Blvd.
Los Angeles, CA 90035
Actress V: 03/30/93

c/o Miller/Boyett
10202 W. Washington Blvd.
Culver City, CA 90232
Forwarded V: 03/30/93

Louise, Tina
310 East 46th St. #18T
New York, NY 10017
Actress V: 12/12/92

9565 Lime Orchard Rd.
Beverly Hills, CA. 90210
Alternate V: 02/21/92

Lounge, John M.
c/o NASA
LBJ Space Center
Houston, TX 77058
Astronaut V: 01/31/93

Lousma, Jack R.
c/o NASA LBJ Space Center
Houston, TX 77058
Astronaut V: 03/03/93

Loveless, Patty
1514 South St.
Nashville, TN 37212
Singer V: 02/03/92

Lovell & Associates
1350 N. Highland Ave. #24
Los Angeles, CA 90028
Talent Agency V: 03/13/93

Lovell Jr., James A.
c/o NASA LBJ Space Center
Houston, TX 77058
Astronaut V: 03/03/93

Loving
c/o ABC-TV
320 W. 66th St.
New York, NY 10023
Production Company V: 03/19/93

Lovitz, John
c/o NBC Prod.
"Saturday Night Live"
30 Rockefeller Plaza
New York, NY 10112
Actor V: 01/10/92

Low, G. David
c/o NASA
LBJ Space Center
Houston, TX 77058
Astronaut V: 01/31/92

Lowe, Rob
c/o Wood\Faley
975 Hancock, #226
Los Angeles, CA 90069
Actor V: 03/26/93

Loy, Myrna
425 E. 63rd St.
New York, NY 10021
Actress V: 05/13/92

c/o Lantz
888 7th Ave.
New York, NY 10106
Alternate V: 02/28/92

LuPone, Patti
8942 Wilshire Blvd.
Beverly Hills, CA 90211
Actress V: 08/22/92

c/o Warner Bros. TV
"Life Goes On"
4000 Warner Blvd.
Burbank, CA 91522
Forwarded V: 12/18/92

Lucas, George
P.O. Box 2009
San Rafael, CA 94912
Producer/Director V: 01/11/93

Lucas, George, contd
3270 Kerner Blvd.
Box 2009
San Rafael, CA 94912
 Alternate V: 09/02/92

Lucas, Sheila
c/o Will Vinton Prod. Inc.
1400 N.W. 22nd Ave.
Portland, OR 97210
 Animator V: 04/16/92

Lucci, Susan
16 Carteret Pl.
Garden City, NJ 11530
 Actress V: 03/16/93

c/o ICM
8942 Wilshire Blvd.
Beverly Hills, CA 90211
 Alternate V: 03/30/93

Lucid, Shannon W.
c/o NASA LBJ Space Center
Houston, TX 77058
 Astronaut V: 03/03/93

Luckinbill, Lawrence
c/o Agency
40 W. 57th St.
New York, NY 10019
 Actor V: 01/07/92

271 Central Park W. #11W
New York, NY 10024
 Alternate V: 09/12/92

c/o Artists Agency
10000 Santa Monica Blvd. #305
Los Angeles, CA 90067
 Forwarded V: 12/05/92

Lucking, William
9229 Sunset Blvd. #607
Los Angeles, CA 90069
 Actor V: 02/04/92

Ludlum, Robert
c/o Heinz Zwack
Harthausener Str. 28
D-8011 Grafbrunnn, Germany
 Author V: 03/17/92

Lulu
c/o Elson
1 Richmond Mews
London W1V 5AG, England
 Actress V: 03/06/92

Lumley, Joanna
c/o MLR
200 Fulham Rd.
London SW10 9PN, England
 Actress V: 03/06/93

Lund, Deanna
545 Howard St.
Salem, VA 24153
 Actress V: 11/11/92

Lund, Lucille
c/o Higgins
3424 Shore Heights Dr.
Malibu, CA 90265
 Actress V: 04/27/92

Lunden, Joan
1965 Broadway #500
New York, NY 10023
 Actress V: 04/27/92

Lundgren, Dolph
29055 Cliffside Dr.
Malibu, CA 90265
 Actor V: 04/10/92

c/o Whitney
1875 Century Park East
Los Angeles, CA 90067-2598
 Alternate V: 12/08/92

2079 Mt. Olympus Dr.
Los Angeles, CA 90046
 L.R.U. V: 01/02/92

Lupino, Ida
11665 Weddington St.
N. Hollywood, CA 91601
 Actress V: 04/27/92

Lupton, John
2528 Tilden Ave.
Los Angeles, CA 90064
 Actor V: 02/04/92

Lupus, Peter
11375 Dona Lisa Dr.
Studio City, CA 91604
 Actor V: 06/18/92

Lyden, Pierce
291 N. Olive St.
Orange, CA 92666
 Actor V: 02/02/92

Lynch, Kelly
804 Woodacres Rd.
Santa Monica, CA 90402
 Actress V: 03/27/93

Lynley, Carol
P.O. Box 2190
Malibu, CA 90265
Actress V: 06/03/92

20522 Pacific Coast Hwy.
Malibu, CA 90265
Alternate V: 01/07/92

Lynn, Amber
4265 Marina City Dr. #215W
Marina del Rey, CA 90292-5829
Adult Films V: 03/11/93

Lynn, Betty
10424 Tennessee Ave.
Los Angeles, CA 90064
Actress V: 07/26/92

Lynn, Loretta
P.O. Box 120369
Nashville, TN 37212-0369
Singer V: 03/04/92

P.O. Box 23470
Nashville, TN 37202
Forwarded V: 06/21/92

1010 18th Ave. S.
Nashville, TN 37212
L.R.U. V: 12/07/92

Lynn, Porche
12439 Magnolia Blvd. #203
N. Hollywood, CA 91607
Adult Films V: 03/11/93

Lynne & Reilly Agency
Toluca Plaza Building
6735 Forest Lawn Dr. #313
Hollywood, CA 90028
Talent Agency V: 03/14/93

M

MAD ABOUT YOU
Tri-Star TV
9336 W. Washington Blvd.
Culver City, CA 90232
Production Company V: 03/26/93

MAJOR DAD
c/o Universal Telvision
Major Dad
100 Univ. City Plz., Bl.426-2E
Universal City, CA 91608
Production Company V: 03/02/92

MANN AND MACHINE
Wolf Films
100 Universal City Plaza
Bldg 69, Suite F
Universal City, CA 91608
Production Company V: 03/26/93

MARRIED WITH CHILDREN
c/o Fox TV
10201 W. Pico Blvd.
Los Angeles, CA 90035
Production Company V: 01/12/92

MATLOCK
c/o Viacom Prod.
10 Universal City Plaza
Universal City, CA 91608
Production Company V: 03/26/93

MCA-TV
100 Universal City Plaza
Universal City, CA 91608
Production Company V: 03/17/92

MGA/Mary Grady Agency
150 E. Olive Ave. #111
Burbank, CA 91502
Talent Agency V: 03/17/93

MGF Magazine
3 W. 18th St.
New York, NY 10011
Entertainment V: 03/03/92

MGM/Warner Bros.
4000 Warner Blvd.
Burbank, CA 91522
Publicity V: 12/15/92

MISS AMERICA PAGEANT
c/o Headquarters
Miss America Pageant
1325 Broadwalk
Atlantic City, NJ 08401
Production Company V: 01/07/92

MOTHER GOOSE & GRIMM
12020 Chandler Blvd. Ste. 200
N. Hollywood, CA 91607
Production Comapny V: 03/18/93

MTM Enterprises
4024 Radford Ave.
Studio City, CA 91604
Production Company V: 03/17/92

MTV/Nichelodeon
1515 Broadway
New York, NY 10036
Production Company V: 11/11/92

MUPPET BABBIES
c/o Jim Henson Prod.
Muppet Babies
117 E. 69th St.
New York, NY 10021
Production Company V: 06/15/92

MURDER SHE WROTE
c/o Universal TV
Murder She Wrote
100 Univ. City Plz., Bldg.507
Universal City, CA 91608
Production Company V: 03/02/92

MURPHY BROWN
c/o Warner Bros. Television
Murphy Brown
4000 Warner Blvd.
Burbank, CA 91522
Production Company V: 03/02/92

MacCorkindale, Simon
c/o The Agency
6380 Wilshire Blvd.
Los Angeles, CA 90048
Actor V: 03/17/92

MacGraw, Ali
1679 Alta Mura Rd.
Pacific Palisades, CA 90272
Actress V: 03/27/93

10345 W. Olympic Blvd.
Los Angeles, CA 90064
L.R.U. V: 07/01/92

MacIntire, Reba
P.O. Box 121996
Nashville, TN 37212
Singer V: 12/10/92

MacKenzie, Giselle
11014 Blix Ave.
N. Hollywood, CA 91602
Actress V: 04/27/92

MacLachlan, Janet
1919 N. Taft Ave.
Los Angeles, CA 90068
Actress V: 05/14/92

MacLachlan, Kyle
760 N. La Cienga
Los Angeles, CA 90069
Actor V: 03/23/93

828 Venezia
Venezia, CA 90291
Alternate V: 07/12/92

MacLachlan, Kyle, contd
9200 Sunset Blvd.
Los Angeles, CA 90069
Alternate V: 02/12/92

MacLaine, Shirley
c/o MacLaine Ent.
25200 Old Malibu Rd.
Malibu, CA 90262
Actress V: 03/01/92

1900 Ave of the Stars #1230
Los Angeles, CA 90067
L.R.U. V: 03/10/92

MacLeod, Gavin
14680 Valley Vista
Sherman Oaks, CA 91403
Actor V: 04/06/93

201 Ocean Ave. #309P
Santa Monica, CA 90402
L.R.U. V: 01/08/92

MacPherson, Elle
40 E. 61st St.
New York, NY 10021
Actress V: 03/27/93

MacRae, Meredith
13659 Victory Blvd. #588
Van Nuys, CA 91401
Actress V: 04/27/92

Mack, Marion
1323 Stonefield St.
Costa Mesa, CA 92626
Actress V: 01/04/92

Mackenzie, Peter
c/o Hermans Head
500 S. Buena Vista St.
Burbank, CA 91521
Actor V: 11/11/92

Macnee, Patrick
235-241 Regent St.
London W1A 2JT, England
Actor V: 03/17/92

P.O. Box 1685
Palm Springs, CA 92263
Alternate V: 07/12/92

39 Guildford Park Rd.
Guildford, Surrey GU2 5NA, England
Alternate V: 03/27/93

16 Berners St.
London W1, England
Forwarded V: 02/19/93

Macy, Bill
10130 Angelo Circle
Beverly Hills, CA 90210
Actor V: 02/28/92

Madden, Dave
1800 N Vine St. #120
Los Angeles, CA 90028
Actor V: 03/01/93

291 S. La Cienega Blvd. #307
Beverly Hills, CA 90211
L.R.U. V: 01/02/92

Madden, John
1 W. 72nd St.
New York, NY 10023
Sportscaster V: 03/19/93

c/o International Mngmt. Group
22 E. 71st St.
New York, NY 10021
Alternate V: 01/05/92

Madden John
c/o CBS Sports
51 W. 52nd St.
New York, NY 10019
Forwarded V: 04/23/92

Madigan, Amy
c/o Agency
10100 Santa Monica Blvd.
Los Angeles, CA 90067
Actress V: 02/24/92

Madonna
8461 Sunset Blvd. #485
W. Hollywood, CA 90069
Singer V: 12/10/92

9045 Oriola Way
Los Angeles, CA 90069
Alternate V: 04/25/91

c/o CAA
9830 Wilshire Blvd.
Beverly Hills, CA 90212
Alternate V: 03/30/93

65 Central Park W.
New York, NY 10023
Forwarded V: 03/10/92

8670 Wilshire Blvd.
Los Angeles, CA 90211
Forwarded V: 05/04/92

930 Stardella Rd.
Los Angeles, CA 90077
L.R.U. V: 07/01/92

Madsen, Virginia
c/o Huston
2204 Stanley Hills Dr.
Los Angeles, CA 90046
Actress V: 06/01/92

c/o Rodkin
8730 Santa Monica Blvd. #1
Los Angeles, CA 90069-4539
Actress V: 04/27/92

Maffay, Peter
c/o Studio 'Red Rooster'
Klenzestr 3a
D-(W) 8132 Tutzing, Germany
Singer V: 01/17/93

Magnuson, Ann
c/o Robinson Ent.
335 N. Maple #250
Actress V: 11/11/92

Mahaffey, John
3100 Richmond Ave. Ste. 500
Houston, TX 77098
Golf V: 01/17/92

Maharis, George
13150 Mulholland Dr.
Beverly Hills, CA 90210
Actor V: 03/27/93

Mahoney, Roger
c/o King Features
216 E. 45th St.
New York, NY 10017
Cartoonist V: 03/11/93

Mailer, Norman
142 Columbia Heights Pl.
Brooklyn, NY 11201
Writer V: 01/18/93

Maitland, Beth
c/o Young and the Restless
7800 Beverly Blvd.
Beverly Hills, CA 90036
Actress V: 06/15/92

Major, John
10 Downing Street
London SW1A 2AA England
Prime Minister V: 06/16/92

Majors, Lee
411 Isle of Capri Dr.
Ft. Lauderdale, FL 33301
Actor V: 03/27/93

Mako
c/o East West Players Inc.
4424 Santa Monica Blvd.
Los Angeles, CA 90029
Actor V: 01/22/92

Malandro, Kristina
10647 Wilkins Ave. #307
Los Angeles, CA 90024
Actress V: 03/27/93

c/o Sunset/Gower Studios
846 N. Cahuenga Blvd.
Los Angeles, CA 90038-3704
Alternate V: 03/03/92

Malandro, Kristina
1750 N. Beverly Dr.
Beverly Hills, CA 90210
Alternate V: 05/16/92

c/o General Hosp./ABC Inc.
4151 Prospect Ave.
Hollywood, CA 90027
Forwarded V: 03/01/92

Malden, Karl
1845 Mandeville Canyon Rd.
Los Angeles, CA 90049
Actor V: 01/11/92

Malkovich, John
346 S. Lucerne Blvd.
Los Angeles, CA 90020
Actor V: 03/27/93

7929 Hollywood Blvd.
Los Angeles, CA 90049
Alternate V: 02/20/92

Malle, Louis
222 Central Park S.
New York, NY 10019
Director V: 03/27/93

Malloy, Larkin
1501 Broadway #703
New York, NY 10036
Actor V: 03/20/93

Malmay-Lurate, Stacy
c/o Dallas Cowboys
One Cowboys Parkway
Irving, TX 75063-4945
Cheerleader V: 08/08/92

Malot, Pierre
10 Ave. George-V
F-75008 Paris, France
Actor V: 02/11/93

Malpaso Productions
4000 Warner Blvd.
Burbank, CA 91522
Production Company V: 03/17/92

Management Jovanovic
Kathi-Kobus-Str. 24
D-(W) 8000 Munchen, 40 Germany
Talent Agency V: 03/15/93

Manchester, Melissa
8800 Sunset Blvd. Ste. 101
Los Angeles, CA 90069
Singer V: 03/02/92

15882 High Knoll Rd.
Encino, CA 91316
Singer V: 04/27/92

Mancini, Henry
c/o Henry Mancini Enter. Inc.
9229 Sunset Blvd. Suite 304
Los Angeles, CA 90069
Composer V: 01/06/92

9200 Sunset Blvd. #1001
Los Angeles, CA 90067
Alternate V: 01/12/92

261 Baroda Dr.
Los Angeles, CA 90024
Forwarded V: 06/02/92

Mancini, Ray 'Boom-Boom'
807 Cambridge Ave.
Youngstown, OH 44502
Boxing Champ V: 05/09/92

750 Bundy Dr. #108
Los Angeles, CA
Forwarded V: 05/09/92

Mancuso, Nick
7160 Grasswood Ave.
Malibu, CA 90265
Actor V: 03/27/93

Mandel, Howie
208 N. Canon Dr.
Beverly Hills, CA 90210
Actor V: 01/02/92

Mandrell, Barbara
P.O. Box 620
Hendersonville, TN 37077-0620
Singer V: 05/16/92

128 River Rd.
Hendersonville, TN 37075
Singer V: 04/27/92

Mandrell, Louise
P.O. Box 800
Hendersonville, TN 37077-0800
Singer V: 11/23/92

30 Music Square
W. Nashville, TN 37203
Alternate V: 01/07/92

1522 Demonbreun St.
Nashville, TN 37203
Forwarded V: 01/07/92

Manetti, Larry
c/o The Artists Group
1930 Century Park W.
Los Angeles, CA 90067
Actor V: 03/17/92

4615 Winnetka Ave.
Woodland Hills, CA 91436
Alternate V: 06/16/92

Manilow, Barry
P.O. Box 933017
Los Angeles, CA 90093
Singer V: 03/01/93

Mann, Carol
6 Cape Chestnut
The Woodlands, TX 76110
Golfer V: 02/04/92

Mann, Jodie
5455 Wilshire Blvd. #1406
Los Angeles, CA 90036
Actress V: 03/01/93

Manning, Irene
3165 La Mesa Dr.
San Carlos, CA 94070
Actress V: 04/27/92

Manoff, Dinah
P.O. Box 5617
Beverly Hills, CA 90213
Actress V: 01/22/92

Mansell, Nigel
c/o Sue Membery
6 Collingwood Close, Pimperne
Near Blandford
Dorset DT11 8XY, England
Race Car Driver V: 01/17/93

Mantle, Mickey
c/o Restaurant & Sports Bar
42 Central Park South
New York, NY 10019
Baseball V: 06/21/92

Mantley, John
4121 Longridge Ave.
Sherman Oaks, CA 91423
Writer V: 01/04/92

13535 Ventura Blvd. Ste. 205
Sherman Oaks, CA 91423
Alternate V: 02/01/92

Maples, Marla
c/o Jones
150 W. 51st St. #802
New York, NY 10019
Actress V: 03/19/93

Marais, Jean
c/o Agence Cineart
34 ave. Champs-Elysees
F-75008 Paris, France
Actor V: 01/17/93

Marceau, Marcel
c/o Compagne De Mime
21 Rue Jean-Mermoz
75008 Paris, France
Mime V: 03/10/92

c/o Theatre De Champs Elyses
15 Ave. Montaigne
75008 Paris, France
Alternate V: 02/18/92

Marceau, Sophie
30 ave. Charles-de-Gaulle
F-92200 Neuilly-sur-Seine, France
Actress V: 01/17/93

Marcell, Joe
c/o NBC Prod.
Fresh Prince of Bel Air
330 Bob Hope Dr.
Burbank, CA 91523
Actor V: 01/09/92

Marchand, Nancy
205 W. 89th St., Ste.6S
New York, NY 10024
Actress V: 04/27/92

Marchetti, Will
P.O. Box 1439
Mill Valley, CA 94942
Actor V: 04/21/92

Marcil, Vanessa
c/o ABC-TV General Hospital
4151 Prospect Ave.
Los Angeles, CA 90027
Actress V: 02/08/93

Marcis, Dave
c/o Marcis Racing
P.O. Box 645
Skyland, NC 28776
 NASCAR Driver V: 03/02/92

Marcos, Imelda
2439 Makiki Dr.
Honolulu, HI 96822
 Celebrity V: 04/27/92

Marcovicci, Andrea
8273 W. Norton Ave.
Los Angeles, CA 90046
 Actress V: 03/25/93

Marcus, Jerry
c/o King Features
216 East 45th St.
New York, NY 10017
 Cartoonist V: 05/01/92

Margolin, Janet
7667 Seattle Pl.
Los Angeles, CA 90046
 Actress V: 06/15/92

Margulies, Jimmy
c/o King Features
216 E. 45th St.
New York, NY 10017
 Cartoonist V: 03/11/93

Marias, Jean
c/o Cineart
31 Ave. des Champs Elysees
F-75008 Paris, France
 Actor V: 03/17/92

Marie, Rose
6916 Chisolm Ave.
Van Nuys, CA 91406
 Actress V: 05/02/92

c/o NBC-TV
3000 W. Alameda Ave.
Burbank, CA 91523
 Forwarded V: 01/13/92

c/o Kummer Assoc.
144 S. McCarty Dr. #201
Beverly Hills, CA 90212-2239
 L.R.U. V: 01/02/92

Marin, Richard 'Cheech'
32020 Pacific Coast Hwy.
Malibu, CA 90265
 Actor V: 03/01/92

Marinaro, Ed
c/o William Morris
151 El Camino Dr.
Beverly Hills, CA 90212
 Actor V: 03/17/92

1466 N. Doheny Dr.
Los Angeles, CA 90069
 Alternate V: 06/17/92

Markham, Monte
P.O. Box 4200
Malibu, CA 90265
 Actor V: 03/21/92

P.O. Box 607
Malibu, CA 90265
 Alternate V: 03/21/92

26328 Ingleside
Malibu, CA 90265
 Forwarded V: 03/21/92

Marlin, Coo Coo
Mahon Rd.
Columbia, TN 38041
 NASCAR Driver V: 03/02/92

Marlin, Sterling
c/o Stavola Racing
P.O. Box 339
Harrisburg, NC 28075
 NASCAR Driver V: 03/02/92

Maroney, Kelli
c/o Media Artists Group
6255 Sunset Blvd. Ste. 627
Los Angeles, CA 90028
 Actress V: 03/26/93

Marsh, Jean
The Pheasant
Chinnor Hill
Oxfordshire OX 4BN, England
 Actress V: 05/16/92

Marsh, Marian
P.O. Box 1
Palm Desert, CA 92260
 Actress V: 06/16/92

Marshall, E.G.
Rural Farm Delivery #2
Mt. Kisco, NY 10549
 Actor V: 02/02/92

Marshall, James
2121 Ave. of the Stars #950
Los Angeles, CA 90067
 Actor V: 02/03/92

Marshall, Penny
1849 Sawtelle Bl. #500
Los Angeles, CA 90025
Actress V: 11/11/92

1888 Century Park E. #1400
Los Angeles, CA 90067
Alternate V: 01/02/92

7150 La Presa Dr.
Los Angeles, CA 90068
Alternate V: 05/16/92

Marshall, Peter
16714 Oakview Dr.
Encino, CA 91316
Celebrity V: 06/16/92

Marshall Agency
8222 Melrose Ave. #302
Los Angeles, CA 90046
Model/Talent Agency V: 03/14/93

Martel, K.C.
c/o Warner Bros. TV
Growing Pains
4000 Warner Blvd.
Burbank, CA 91522
Actor V: 12/03/92

Martel Agency
1680 N. Vine St. #203
Hollywood, CA 90028
Talent Agency V: 02/19/93

Martens, Wilford
Wetstraat 16
1000 Brussel, Belgium
Prime Minister V: 03/01/92

Martens, Wilford
24 Desire Van Monckhovenstraat
900 Gent, Belgium
Forwarded V: 03/09/92

Marter, Ian
c/o David Preston
74 New Bond St.
London, W1Y 9DA England
Actor V: 02/01/92

Martin, Andrea
40 W. 57th St.
New York, NY 10019
Actress V: 02/22/92

Martin, Dean
1900 Ave. of Stars Ste. 1230
Los Angeles, CA 90067
Actor V: 04/22/92

Martin, Dean, contd
12722 Ventura Blvd. #440
Studio City, CA 91601
Alternate V: 11/11/92

613 N. Linden Dr.
Beverly Hills, CA 90210
Forwarded V: 01/07/92

Martin, Greg
c/o KY Headhunters
192 Ridge Crest Drive
Goodlettsville, TN 37072
Celebrity V: 03/26/93

Martin, Helen
1440 N. Fairfax #109
Los Angles, CA 90046-3939
Actress V: 04/27/92

Martin, Joe
c/o King Features
216 East 45th St.
New York, NY 10017
Cartoonist V: 04/23/92

Martin, Kellie
c/o Warner Bros. TV
Life Goes On
4000 Warner Blvd.
Burbank, CA 91522
Actress V: 12/18/92

Martin, Mark
c/o Roush Racing
P.O. Box 1089
Liberty, NC 27298
NASCAR Driver V: 03/02/92

Martin, Pamela Sue
P.O. Box 25578
Los Angeles, CA 90025
Actress V: 03/27/93

Martin, Steve
c/o R&C
10000 Santa Monica Blvd.
Los Angeles, CA 90067
Actor V: 01/09/92

P.O. Box 929
Beverly Hills, CA 90213
Alternate V: 12/12/92

Martineck, Sarah
c/o Universal Television
100 Universal City Plaza 422-2
Universal City, CA 91608
Actress V: 05/15/92

Martinez, A
6835 Wildlife Rd.
Malibu, CA 90265
Actor V: 01/16/93

Mascolo, Joe
c/o General Hosp./ABC Inc.
4151 Prospect Ave.
Hollywood, CA 90027
Actor V: 03/01/92

Masina, Giulietta
Via Margutta 110
Rome 00187, Italy
Actress V: 02/28/92

Mason, Marsha
10100 Santa Monica Blvd. #496
Los Angeles, CA 90067
Actress V: 05/19/92

1200 Turquesa Lane
Pacific Palisades, CA 90272
Alternate V: 06/16/92

10745 Chalon Rd.
Los Angeles, CA 90077
Forwarded V: 01/29/92

Massey, Daniel
c/o Leading Artists
68 Saint James St.
London SW1, England
Actor V: 02/16/92

c/o Agency
388 Oxford St.
London W1, England
Alternate V: 02/28/92

Mast, Rick
c/o Precision Prod. Racing
P.O. Box 569
Denver, NC 28037
NASCAR Driver V: 03/02/92

Mastroianni, Marcello
c/o Giovanna Cau
Via M. Adelaide 8
I-00196 Rome, Italy
Actor V: 01/17/93

Matera, Fran
c/o King Features
216 East 45th St.
New York, NY 10017
Cartoonist V: 02/14/92

Matheson, Tim
1221 Stone Canyon Rd.
Los Angeles, CA 90077-2919
Actor V: 03/03/92

Mathews, Banjo
P.O. Box 426
Arden, NC 28704
NASCAR Driver V: 03/02/92

Mathews, Carmen
101 Marchant Rd.
W. Redding, CT 06896
Actress V: 03/23/92

Mathias, Bob
7469 E. Pine Ave.
Fresno, CA 93727
Track Star V: 02/01/92

Mathis, Johnny
1469 Stebbins Terr.
Los Angeles, CA 90069
Singer V: 01/02/93

3500 W. Olive Ave. #750
Burbank, CA 91505
Alternate V: 03/03/92

P.O. Box 69278
Los Angeles, CA 90069-0278
Forwarded V: 03/03/92

Matlin, Marlee
121 N. San Vincente Blvd.
Beverly Hills, CA 90211
Actress V: 02/14/92

Mattea, Kathy
P.O. Box 158482
Nashville, TN 37215
Singer V: 01/25/93

Matthau, Walter
10100 Santa Monica Blvd. #2200
Los Angeles, CA 90067
Actor V: 04/01/92

c/o Warner Bros.
4000 Warner Blvd.
Burbank, CA 91522
Alternate V: 03/14/93

Matthews, Kerwin
67-A Buena Vista Terr.
San Francisco, CA 94117
Actor V: 03/16/93

Matthews, Lisa
c/o Playboy Ent.
8560 Sunset Blvd.
Los Angeles, CA 90069
Playmate V: 11/11/92

Mattingly, Thomas K.
c/o NASA LBJ Space Center
Houston, TX 77058
Astronaut V: 03/03/93

Mattioli, Dr. Joseph
Pocono Int'l Raceway
P.O. Box 500
Long Pond, PA 18334
NASCAR Official V: 03/02/92

Mature, Victor
P.O. Box 706
Rancho Santa Fe, CA 92067
Actor V: 02/27/93

Mauldin, Bill
c/o North American Synd.
2821 Europa Dr.
Costa Mesa, CA 92626-3525
Cartoonist V: 01/02/92

1703 Kaiser Ave.
P.O. Box19620
Irvine, CA 92714
L.R.U. V: 02/01/93

Maule, Brad
c/o General Hosp./ABC Inc.
4151 Prospect Ave.
Hollywood, CA 90027
Actor V: 03/01/92

Max, Peter
118 Riverside Dr.
New York, NY 10024
Artist V: 04/16/92

Maxwell, Frank
c/o General Hosp./ABC Inc.
4151 Prospect Ave.
Hollywood, CA 90027
Actor V: 03/01/92

Maxwell-Reid, Daphne
18034 Ventura Blvd. Ste.318
Encino, CA 91316
Actress V: 11/10/92

c/o Timalove Prod., 32nd Fl.
10 Universal City Plaza
Universal City, CA 91608-1097
Alternate V: 11/10/92

May, Robert Alden
c/o Alden Prod.
P.O. Box 30
Big Pine, CA 93513
FX Master V: 04/01/92

c/o Cine-F/X Studios
190 Main St.
Big Pine, CA 93513
Alternate V: 04/01/92

Mayehoff, Eddie
369 Paseo de Playa #411
Ventura, CA 93001
Actor V: 03/20/92

Maynard, Don
6545 Butterfield Dr.
El Paso, TX 79932
Football V: 02/13/92

Mayo, Virginia
109 E. Avenida de los Aboles
Thousand Oaks, CA 91360
Actress V: 03/02/92

c/o Jack Rose
6430 Sunset Blvd.
Los Angeles, CA 90028
Forwarded V: 01/07/92

Mayo, Whitman
3210 W. 80th St.
Inglewood, CA 90305
Actor V: 06/16/92

Mayron, Melanie
c/o Wm. Morris
151 El Camino
Beverly Hills, CA 90210
Actress V: 08/09/92

1418 N. Ogden Drive
Los Angeles, CA 90046
Actress V: 03/23/92

1017 N. Orange Grove
Los Angeles, CA 90046
Alternate V: 03/12/92

Mays, Willie
c/o Ballys Park Place
Boardwalk and Place
Atlantic City, NJ 08401
Baseball V: 01/12/92

Mazzucchelli
326 Washington
Hoboken, NJ 07030
Artist V: 02/21/92

McKellar, Danica
4151 Prospect Ave.
Hollywood, CA 90027
Actress V: 03/01/93

McArdle, Andrea
713 Disston St.
Philadelphia, PA 19111
Actress V: 03/23/92

McArthur, Alex
c/o Bymel
1724 N. Vista St.
Los Angeles, CA 90046-2235
Actor V: 03/12/92

McArthur Jr., William S.
c/o NASA LBJ Space Center
Houston, TX 77058
Astronaut V: 03/03/93

McBride, Jon A.
c/o NASA LBJ Space Center
Houston, TX 77058
Astronaut V: 03/03/93

McBroom, Amanda
1608 N. Las Palmas
Hollywood, CA 90028
Actress V: 06/15/92

McCall, Mitzi
3635 Wrightwood Dr.
Studio City, PA 91604
Actress V: 03/23/92

McCalla, Irish
c/o McIntyres
920 Oak Terrace
Prescott, AZ 86301
Actress V: 02/01/92

McCallister, Lon
P.O. Box 396
Little River, CA 95456
Actor V: 06/15/92

McCallum, David
40 E. 62nd St.
New York, NY 10021
Actor V: 01/06/92

c/o Agency
388 Oxford St.
London, England
Alternate V: 07/18/92

10 E. 44th St.
New York, NY 10017
Alternate V: 03/17/92

McCallum, David, contd
c/o Hilary Gagan
91, The Grove
London N13 5JS, England
Alternate V: 02/28/92

McCambridge, Mercedes
1001 Gentry St. Ste.8-I
La Jolla, CA 92037
Actress V: 03/23/92

McCandless, Bruce
c/o NASA LBJ Space Center
Houston, TX 77058
Astronaut V: 03/03/93

McCarthy, Andrew
4708 Vesper Ave.
Sherman Oaks, CA 91403
Actor V: 03/27/93

McCarthy, Joseph J.
2305 Lawson Rd., Apt.D
Delray Beach, FL 33445
Medal of Honor V: 03/17/92

McCarthy, Nobu
c/o Cuthbert
372 N. Encinitas
Monrovia, CA 91016
Actress V: 03/23/92

McCashin, Constance
2037 Desford Dr.
Beverly Hills, CA 90210
Actress V: 03/23/92

McCay, Peggy
8811 Wonderland Ave.
Los Angeles, CA 90046
Actress V: 03/23/92

McClanahan, Rue
c/o Witt/Thomas
Golden Palace
846 N. Cahuenga Blvd. Bldg.G
Hollywood, CA 90038
Actress V: 02/17/92

16001 Woodvale Rd.
Encino, CA 91436
Actress V: 03/23/92

c/o ICM
8942 Wilshire Blvd.
Beverly Hills, CA 90210
Alternate V: 01/04/92

McClory, Sean
6612 Whitley Terr.
Los Angeles, CA 90069
Actor   V: 06/14/92

McClure, Doug
151 S. El Camino Dr.
Beverly Hills, CA 90212
Actor   V: 02/21/92

McClure, Morgan
c/o McClure Racing
Rt.10, Box 780
Abington, VA 24210
NASCAR Owner   V: 03/02/92

McConnell, Judith
c/o ABC-TV/Santa Barbara
3000 W. Alemeda Ave.
Burbank, CA 91523
Actress   V: 01/16/92

3300 Bennett Dr.
Los Angeles, CA 90068
Actress   V: 03/23/92

McCoo, Marilyn
P.O.Box 7905
Beverly Hills, CA 90212
Singer   V: 06/13/92

McCook, John
c/o Bell-Phillip Prod.
Bold & Beautiful
7800 Beverly Blvd., Ste.3371
Los Angeles, CA 90036
Actor   V: 06/15/92

McCord, Kent
1738 N. Orange Grove
Los Angeles, CA 90046
Actor   V: 03/15/93

McCormack, Patty
12731 Moorpark #3
Studio City, CA 91604
Actress   V: 03/23/92

McCormick, Maureen
c/o Cummings
2812 N. Shellcreek Pl.
Westlake Village, CA 91361
Actress   V: 03/27/93

McCoy, Sylvester
c/o BBC-TV Center
Wood Lane
London, W12 8QT England
Actor   V: 03/01/92

McCulley, Michael J.
c/o NASA
LBJ Space Center
Houston, TX 77058
Astronaut   V: 01/31/92

McCullough, Kimberly
c/o General Hosp./ABC Inc.
4151 Prospect Ave.
Hollywood, CA 90027
Actress   V: 03/01/92

McDivitt, James A.
c/o Defence Electronics Ops.
Rockwell Int'l
3370 Miraloma Ave.
Anaheim, CA 92803
Astronaut   V: 03/17/92

c/o Rockwell Int'l
1745 Jeff Davis Hwy. #1200
Arlington, VA 22202
Astronaut   V: 03/30/93

c/o NASA LBJ Space Center
Houston, TX 77058
Forwarded   V: 03/03/93

McDonald, Country Joe
P.O. Box 7158
Berkeley, CA 94707-0158
Singer   V: 03/15/92

McDowell, Malcolm
c/o Agency
388 Oxford St.
London W1, England
Actor   V: 02/18/92

McDowell, Roddy
3110 Brookdale Rd.
Studio City, CA 91604
Actor   V: 02/18/92

McEnery, Peter
c/o Peters Ltd.
10 Buckingham St.
London W1, England
Actor   V: 01/12/92

c/o Norman Boyack
9 Cork St.
London W1, England
Alternate   V: 02/28/92

McEnroe, John
23712 Malibu Colony Dr.
Malibu, CA 90265
Tennis   V: 03/02/92

McEnroe, John, contd
22240 Pacific Coast Hwy.
Malibu, CA 90265
L.R.U. V: 06/01/92

McEntire, Reba
511 Fairgrounds Ct.
Nashville, TN 37204
Singer V: 04/12/92

P.O Box 121996
Nashville, TN 37212
Singer V: 03/23/92

McEwan, Geraldine
c/o Marmont
Langham House
302-308 Regent St.
London, W1R 5AL, England
Actress V: 03/06/93

McFadden, Gates
c/o Star Trek-TNG Paramount
5555 Melrose Ave.
Hollywood, CA 90038
Actress V: 03/04/93

121 N. San Vicente Blvd.
Beverly Hills, CA 90211
Alternate V: 12/07/92

2510 Canyon Dr.
Los Angeles, CA 90068
Alternate V: 01/23/93

McFarland, George (Spanky)
P.O. Box 80202
Ft. Worth, TX 76180
Actor V: 02/27/92

8500 Buckner Lane
Ft. Worth, TX 76180
Alternate V: 03/12/92

McGavin, Darren
470 Park Ave.
New York, NY 10022
Actor V: 03/17/93

8643 Holloway Plaza
Los Angeles, CA 90069
Alternate V: 03/02/92

151 S. El Camino Dr.
Beverly Hills, CA 90212
L.R.U. V: 01/02/92

McGee, Henry
47 Courtfield Rd. Apt. 20
London SW7 4DB, England
Actor V: 03/17/93

McGill, Bruce
Paramount/MacGyver
5555 Melrose Ave.
Los Angeles, CA 90038
Actor V: 12/07/92

McGillis, Kelly
13428 Maxella Ave. #513
Marina del Rey, CA 90292
Actress V: 03/27/93

c/o Agency
40 W. 57th St.
New York, NY 10019
Alternate V: 03/17/92

c/o Studio Fan Mail
1122 S. Robertson Blvd.
Los Angeles, CA 90035
Alternate V: 03/30/93

2699 S. Bayshore Dr. #400
Miami, FL 33133-5408
Forwarded V: 03/30/93

9595 Wilshire Blvd. #505
Beverly Hills, CA 90212
L.R.U. V: 04/01/92

McGinnis, Doug
5341 Silverlode Dr.
Placerville, CA 95667
Stuntman V: 11/11/92

McGlynn, Dennis
Dover Downs Int'l Speedway
P.O. Box 843
Dover, DE 19903
NASCAR Official V: 03/02/92

McGoohan, Patrick
16808 Bollinger Dr.
Pacific Palisades, CA 90272
Actor V: 02/14/93

McGovern, Elizabeth
17319 Magnolia Blvd.
Encino, CA 91316
Actress V: 03/21/92

McGovern, George S.
Friendship Station
Box 5591
Washington, DC 20016
Politician V: 03/20/93

McGovern, Maureen
529 W. 42nd St. #7F
New York, NY 10036
Singer V: 03/23/92

McGowan, Ross
c/o KTVU
P.O. Box 22222
Oakland, CA 94623
TV Host V: 01/17/93

McGraw, Ali
c/o Bauman & Hiller
5750 Wilshire Blvd. #512
Los Angeles, CA 90036
Actress V: 03/19/93

1679 Alta Mora Rd.
Pacific Palisades, CA 90272
L.R.U. V: 07/31/92

McGraw, Tug
P.O. Box 7575
Philadelphia, PA 19101
Baseball V: 01/12/92

1 Dale Lane
Wallingford, PA 19086
Alternate V: 12/10/92

McGuire, Dorothy
10351 Santa Monica Blvd. #300
Los Angeles, CA 90025
Actress V: 03/04/92

121 Copley Pl.
Beverly Hills, CA 90210
Forwarded V: 03/22/92

P.O. Box 25940
Los Angeles, CA 90025
L.R.U. V: 01/02/92

McHugh Talent Angency
8150 Beverly Blvd. #303
Los Angeles, CA 90048
Talent Agency V: 03/11/93

McIntosh, Craig
c/o King Features
216 E. 45th St.
New York, NY 10017
Cartoonist V: 03/11/93

McIntyre, John
1417 Samoa Way
Laguna Beach, CA 92651
Actor V: 06/15/92

McKay, Gardner
445 Kawailoa Rd. #10
Kailua, HI 96734-3167
Actor V: 02/12/92

McKay, Sunny
c/o Five K Sales Co.
9420 Reseda Blvd., #836
Northridge, CA 91324
Adult Films V: 03/03/93

McKay, Woody
Darlington Raceway
P.O. Box 500
Darlington, SC 29532
NASCAR Official V: 03/02/92

McKearn, Leo
c/o Hatton & Baker
18 Jermyn St.
London SW1Y 6HN, England
Actor V: 02/28/92

McKee, Todd
c/o Bell-Phillip Prod.
Bold & Beautiful
7800 Beverly Blvd., Ste.3371
Los Angeles, CA 90036
Actor V: 06/15/92

McKellar, Danica
c/o New World TV
The Wonder Years
1440 S. Sepulveda Blvd.
Los Angeles, CA 90025
Actress V: 12/11/92

McKenna, Virginia
c/o Cherry Tree Cottage
Cold Harbour, Dorking
Surry RH5 6HA, England
Actress V: 02/17/92

McKeon, Nancy
P.O. Box 6778
Burbank, CA 91510
Actress V: 06/17/92

McKern, Leo
c/o Agency
388-396 Oxford St.
London W1 9HE, England
Actor V: 03/17/92

McKinney, Kurt
c/o General Hosp./ABC Inc.
4151 Prospect Ave.
Hollywood, CA 90027
Actor V: 03/01/92

McKuen, Rod
1155 Angelo Dr.
Beverly Hills, CA 90210
Singer V: 01/18/92

McLachlan, Sarah
1717 W. 4th Ave.
Vancouver, B.C. V6J 1M2, Canada
Singer V: 03/02/93

McLaughlin, Lise-Ann
c/o Stone
9 Newburgh St.
London W1V 1LH, England
Actress V: 03/06/93

McLean, Don
Old Mountain Rd.
Garrison, NY 10524
Golf V: 03/30/93

P.O. Box 102
Castine, ME 04421-0102
Forwarded V: 03/30/93

McLeod, Catherine
c/o Keefer
4146 Allott Ave.
Sherman Oaks, CA 91403
Actress V: 02/20/92

McLerie, Allyn Ann
3344 Campanil Dr.
Santa Barbara, CA 93109
Actress V: 03/23/92

McLish, Rachel
3114 Abington St.
Beverly Hills, CA 90210
Actress V: 03/23/92

McMahon, Ed
1050 Summit Dr.
Beverly Hills, CA 90210-2832
Celebrity V: 02/22/92

c/o Dick Clark Prod.
"Super Bloopers"
3003 W. Olive
Burbank, CA 91505
Forwarded V: 01/07/92

McMahon, Jim
c/o Zucker Sports Mgmt.
5 Revere Dr., Ste.201
Northbrook, IL 60062
Football V: 07/14/92

McMonagle, Donald R.
c/o NASA
LBJ Space Center
Houston, TX 77058
Astronaut V: 01/31/92

McMurray, Sam
"Dinosaurs"
4024 Radford Ave., Bldg. 2, Rm. 11
Studio City, CA 91604
Actor V: 06/15/92

McMyler, Pamela
1680 N. Vine St. Ste. 203
Hollywood, CA 90028
Actress V: 05/07/92

McNamara, Robert S.
1455 Pennslyvania Ave. N.W.
Suite 515
Washington, DC 20004
Politician V: 04/14/92

2412 Tracy Place
Washington, DC 20008
Forwarded V: 02/14/92

McNaught, Judith
5237 W. Plano Pkwy.
Plano, TX 75075
Author V: 01/16/92

McNeil, Kate
c/o GTG Ent./Culver Studios
9336 W. Washington Blvd.
Culver City, CA 90232
Actress V: 05/15/92

3248 Oakshire Dr.
Los Angeles, CA 90068
Actress V: 03/23/92

McNichol, Jimmy
P.O. Box 5813
Sherman Oaks, CA 91413-5813
Actor V: 04/12/92

McNichol, Kristy
P.O. Box 5813
Sherman Oaks, CA 91413-5813
Actress V: 01/22/92

14355 Millbrook Dr.
Sherman Oaks, CA 91423
Alternate V: 04/12/92

c/o Empty Nest
500 S. Buena Vista St.
Burbank, CA 91521
Forwarded V: 11/11/92

McPartlin, Steve
c/o KTVU
P.O. Box 22222
Oakland, CA 94623
TV Host V: 01/17/93

McQuagg, Sam
8886 Hamilton Rd.
Midland, GA 31820
NASCAR Driver V: 03/02/92

McQueen, Butterfly
3060-A Dent St.
Terrace Manor
Augusta, GA 30906
Actress V: 01/14/93

31 Hamilton Terr. #3
New York, NY 10031
L.R.U. V: 01/03/92

McQueeny, Pat
146 N. Almont Dr. Apt.8
Beverly Hills, CA 90211
Actress V: 01/06/92

McRae, Carmen
2200 Summit Ridge Dr.
Beverly Hills, CA 90210
Singer V: 06/17/92

McRaney, Gerald
329 N. Wetherly Dr. #101
Beverly Hills, CA 90211
Actor V: 03/27/93

c/o Spanish Trail Prod.
100 Universal City Plaza
Universal City, CA 91608
Forwarded V: 04/01/92

c/o Universal Television
Major Dad
100 Univ. City Plz., BL.426-2E
Universal City, CA 91608
Forwarded V: 03/02/92

McRoberts, Briony
c/o Green
2 Conduit St.
London W1R 9TG, England
Actress V: 03/06/92

McShane, Ian
388 Oxford St.
London W1, England
Actor V: 03/14/92

999 N. Doheny Dr. #PH
Los Angeles, CA 90069
Alternate V: 03/27/93

McVey, Tyler
4717 Laurel Cyn. Blvd. Ste.206
N. Hollywood, CA 91607
Actor V: 07/03/92

McVicar, Daniel
c/o Bell-Phillip Prod.
Bold & Beautiful
7800 Beverly Blvd., Ste.3371
Los Angeles, CA 90036
Actor V: 06/15/92

McVie, Christine
9744 LLoydcrest Dr.
Beverly Hills, CA 90210
Singer V: 06/17/92

McWilliams, Carolyn
2915 Mandeville Canyon Rd.
Los Angeles, CA 90049
Actress V: 03/23/92

Mclaughlin, Emily
c/o General Hosp./ABC Inc.
4151 Prospect Ave.
Hollywood, CA 90027
Actress V: 03/01/92

Mcliam, John
12429 Laurel Terrace Dr.
Studio City, CA 91604
Actor V: 07/03/92

Meade, Carl J.
c/o NASA
LBJ Space Center
Houston, TX 77058
Astronaut V: 01/31/92

Meadows, Audrey
350 Trousdale Pl.
Beverly Hills, CA 90210
Actress V: 02/14/92

c/o Universal Television
100 Universal City Plaza 422-2
Universal City, CA 91608
Alternate V: 05/15/92

Meadows, Jane
16185 Woodvale Rd.
Encino, CA 91436
Actress V: 03/23/92

Meaney, Colm
c/o The Gage Group
9255 Sunset Blvd., #515
Los Angeles, CA 90069
Actor V: 02/23/93

c/o Star Trek-DS9
5555 Melrose Ave.
Hollywood, CA 90036
Alternate V: 02/23/93

Meaney, Kevin
c/o Universal Television
100 Universal City Plaza 422-2
Universal City, CA 91608
 Actor V: 05/15/92

Means, Jimmy
102 Greenbriar Dr.
Forest City, NC 28043
 NASCAR Driver V: 03/02/92

Meara, Anne
118 Riverside Dr. #5-A
New York, NY 10024
 Actress V: 03/23/92

Media Artist Group
6255 Beverly Blvd. Ste.627
Los Angeles, CA 90028
 Talent Agency V: 03/11/93

Media/Fox Pictures
P.O. Box 900
Beverly Hills, CA 90213
 Publicity V: 12/15/92

Medina, Hazel
12429 Laurel Terrace Dr.
Studio City, CA 91604
 Actress V: 01/12/92

Medley, Bill
9841 Hot Springs Dr.
Hunting Beach CA 92646
 Singer V: 02/14/92

Meeker, Ken
c/o One Life to Live
56 W. 66th St.
New York, NY 10023
 Actor V: 01/09/92

Mehta, Zubin
1015 Gayley Ave., Box 1101
Los Angeles, CA 90024
 Conductor V: 11/11/92

Mellencamp, John Cougar
Rt.1 Box 361
Nashville, TN 47448
 Singer V: 02/12/92

Belmont Mall Studio
Belmont, IN 47401
 Alternate V: 02/11/92

Melling, Harry
P.O. Box 665
Dawsonville, GA 28677
 Race Driver V: 03/12/93

Melman, Larry "Bud"
c/o UN Prod.
130 Engle St.
Englewood, NJ 07631
 Actor V: 04/01/92

Melnick, Bruce E.
c/o NASA
LBJ Space Center
Houston, TX 77058
 Astronaut V: 01/31/92

Melton, Sid
5347 Cedros Ave.
Van Nuys, CA 91410
 Actor V: 06/04/92

Melvin, Allan
271 N. Bowling Green Way
Los Angeles, CA 90049
 Actor V: 09/16/92

Melvin, Murry
c/o Joy Jameson Ltd.
7 West Eaton Place Mews
London, SW1 1X8LY England
 Actor V: 03/16/92

Menot, Roya
c/o St. Laurent & Assoc.
1410 York Ave. 4D
New York, NY 10021
 Actress V: 04/01/92

Menzies, Heather
15930 Woodvale Rd.
Encino, CA 91436
 Actor V: 04/02/92

Mercer, Marian
25901 Pluma
Calabasas, CA 91302
 Actress V: 03/23/92

Mercouri, Melina
25 Anagnostopoulos St.
Kolonaki
Athens 10673, Greece
 Actress V: 02/28/92

Meredith, Burgess
25 Malibu Colony Rd. Box 757
Malibu, CA 90265
 Actor V: 04/01/92

P.O. Box 757
Malibu, CA 90265
 Alternate V: 03/30/93

Meredith, Burgess, contd
23736 Malibu Colony Dr.
Malibu, CA 90265
Forwarded V: 03/21/92

Meredith, Don
P.O. Box 597
Santa Fe, NM 87504
Actor V: 02/17/92

Meredith, Lucille
c/o Viacom Prod.
Matlock
100 Universal City Plaza, Bl. 448
Universal City, CA 91608
Actress V: 12/01/92

Meriwether, Lee
P.O. Box 260402
Encino, CA 91426
Actress V: 02/18/92

Merkle, Angela
Schonhauser Allee 104
D-(0) 1071 Berlin
Germany
Politician V: 02/01/93

Merlin, Jan
c/o Screen Actors Guild
7065 Hollywood Blvd.
Hollywood, CA 90028
Actor V: 12/12/92

Merrick, Dawn
c/o General Hosp./ABC Inc.
4151 Prospect Ave.
Hollywood, CA 90027
Actress V: 03/01/92

Merriman, Amy
c/o Dallas Cowboys
One Cowboys Parkway
Irving, TX 75063-4945
Cheerleader V: 08/08/92

Merritt, Teresa
192-06 110th Rd.
St. Alban, NY 11412
Actress V: 03/23/92

Metcalf, Laurie
c/o Carsey-Werner/CBS-MTM
Roseanne
4024 Radford Ave.
Studio City, CA 91604
Actress V: 12/07/92

Metcalf, Mark
c/o Hagan Racing
P.O. Box 2010
Thomasville, NC 27360
NASCAR Crew V: 02/27/93

Metro-Goldwyn-Meyer
10000 W. Washington Blvd.
Culver City, CA 90232
Production Company V: 03/17/92

Metropolitan Talent
c/o Metro. Talent Agency
9320 Wilshire Blvd. 3rd Fl.
Beverly Hills, CA 90212
Talent Agency V: 02/23/93

Meyers, Ari
301 N. Canon Dr. #203
Beverly Hills, CA 90210
Actress V: 03/23/92

Meyers, David
10 Summit Ave.
Mill Valley, CA 94941
Producer V: 03/25/92

Meyers, Mike
c/o SNL NBC-TV
30 Rockefeller Plaza
New York, NY 10112
Actor V: 11/11/92

Meyers, Russell
770 N. Orange Ave.
Orlando, FL 32801
Cartoonist V: 02/14/92

c/o Tribune Media Services
64 E. Concord St.
Orlando, FL 32800
Alternate V: 01/12/92

Miami Dolphins
Joe Robbie Stadium
2269 NW 199th St.
Miami, FL 33056
Team Offices V: 05/15/92

Miami Sound Machine
1575 N.W. 27th Ave.
Miami, FL 33125
Musical Group V: 01/03/92

8730 Sunset Blvd. #600
Los Angeles, CA
Alternate V: 01/09/92

Miami Sound Machine, contd
8390 SW 4 St.
Miami, FL 33144
 Forwarded V: 03/15/92

Michael, George
P.O. Box 302
San Francisco, CA 94101
 Singer V: 03/01/92

#2 Elgin Mews
London W9, England
 Alternate V: 06/17/92

2 Eden Place
London W8, England
 Alternate V: 02/01/92

Michel, F. Curtis
c/o NASA LBJ Space Center
Houston, TX 77058
 Astronaut V: 03/03/93

Michell Agency
11425 Moorpark St.
Studio City, CA 91602
 Talent Agency V: 03/17/93

Midler, Bette
P.O. Box 46039
Hollywood, CA 90046
 Actress V: 03/01/93

c/o Disney/All Girl Prod.
500 S. Buena Vista St.
Burbank, CA 91521
 Alternate V: 05/12/92

9481 Readcrest Dr.
Beverly Hills, CA 90210
 L.R.U. V: 05/04/92

Mifune, Toshiro
9-30-7, Seijyo, Setagayaku
Tokyo, Japan
 Actor V: 03/12/92

Milano, Alyssa
c/o Columbia Pictures TV
"Who's the Boss"
1438 N. Gower Blvd.
Los Angeles, CA 90028
 Actress V: 12/01/92

Miles, Sarah
c/o G.R.F. International
82 Brook St.
London W1Y 1YG, England
 Actress V: 03/23/92

Miles, Sarah, contd
c/o Marina Martin
6A Danbury St.
London N1 8JJ, England
 Alternate V: 02/28/92

Miles, Sylvia
240 Central Park South
New York City, NY 10019
 Actress V: 03/01/92

Miles, Vera
P.O. Box 1704
Big Bear Lake, CA 92315-1704
 Actress V: 04/01/92

Miller, Ann
151 Ainslie St.
Brooklyn, NY 11211
 Actress V: 10/01/92

Miller, Arthur
Rural Route 1, Box 320
Tophet Road
Roxbury, CT 06783
 Author V: 09/22/92

Miller, Butch
c/o Miller Fan Club
2750 Pineridge Dr., Suite D
Grand Rapids, MI 49504
 BGN Driver V: 02/27/93

Miller, David Wiley
c/o King Features
216 East 45th St.
New York, NY 10017
 Cartoonist V: 07/30/92

Miller, Dennis
9200 Sunset Blvd. #428
Los Angeles, CA 90069
 Actor V: 01/07/92

c/o NBC Prod.
Saturday Night Live
30 Rockefeller Plaza
New York, NY 10112
 Forwarded V: 01/10/92

Miller, Dick
8852 Wonderland Ave.
Los Angeles, CA 90046
 Actor V: 01/17/92

Miller, Jeremy
c/o Growing Pains
4000 Warner Blvd.
Burbank, CA 91522
 Actor V: 12/03/92

Miller, Johnny
P.O. Box 2260
Napa, CA 94558-2260
Golf V: 02/18/92

Miller, Mitch
345 W. 58th St.
New York, NY 10019
Band Leader V: 01/11/92

Miller, Penelope
2121 Ave. of the Stars #950
Los Angeles, CA 90067
Actress V: 03/19/92

Miller, Sharron
15301 Ventura Blvd. #345
Sherman Oaks, CA 91403
Director V: 03/01/93

Million, Tiffany
c/o 5K Sales
9420 Reseda Blvd., Ste.836
Northridge, CA 91324
Adult Films V: 01/17/93

Mills, Ally
8995 Norma Pl.
Los Angeles, CA 90069
Actress V: 02/20/92

c/o New World TV
"The Wonder Years"
1440 S. Sepulveda Blvd.
Los Angeles, CA 90025
Forwarded V: 12/11/92

Mills, Billy
632 S. 2nd St.
P.O. Box 670
Raton, NM 87740-0670
Olympian V: 07/01/92

Mills, Donna
822 S. Robertson Blvd. #200
Los Angeles, CA 90035
Alternate V: 04/05/93

3970 Overland Ave.
Culver City, CA 90230
Forwarded V: 01/12/92

8966 Sunset Blvd.
Hollywood, CA 90069
L.R.U. V: 10/10/92

Mills, Hayley
15 Golden Square
London W2, England
Actress V: 03/02/93

Mills, Hayley, contd
81 High St.
Hampton, Middlesex, England
Alternate V: 02/01/92

c/o Agency
388 Oxford St.
London W1, England
Forwarded V: 03/11/92

c/o Chatto
Prince of Wales Theatre
Coventry St.
London W1V 7FE, England
Forwarded V: 03/06/92

Mills, John
c/o Agency
388 Oxford St.
London W1, England
Actor V: 03/11/92

c/o Thames TV Ltd.
306-316 Euston Rd.
London NW1 3BB, England
Alternate V: 03/22/92

Denham Village
Hill House
Buckinghamshire, England
Forwarded V: 03/17/93

Mills, Juliet
4036 Foothill Rd.
Carpinteria, CA 90313
Actress V: 02/12/92

Mills, Tonisha
P.O. Box 1026
Studio City, CA 91604
Adult Films V: 03/11/93

Milmoe, Caroline
c/o Martin-Smith
Half Moon Chamber
Chapel Walks
Manchester M2 1HN, England
Actress V: 06/03/92

Milwaukie Brewers
Milwaukie County Stadium
Milwaukie, WI 53214
Team Office V: 05/15/92

Miner, Jan
300 E. 46th St. Ste.9J
New York, NY 10017
Actress V: 03/23/92

Minnelli, Liza
150 E. 69th St. #21-G
New York, NY 10021
Actress V: 02/11/92

40 W. 57th St.
New York, NY 10019
Alternate V: 07/27/92

Minnesota Twins
501 Chicago Ave. S.
H.H. Humphrey Metrodome
Minneapolis, MN 55415
Team Office V: 05/15/92

Minnesota Vikings
9520 Viking Dr.
Eden Prairie, MN 55344
Team Offices V: 05/15/92

Miramar Agency
9157 Sunset Blvd. Ste.300
Los Angeles, CA 90069
Model/Talent Agency V: 03/19/93

Mirren, Helen
c/o Al Parker
55 Park Lane
London W1, England
Actress V: 02/28/92

Mishkin Agency
2355 Benedict Canyon
Beverly Hills, CA 90210
Talent Agency V: 04/01/93

Mitchell, Cameron
9744 Wilshire Blvd. #308
Beverly Hills, CA 90212
Actor V: 01/02/92

Mitchell, Edgar D.
c/o NASA LBJ Space Center
Houston, TX 77058
Astronaut V: 03/03/93

Mitchell, Guy
P.O. Box 43336
Las Vegas, NV 89116
Actor V: 11/11/92

Mitchell, Sam
c/o Minnesota Timberwolves
600 1st Ave. N.
Minneapolis, MN 55403-1416
Sports V: 05/29/92

730 Hennepin Ave. #500
Minneapolis, MN 55403
L.R.U. V: 05/29/92

Mitchell, Sasha
9057 #A Nemo St.
W. Hollywood, CA 90069
Actress V: 03/23/92

Mitchell, Sharon
9420 Reseda Blvd., #836
Northridge, CA 91324
Adult Films V: 03/03/93

Mitchell, Susan
c/o Dallas Cowboys
One Cowboys Parkway
Irving, TX 75063-4945
Cheerleader V: 08/08/92

Mitchum, Carrie
c/o Bold & Beautiful
7800 Beverly Blvd., Ste.3371
Los Angeles, CA 90036
Actress V: 06/15/92

Mitchum, John
15612 Liberty Circle
Neveda City, CA 95959
Actor V: 08/03/92

c/o Mitchum/Callow Prod.
808 N. Vine St.
Falbrook, CA 92028
Alternate V: 01/02/92

87 Snell St.
Sonora, CA 95370
Alternate V: 06/14/92

Mitchum, Robert
P.O. Box 5216
Montecito, CA 93108
Actor V: 06/01/92

860 San Ysidro Rd.
Santa Barbara, CA 93108
Alternate V: 04/10/92

Miyamura, Hiroshi H.
1905 Mossman
Gallup, NM 87301
Medal of Honor V: 02/04/92

Miyori, Kim
8033 Sunset Blvd. #770
Los Angeles, CA 90046
Actress V: 03/27/92

Mobley, Mary Ann
2751 Hutton Dr.
Beverly Hills, CA 90210
Actress V: 03/13/92

Mod Model/Talent Agency
6404 Wilshire Blvd. Ste.900
Los Angeles, CA 90048
Model/Talent Agency V: 02/12/92

Modine, Matthew
1632 N. Beverly Dr.
Beverly Hills, CA 90210
Actor V: 04/01/93

Modrzejewski, Robert J.
4725 Oporto Dr.
San Diego, CA 92124
Medal of Honor V: 01/16/92

Moechel Agency
200 N. Robertson Blvd. Ste.224
Beverly Hills, CA 90211
Talent Agency V: 01/26/93

Moffet, Randy
110 Lakeover Dr.
Athens, GA 30606
Baseball V: 12/10/92

Moise, Patty
c/o NASCAR
1811 Volusia Ave.
Daytona Beach, FL 32015
NASCAR Driver V: 03/02/92

Moll, Richard
c/o Warner Bros. TV
"Night Court"
4000 Warner Blvd., Office 12A
Burbank, CA 91521
Actor V: 01/12/92

Moller, Ralph
555 S. Barrington Ave. #325
Los Angeles, CA 90049
Bodybuilder V: 01/17/93

Moncrieff, Karen
c/o Price
1848 Bagley Ave.
Los Angeles, CA 90035
Actress V: 03/23/92

Mondale, Walter
2200 First Bank Place E.
Minneapolis, MN 55402
Former Vice-Pres. V: 02/21/92

Money, Eddie
P.O. Box 1994
San Francisco, CA 94101
Singer V: 03/01/92

Monroe, Tami
4354 Laurel Canyon Blvd. #144
Studio City, CA 91604
Adult Films V: 03/11/93

Montalban, Ricardo
9256 Robin Dr.
Los Angeles, CA 90069
Actor V: 02/11/92

15301 Ventura Blvd #345
Sherman Oaks, CA 91403
Alternate V: 08/20/92

c/o ABC-TV
4151 Prospect Ave.
Los Angeles, CA 90027
Alternate V: 03/30/93

Montana, Joe
711 Nevada St.
Redwood, CA 94061
Football V: 06/01/92

c/o SF 49ers
4949 Centennial Blvd.
Santa Clara, CA 95054-1229
Alternate V: 06/01/92

Montana, Monte
10234 Escondito Canyon
Aqua Dulce, CA 91350
Actor V: 03/02/92

10326 Montana Ln.
Aqua Dulce, CA 91350
Alternate V: 05/22/92

520 Murray Canyon
Palm Springs, CA 92264
Actor V: 05/22/92

Montgomery, Belinda
c/o Steven Bochco Prods.
"Doogie Howser, M.D."
10201 W. Pico Blvd.
Los Angeles, CA 90035
Actress V: 12/15/92

Montgomery, Elizabeth
1230 Benedict Canyon Dr.
Beverly Hills, CA 90210
Actress V: 04/22/92

Montgomery, George
c/o Sagebrush Inc.
P.O. Box 69983
Los Angeles, CA 90069
Actor V: 03/02/92

Montiel, H. Pierre
103 W. 73rd St.
New York, NY 10023
Artist V: 01/09/92

Montreal Expos
P.O. Box 500, Station M
Olympic Stadium
Montreal, Quebec, Canada H1V 3P2
Olympic Office V: 05/15/92

Moody, Bobby
c/o Childress
P.O. Box 1189 Industrial Dr.
Welcome, NC 27374
Race Driver V: 03/12/93

Moody, Ron
Ingleside 41, The Green
Southgate
London N14, England
Actor V: 01/08/92

Moore, Alvy
8546 Amestoy Ave.
Northridge, CA 91324
Actor V: 03/10/92

Moore, Bud
4 Duck Lane
Isle of Pines, SC 29451
NASCAR Driver V: 03/02/92

400 N. Fairview Ave.
Spartanburg, SC 29304
Alternate V: 03/02/92

Moore, Clayton
4720 Park Olivo
Calabasas, CA 91302
Actor V: 02/04/92

Moore, Constance
1661 Ferrari Dr.
Beverly Hills, CA 90210
Actress V: 03/02/92

Moore, Demi
9830 Wilshire Blvd.
Beverly Hills, CA 90212
Actress V: 01/16/92

13511 Mulholland Dr.
Beverly Hills, CA 90210
L.R.U. V: 01/02/92

Moore, Dudley
73 Market St.
Venice, CA 90291
Actor V: 12/08/92

Moore, Dudley, contd
5505 Ocean Front Walk
Marina del Rey, CA 90291
Alternate V: 04/01/93

Moore, Gary
P.O.Box 533
Northeast Harbor, ME 04662
TV Host V: 02/05/92

Moore, John Travers
827 N. Justice
Hendersonville, NC 28739
Author V: 01/11/92

Moore, Juanita
3802-L Dunsford Lane
Inglewood, CA 90305
Actress V: 02/18/92

Moore, Mary Tyler
c/o MTM Enterprises
4024 Radford Ave.
Studio City, CA 91604
Actress V: 07/03/92

927 5th Ave.
New York, NY 10021
Forwarded V: 06/17/92

Moore, Melanie
P.O Box 15567
Beverly Hills, CA 90209
Adult Films V: 03/11/93

Moore, Melba
200 Central Park S. Ste.8R
New York, NY 10019
Singer V: 02/18/92

Moore, Melissa Anne
11288 Ventura Blvd. Ste.B 389
Studio City, CA 91604
Actress V: 03/03/93

7060 Hollywood Bl. #1216
Hollywood, CA 90028
L.R.U. V: 12/10/92

Moore, Roger
Chalet Fenil, Grund Bei
Staad, Switzerland
Actor V: 03/10/92

c/o Agency
388-396 Oxford St.
London W1 9HE, England
Forwarded V: 03/17/92

Moreau, Jean
c/o George Beaume
3 Quia Malquais
Paris 75006, France
Actress V: 03/02/92

193 rue de l'Universite
75 007 Paris, France
Alternate V: 06/17/92

Moreno, Rita
c/o Wm Morris
151 El Camino Dr.
Beverly Hills, CA 90212
Actress V: 05/15/92

1620 Amalfi Dr.
Pacific Palisades, CA 90272
Alternate V: 05/12/92

c/o Wm. Morris Agency
1350 Ave. of the Americas
New York, NY 10009
Forwarded V: 06/01/92

Moret, Angelique
2151 El Camino #1115
Beverly Hills, CA 90210
Actress V: 02/21/92

Morey, Bill
6310 San Vicente Blvd.
Beverly Hills, CA 90211
Actor V: 01/16/93

Morgan, Britt
P.O. Box 1382
Hollywood, CA 90078
Adult Films V: 03/11/93

Morgan, Harry
13172 Boca de Canon Rd.
Los Angeles, CA 90049
Actor V: 01/15/93

Morgan, Lorrie
c/o Moress, Nanas, Shea
1209 16th Ave. S.
Nashville, TN 37212
Singer V: 01/20/93

Morgan, Reed
12524 Culver Blvd. #17
Los Angeles, CA 90066
Actor V: 06/15/92

Morgan, Renee
9333 Oso Ave.
Chatsworth, CA 91311
Actress V: 09/06/92

Moriarty, Cathy
9005 Burton Way #601
Los Angeles, CA 90048
Actress V: 03/27/93

Moriarty, Michael
c/o Witt/Thomas
"Law & Order"
100 Universal City Plaza, Bl.G
Universal City, CA 91608
Actor V: 01/12/92

Morin, Jim
c/o King Features
216 E. 45th St.
New York, NY 10017
Cartoonist V: 03/11/93

Morison, Patricia
400 S. Hauser Blvd. Ste.9-L
Los Angeles, CA 90036
Actress V: 04/16/92

Morita, Pat
P.O. Box 491278
Los Angeles, CA 90049-9278
Actor V: 02/28/92

Morris, Gary
c/o Singers & Songwriters
6027 Church Dr.
Sugarland, TX 77478
Actor V: 01/22/92

Morris, Phil
c/o GTG Ent./Culver Studios
9336 W. Washington Blvd.
Culver City, CA 90232
Actor V: 05/15/92

Morris Agency
151 El Camino
Beverly Hills, CA 90212
Talent Agency V: 01/24/93

Morrison, Glenn
c/o Dallas Cowboys
One Cowboys Parkway
Irving, TX 75063-4945
Cheerleader V: 08/08/92

Morrison, James
c/o ABC-TV
General Hospital
4151 Prospect Ave.
Hollywood, CA 90027
Actor V: 06/15/92

Morrow, Jeff
4828 Balboa Ave. #B
Encino, CA 91316
Actor V: 02/21/92

Morrow, Rob
c/o Pipeline Prod.
7140 180th Ave. N.E.
Redmond, WA 98052
Actor V: 03/05/93

c/o Cine-Nevada Inc.
Northern Exposure
3000 Olympic Blvd., Ste.2575
Santa Monica, CA 90404
Alternate V: 05/15/92

Morse, Barry
P.O. Box 1572
Jasper, T0E JE0 Alberta
Canada
Actor V: 04/23/92

Morse, David
c/o Bikoff Agency
9120 Sunset Blvd.
Los Angeles, CA 90069
Actor V: 03/17/92

Morse, Helen
147A King St.
Sydney, NSW 2000, Australia
Actress V: 03/02/92

Morton, Joe
c/o Orion
Equal Justice
1888 Century Park East
Los Angeles, CA 90067
Actor V: 12/18/92

Moscone, Willie
1804 Prospect Ridge Blvd.
Hardon Heights, NJ 08035
Billiard Pro V: 02/01/92

Mosley, Bryan
c/o Granada TV
36 Golden Square
London W1R 4AH, England
Actor V: 03/17/92

Mosley, Roger E.
c/o Aimee Ent.
13743 Victory Blvd.
Van Nuys, CA 91401
Actor V: 03/17/92

Moss, Ronn
c/o CBS-TV/Young & Restless
7800 Beverly Blvd.
Los Angeles, CA 90036
Actor V: 03/04/92

Moss & Associates
8019 1/2 Melrose Ave. #3
Los Angeles, CA 90046
Talent Agency V: 03/14/93

Motion Picture Arts & Sciences
8949 Wilshire Blvd.
Beverly Hills, CA 90211
Academy Office V: 03/17/92

Motion Picture Assn.
14144 Ventura Blvd.
Sherman Oaks, CA 91423
Production Company V: 03/17/92

Movie Channel
1633 Broadway
New York, NY 10019
Network HQ V: 03/01/92

100 Universal City Plz.31st Fl
Unversal City, CA 91608
Alternate V: 03/17/92

Moviecorp VII Inc.
3131 Lakeshore Blvd. W.
Toronto, M8V 1K9 Ontario
Canada
Company HQ V: 03/01/92

92 Isabella St.
Toronto, M4Y 1N4 Ontario
Canada
Alternate V: 03/01/92

Movieline
1141 S. Beverly Drive
Los Angeles, CA 90099-2024
Magazine V: 03/21/92

Movies USA
8010 Roswell Rd.
Atlanta, GA 30350
Magazine V: 03/03/92

Moving Image & Sound Archives
395 Wellington St.
Ottawa, Ontario K1A ON3 Canada
Archive V: 03/14/93

Movita
2766 Motor Ave.
Los Angeles, CA 90064
Actress V: 02/18/92

Mr. T
395 Green Bay Rd.
Lake Forest, IL 60045
Actor V: 03/04/93

Mrecouri, Melina
Anagnostropoulon 25
Athens, Greece
Actress V: 03/23/92

Mubarak, M.
c/o Soheil Lasheen
Office Of The President
Cairo, Egypt
President V: 03/21/92

Mudd, Roger
7167 Old Dominion Dr.
McLean, VA 22101
Newsman V: 03/01/92

3620 27th St. South
Arlington, VA 22206
Alternate V: 02/16/92

Mueller-Stahl, Armin
Gartnweg 31
D-(W) 2430 Sirksdprf, Germany
Actor V: 01/17/93

c/o ZBF Agentur
Ordensmeisterstr. 15-16
D-(W) 1000 Berlin 42
Germany
Alternate V: 02/11/93

Muir, Esther
587 Heritage Hills Dr. Ste.D
Somers, NY 10589-1908
Actress V: 02/18/92

Muldaur, Diana
259 Quadro Vecchio Dr.
Pacific Palisades, CA 90272
Actress V: 04/18/92

Muldaur, Maria
P.O. Box 5535
Mill Valley, CA 94942-5525
Singer V: 02/27/93

Mulgrew, Kate
11938 Foxboro Dr.
Los Angeles, CA 90049
Actress V: 03/27/93

Mulhern, Matt
9350 Wilshire Blvd. #324
Beverly Hills, CA 90212
Actor V: 01/16/93

Mull, Martin
338 Chadbourne Ave.
Los Angeles, CA 90049
Actor V: 01/22/92

Mullane, Richard
c/o NASA LBJ Space Center
Houston, TX 77058
Astronaut V: 03/03/93

Mullard, Arthur
c/o Essannay Ltd.
75 Hammersmith Rd.
London W14, England
Actor V: 02/27/92

Mullen, Chris
c/o Golden State Warriors
Oakland Coliseum
Oakland, CA 94621
Basketball V: 12/16/92

Mullen, Patricia
233 Park Ave. S. 10th Fl.
New York, NY 10017
Actress V: 12/20/92

Muller, Marius
c/o ZBF Agentur
Leopoldstr. 19
D-(W) 8000 Munchen 40, Germany
Actor V: 01/17/93

Mulligan, Richard
145 S. Beachwood Dr.
Los Angeles, CA 90004
Actor V: 03/24/92

Mulloy, John
c/o Childress
P.O. Box 1189 Industrial Dr.
Welcome, NC 27374
Race Crew V: 03/12/93

MultiMedia Films
10401 W. Jefferson Blvd.
Culver City, CA 90232
Production Company V: 03/17/92

Mumy, Bill
2419 Laurel Pass Ave.
Los Angeles, CA 90046
Actor V: 01/02/92

9169 Sunset Blvd.
Los Angeles, CA 90069
Alternate V: 11/11/92

Munro, Caroline
1348 Fern Ave.
Reading, PA 19607
 Actress V: 03/01/92

22 Grafton St.
London W1, England
 Alternate V: 01/17/92

Murphy, Ben
3601 Vista Pacifica #17
Malibu, CA 90265
 Actor V: 06/17/92

Murphy, Eddie
2727 Benedict Canyon
Beverly Hills, CA 90210
 Actor V: 06/17/92

5555 Melrose Ave.
Hollywood, CA 90038-3197
 Alternate V: 01/11/92

Murphy, John Cullen
c/o King Features
216 East 45th St.
New York, NY 10017
 Cartoonist V: 04/01/93

Murphy Agency
6014 Greenbush Ave.
Van Nuys, CA 91401
 Talent Agency V: 02/19/93

Murray, Anne
4881 Yonge St. #412
Toronto, M2N 5X3 Ontario
Canada
 Singer V: 01/23/92

Murray, Barbara
c/o Rank Organization
6 Connaught Pl.
London W2 2EZ, England
 Actress V: 01/17/92

Murray, Bill
P.O. Box 573
Palisades, NY 10964
 Actor V: 03/27/93

375 Greenwich St.
New York, NY 10013
 L.R.U. V: 07/01/92

Murray, Don
440 Santa Rosa
Santa Rosa, CA 93108
 Actor V: 02/05/92

Murray, Don, contd
c/o Paramount Pictures
5555 Melrose Ave., Wilder #214
Los Angeles, CA 90038
 Forwarded V: 05/15/92

Murray, Jan
1157 Calle Vista Dr.
Beverly Hills, CA 90210
 Actor V: 09/09/92

Murray, Ken
2370 Bowmont Dr.
Beverly Hills, CA 90210
 Actor V: 06/23/92

Murray, Linda
P.O. Box 3998
Centerline, MI 48015-0998
 Ms. Olympia V: 11/11/92

Murtagh, Kate
15146 Moorpark St.
Sherman Oaks, CA 91403
 Actress V: 06/17/92

Museum of Broadcasting
1 East 53rd St.
New York, NY 10022
 Archive V: 01/30/93

Museum of Jewish Heritage
342 Madison Ave., Room 717
New York, NY 10017
 Archive V: 01/30/93

Museum of Modern Art
Dept. of Film
11 W. 53rd St.
New York, NY 10019
 Archive V: 03/20/93

Museum-Broadcast Comm.
233 N. Michigan Ave., Ste 1911
Chicago, IL 60601
 Archive V: 03/20/93

Musgrave, Ted
c/o Radius Motorsports
P.O. Box 950
Denver, NC 28037
 NASCAR Driver V: 03/02/92

Musgrove, F. Story
c/o NASA LBJ Space Center
Houston, TX 77058
 Astronaut V: 03/03/93

Mussolini, Alessandra
Camera di Deputati
Gruppo del MSI-DN
I-00100 Rome, Italy
Politician V: 12/19/92

Muti, Ornella
17a Via N. Martelli 3
Rome, Italy
Actress V: 01/17/93

Myers, Danny
c/o Childress
P.O. Box 1189 Industrial Dr.
Welcome, NC 27374
Race Crew V: 03/12/93

Myers, Mike
RFD #1, Box 250A
Washington Station
Palisades, NY 10964
Actor V: 01/07/92

Mynx, Tiffany
P.O. Box 93607
Los Angeles, CA 90093
Adult Films V: 03/11/93

N

NAME YOUR ADVENTURE
Big Daddy Prod.
P.O. Box 7304
N. Hollywood, CA 91603
Production Company V: 03/26/93

NASA
LBJ Space Center
Houston, TX 77058
Test Center V: 03/15/92

NASA Magazine
c/o Internal Comm. Branch
Code P-2 NASA Headquarters
Washington, DC 20402
Magazine V: 03/03/92

NBA INSIDE STUFF
c/o NBA Enter.
38 E. 32nd St., 4th Fl.
New York, NY 10016
Production Company V: 06/15/92

NBC-TV
30 Rockefeller Plaza
New York, NY 10112
Network HQ V: 03/01/92

NBC-TV
3000 W. Alemeda
Burbank, CA 91523
Alternate V: 03/01/92

NIGHT COURT
Warner Bros. Television
4000 Warner Blvd.
Office 12A
Burbank, CA 91522
Production Company V: 03/26/93

NIGHTLINE
c/o ABC-TV
1717 DeSales St. NW
Washington, DC 20036
Production Company V: 03/19/93

NIGHTMARE CAFE
Wes Craven Prod. 3016C
10000 W. Washington Blvd.
Culver City, CA 90232
Production Company V: 03/26/93

NORTHERN EXPOSURE
c/o Cine-Nevada Inc.
Northern Exposure
3000 Olympic Blvd., Ste.2575
Santa Monica, CA 90404
Production Company V: 05/15/92

c/o Pipeline Prod.
Northern Exposure
1600 132nd Ave. N.E.
Bellevue, WA 98005
Alternate V: 06/15/92

NURSES
Witt, Thomas, Harris Prod.
846 N. Cahuenga Blvd.
Los Angeles, CA 90038
Production Company V: 03/26/93

NYC Dept./Records & Info.
Municipal Archives
31 Chambers St., Rm. 101
New York, NY 10007
Archive V: 03/20/93

Nabors, Jim
151 El Camino
Beverly Hills, CA 90212
Actor V: 01/21/92

215 Kulamanu
Honolulu, HI 96816
Alternate V: 04/01/92

Nabors, Jim, contd
P.O. Box 707
Honokaa, HI 96726
L.R.U. *V: 04/01/92*

Nader, Ralph
P.O. Box 19367
Washington, DC 20036
Consumer Advocate *V: 09/02/92*

Nagel, Steven R.
c/o NASA LBJ Space Center
Houston, TX 77058
Astronaut *V: 03/03/93*

Namath, Joe
300 E. 51st St. #11A
New York, NY 10022
Football *V: 12/10/92*

Napier, Charles
Star Route Box 60H
Caliente, CA 93518
Actor *V: 02/12/92*

c/o MTA
9320 Wilshire Blvd. #324, 3rd Fl.
Beverly Hills, CA 90212
Alternate *V: 01/16/93*

Napier, Hugo
c/o General Hosp./ABC Inc.
4151 Prospect Ave.
Hollywood, CA 90027
Actor *V: 03/01/92*

Nashville Network
2806 Opryland Dr.
Nashville, Tn 37214
Network HQ *V: 03/01/92*

Nat'l Archives/Records Adm.
Motion Picture, Sound & Video Branch
Pennsylvania Ave. at 8th St. N.W.
Washington, DC 20408
Archive *V: 01/30/93*

Nat'l Assn. of Fan Clubs
c/o Ms. Linda Kay
P.O. Box 7487
Burbank, CA 91510
Central Office *V: 12/12/92*

Nat'l Center Film & Video
The American Film Institute
P.O. Box 27999
2021 N. Western Ave.
Los Angeles, CA 90027
Archive *V: 03/20/93*

Nat'l Center for Jewish Film
Brandeis University
Lown Building #102
Waltham, MA 02254
Archive *V: 03/20/93*

Nat'l Football League
410 Park Ave.
New York, NY 10022
League HQ *V: 12/10/92*

Nat'l Lampoon Films
11255 W. Olympic Blvd.
Los Angeles, CA 90064
Production Company *V: 03/17/92*

3619 Motor Ave. #300
Los Angeles, CA 90034
Alternate *V: 03/17/92*

Nat'l League HQ
350 Park Ave.
New York, NY 10022
Team Office *V: 05/15/92*

Nat'l Library of Medicine
Nat. Medical Historical Film Coll.
Audio-Visual Resource Section
8600 Rockville Pike
Bethesda, MD 20894
Archive *V: 03/20/93*

Nat'l Theatre Archive
1321 Pennsylvania Ave. NW
Washington, DC 20004
Archive *V: 03/20/93*

Nathe & Associates
8281 Melrose Ave. #200
Los Angeles, CA 90046
Talent Agency *V: 02/19/93*

Natividad, Kitten
P.O. Box 48938
Los Angeles, CA 90048
Actress *V: 03/26/93*

Natwick, Mildred
1001 Park Ave.
New York, NY 10028
Actress *V: 06/17/92*

14 Sutton Pl. South. 6B
New York, NY 10022
Alternate *V: 03/14/93*

Naud, Melinda
12330 Viewcrest Rd.
Studio City, CA 91604
Actress *V: 02/18/92*

Neal, Patricia
P.O. Box 1043
Edgartown, MA 02539
Actress V: 03/03/92

Neal, Patricia
9869 Santa Monica Blvd. #207
Beverly Hills, CA 90212
Alternate V: 03/15/92

Needham, Connie
8075 W. 3rd St. #303
Beverly Hills, CA 90211
Actress V: 02/01/92

Neely, Cam
c/o Boston Bruins
150 Causeway St.
Boston, MA 02114
Hockey V: 04/05/93

Neill, Noel
331 Sage Lane
Santa Monica, CA 90402
Actress V: 03/02/92

Nelson, Byron
Rt.2, Fairway Ranch, Litsey Rd.
Roanoake, TX 76262
Golf V: 02/04/92

Nelson, Craig T.
28872 Boniface Dr.
Malibu, CA 90265
Actor V: 01/12/92

c/o Universal TV
Coach
100 Universal Plaza, Bung.78
Universal City, CA 91608
Forwarded V: 12/18/92

Nelson, Gary
c/o NASCAR
1811 Volusia Ave.
Daytona Beach, FL 32015
NASCAR Inspector V: 03/02/92

Nelson, Gene
c/o KSFO
300 Broadway
San Francisco, CA 94133
Radio Host V: 04/18/93

Nelson, George D.
c/o NASA LBJ Space Center
Houston, TX 77058
Astronaut V: 03/03/93

Nelson, Judd
P.O. Box 69170
Los Angeles, CA 90069
Actor V: 01/16/93

Nelson, Ray Faraday
333 Ramona Ave.
El Cerrito, CA 94530
Inventor V: 03/01/92

Nelson, Tracy
405/407 Sycamore Rd.
Santa Monica, CA 90402
Actress V: 08/15/92

Nelson, Willie
Rt.1 Briarcliff 2
Spicewood, TX 78669
Singer V: 01/02/92

P.O. Box 33280
Austin, TX 78764
Alternate V: 03/27/93

Nemechek, Joe
P.O. Box 1131
Mooresville, NC 28115
Race Driver V: 03/12/93

Nena
c/o Bernd Reisig GmbH
Merianstr. 39
D-(W) 6000 Frankfurt/Main 1, Germany
Singer V: 01/17/93

Nero, Franco
Via di Monte del Gallo 26
I-00165 Rome, Italy
Actor V: 01/17/93

Nesmith, Michael
c/o Pacific Arts Video
P.O. Box 7408
Carmel, CA 93921
Producer V: 04/01/92

Nettles, John
c/o Saraband Assoc.
265 Liverpool Rd.
London N1 1LX, England
Actor V: 03/17/92

Nettleton, Lois
c/o Mann
11762-G Moorpark St.
Studio City, CA 91604-2120
Actress V: 11/11/92

Neuwirth, Bebe
Paramount/Cheers
5555 Melrose Ave./Ball RM105
Hollywood, CA 90038
Actress V: 01/07/92

New Century Vista
5757 Wilshire Blvd. #723
Los Angeles, CA 90036
Distributor V: 03/17/92

New Century Vista
1875 Century Park E. Suite 200
Los Angeles, CA 90067
Alternate V: 03/01/92

New England Patriots
Sullivan Stadium, Rt.1
Foxboro, MA 02035
Team Offices V: 05/15/92

New Horizon Pictures
11600 San Vincente Blvd.
Los Angeles, CA 90049
Production Company V: 03/17/92

New Kids on the Block
P.O. Box 7001
Quincey, MA 02269
Band V: 03/04/93

New Orleans Saints
6928 Saints Ave.
Metairie, LA 70003
Team Offices V: 05/15/92

New Vision Entertainment
5757 Wilshire Blvd. #600
Los Angeles, CA 90036
Film Distributor V: 03/17/92

New World Entertainment
1440 S. Sepulveda Blvd.
Los Angeles, CA 90025
Production Company V: 03/17/92

New York Giants
Giants Stadium
East Rutherford, NJ 07073
Team Offices V: 05/15/92

New York Jets
598 Madison Ave.
New York, NY 10022
Team Offices V: 05/15/92

1000 Fulton Ave.
Hempstead, NY 11550
Alternate V: 05/15/92

New York Mets
Shea Stadium
Flushing, NY 11368
Team Office V: 05/15/92

New York Public Library
Performing Arts Reserch Center
Dance Collection
111 Amsterdam Ave.
New York, NY 10009
Archive V: 03/20/93

New York Yankees
Yankee Stadium
Bronx, NY 10451
Team Office V: 05/15/92

Newhart, Bob
c/o Newhart MTM Prod.
4024 Radford
Studio City, CA 91604
Actor V: 01/02/92

Newly, Anthony
4419 Van Nuys Blvd. Ste.304-B
Sherman Oaks, CA 91403
Actor V: 01/14/92

3249 Hutton Dr.
Beverly Hills, CA 90210
L.R.U. V: 04/12/92

Newman, James H.
c/o NASA LBJ Space Center
Houston, TX 77058
Astronaut V: 03/03/93

Newman, Laraine
10480 Ashton Ave.
Los Angeles, CA 90024
Actress V: 01/02/92

Newman, Nancy
c/o CNN-Sport Dept.
1050 Techwood Dr. NW
Atlanta, GA 30318
Commentator V: 11/30/92

Newman, Nanette
c/o Chatto
Prince of Wales Theatre
Coventry St.
London W1V 7FE, England
Actress V: 03/06/93

c/o Agent
The Bookshop, Virginia Water
Surrey, England
Alternate V: 04/06/93

Newman, Paul
1120 5th Ave. #1C
New York, NY 10128
Actor V: 08/30/92

477 Madison Ave.
New York, NY 10022-5802
Alternate V: 11/01/92

Newman, Wendy
c/o Dallas Cowboys
One Cowboys Parkway
Irving, TX 75063-4945
Cheerleader V: 08/08/92

Newmar, Julie
204 S. Carmelina Ave.
Los Angeles, CA 90049
Actress V: 10/10/92

c/o Eat A Pita
465 Fairfax Ave.
Los Angeles, CA 90036
Alternate V: 04/21/92

Newton, Richard
c/o Viacom Prod.
Matlock
100 Universal City Plaza, Bl. 448
Universal City, CA 91608
Actor V: 12/01/92

Newton, Wayne
4220 S. Maryland Parkway
Building B Suite 401
Las Vegas, NV 89119
Actor V: 03/02/92

6000 S. Eastern Ave. Ste.7B
Las Vegas, NV 89119
Alternate V: 01/06/92

c/o Flying Eagle Inc.
3422 Happy Lane
Las Vegas, NV 89120
Alternate V: 03/30/93

Newton-John, Olivia
P.O. Box 2710
Malibu, CA 90265
Actress V: 02/22/92

7204 3/4 Melrose Ave.
Los Angeles, CA 90036
Forwarded V: 01/07/92

Nichols, Bobby
8681 Glenlyon Ct.
Ft. Meyers, FL 33912
Golfer V: 02/04/92

Nichols, Mike
35 E. 76th St.
New York, NY 10021
Actor V: 02/11/92

Nichols, Nichelle
c/o Florence Butler
P.O. Box 1051
Silver Spring, MD 20910
Actress V: 03/01/92

23281 Leonora Dr.
Woodland Hills, CA 91367
Forwarded V: 03/16/92

22647 Ventura Blvd. #121
Woodland Hills, CA 91364
L.R.U. V: 01/04/92

Nichols, Stephen
NBC Daytime Programming
3000 W. Alameda Ave.
Burbank, CA 91523
Actor V: 09/01/92

Nicholson, Jack
12850 Mulholland Dr.
Beverly Hills, CA 90210
Actor V: 03/15/92

911 W. Pico Blvd. #PH-A
Los Angeles, CA 90035
Alternate V: 01/16/92

Nickelodeon/MTV
1515 Broadway
New York, NY 10036
Network HQ V: 11/11/92

Nicklaus, Jack
11780 U.S. HWY 1
Palm Beach, FL 33408
Golf V: 11/11/92

11397 Old Harbor Rd.
N. Palm Beach, FL 33408
Alternate V: 11/11/92

1208 US HWY 1
N. Palm Beach, FL 33408
Forwarded V: 01/02/92

Nicks, Stevie
c/o Ginny Kamano
P.O. Box 6907
Alhambra, CA 91802
Singer V: 08/09/92

Nickson, Julia
c/o Soul
2232 Moreno Dr.
Los Angeles, CA 90030-3044
 Actress V: 06/17/92

Niekro, Joe
39 Shadow Ln.
Lakeland, FL 33813
 Baseball V: 12/10/92

Nielson, Brigitte
12400 Wilshire #930
Los Angeles, CA 90025
 Actress V: 04/01/92

Nielson, Leslie
1622 Viewmont Dr.
Los Angeles, CA 90069
 Actor V: 01/12/92

Niemi, Lisa
9057 Nemo St. #A
W. Hollywood, CA 90069
 Actress V: 01/16/93

Nillowitsch, Willi
Vinzenzallee 11
D-(W) 5000 Koln 40
Germany
 Actor V: 02/11/93

Nilsson, Harry
23960 Long Valley Rd.
Hidden Hills, CA 91302
 Singer V: 03/27/93

10549 Rocca Pl.
Los Angeles, CA 90049
 Alternate V: 06/17/92

Nimmo, Derek
Grafton House, Ste. 42-43
2-3 Golden Square
London W1R 3AD, England
 Actor V: 03/17/93

Nimoy, Leonard
328 S. Beverly Dr. #A
Beverly Hills, CA 90212
 Director V: 02/02/92

17 Gateway Dr.
Batavia, NY 14020
 Alternate V: 11/11/92

c/o Francis/Freeman
501 S. Beverly Dr. 3rd Fl.
Beverly Hills, CA 90212-4514
 Alternate V: 03/30/93

Nimoy, Leonard, contd
P.O. Box 5617
Beverly Hills, CA 90210
 Forwarded V: 06/11/92

Nixon, Pat
577 Chestnut Ridge Rd.
Woodcliff Lake, NJ 07675
 Former First Lady V: 03/04/93

Nixon, Richard
577 Chestnut Ridge Rd.
Woodcliff Lake, NJ 07675
 Former President V: 03/21/92

Nolan, Jeanette
1417 Samona Way
Laguna Beach, CA 92651
 Actress V: 03/01/92

Nolan, Kathleen
360 E. 55th St., #PH
New York, NY 10022
 Actress V: 02/18/92

Nolte, Nick
6173 Bonsall Dr.
Malibu, CA 90265
 Actor V: 06/17/92

Noone, Kathleen
130 W. 42nd St. #1804
New York, NY 10036
 Actress V: 07/01/92

Norcross, Clayton
951 Galloway St.
Pacific Palisades, CA 90272
 Actor V: 01/16/93

Norman, Greg
1 Erieview Plaza
Cleveland, OH 44114-1782
 Golfer V: 02/04/92

Norris, Chuck
8200 Wilshire Blvd.
Beverly Hills, CA 90212
 Actor V: 06/14/92

P.O. Box 872
Navasota, TX 77868
 Alernate V: 11/11/92

North, Chris
c/o Witt/Thomas
"Law & Order"
100 Universal City Plaza, Bl.G
Universal City, CA 91608
 Actor V: 01/12/92

North, Oliver
703 Kentland Dr.
Great Falls, VA 22066
Soldier V: 02/01/92

North, Sheree
27 Village Park Way
Santa Monica, CA 90405
Actress V: 03/03/93

Northeast Historic Film
Blue Hill Falls, ME 04615
Archive V: 03/20/93

Norton-Taylor, Judy
6767 Forest Lawn Dr. #115
Los Angeles, CA 90068
Actress V: 03/27/93

Norville, Deborah
829 Park Ave. #10A
New York, NY 10022
TV Hostess V: 03/27/93

Notre Dame Football
c/o Manager
P.O. Box 518
Notre Dame, IN 46556
Team Office V: 02/01/92

Nova, Kassi
c/o Five K Sales Co.
9420 Reseda Blvd., #836
Northridge, CA 91324
Adult Films V: 03/03/93

Novak, Kim
24700 Outlook Dr.
Carmel, CA 93923
Actress V: 04/01/92

Rt. 3 Box 524
Carmel, CA 93921
Forwarded V: 02/21/92

Novello, Don
P.O. Box 245
Fairfax, CA 94930
Actor V: 06/17/92

Nuyen, France
1800 Franklin Canyon Terr.
Beverly Hills, CA 90210
Actress V: 06/17/92

Nye, Carrie
109 E. 79th St. #2C
New York, NY 10021
Actress V: 02/18/92

O

O'Brian, Hugh
3195 Benedict Canyon Rd.
Beverly Hills, CA 90210
Actor V: 03/16/92

O'Brien, Margaret
1250 La Preresa Dr.
Thousand Oaks, CA 91362
Actress V: 02/12/92

O'Brien, Richard
c/o Chatto
Prince of Wales Theatre
Coventry St.
London W1V 7FE, England
Actor V: 03/17/92

O'Connell, Helen
c/o Chamales
1260 S. Beverly Glen #108
Los Angeles, CA 90025
Actress V: 06/17/92

O'Connor, Bryan D.
c/o NASA
LBJ Space Center
Houston, TX 77058
Astronaut V: 01/31/92

O'Connor, Carroll
c/o Ugo Productions
P.O. Box 49935
Los Angeles, CA 90049-0935
Actor V: 07/21/92

30826 Broad Beach Rd.
Malibu, CA 90265
Actor V: 06/17/92

c/o MGM/UA Comm.
In the Heat of the Night
1000 W. Washington Blvd.
Culver City, CA 90232
Forwarded V: 01/07/92

O'Connor, Donald
P.O. Box 4524
Valley Village Station
N. Hollywood, CA 91607
Actor V: 06/01/92

3715 Alomar Rd.
Sherman Oaks, CA 91423
Forwarded V: 05/24/92

O'Connor, Hugh
"In the Heat of the Night"
1000 W. Washington Blvd.
Culver City, CA 90232
Actor V: 01/07/92

O'Connor, Sinead
10 Halsey House
13 Red Lion Square
London WC1, England
Singer V: 05/02/92

O'Connor, Tim
10000 Santa Monica Blvd. #305
Los Angeles, CA 90067
Actor V: 03/15/92

O'Day, Molly
P.O. Box 2123
Avila Beach, CA 93424
Actress V: 02/18/92

O'Driscoll, Martha
c/o Appleton
22 Indian Circle Dr.
Miami Beach, FL 33154
Actress V: 02/18/92

O'Hara, Maureen
Lugdine Park Glengariff
County Cork, Ireland
Actress V: 03/12/92

c/o Blair
P.O. Box 1400
Christieansted, VI 00821
Actress V: 03/02/93

O'Keefe, Michael
c/o CAA
9830 Wilshire Blvd.
Beverly Hills, CA 90212
Actor V: 01/16/93

O'Keefe, Miles
P.O. Box 216
Malibu, CA 90265
Actor V: 03/27/93

c/o Irv Schecter Co.
9300 Wilshire Blvd. Ste.410
Beverly Hills, CA 90212
Alternate V: 04/01/92

O'Leary, Brian T.
c/o NASA LBJ Space Center
Houston, TX 77058
Astronaut V: 03/03/93

O'Leary, Hazel
Dept. of Energy
1000 Independence Ave. S.W.
Washington, DC 20585
Secretary of Energy V: 01/31/93

O'Neal, Ryan
21368 Pacific Coast Hwy.
Malibu, CA 90265
Actor V: 03/12/92

328 S. Beverly Dr. #A
Beverly Hills, CA 90212
Alternate V: 01/11/92

O'Neal, Tatum
23712 Malibu Colony Dr.
Malibu, CA 90265
Actress V: 04/01/92

O'Neill, Ed
2607 Grand Canal
Venice, CA 90291
Actor V: 03/27/93

10201 W. Pico Blvd.
Los Angeles, CA 90035
Forwarded V: 01/12/92

O'Neill, Jennifer
32356 Mulholland Hwy.
Malibu, CA 90265
Actress V: 03/27/93

O'Sullivan, Maureen
1839 Union St.
Schenectady, NY 12309
Actress V: 02/12/92

O'Toole, Annette
360 Morton St.
Ashland, OR 97520-3065
Actress V: 03/07/92

O'Toole, Peter
98 Heath St.
London, NW3 England
Actor V: 03/15/92

ONE LIFE TO LIVE
c/o ABC-TV
33 W. 60th St. 7th Fl.
New York, NY 10023
Actress V: 03/19/93

OUT ALL NIGHT
NBC/Raleigh Studios
5300 Melrose Ave.
Los Angeles, CA 90038
Production Company V: 03/26/93

Oak Ridge Boys
329 Rockland Rd.
Hendersonville, TN 37075
Singers V: 03/15/92

Oakes, Randi
c/o Harrison
3681 Alomar Dr.
Sherman Oaks, CA 91423
Actress V: 03/27/93

Oakland A's
Oakland-Alemeda County Stadium
Oakland, CA 94621
Team Office V: 05/15/92

Oberman, Claire
c/o Burnett
Grafton House, Ste. 42-43
2-3 Golden Square
London, W1R 3AD England
Actress V: 03/20/92

Ocasek, Ric
R20 110 W. 57th St., 7th Fl.
New York, NY 10019
Singer V: 01/16/93

Ochoa, Ellen
c/o NASA LBJ Space Center
Houston, TX 77058
Astronaut V: 03/03/93

Odyssey Distributors
6500 Wilshire Blvd. #400
Beverly Hills, CA 90211
Distributor V: 03/17/92

Oerter, Al
5485 Avenieda Pescadera
Fort Meyers, FL 33931-4209
Olympian V: 11/11/92

Ogilvy, Ian
c/o Whitehall
125 Gloucester Rd.
London SW7 4TE, England
Actor V: 03/17/92

Oh, Soon-Tek
8235 Santa Monica Blvd. #202
Los Angeles, CA 90046
Actor V: 02/01/92

Oldman, Gary
c/o Duncan Heath
162-170 Wardour St.
London W1V 3AT, England
Actor V: 02/11/93

Olmos, Edward James
10000 Santa Monica Blvd. #305
Los Angeles, CA 90067
Actor V: 05/02/92

5225 Colins Ave. #415
Miami Beach, FL 33140
L.R.U. V: 01/02/92

Olsen, Ashley Fuller
c/o Lorimar Telepicture Prods.
Full House
10201 W. Pico Blvd.
Los Angeles, CA 90035
Actress V: 12/15/92

Olsen, Mary Kate
c/o Lorimar Telepicture Prods.
"Full House"
10201 W. Pico Blvd.
Los Angeles, CA 90035
Actress V: 12/15/92

Olson, Eric
c/o King Features
216 E. 45th St.
New York, NY 10017
Cartoonist V: 03/11/93

Olson, Nancy
c/o Livingston
945 N. Alpnie Dr.
Beverly Hills, CA 90210
Actress V: 02/18/92

Omni Artists Int'l
9107 Wilshire Blvd. #602
Beverly Hills, CA 90210
Talent Agency V: 02/19/93

Omnipop Inc.,
10700 Ventura Blvd. 2nd Fl.
Studio City, CA 91604
Talent Agency V: 03/11/93

Ono, Yoko
1 W. 72nd St.
New York, NY 10023
Singer V: 03/15/92

Ontkean, Michael
7120 Grasswood Ave.
Malibu, CA 90265
Actor V: 03/27/93

Oosterhuis, Peter
c/o Forsgate Country Club
Forsgate Dr.
Jamesbury, NJ 08831
Golfer V: 02/04/92

Oravetz, Ernie
4417 W. Paul Ave.
Tampa, FL 33611
Baseball V: 01/06/92

Orion Pictures and TV
1888 Century Park E. 6th Fl.
Los Angeles, CA 90067
Production Company V: 03/17/92

Orlando, Tony
804 N. Crescent Dr.
Beverly Hills, CA 90210
Singer V: 08/16/92

Osborne, John
c/o Agent
91 Regent St.
London W1, England
Playwright V: 03/15/92

Osburn, Julie
c/o NBC-TV
"Another World"
79 Madison Ave., 5th Fl.
New York, NY 91523
Actress V: 06/15/92

Oslin, K.T.
27 Music Square E. #180
Nashville, TN 37203
Singer V: 03/07/92

Osmond, Donny
c/o Ent. Corp.
1570 Brookhollow #118
Santa Ana, CA 92705
Actor V: 03/02/92

Osmond, Ken
9863 Wornam Ave.
Sunland, CA 91040
Musician V: 03/04/93

Osmond, Marie
P.O. Box 6000
Provo, UT 84603
Singer V: 06/25/92

Osterhage, Jeff
210 N. Cordova #D
Burbank, CA 91505
Actor V: 03/22/93

Oswald, Steven S.
NASA/LBJ Space Center
Houston, TX 77058
Astronaut V: 01/31/92

Overall, Park
c/o Flannagan Agency
1501 Broadway Ste. 404
New York, NY 10036
Actress V: 12/10/92

4904 Sancola Ave.
N. Hollywood, CA 91602
Alternate V: 03/27/93

c/o Empty Nest
500 S. Buena Vista St.
Burbank, CA 91521
Forwarded V: 11/11/92

Overmeyer, Robert F.
c/o NASA
LBJ Space Center
Houston, TX 77058
Astronaut V: 03/03/93

Overstreet, Paul
P.O. Box 2977
Hendersonville, TN 37007
Singer V: 01/11/93

Owen, Bill
c/o Stone
18 York Bldg.
London, WC2N 6JU England
Actor V: 03/15/92

25 Whitehall
London SW1A 2BS, England
Alternate V: 03/17/92

Owens, Buck
1225 N. Chester Ave.
Bakersfield, CA 93308
Singer V: 08/03/92

Owens, Gary
KJQI-1500 Cotner
Los Angeles, CA 90025
Radio/TV DJ V: 04/21/93

Oxenberg, Catherine
P.O.Box 25909
Los Angeles, CA 90025
Actress V: 02/28/92

P

PACIFIC STATION
500 S. Buena Vista St.
Vista Bungalow
Burbank, CA 91521
Production Company V: 03/26/93

PBS-TV
1320 Braddock Place
Alexandria, VA 22314
Public TV HQ *V: 03/01/92*

PERFECT SCORE
Go for Productions
Schulman Video
861 Seward St.
Los Angeles, CA 90038
Production Company *V: 03/18/93*

PERFECT STRANGERS
c/o Lorimar
Perfect Strangers
3970 Overland Ave.
Culver City, CA 90230
Production Company *V: 12/15/92*

PERRY MASON MOVIES
Viacom Prod.
100 Universal City Plaza
Universal City, CA 91608
Production Company *V: 03/26/93*

PERSONALS
Stephen J. Cannell Prod.
7083 Hollywood Blvd.
Hollywood, CA 90028
Production Company *V: 03/18/93*

PICKET FENCES
20th Century Fox TV
10201 West Pico Blvd.
Build. 80
Los Angeles, CA 90035
Production Company *V: 03/14/93*

PMK
955 S. Carillo Dr. #200
Los Angeles, CA 90048
Talent Agency *V: 03/13/93*

1776 Broadway, 8th Fl.
New York, NY 10019
Alternate *V: 03/20/93*

POWERS THAT BE
Columbia Pictures
1438 N. Gower St.
Stage 12
Los Angeles, CA 90028
Production Company *V: 03/26/93*

PRICE IS RIGHT
c/o Goodson Prod.
The Price is Right
5750 Wilshire Blvd. #475 W
Los Angeles, CA 90036
Production Company *V: 06/15/92*

Paar, Jack
9 Chateau Ridge Dr.
Greenwich, CT 06830
Celebrity *V: 03/04/93*

Pace, Judy
4139 Cloverdale
Los Angeles, CA 90008
Actress *V: 06/17/92*

Pacific Artists
515 N. La Cienega Blvd.
Los Angeles, CA 90048
Talent Agency *V: 03/11/93*

Pacific Film Archive
Art Museum/UC-Berkeley
2625 Durant Ave.
Berkeley, CA 94720
Archive *V: 03/20/93*

Pacino, Al
301 W. 57th St. #16-C
New York, NY 10019
Actor *V: 03/27/93*

9 E. 68th St.
New York, NY 10021
L.R.U. *V: 01/02/92*

Page, Patti
1412 San Lucas Ct.
Solana Beach, CA 92075
Actress *V: 11/11/92*

151 El Camino
Beverly Hills, CA 90210
Alternate *V: 02/18/92*

314 Huntley Dr.
Beverly Hills, CA 90211
Alternate *V: 01/06/92*

P.O. Box 1105
Rancho Santa Fe, CA 92067
L.R.U. *V: 01/02/92*

Paige, Janis
c/o Rosner
1642 Westwood Blvd.
Los Angeles, CA 90024
Actress *V: 04/23/92*

1700 Rising Glen Rd.
Los Angeles, CA 90069
Alternate *V: 04/21/92*

c/o General Hosp./ABC Inc.
4151 Prospect Ave.
Hollywood, CA 90027
Forwarded *V: 03/01/92*

Palance, Holly
2753 Roscomare Rd.
Los Angeles, CA 90077
Actress V: 02/18/92

Palance, Jack
c/o Hatch Entertainment
10880 Wilshire Blvd. #911
Los Angeles, CA 90024
Actor V: 06/14/92

c/o Vision Int.
3330 W. Cahuenga Blvd.
Los Angeles, CA 90068
Alternate V: 01/13/93

Star Rt. 1, Box 805
Tehachapi, CA 93561
Alternate V: 03/27/93

Palin, Michael
c/o BBC-TV Center
London, W12 England
Actor V: 02/23/92

c/o Mayday Mgmt.
68A Delancy St.
London NW7 7RY, England
Alternate V: 07/30/92

Pall, Gloria
12828 Victory Blvd. #1
N. Hollywood, CA 91606
Actress V: 03/30/93

Palmer, Arnold
P.O. Box 52
Youngstown, PA 15696
Golfer V: 04/11/92

P.O. Box 616
Latrobe, PA 15650
Forwarded V: 04/16/92

Palmer, Betsy
129 Howland Ave.
River Edge, NJ 07661
Actress V: 05/26/92

Palmer, Geoffrey
c/o Spotlight
7 Leicester Place
London WC2H 7BP, England
Actor V: 03/17/92

Palmer, Tom
c/o Young and the Restless
7800 Beverly Blvd.
Beverly Hills, CA 90036
Actor V: 06/15/92

Palmer, Tony
4 Kensington Park Gardens
London W11 3HB, England
Writer V: 07/06/92

Pankin, Stuart
9200 Sunset Blvd.   Ste. 428
Los Angeles, CA 90069
Actor V: 01/21/92

c/o Dinosaurs
500 S. Buena Vista St.
Burbank, CA 91521
Alternate V: 11/11/92

c/o Jacobs-Henson Prod.
Dinosaurs
4024 Radford Ave.
Bldg.2 Rm.11
Studio City, CA 91604
Alternate V: 01/03/93

Paradis, Vanessa
c/o Artmedia
10 Ave. George-V
F-75008 Paris, France
Actress V: 02/11/93

Paramount Motion Pictures
15260 Ventura Blvd. #1140
Sherman Oaks, CA 91403
Distributor V: 03/17/92

Paramount Studios
5555 Melrose Ave.
Hollywood, CA 90038
Studio HQ V: 04/02/92

Pare, Michael
2804 Pacific Ave.
Venice, CA 90291
Actor V: 03/27/93

Paris, Victoria
c/o 5K Sales
9420 Reseda Blvd., Ste.836
Northridge, CA 91324
Adult Films V: 01/17/93

Parke, Dorothy
9200 Sunset Blvd. #625
Los Angeles, CA 90069
Actress V: 02/01/92

Parker, Brant
c/o King Features
216 East 45th St.
New York, NY 10017
Cartoonist V: 02/15/92

Parker, Brant, contd
5668 Thorndyke Ct.
Centreville, VA 22020
Alternate V: 12/18/92

Parker, Cecelia
5287 Teton Lane
Ventura, CA 93003
Actress V: 06/17/92

Parker, Col. Tom
P.O. Box 220
Madison, TN 37118
Manager V: 01/08/92

Parker, Eleanor
2195 La Paz Way
Palm Springs, CA 92262
Actress V: 02/18/92

2814 La Paz Way
Palm Springs, CA 92262
L.R.U. V: 03/02/92

Parker, Fess
495 Santiago Way
Palm Springs, CA 92262
Actor V: 03/03/92

633 E. Cabrillo Blvd.
Santa Barbara, CA 93103
Alternate V: 01/20/92

P.O. Box 50440
Santa Monica, CA 93150-0440
Alternate V: 05/21/92

P.O. Box 908
Los Olivos, CA 93441
Alternate V: 11/11/92

Parker, James
5448 Wingbourne Ct.
Columbia, MD 21045
Football V: 05/14/92

Parker, Jameson
151 El Camino
Beverly Hills, CA 90212
Actor V: 01/16/93

Parker, Jean
617 Columbus Ste.E
Glendale, CA 91205
Actress V: 02/18/92

Parker, Jennifer
P.O. Box 3002
Los Angeles, CA 90078
Actress V: 03/17/92

Parker, Kay
c/o 5K Sales
9420 Reseda Blvd., Ste.836
Northridge, CA 91324
Adult Films V: 01/17/93

Parker, Robert A.
c/o NASA LBJ Space Center
Houston, TX 77058
Astronaut V: 03/03/93

Parker, Sarah Jessica
300 S. Doheny Dr. #620
Los Angeles, CA 90048
Actress V: 03/22/93

1494 N. Kings Rd.
Los Angeles, CA 90069
Alternate V: 06/17/92

Parkinson, Dian
The Price is Right #101
c/o Mark Goodson Prod.
5750 Wilshire Blvd.
Los Angeles, CA 90036-3697
Celebrity V: 03/27/93

4655 Natick Ave. #1
Sherman Oaks, CA 91403
Alternate V: 02/18/92

Parks, Dorothy
9220 Sunset Bl. #625
Los Angeles, CA 90069
Actress V: 11/11/92

Parks, Michael
1320 Armacost Ave. Ste. #12
Los Angeles, CA 90025
Actor V: 03/27/93

Parks, Rosa
231 W. Layfayette St.
Dearborn, MI 48226
Activist V: 06/17/92

Parnell, Robert
c/o Grimme Agency
207 Powell St.
San Francisco, CA 94102
Actor V: 04/21/92

Parsons, Benny
c/o NASCAR
1811 Volusia Ave.
Daytona Beach, FL 32015
NASCAR Driver V: 03/02/92

Parsons, Estelle
505 West End Ave.
New York, NY 10024
Actress V: 06/17/92

Parsons, Phil
1811 Volusia Ave.
Daytona Beach, FL 32015
NASCAR Driver V: 03/02/92

Partch, Virgil
c/o King Features
216 East 45th St.
New York, NY 10017
Cartoonist V: 02/01/92

Parton, Dolly
Rt.1, Crockett Rd.
Brentwood, TN 37027
Singer V: 03/01/92

9035 Norma Pl.
Los Angeles, CA 90069
Alternate V: 03/04/93

1888 Century Park E. #1400
Los Angeles, CA 90036
Alternate V: 11/22/92

700 Dollywood Ln.
Pigeon Forge, TN 37863-4101
Alternate V: 04/01/92

P.O. Box 1976
Nolensville, TN 37135
Forwarded V: 07/03/92

Partos Company
3630 Barham Blvd. Ste.Z108
Los Angeles, CA 90068
Talent Agency V: 03/17/93

Paschall, Jim
Rt.2, Box 450
Denton, NC 27238
NASCAR Driver V: 03/02/92

Pasdar, Adrian
3176 Lindo St.
Los Angeles, CA 90068
Actor V: 03/27/93

5 Westminister Ave. #2
Venice, CA 90291
L.R.U. V: 05/29/92

Pasquesi, David
9350 Wilshire Blvd. #324
Beverly Hills, CA 90212
Actor V: 01/16/93

Pastorelli, Robert
2751 Holly Ridge Dr.
Los Angeles, CA 90068
Actor V: 03/01/92

c/o Warner Bros. TV
"Murphy Brown"
4000 Warner Blvd.
Burbank, CA 91522
Forwarded V: 03/02/92

Pate, Jerry
1255 Country Club Rd.
Gulf Breeze, FL 32561
Golfer V: 02/04/92

Pathe Communications
640 S. San Vicente Blvd.
Beverly Hills, CA 90211
Distributor V: 03/17/92

Patrick, Butch
P.O. Box 857
Farmington, NY 11738
Actor V: 03/04/93

2113-B Rabb Rd.
Austin, TX 78704
L.R.U. V: 01/02/92

Patrick, Robert
c/o La Mama
74-A E. 4th St.
New York, NY 10003
Writer V: 02/23/93

Patterson, Floyd
P.O. Box 336
New Paltz, NY 12561
Boxing V: 04/01/92

Patterson, Lorna
5028 Willowcrest Ave.
N. Hollywood, CA 91601
Actress V: 02/18/92

Patterson, Neva
2498 Mandeville Canyon Rd.
Los Angeles, CA 90049
Actress V: 02/18/92

Patton III, George S.
650 Ashbury St. S.
Hamilton, MA 01982
Celebrity V: 05/22/92

Paul, Arthur
175 E. Delawaree Pl.
Chicago, IL 60611
Artist V: 11/11/92

Pavarotti, Luciano
941 Via Giardini
41040 Saliceta S.
Guiliano, Modena, Italy
Opera Tenor V: 04/02/92

Pavlav, Muriel
10 Batchworth Heath
Nr. Richmansworth
Herts., England
Actress V: 01/02/92

Pays, Amanda
2114 Kew Dr.
Los Angeles, CA 90046
Actress V: 05/13/92

Payton, Walter
1700 E. Golf Rd.#1100
Schaumburg, IL 60173
Football V: 12/10/92

Payton-Wright, Pamela
21 E. 93rd St.
New York, NY 10028
Actress V: 07/01/92

Pearson, David
P.O. Box 8099
Spartanburg, SC 29305
NASCAR Driver V: 03/02/92

Pearson, Larry
c/o NASCAR
1811 Volusia Ave.
Daytona Beach, FL 32015
NASCAR Driver V: 03/02/92

Pease, Patricia
13538 Valleyheart Dr.
Sherman Oaks, CA 91403
Actress V: 02/18/92

Peck, Gregory
P.O. Box 837
Beverly Hills, CA 90213-0837
Actor V: 03/31/92

375 N. Carolwood Dr.
Los Angeles, CA 90024
Alternate V: 11/06/92

1888 Century Park E.
Los Angeles, CA 90067
Alternate V: 06/14/92

Peck, Tom
P.O. Box 249
McConnellsburg, PA 17233
Race Driver V: 03/12/93

Peeples, Nia
26012 Froma Cr.
Calabasas, CA 91302
Actress V: 07/31/92

3575 Cahuenga Blvd. W. #520
Los Angeles, CA 90068
Alternate V: 08/15/92

Pellegrini, Margaret
5018 N. 61st Ave.
Glendale, AZ 85301
Actress V: 01/21/92

Pemberton, Ryan
c/o Yates Racing
115 Dwelle St.
Charlotte, NC 27374
NASCAR Crew V: 02/27/93

Pena, Anthony
c/o Young and the Restless
7800 Beverly Blvd.
Beverly Hills, CA 90036
Actor V: 06/15/92

Pena, Federico
Dept. of Transportation
400 7th Street, S.W.
Washington, DC 20590
Dept. Head V: 01/31/93

Penn, Sean
c/o Clyde Is Hungry Prod. Inc.
22333 Pacific Coast Hwy.
Malibu, CA 90265-2630
Actor V: 04/13/92

6728 Zumerez Dr.
Malibu, CA 90265
Alternate V: 03/23/92

P.O. Box 2630
Malibu, CA 90265
Alternate V: 01/16/93

Penn & Teller
c/o Earth's Center
P.O. Box 1196
New York, NY 10185-0010
Comedy Team V: 07/14/92

Pennington, Janice
The Price is Right #101
c/o Mark Goodson Prod.
5750 Wilshire Blvd.
Los Angeles, CA 90036-3697
Celebrity V: 03/27/93

Penny, Joe
c/o Moress
2128 W. Pico Blvd.
Santa Monica, CA 90485
Actor V: 04/18/92

10453 Sarah St.
N. Hollywood, CA 91602
Alternate V: 03/17/93

c/o Viacom Prod.
Bldg. 69, Rm.203
100 Universal City Plaza
Universal City, CA 91608
Forwarded V: 04/01/92

Penny, Sydney
c/o NBC-TV 'Santa Barbara'
3000 W. Alameda Ave.
Burbank, CA 91523
Actor V: 10/09/92

3090 Calvet Ct.
Camarillo, CA 93010
Actress V: 02/18/92

Penske, Roger
c/o Penske Racing
6 Knob Hill Rd.
Mooreville, NC 28115
NASCAR Owner V: 03/02/92

People Weekly
Time & Life Bldg.
Rockefeller Plaza
New York, NY 10020-1393
Publishers V: 03/01/92

Pep, Willie
166 Bunce Rd.
Wethersfield, CT 06109-3213
Boxing V: 03/30/93

Peppard, George
c/o Marian Taylor
P.O. Box 1643
Beverly Hills, CA 90213
Actor V: 03/25/92

c/o Studio Fan Mail
1122 S. Robertson Blvd.
Los Angeles, CA 90035
Alternate V: 05/13/92

Perez, Rosie
1135 Keniston Ave.
Los Angeles, CA 90019
Actress V: 02/18/92

Perkins, Millie
4311 Alcove Ave. #9
Studio City, CA 91604
Actress V: 02/18/92

Perlman, Itzhak
40 W. 57th St.
New York, NY 10019
Violinist V: 05/03/92

Perlman, Rhea
31020 Broad Beach
Malibu, CA 90285
Actress V: 03/17/93

Paramount/Cheers
5555 Melrose Ave./Ball RM105
Hollywood, CA 90038
Alternate V: 01/07/91

P.O. Box 27365
Los Angeles, CA 90027
L.R.U. V: 03/03/93

Perlman, Ron
345 N. Maple Dr. #183
Beverly Hills, CA 90210
Actor V: 03/17/93

Perot, H. Ross
c/o Perot Syst. Corp.
12372 Merit Dr. #1600
Dallas, TX 75251
Politician V: 11/16/92

1700 Lakeside Sq.
Dallas, TX 75251
Alternate V: 10/06/92

Perreau, Gigi
268 N. Bowling Green Way
Los Angeles, CA 90049
Actress V: 03/17/93

Perrine, Valerie
c/o Bernie Francis
328 S. Beverly Dr.
Beverly Hills, CA 90212
Actress V: 05/12/92

Perry, Steve
P.O. Box 97
Larkspur, CA 94939
Actor V: 03/27/93

Pertwee, Jon
24 Calthope Gardens
Sutton, Surry SM1 3DF
England
Actor V: 01/13/93

Pertwee, John, contd
c/o Spotlight
7 Leicester Place
London WC2H 7BP, England
Alternate V: 03/17/92

3 Church Rd., Penny Lane
Wavertree, Liverpool, England
Forwarded V: 03/17/92

Pesci, Joe
c/o Fallu Prod.
149 Harrison St.
Bloomfield, NJ 07003
Actor V: 03/30/93

Pescow, Donna
9285 Flicker Pl.
Los Angeles, CA 90069
Actress V: 02/18/92

P.O. Box 93575
Los Angeles, CA 90093
L.R.U. V: 07/01/92

Peter, Paul, and Mary,
27 W. 67th St.
New York, NY 10023
Singers V: 03/10/92

P.O. Box 135
Bearsville, NY 12409
Alternate V: 04/22/92

Peters, Bernadette
8651 Pine Tree Place
Los Angeles, CA 90069
Actress V: 02/26/92

277 West End Ave.
New York, NY 10023
Actress V: 02/18/92

P.O. Box 8156
N. Hollywood, CA 91608
Alternate V: 03/02/92

323 W. 80th St.
New York, NY 10024
Forwarded V: 03/02/92

Peters, Jean
507 N. Palm Dr.
Beverly Hills, CA 90210
Actress V: 01/14/92

Peters, Mike
c/o Grimmy Inc.
P.O. Box 35357
Sarasota, FL 34242-5357
Cartoonist V: 04/16/92

Peters, Jr., House
12027 Borden Rd. #91
Escondido, CA 92026
Actor V: 11/27/92

Petersen, Wolfgang
c/o The Chasin Agency
190 N. Canon Dr. #201
Beverly Hills, CA 90210
Director V: 01/17/93

Peterson, Cassandra
P.O. Box 38246
Hollywood, CA 90038
Elvira V: 11/10/92

Peterson, Donald H.
c/o NASA LBJ Space Center
Houston, TX 77058
Astronaut V: 03/03/93

Peterson, William
c/o CAA
1888 Century Park E. #1400
Los Angeles, CA 90067
Actor V: 02/02/92

Pett, Joel
c/o King Features
216 E. 45th St.
New York, NY 10017
Cartoonist V: 03/11/93

Petty, Kyle
830 W. Lexington
High Point, NC 27262
NASCAR Driver V: 02/17/92

c/o Sabco Racing
P.O. Box 560579
Charlotte, NC 28256
Alternate V: 03/02/92

Petty, Lee
c/o Petty Enterprises
Rt.4, Box 86
Randleman, NC 27317
NASCAR Driver V: 03/02/92

Petty, Lynda
c/o Petty Enterprises
Rt.4, Box 86
Randleman, NC 27317
NASCAR Driver V: 03/02/92

Petty, Maurice
c/o Petty Enterprises
Rt.4, Box 86
Randleman, NC 27317
NASCAR Driver V: 03/02/92

Petty, Richard
Rt. 3, Box 631
Randleman, NC 27317
NASCAR Driver V: 03/01/92

Route 4, Box 86
Randleman, NC 27317
L.R.U. V: 01/08/92

Peyser, Penny
9200 Sunset Blvd. #710
Los Angeles, CA 90069
Actress V: 01/16/93

Pflug, Jo Ann
200 Jungle Rd.
Palm Beach, FL 33480-4812
Actress V: 06/14/92

1430 Alabama Dr.
Winter Park, FL 32789
Actress V: 07/01/92

Phelps, Doug
c/o KY Headhunters
192 Ridge Crest Drive
Goodlettsville, TN 37072
Celebrity V: 03/26/93

Phelps, Peter
c/o Barbara Lean
261 Miller St.
N. Sydney
NSW, Australia
Actor V: 03/01/93

Philadelphia Eagles
Broad St. & Pattison Ave.
Philadelphia, PA 19148
Team Offices V: 05/15/92

Philadelphia Phillies
P.O. Box 7575
Veterans Stadium
Philadelphia, PA 19101
Team Office V: 05/15/92

Philbin, Mary
8788 Coral Springs Ct. #8202
Huntington Beach, CA 92646
Actress V: 02/18/92

Philbin, Regis
c/o Live
7 Lincoln Sq., 5th Fl.
New York, Ny 10023
Celebrity V: 03/30/92

Phillips, Chynna
938 2nd St. #302
Santa Monica, CA 90403
Actress V: 04/16/93

Phillips, Julia
2534 Benedict Canyon Dr.
Beverly Hills, CA 90210
Actress V: 02/18/92

Phillips, Leslie
c/o Agency
388 Oxford St.
London W1, England
Actor V: 03/12/92

Phillips, Lou Diamond
1999 Ave. of the Stars #2850
Los Angeles, CA 90067
Actor V: 03/16/93

2121 Ave. of the Stars #950
Los Angeles, CA 90067
Alternate V: 12/12/92

Phillips, Michelle
10557 Troon Ave.
Los Angeles, CA 90064
Actress V: 06/12/92

Phillips, Wendy
3231 Greenfield Ave.
Los Angeles, CA 90034
Actress V: 02/18/92

Phillips, Wilson
c/o Fan Emporium
P.O. Box 679
Branford, CT 06405
Singers V: 06/15/92

Phoenix Cardinals
P.O. Box 888
Phoenix, AZ 85001
Team Offices V: 05/15/92

Picardo, Robert
c/o New World TV
"The Wonder Years"
1440 S. Sepulveda Blvd.
Los Angeles, CA 90025
Actor V: 12/11/92

Picasso, Paloma
1021 Park Ave.
New York, NY 10021
Designer V: 05/15/92

Pickett, Cindy
151 El Camino Dr.
Beverly Hills, CA 90212
Actress V: 03/22/93

Pickle Family Circus
400 Missouri St.
San Francisco, CA 94107
Family Act V: 02/01/92

Pickles, Christina
137 S. Westgate Ave.
Los Angeles, CA 90049
Actress V: 05/15/92

Pierce, Devon
c/o Young and the Restless
7800 Beverly Blvd.
Beverly Hills, CA 90036
Actress V: 06/15/92

Pierpoint, Eric
10929 Morrison St. #14
N. Hollywood, CA 91601
Actor V: 03/27/93

Pilcher, Andrew
c/o King Features
216 E. 45th St.
New York, NY 10017
Cartoonist V: 03/11/93

Pinchot, Bronson
9200 Sunset Blvd. Ste.428
Los Angeles, CA 90069
Actor V: 01/21/92

10202 W. Washington Blvd.
B.P. 27 Myrna Loy
Culver City, CA 90232
Alternate V: 01/02/92

c/o Lorimar
"Perfect Strangers"
3970 Overland Ave.
Culver City, CA 90230
Forwarded V: 12/15/92

Pintauro, Danny
c/o Columbia Pictures TV
"Who's the Boss"
1438 N. Gower Blvd.
Los Angeles, CA 90028
Actor V: 12/01/92

Pistone, Tom
7858 Old Concord Rd.
Charlotte, NC 28213
NASCAR Driver V: 03/02/92

Pitney, Gene
8901-6 Miles Rd.
Caledonia, WS 53108
Singer V: 03/02/92

6046 37th Ave.
Kenosha, WI 53142
L.R.U. V: 03/03/93

Pitt, Ingrid
4 Waterloo Pl.
London SW1Y 4AW, England
Actress V: 03/06/92

4 Court Lodge, 48 Sloane Sq.
London SW1, England
Alternate V: 11/22/92

c/o Barry Langford
11-15 Betteston
Covent Garden
London W1R 3AG, England
Alternate V: 02/28/92

Pittsburgh Pirates
P.O. Box 7000
Three Rivers Stadium
Pittsburgh, PA 15212
Team Office V: 05/15/92

Pittsburgh Steelers
Three Rivers Stadium
300 Stadium Circle
Pittsburgh, PA 15212
Team Offices V: 05/15/92

Place, Mary Kay
2739 Motor Ave.
Los Angeles, CA 90064
Actress V: 06/17/92

Plank, Scott
c/o Paramount Pictures
5555 Melrose Ave., Wilder #214
Los Angeles, CA 90038
Actor V: 05/15/92

Playboy Fan Mail
8560 Sunset Blvd.
Los Angeles, CA 90069
Production Company V: 03/17/92

Playboy Magazine
680 N. Lake Shore Drive
Chicago, IL 60611
Corp. Office V: 04/16/92

919 N. Michigan Ave.
Chicago, IL 60611
Alternate V: 03/01/92

Playboy Products
P.O. Box 1554
Elk Grove Village, IL 60007
Playmate Ephemera V: 03/10/92

Player, Gary
c/o Intl. Mngmt. Grp.
1 Erieview Plaza
Cleveland, OH 44114
Golf V: 01/16/92

P.O. Box 785629
Sandton 2146, South Africa
Alternate V: 07/04/92

Playmate Fan Mail
500 N. Michigan Ave. #1920
Chicago, IL 60611
Reader Services V: 12/15/92

8560 Sunset Blvd.
Los Angeles, CA 90069
Alternate V: 12/15/92

Playmate Promotions
8560 Sunset Blvd.
Los Angeles, CA 90069
Playmate Mail V: 04/16/92

Pleasance, Donald
7 W. Eaton Place Mews
London W1, England
Actor V: 03/26/93

Plenty, Patty
1350 E. Flamingo #150
Las Vegas, NV 89119
Actress V: 04/12/92

Pleshette, Suzanne
c/o CBS TV
7800 Beverly Blvd.
Los Angeles, CA 90036
Actress V: 01/04/92

P.O. Box 1492
Beverly Hills, CA 90213
Actress V: 04/21/92

Plummer, Christopher
49 Wampum Hill Rd.
Weston, CT 06883
Actor V: 03/24/92

Pogue, William R.
c/o NASA LBJ Space Center
Houston, TX 77058
Astronaut V: 03/03/93

Pohl, Dan
11609 S. Tusaye Ct.
Phoenix, AZ 85044
Golfer V: 02/04/92

Pohl, Witta
Brabandstr. 63a
D-(W) 2000 Hamburg 60
Germany
Actress V: 02/11/93

Pointer, Anita
12060 Crest Ct.
Beverly Hills, CA 90210
Singer V: 05/15/92

Pointer, Priscilla
2051 N. Vine St.
Los Angeles, CA 90068
Singer V: 05/15/92

Pointer, Ruth
29652 Cuthbert Rd.
Malibu, CA 90265
Singer V: 05/15/92

Poitier, Sidney
c/o Verdon Prod.
9359 Wilshire Blvd.
Beverly Hills, CA 90212
Actor V: 02/22/92

1007 Cove Way
Beverly Hills, CA 90210
Alternate V: 07/14/92

Pollack, Sydney
c/o Mirage
100 Universal City, Plz.#414
Universal City, CA 91608
Director V: 07/04/92

Pollard, Larry
c/o NASCAR
1811 Volusia Ave.
Daytona Beach, FL 32015
NASCAR Driver V: 03/02/92

Pollard, Michael J.
c/o August Entertainment
838 N. Fairfax Ave.
Los Angeles, CA 90046
Actor V: 05/04/92

520 S. Burnside #12A
Los Angeles, CA 90036
Alternate V: 03/16/93

Polt, Gerhard
Breitensteinstr. 19a
D-(W) 8162 Schliersee 2
Germany
Actor V: 01/19/93

Ponce, Dany
14539 Teton Dr.
Hacienda Heights, CA 91302
Actor V: 03/27/93

Ponti, Carlo
Chalet Daniel
Burgenstock
Nidwalden, Switzerland
Producer V: 09/27/92

Porizkova, Paulina
1775 Broadway, 7th Fl.
New York, NY 10019
Model V: 01/16/93

111 E. 22nd St. #200
New York, NY 10010
Alternate V: 02/20/92

Porter, Don
1900 Ave. of Stars #2270
Los Angeles, CA 90067
Actor V: 04/13/92

Post, Markie
10153 1/2 Riverside Dr. #333
Toluca Lake, CA 91602
Actress V: 11/11/92

4425 Talofa Ave.
N. Hollywood, CA 91602
Alternate V: 03/12/93

c/o Sterling/Winter Co.
1900 Ave. of the Stars Ste.739
Los Angeles, CA 90067
Alternate V: 02/20/92

c/o Warner Bros. TV
"Night Court"
4000 Warner Blvd., Office 12A
Burbank, CA 91521
Forwarded V: 01/17/92

Poston, Tom
2830 Deep Canyon Dr.
Beverly Hills, CA 90210-1010
Actor V: 05/16/92

P.O. Box 1865
Studio City, CA 91604
Alternate V: 04/01/92

Poston, Tom, contd
415 Greencraig Rd.
Los Angeles, CA 90049
Alternate V: 01/19/92

Potomac Productions
21724 Ventura Blvd. #195
Woodland Hills, CA 91364
Publicity V: 12/15/92

P.O. Box 5973-215
Sherman Oaks, CA 91413
Alternate V: 12/10/92

Potts, Annie
1601 Campbell Dr.
Glendale, CA 91207
Actress V: 03/26/93

Columbia Plaza/Mozark
"Designing Women"
Prod.Bl.8 #147
Burbank, CA 91505
Forwarded V: 02/03/93

Potts, Cliff
21423 Highvale Ter.
Topanga, CA 90290
Actor V: 03/20/93

Poulot, Jean S.
c/o Will Vinton Prod. Inc.
1400 N.W. 22nd Ave.
Portland, OR 97210
Animator V: 04/16/92

Pounder, CCH
c/o Smith
121 N. San Vicente Blvd.
Beverly Hills, CA 90211
Actress V: 05/15/92

Poundstone, Paula
801 Westmount Dr.
Los Angeles, CA 90069
Comic V: 02/01/92

1027 Chelsea Ave.
Santa Monica, CA 90403
Alternate V: 05/14/92

Pousette, Lena
1177 Latigo Canyon Rd.
Malibu, CA 90265
Actress V: 05/15/92

Povich, Maury
250 W. 57th St. #26-W
New York, NY 10019
Journalist V: 01/16/93

Powell, Jane
1560 Broadway
New York, NY 10036
Actress V: 01/02/92

230 W. 55th St., #14-B
New York, NY 10019
Forwarded V: 06/01/92

Powell, Norman S.
12070 Mound View Pl.
Studio City, CA 91604
Producer V: 02/01/92

Powell, Robert
c/o Agency
388 Oxford St.
London W1, England
Actor V: 02/24/92

Powers, Mala
151 S. El Camino Dr.
Beverly Hills, CA 90212
Actress V: 01/16/92

10543 Valley Spring Ln.
Toluca Lake, CA 91602
Alternate V: 03/17/93

Powers, Stefanie
2661 Hutton Dr.
Beverly Hills, CA 90210
Actress V: 05/09/92

P.O. Box 5087
Sherman Oaks, CA 91403
Alternate V: 06/25/92

Powers, Udana
838 N. Doheny Dr. #1402
Los Angeles, CA 90069
Actress V: 07/01/92

Powers, Warren
c/o Broncos
13655 Broncos Parkway
Englewood, CO 80112
Football V: 08/26/92

Prange, Laurie
1519 Sargent Pl.
Los Angeles, CA 90026
Actress V: 05/15/92

Prather, Joan
31647 Sea Level Dr.
Malibu, CA 90265
Actress V: 05/15/92

Precourt Jr., Charles J.
c/o NASA LBJ Space Center
Houston, TX 77058
Astronaut V: 03/03/93

Prell, Jerry
c/o" Young and the Restless"
7800 Beverly Blvd.
Beverly Hills, CA 90036
Actor V: 06/15/92

Premiere
2 Park Ave.
New York, NY 10016
Magazine V: 03/21/92

Prentice, John
c/o King Features
216 East 45th St.
New York, NY 10017
Cartoonist V: 04/13/93

Prentiss, Paula
719 N. Foothill Rd.
Beverly Hills, CA 90210
Actress V: 02/16/92

Presle, Micheline
6 rue Anton Dubois
F-75006 Paris, France
Actress V: 05/15/92

Presley, Lisa Marie
c/o Keough
12614 Promontory Rd.
Los Angeles, CA 90049
Actress V: 04/13/92

113 N. Robertson Blvd.
Beverly Hills, CA 90211
L.R.U. V: 07/01/92

Presley, Pricilla
1167 Summit Dr.
Beverly Hills, CA 90210
Actress V: 03/28/92

151 El Camino Dr.
Beverly Hills, CA 90212
Alternate V: 03/20/92

Graceland
P.O. Box 16508
Memphis, TN 38186-0508
Alternate V: 09/21/92

Pressman, Lawrence
15033 Encanto Dr.
Sherman Oaks, CA 91403
Actor V: 03/12/92

Preston, Kelly
c/o MTA
9320 Wilshire Blvd., 3rd Fl.
Beverly Hills, CA 90212
Actress V: 06/01/92

23906 DeVille Way #D
Malibu, CA 90265
L.R.U. V: 07/01/92

Previn, Andre
135 N Grand Ave.
Los Angeles, CA 90067
Composer V: 02/01/92

2049 Century Park E. #3700
Los Angeles, CA 90067
Forwarded V: 04/25/92

Price, Paula
c/o Five K Sales Co.
9420 Reseda Blvd., #836
Northridge, CA 91324
Adult Films V: 03/03/93

Price, Vincent
9255 Swallow Dr.
Los Angeles, CA 90069
Actor V: 04/21/92

Priddy, Nancy
c/o CED
261 S. Robertson Blvd.
Beverly Hills, CA 90211
Actress V: 01/16/93

Pride, Charlie
P.O. Box 670507
Dallas, TX 75367
Singer V: 01/12/92

Priest, Pat
P.O. Box 1298
Hatley, ID 83334
Actress V: 03/30/93

P.O. Box 1298
Ketchum, ID 83333-1298
Alternate V: 05/15/92

Priestly, Jason
8961 Sunset Blvd. #2A
Los Angeles, C 90069
Actor V: 06/21/92

Prince
c/o E. Murton
P.O. Box 310
Croydon CR96AP, England
Singer V: 04/10/92

Prince, contd
9401 Kiowa Trail
Chanhassen, MN 5317
Alternate V: 03/17/93

Prince Albert
Palais de Monaco
98015 Monte Carlo 518, Monaco
Royalty V: 02/20/92

Place du Musee
MC 98000, Monaco
Alternate V: 02/20/92

Princess Caroline
Palais de Monaco
98015 Monte Carlo, 518, Monaco
Royalty V: 03/12/92

Princess Stephanie
Palais de Monaco
98015 Monte Carlo, 518, Monaco
Royalty V: 03/12/92

Principal, Victoria
10000 Santa Monica Blvd. #400
Los Angeles, CA 90067
Actress V: 01/16/93

814 Cynthia St.
Beverly Hills, CA 90210-3519
Alternate V: 01/02/92

9755 Oak Pass Rd.
Beverly Hills, CA 90210
L.R.U. V: 01/02/92

Prine, Andrew
c/o Gores & Fields
10100 Santa Monica Blvd. #700
Los Angeles, CA 90067
Actor V: 04/01/92

Privilege Agency
8344 Beverly Blvd. 2nd Fl.
Los Angeles, CA 90048
Talent Agency V: 03/19/93

Pro-Sport & Entertainment
1161 San Vicente Blvd. #303
Los Angeles, CA 90049
Talent Agency V: 04/01/93

Prochnow, Jurgen
c/o Willaim Morris Agency
151 El Camino Dr.
Beverly Hills, CA 90212
Actor V: 01/17/93

Producers Guild
400 S. Beverly Dr., Ste.211
Beverly Hills, CA 90212
Guild Office *V: 01/12/92*

Progressive Artists Agency
400 S. Bevrly Dr. #216
Beverly Hills, CA 90212
Talent Agency *V: 03/17/93*

Props, Rene
c/o CBS-TV "ATWT"
524 W. 57th St. #5330
New York, NY 10019
Actress *V: 07/01/92*

Prosky, Robert
4024 Radford Ave.
Studio City, CA 91604
Actor *V: 04/10/92*

c/o Freedman
121 N. San Vicente Blvd.
Beverly Hills, CA 90211
Alternate *V: 03/17/92*

Provenza, Paul
c/o Empty Nest
500 S. Buena Vista St.
Burbank, CA 91521
Actor *V: 11/11/92*

Provost, Jon
627 Montclair Dr.
Santa Rosa, CA 95409
Actor *V: 09/06/92*

Prowse, Dave
7 Carlyle Rd.
Croydon CR0 7HN, England
Actor *V: 02/14/92*

c/o Prowse Fitness Center
12 Marshalsea Rd.
London SE1, England
Alternate *V: 04/13/92*

Prowse, Juliet
343 S. Beverly Glen Blvd.
Los Angeles, CA 90024
Actress *V: 05/22/92*

Pryor, Richard
c/o Indigo Products
Columbia Plaza
Burbank, CA 91505
Actor *V: 06/28/92*

Public Broadcastive Service
1330 Braddock Pl.
Alexandria, VA 22314
Archive *V: 03/20/93*

Punch, Jerry
1811 Volusia Ave.
Daytona Beach, FL 32015
NASCAR MC *V: 03/02/92*

Purcell, Lee
1930 Century Park W. #303
Los Angeles, CA 90067
Actress *V: 01/04/92*

19528 Ventura Blvd.
Tarzana, CA 91356
Alternate *V: 05/14/92*

Purcell, Sarah
6525 Sunset Blvd. #600
Los Angeles, CA 90038
Actress *V: 01/16/93*

460 Lincoln Blvd.
Santa Monica, CA 90402-1936
L.R.U. *V: 12/01/92*

Purdee, Nathan
c/o"Y & R"/7800 Beverly Blvd.
Beverly Hills, CA 90036
Actor *V: 06/15/92*

Purdue University
Public Affairs Video Archives
West Lafayette, IN 47907
Archive *V: 03/20/93*

Purl, Linda
10417 Ravenwood Ct.
Los Angeles, CA 90077
Actress *V: 03/26/93*

Purvis, Jeff
1811 Volusia Ave.
Daytona Beach, FL 32015
NASCAR Driver *V: 03/26/93*

Pyle, Denver
10614 Whipple St.
N. Hollywood, CA 91602
Actor *V: 03/01/92*

Pyne, Natasha
43-A Princess Rd.
Regents Park
London NW1 8JS, England
Actress *V: 12/23/92*

Q

QUANTUM LEAP
100 Universal City Plaza
Universal City, CA 91608
Production Company V: 01/12/92

Quaid, Dennis
P.O. Box 742625
Houston, TX 77274
Actor V: 03/04/92

Quaid, Randy
15760 Ventura Blvd. #1730
Encino, CA 91436
Actor V: 03/26/93

P.O. Box 742405
Houston, TX 77274
Alternate V: 02/19/92

Quarterflash
P.O. Box 8231
Portland, OR 97207
Musical Group V: 07/14/92

Quayle, Daniel
7 N. Jefferson St.
Huntington, IN 46750
Former V.P.-USA V: 09/27/92

Questel, Mae
27 E. 65th St.
New York, NY 10021
Actress V: 01/14/92

Quigley, Joan
1055 California St. #14
San Francisco, CA 94108
Astrologer V: 03/17/93

Quigley, Linnea
13659 Victory Blvd. #467
Van Nuys, CA 91401
Actress V: 03/20/93

12710 Blythe St.
N. Hollywood, CA 91605
Actress V: 06/17/92

Quinlan, Kathleen
9000 Sunset Blvd. #1200
Los Angeles, CA 90069
Actress V: 01/30/92

P.O. Box 2465
Malibu, CA 90265
Alternate V: 01/19/92

Quinn, Anthony
c/o McCartt-Oreck-Barrett
10390 Santa Monica Blvd. #310
Los Angeles, CA 90025
Actor V: 07/14/92

8966 Sunset Blvd.
Hollywood, CA 90069
Forwarded V: 01/12/92

2 E. 86th St.
New York, NY 10028
L.R.U. V: 01/02/92

Quinn, Martha
3562 Laurelvale Dr.
Studio City, CA 91604-4136
Actress V: 05/15/92

Quo, Beulah
c/o ABC-TV
General Hospital
4151 Prospect Ave.
Hollywood, CA 90027
Actress V: 06/15/92

R

RAVEN
Invader Prod./Columbia TV
3400 Riverside Dr., Ste. 695
Burbank, CA 91505
Production Company V: 03/14/93

REASONABLE DOUBTS
300 S. Lorimar Plaza
Bldg. 140, Room 247
Burbank, CA 91505
Production Company V: 03/26/93

REGIS & CATHY LEE
c/o Live
7 Lincoln Sq., 5th Fl.
New York, Ny 10023
Production Company V: 03/30/92

RESCUE 911
Arnold Shapiro Prod.
1438 N. Gower Ave., Box 53
Hollywood, CA 90028
Production Company V: 03/13/93

Shapiro/Rescue 911
5800 Sunset Blvd.
Hollywood, CA 90028
Alternate V: 05/15/92

RHYTHM AND BLUES
Twentieth TV
10201 W. Pico Blvd.
Los Angeles, CA 90035
Production Company V: 03/26/93

ROSEANNE
c/o CBS-MTM
Roseanne
4024 Radford Ave.
Studio City, CA 91604
Production Company V: 12/07/92

ROUND TABLE
Aaron Spelling Prod.
5700 Wilshire Blvd.
Ste. 575
Los Angeles, CA 90036
Production Company V: 03/26/93

Rabbit Ears/UA
100 Universal City Plz.
Universal City, CA 91608
Publicity V: 12/15/92

Rabbitt, Eddie
c/o Moress
1209 16th Ave. S.
Nashville, TN 37212
Singer V: 10/18/92

Rachins, Alan
c/o Artists Agency
10000 Santa Monica Blvd.
Los Angeles, CA 90067
Actor V: 03/17/92

c/o L.A. Law
P.O. Box 900
Beverly Hills, CA 90213
Forwarded V: 01/12/92

Rae, Charlotte
P.O. Box 49991
Los Angeles, CA 90049
Actress V: 01/16/93

P.O. Box 49991
Los Angeles, CA 90049
Actress V: 05/15/92

Rael Company
1720 N. La Brea Ave.
Los Angeles, CA 90046
Model/Talent Agency V: 02/12/92

Rafferty, Bill
151 El Camino
Beverly Hills, CA 90212
Comedian V: 02/01/92

Rafferty, Frances
22141 Burbank Blvd. #4
Woodland Hills, CA 91367
Actress V: 05/15/92

Raffin, Deborah
301 N. Canon Dr. #203
Beverly Hills, CA 90210-4724
Actress V: 05/29/92

2630 Eden Place
Beverly Hills, CA 90210
Alternate V: 12/10/92

750 Ventura Blvd. #202
Studio City, CA 91604
Forwarded V: 05/29/92

Ragar, Ken
c/o NASCAR
1811 Volusia Ave.
Daytona Beach, FL 32015
NASCAR Driver V: 03/02/92

Ragsdale, William
c/o Hermans Head
500 S. Buena Vista St.
Burbank, CA 91521
Actor V: 11/11/92

Railsback, Steve
P.O. Box 1308
Los Angeles, CA 90078
Actor V: 07/23/92

P.O. Box 1308
Hollywood, CA 90078
Actor V: 04/06/93

Rainer, Luise
Vico Morcote
Lake Lugano
Switzerland CH-6911
Actress V: 01/03/93

c/o Knittel
Vico Morcote
6911 Switzerland
Alternate V: 03/26/93

Rainey, Ford
3821 Carbon Canyon Rd.
Malibu, CA 90265
Actor V: 02/01/92

Rainwater, Gregg
P.O. Box 291836
Los Angeles, CA 90078
Actor V: 04/01/93

Raitt, Bonnie
P.O. Box 626
Los Angeles, CA 90078
Singer V: 01/16/92

Ralph, Sheryl Lee
938 S. Longwood Ave.
Los Angeles, CA 90019
Actress V: 05/15/92

Ralston, Esther
35 Heather Way
Ventura, CA 93004
Actress V: 01/04/92

Ralston, Vera
4121 Cresciente Dr.
Santa Barbara, CA 93110
Actress V: 01/30/92

4121 Crescienta Dr.
Santa Barbara, CA 93110
Actress V: 05/15/92

Rambis, Kurt
c/o Phoenix Suns
2910 N. Central
Phoenix, AZ 85012
Basketball V: 01/12/92

Rambo, Dack
c/o NBC-TV
"Another World"
79 Madison Ave., 5th Fl.
New York, NY 91523
Actor V: 06/15/92

Ramis, Harold
14198 Alisal Ln.
Santa Monica, CA 90402
Actor V: 03/27/93

Ramos, Rudy
280 S. Beverly Dr. #400
Beverly Hills, CA 90212
Actor V: 03/01/92

Rampling, Charlette
c/o Boreau J. Bonnet
78 Ave. des Champs Elysees
Paris 75008, France
Actress V: 03/02/92

c/o London Mgmt.
235 Regent St.
London W1, England
Alternate V: 02/28/92

Ramsey, Logan
12923 Killion St.
Van Nuys, CA 91401
Actor V: 07/01/92

Randall, Tony
1 W. 81st. St. #6D
New York, NY 10024
Actor V: 02/11/93

888 7th Ave.
New York, NY 10019
Alternate V: 01/11/89

145 Central Park W. #6c
New York, NY 10023
L.R.U. V: 04/21/92

Randolph, Boots
4798 Lickton Pike
Whites Creek, TN 37189
Musician V: 04/04/92

Randolph, John
1850 N. Whitley Pl.
Los Angeles, CA 90028
Actor V: 03/27/93

Randolph, Joyce
295 Central Park W. Ste.18A
New York, NY 10024
Actress V: 03/12/92

Randolph, Ty
c/o Five K Sales Co.
9420 Reseda Blvd., #836
Northridge, CA 91324
Adult Films V: 03/03/93

Ranford, Bill
c/o Edmonton Oilers
Northlands Coliseum
Edmunton, Alberta T5B 4M9
Canada
Hockey V: 04/05/93

Raphael, Sally Jessy
510 W. 57th St. #200
New York, NY 10019
TV Host V: 03/17/93

Rashad, Phylicia
448 W. 44th St.
New York, NY 10036
Actress V: 04/10/92

10000 Santa Monica Blvd.
Los Angeles, CA 90067
Forwarded V: 03/20/92

Ratcliff, Tammi
c/o Dallas Cowboys
One Cowboys Parkway
Irving, TX 75063-4945
Cheerleader V: 08/08/92

Ratzenberger, John
c/o The Agency
10351 Santa Monica Blvd.
Los Angeles, CA 90025
Actor V: 03/17/92

c/o Paramount
"Cheers"
5555 Melrose Ave./Ball RM105
Hollywood, CA 90038
Forwarded V: 01/07/92

Rawls, Lou
9255 Sunset Blvd. Suite 706
Los Angeles, CA 90069
Singer V: 04/12/92

109 Fremont Place
Los Angeles, CA 90005
Alternate V: 09/12/92

Rawls, Sam C.
c/o King Features
216 East 45th St.
New York, NY 10017
Cartoonist V: 05/13/92

Ray, Marguerite
1329 N. Vista St. #106
Los Angeles, CA 90046
Actress V: 05/15/92

Rayburn, Gene
Seaview Ave.
Osterville, MA 02655
Celebrity V: 06/05/92

Raye, Martha
1153 Roscomare Rd.
Los Angelas, CA 90024
Actress V: 01/06/92

Rayhal, Bobby
934 Crescent Blvd.
Glenellyn, IL 60137
Race Driver V: 03/01/92

Raymond, Gene
250 Trino Way
Pacific Palisades, CA 90272
Actor V: 04/22/92

Raymond, Paula
P.O. Box 86
Beverly Hills, CA 90213
Actress V: 05/15/92

P.O. Box 86
Beverly Hills, CA 90213
Actress V: 04/06/93

Rayne
c/o Five K Sales Co.
9420 Reseda Blvd., #836
Northridge, CA 91324
Adult Films V: 03/03/93

Rea, Peggy
432 Curson Ave. Ste.2K
Los Angeles, CA 90036
Actress V: 05/15/92

Readdy, William F.
c/o NASA
LBJ Space Center
Houston, TX 77058
Astronaut V: 01/31/92

Reagan, Michael
10880 Wilshire Blvd. 7th Fl.
Los Angeles, CA 90024
Actor V: 02/02/92

4740 Aliott Ave.
Sherman Oaks, CA 91423
Forwarded V: 03/22/92

Reagan, Nancy
11000 Wilshire Blvd.
Los Angeles, CA 90024
Former First Lady V: 11/07/92

Reagan, Ronald
11000 Wilshire Blvd.
Los Angeles, CA 90024
Former US President V: 11/07/92

Rancho del Cielo
Santa Barbara, CA 93108
Alternate V: 03/18/93

Reagan, Ronald, Jr.
1283 Devon Ave.
Los Angeles, CA 90024
Celebrity V: 03/16/93

Reason, Rex
20105 Rhapsody Rd.
Walnut Creek, CA 91789
Actor V: 02/01/92

Rechin, Bill
c/o King Features
216 East 45th St.
New York, NY 10017
Cartoonist V: 04/26/92

Recht, Tracy E.
c/o Young and the Restless
7800 Beverly Blvd.
Beverly Hills, CA 90036
Actress V: 06/15/92

Redbone, Leon
179 Aquetong Rd.
New Hope, PA 18938
Singer V: 02/23/93

Redd, Veronica
c/o Young and the Restless
7800 Beverly Blvd.
Beverly Hills, CA 90036
Actress V: 06/15/92

Redding, Juli
115 N. Carolwood Dr.
Los Angeles, CA 90077
Actress V: 05/15/92

Redeker, Quinn
c/o Young and the Restless
7800 Beverly Blvd.
Beverly Hills, CA 90036
Actor V: 06/15/92

Redenbacher, Orville
1780 Ave. del Mundo #704
Coronado, CA 92118
Popcorn King V: 01/19/92

Redford, Robert
1223 Wilshire Blvd. #412
Santa Monica, CA 90403
Director V: 01/16/93

R.R.3 Box A1
Provo, Utah 84604
Alternate V: 05/02/92

c/o Wildwood Entertainment
4000 Warner Blvd.
Burbank, CA 91522
Forwarded V: 03/02/92

Redgrave, Lynn
P.O.Box 186
Topanga, CA 90290
Actress V: 04/16/92

Redgrave, Lynn, contd
21342 Colina Dr.
Topanga, CA 90290
Alternate V: 06/17/92

Redgrave, Vanessa
c/o Wm. Morris Agency
147 Wardour St.
London W1, England
Actress V: 07/03/92

1 Ravenscourt Rd.
London W6 England
Alternate V: 06/17/92

c/o James Sharkey-3rd Fl.
15 Golden Square
London W1R 3AG, England
Alternate V: 02/28/92

31/32 Soho Sq.
London W1 England
Alternate V: 03/11/93

Redmond, Marcus
c/o Doogie Howser, M.D.
10201 W. Pico Blvd.
Los Angeles, CA 90035
Actor V: 12/15/92

Redmond, Marge
101 Central Park W.
New York, NY 10023
Actress V: 05/15/92

Reed, Andre
c/o Buffalo Bills
1 Bills Dr.
Orchard Park, NY 14127
Football V: 11/14/92

Reed, Erin
c/o NBC-TV
3000 W. Alemeda
Burbank, CA 91523
Actress V: 11/07/92

Reed, Jerry
45 Music Square W.
Nashville, TN 37203
Actor V: 03/21/92

Reed, Lou
38 East 68th St.
New York, NY, 10021
Singer V: 02/21/93

c/o ATI
888 7th Ave.
New York, NY 10019
Alternate V: 03/14/92

Reed, Oliver
The Maddens
500 Reigate Rd., Tadworth
Surrey K2O 5PF, England
Actor V: 02/28/92

Reed, Rex
435 N. Michigan Ave.
Chicago, IL 60611
Critic V: 02/04/92

1 W. 72nd St.
New York, NY 10023
Alternate V: 03/25/92

Reed, Shanna
c/o Universal Television
"Major Dad"
100 Univ. City Plz., Bl.426-2E
Universal City, CA 91608
Actress V: 03/02/92

Reed, Walter
4222 Gull Cove Way
Capitola, CA 95010
Director V: 02/02/92

Reed Hall, Alaina
215 S. La Cienega Blvd. #203
Beverly Hills, CA 90211
Actress V: 01/16/93

Reed-Forest, Veronica
10351 Santa Monica Blvd. #211
Los Angeles, CA 90025
Actress V: 01/16/93

Rees, Roger
c/o Paramount
"Cheers"
5555 Melrose Ave./Ball RM105
Hollywood, CA 90038
Actor V: 01/07/92

Reese, Della
1910 Bel Air Rd.
Los Angeles, CA 90077
Singer V: 06/17/92

Reeve, Christopher
P.O. Box 461
New York, NY 10024
Actor V: 01/02/92

29 E. 22nd St. #12N
New York, NY 10010-5305
Alternate V: 03/30/93

Reeves, Keanu
7920 Sunset Blvd. #250
Los Angeles, CA 90046
Actor V: 04/05/93

Reeves, Ronna
c/o C & M Prod.
5114 Albert Dr.
Brentwood, TN 37027
Singer V: 10/22/92

Reeves, Steve
c/o Classic Images
P.O. Box 807
Valley Center, CA 92082
Actor V: 03/12/92

Regalbuto, Joe
c/o Wm. Morris
151 El Camino
Beverly Hills, CA 90210
Actor V: 03/17/92

724 24th St.
Santa Monica, CA 90405
Actor V: 04/06/93

c/o Warner Bros. Television
"Murphy Brown"
4000 Warner Blvd.
Burbank, CA 91522
Forwarded V: 03/02/92

Regher, Duncan
2401 Main St.
Santa Monica, CA 90405
Actor V: 03/17/93

Reich, Robert B.
Dept. of Labor
200 Constitution Ave, N.W.
Washington, DC 20210
Secretary of Labor V: 01/31/93

Reid, Beryl
36 Michaelham Gardens
Strawberry Hill
Twickenham TW1
London, England
Actor V: 02/18/93

Reid, Tim
16030 Ventura Blvd. Ste.380
Encino, CA 91436
Actor V: 11/10/92

16540 Aldon Rd.
Encino, CA 91436
Alternate V: 11/10/92

Reid, Tim, contd
11342 Dona Lisa
Studio City, CA 91604
Alternate V: 03/02/92

c/o Timalove Prod., 32nd Fl.
10 Universal City Plaza
Universal City, CA 91608-1097
Forwarded V: 10/11/92

Reightler Jr., Kenneth S.
c/o NASA
LBJ Space Center
Houston, TX 77058
Astronaut V: 01/31/92

Reilly, Charles Nelson
2341 Gloaming Way
Beverly Hills, CA 90210
Actor V: 06/17/92

Reilly, John
c/o General Hosp./ABC Inc.
4151 Prospect Ave.
Hollywood, CA 90027
Actor V: 03/01/92

Reiner, Carl
714 N. Rodeo Dr.
Beverly Hills, CA 90210
Actor V: 06/17/92

311 S. Bristol Ave.
Los Angeles, CA 90049-3729
Alternate V: 06/21/92

Reiner, Rob
255 Chadbourne Ave.
Los Angeles, CA 90049
Actor V: 05/16/92

311 S. Bristol Ave.
Los Angeles, CA 90049-3729
Alternate V: 06/21/92

Reinhardt, Sandra
c/o NBC-TV/"Another World"
79 Madison Ave., 5th Fl.
New York, NY 91523
Actress V: 06/15/92

Reinhold, Judge
8942 Wilshire Blvd.
Beverly Hills, CA 90211
Actor V: 03/22/93

Reiser, Paul
9200 Sunset Blvd. Ste.#915
Los Angeles, CA 90069
Actor V: 01/18/92

Remar, James
151 S. El Camino Dr.
Beverly Hills, CA 90212
Actor V: 06/02/92

Renee, Kim
7790 Royal Oaks Rd.
Las Vegas, NV 89123
Stunt Person V: 03/17/92

Reno, Janet
Dept. of Justice
10th St. and Constitution Ave., N.W.
Washington, DC 20530
Attorney General V: 03/22/93

Republic Pictures
12636 Beatrice St.
Los Angeles, CA 90066
Distributor V: 03/17/92

Ress, Roger
8942 Wilshire Blvd.
Beverly Hills, CA 90211
Actor V: 03/17/92

Rettig, Tommy
13802 NW Passage #302
Marina del Rey, CA 90291
Actor V: 01/02/92

Reuhl, Mercedes
129 Macdougal St.
New York, NY 10012-1265
Actress V: 05/04/92

Revill, Clive
c/o Duncan Heath
162 Wardour St.
London W1, England
Actor V: 02/28/92

Reynolds, Allie
2709 Cashion Pl.
Oklahoma City, OK 73112
Baseball V: 06/02/92

Reynolds, Burt
16133 Jupiter Farms Rd.
Jupiter, FL 33478
Actor V: 03/12/92

1061 Indian Town Rd.
Jupiter, FL 33458
Actor V: 03/26/93

c/o "Evening Shade"
4024 Radford Ave., Bl.5, Rm.104
Studio City, CA 91604
Forwarded V: 05/15/93

Reynolds, Debbie
11595 La Maida St.
N. Hollywood, CA 91602
Actress V: 02/09/92

Reynolds, James
c/o Days/ NBC-TV
3000 W. Alemeda Ave.
Burbank, CA 91523
Actor V: 01/11/92

Rez
4707 N. Malden
Chicago, IL 60640
Musical Group V: 02/04/92

Rhode Island Hist. Society
110 Benevolent St.
Providence, RI 02906
Archive V: 03/02/93

Rhue, Madlyn
148-D S. Maple Dr. Ste.D
Beverly Hills, CA 90212
Actress V: 05/15/92

Rice-Taylor, Allyson
c/o CBS-TV As the World Turns
51 W. 52nd St.
New York, NY 10019
Actress V: 11/18/92

Rich, Christopher
15760 Ventura Blvd. #1730
Encino, CA 91436
Actor V: 08/06/92

Richard, Cliff
St. George's Hill
Weybridge, England
Actor V: 08/16/92

Richard, Wendy
c/o Mahoney
94 Gloucester Place, Lower Fl.
London, W1H 3DA, England
Actress V: 03/20/92

Richards, Ann
P.O. Box 12428
Austin, TX 78711
Politician V: 05/15/92

Richards, Beah
1308 S. New Hampshire
Los Angeles, CA 90019
Actress V: 05/15/92

Richards, Natasha
180 W. 58th St.
New York, NY 10019
Actress V: 05/15/92

Richards, Raven
c/o Five K Sales Co.
9420 Reseda Blvd., #836
Northridge, CA 91324
Adult Films V: 03/03/93

Richards, Richard N.
c/o NASA
LBJ Space Center
Houston, TX 77058
Astronaut V: 01/31/92

Richards, Rusty
Box 100, Star Route
Modjeska, CA 92676-9801
Music Legend V: 11/11/92

Richardson, Bobby
P.O. 20000
Lynchburg, VA 24506-8001
Baseball V: 04/16/92

Richardson, Cheryl
c/o ABC-TV
General Hospital
4151 Prospect Ave.
Hollywood, CA 90027
Actress V: 06/15/92

Richardson, Natasha
180 W. 58th St.
New York, NY 10019
Actress V: 03/30/93

5555 Melrose Ave.
Los Angeles, CA 90038
L.R.U. V: 12/02/92

Richardson, Patricia
c/o Wm. Morris
151 El Camino
Beverly Hills, CA 90210
Actress V: 03/02/93

c/o Home Improvements
500 S. Buena Vista St.
Burbank, CA 91521
Forwarded V: 11/11/92

Richer, Stephane
c/o New Jersey Devils
Meadowlands Arena
E. Rutherford, NJ 07073
Hockey V: 04/05/93

Rickles, Don
925 N. Alpnie Dr.
Beverly Hills, CA 90210
Actor V: 05/16/92

8966 Sunset Blvd.
Hollywood, CA 90069
Alternate V: 01/12/92

Ride, Sally K.
c/o NASA
LBJ Space Center
Houston, TX 77058
Astronaut V: 01/19/92

c/o Harry Rhoads Jr.
Washington Speakers Bureau
123 N. Henry St.
Alexandria, VA 22314
Alternate V: 03/17/92

Rider, Chuck
c/o Bahari Racing
47 Rolling Hills Rd.
Mooresville, NC 28115
NASCAR Owner V: 03/02/92

Ridgeway, Frank
c/o King Features
216 East 45th St.
New York, NY 10017
Cartoonist V: 07/21/92

Ridgeway, Matthew
918 W. Waldheim Rd. Fox Chapel
Pittsburgh, PA 15215
Military Leader V: 05/22/92

Rigby, Cathy
c/o McCoy/Rigby
110 E. Wilshire Ave., #200
Fullerton, CA 92632
Olympian V: 04/22/92

Rigg, Diana
2-4 Noel St.
London W1V 3RB, England
Actress V: 03/22/93

c/o London Mgmt.
235-241 Regent St.
London W1A 2JT, England
Alternate V: 01/04/92

Rightous Brothers
c/o Barry Riclera
9841 Hot Springs Dr.
Huntington Beach, CA 92646
Singers V: 02/15/92

Rightous Brothers, contd
c/o Frontier Hotel & Casino
Las Vegas, NV 89102
Alternate V: 03/12/92

Riley, Jeannie C.
P.O. Box 454
Brentwood, TN 37027
Singer V: 04/19/92

Riley, Richard W.
Dept. of Education
400 Maryland Ave. S.W.
Washington, DC 20202
Secretary of Education V: 01/31/93

Rinfro, Chico
c/o WIGO INC
1526 Howell Mill Rd.
Atlanta, GA 30318-7651
Baseball V: 02/18/92

1423 W. Peachtree NW
Atlanta, GA 30301
Forwarded V: 02/18/92

Ringwald, Molly
8942 Wilshire Blvd.
Beverly Hills, CA 90211
Actress V: 01/02/92

7680 Mulholland Dr.
Los Angeles, CA 90046
Actress V: 05/15/92

120 El Camino Dr. #104
Beverly Hills, CA 90212
L.R.U. V: 12/08/92

Ritenour, Lee
P.O. Box 6774
Malibu, CA 90265
Singer V: 06/17/92

Ritter, John
236 Tigertail Rd.
Los Angeles, CA 90049
Actor V: 03/01/92

c/o Adam Prod./20th Cent./Fox
P.O. Box 900
Beverly Hills, CA 90213
Alternate V: 04/22/92

Rivers, Joan
The Joan Rivers Show
524 W. 57th St.
New York, NY 10019
Comedian/TV Host V: 01/16/93

Rivers, Joan, contd
P.O. Box 49774
Los Angeles, CA 90049-0774
Alternate V: 11/07/92

310 S. Almont Dr.
#212
Sherman Oaks, CA 90048
Alternate V: 11/11/92

1084 Ambazac Way
Los Angeles, CA 90077
Forwarded V: 06/23/92

Roarke, Adam
c/o Film Actor Cars
6311 N. O'Conner Rd.
Irving, TX 75039-3510
Actor V: 01/04/92

Robards, Jason
c/o Wm. Morris
1350 Ave. of the Americas
New York, NY 10019
Actor V: 02/12/92

Robbins, Brian
c/o Warner Brothers TV
Head of the Class
100 North Pass Rd.
Burbank, CA 91505
Actor V: 12/18/92

Robbins, Harold
990 N. Patencio Rd.
Palm Springs, CA 92262
Author V: 02/17/92

Roberts, Beverly
30912 Ariana Ln.
Laguna Niguel, CA 92677
Actress V: 05/15/92

Roberts, Doris
6225 Quebec Dr.
Los Angeles, CA 90068
Actress V: 06/17/92

Roberts, Julia
c/o ICM
8942 Wilshire Blvd.
Beverly Hills, CA 90211
Actress V: 01/16/93

8942 Wilshire Blvd.
Beverly Hills, CA 90211
Actress V: 05/15/92

500 S. Buena Vista St.
Burbank, CA 91521
Alternate V: 05/22/92

Roberts, Julia, contd
1776 Broadway 8th Fl.
New York, NY 10019
Forwarded V: 03/17/92

Roberts, Pernell
20395 Seaboard Rd.
Malibu, CA 90265
Actor V: 06/17/92

P.O. Box 5617
Beverly Hills, CA 90213
Alternate V: 01/16/93

Roberts, Tanya
2175 Summitridge Dr.
Beverly Hills, CA 90210-1523
Actress V: 12/12/92

10090 Cielo Dr.
Beverly Hills, CA 90210-2025
L.R.U. V: 07/01/92

Robertson, Cliff
P.O. Box 55049
Sherman Oaks, CA 91413
Actor V: 05/23/92

325 Dunemere Dr.
La Jolla, CA 92037
Alternate V: 03/26/93

40 W. 57th St.
New York, NY 10019
Alternate V: 03/29/92

P.O. Box 940
Water Mill, NY 11976
Alternate V: 03/14/93

Robertson, Dale
13263 Ventura Blvd. #4
N. Hollywood, CA 91604
Actor V: 08/15/92

P.O. Box 850707
Yukon, OK 73085
Alternate V: 03/26/93

Robey
3662 Barham Blvd. #M
Los Angeles, CA 90068
Actor V: 03/17/93

Robinson, Alexia
ABC-TV
General Hospital
4151 Prospect Ave.
Hollywood, CA 90027
Actress V: 06/15/92

Robinson, Dolores
335 N. Maple Dr. #250
Beverly Hills, CA 90210
Talent Agency V: 02/05/93

Robinson, Holly
7743 Woodrow Wilson Dr.
Los Angeles, CA 90046
Actress V: 03/16/93

335 N. Maple Dr.
La Jolla, CA 92037
Alternate V: 05/16/92

Robinson, John
c/o L.A. Rams
2327 W. Lincoln Blvd.
Anaheim, CA 92801
Football V: 01/12/92

Robinson, Smokey
P.O. Box 3144
Hollywood, CA 90078
Singer V: 04/22/92

17085 Rancho St.
Encino, CA 91316
Alternate V: 03/17/93

Robinson, T. Wayne
P.O. Box 249
McConnellsburg, PA 17233
Race Driver V: 03/12/93

Rocco, Alex
P.O. Box 1303
Carpenteria, CA 93014-1303
Actor V: 01/10/92

1755 Ocean Oaks Rd.
Carpenteria, CA 93013
Alternate V: 03/01/92

Roche, Eugene
451 1/2 Kelton Ave.
Los Angeles, CA 90024
Actor V: 03/25/92

Rockwell, Robert
650 Toyopa Dr.
Pacific Palisades, CA 90272
Actor V: 02/15/92

Rocky Horror Picture Show
c/o Sal Piro
204 W. 20th St.
New York, NY 10011
Fan Club V: 03/16/92

Rodd, Marcia
11738 Moorpark St. Ste.C
Studio City, CA 91604
Actress V: 05/15/92

Rodriguez, Paul
2036 Hanscom Dr.
S. Pasadena, CA 91030
Actor V: 03/26/93

Rogers, Charles "Buddy"
1147 Pickfair Way
Beverly Hills, CA 90210
Actor V: 06/17/92

Rogers, Fred
c/o Mr. Rogers
4802 5th Ave.
Pittsburgh, PA 15213
Educator V: 02/12/92

Rogers, Ginger
18745 Crater Lake Hwy #62
Eagle Point, OR 97524
Actress V: 06/01/92

4460 Pioneer Rd.
Medford, OR 97501-9643
Actress V: 03/22/93

Rogers, Jane
c/o Bell-Phillip Prod.
Bold & Beautiful
7800 Beverly Blvd., Ste.3371
Los Angeles, CA 90036
Actress V: 06/15/92

Rogers, Jimmie
1961 Falcon Ct.
Thousand Oaks, CA 91362
Celebrity V: 05/16/92

Rogers, Kenny
P.O. Box 24240
Nashville, TN 37202-4240
Singer V: 12/12/92

1112 N. Shelborne Dr.
Los Angeles, CA 90069
Alternate V: 03/30/92

Rt.1, Box 100
Colbert, GA 30628-0100
Alternate V: 06/02/92

700 Dollywood Ln.
Pigeon Forge, TN 37863-4101
Alternate V: 05/05/92

Rogers, Melody
2051 Nichols Canyon Rd.
Los Angeles, CA 90046
 Actress V: 05/15/92

Rogers, Roy
15650 Seneca Rd.e Dr.
Victorville, CA 92392
 Actor V: 03/16/92

Rogers, Suzanne
11266 Canton Dr. #301
Studio City, CA 91604
 Actress V: 05/15/92

Rogers, Tristan
c/o General Hosp./ABC Inc.
4151 Prospect Ave.
Hollywood, CA 90027
 Actor V: 03/01/92

8550 Holloway Dr. #301
Los Angeles, CA 90069
 Alternate V: 03/26/93

Rogers, Wayne
11828 La Grange Ave.
Los Angeles, CA 90025
 Actor V: 03/26/93

Roker, Roxie
4061 Cloverdale Ave.
Los Angeles, CA 90008
 Actress V: 05/15/92

Roland, Gilbert
518 N.Roxbury Dr.
Beverly Hills, CA 90210
 Actor V: 03/01/92

Rolle, Esther
P.O Box 8986
Los Angeles, CA 90008
 Actress V: 05/15/92

Rolling Stone Magazine
745 Fifth Ave.
New York, NY 10151
 Publishers V: 03/01/92

Rollins, Howard
"In the Heat of the Night"
1000 W. Washington Blvd.
Culver City, CA 90232
 Actor V: 01/07/92

Roman, Phil
10635 Riverside Dr.
Toluca Lake, CA 91602
 Cartoonist V: 02/04/92

Roman, Phil, contd
P.O. Box 7706
N. Hollywood, CA 91617-7706
 Alternate V: 03/30/93

Roman, Ruth
1220 Cliff Dr.
Laguna Beach, CA 92651
 Actress V: 05/15/92

Romay, Lina
1303 Lyndon St. #6
S. Pasadena, CA 91362
 Actress V: 05/15/92

Romero, Cesar
12115 San Vicente Blvd. #302
Los Angeles, CA 90049
 Actor V: 02/02/92

Ronstadt, Linda
c/o Asher/Krost Management
644 N. Doheny Dr.
Los Angeles, CA 90069
 Singer V: 09/10/92

Rooney, Andy
51 W. 52nd St.
New York, NY 10019
 Humorist V: 04/14/92

Rooney, Mickey
4165 Thousand Oaks Blvd. #300
Westlake Village, CA 91362
 Actor V: 03/26/93

7500 De Vista Dr.
Los Angeles, CA 90046
 Alternate V: 02/19/92

Roosa, Stuart A.
c/o NASA LBJ Space Center
Houston, TX 77058
 Astronaut V: 03/03/93

Rosamund, John
4 Deans Yard
London SW1P, England
 Actor V: 03/01/92

Rose, Axl
Bebel Str. 37
6720 Speyer, Germany
 Singer V: 11/16/92

2738 Holly Ridge
Los Angeles, CA 90068
 Alternate V: 03/18/93

Rose, David
216 E. 45th St.
New York, NY 10017
Cartoonist V: 03/11/93

Rose, Murray
3305 Carse Dr.
Los Angeles, CA 90068
Swimmer V: 06/17/92

Rose, Pete
10415 Honebridge Blvd.
Boca Raton, FL 33498
Baseball Manager V: 01/16/93

Rosemarie
6918 Chisholm Ave.
Van Nuys, Ca 91406
Actress V: 03/26/93

Rosenberg Office
8428 Melrose Pl., Ste.C
Los Angeles, CA 90046
Talent Agency V: 02/23/93

Ross, Charlotte
8715 Burton Wy. #1
Los Angeles, CA 90048
Actress V: 04/01/93

Ross, Diana
P.O. Box 11059
Glenville Station
Greenwich, CT 06831-1059
Singer V: 01/11/92

22028 Pacific Coast Hwy.
Malibu, CA 90265
Alternate V: 05/15/92

Ross, Donald K.
15871 Glenwood Rd. SW
Port Orchard, WA 98366
Medal of Honor V: 03/17/92

Ross, Jerry L.
NASA/LBJ Space Center
Houston, TX 77058
Astronaut V: 03/03/93

Ross, Katherine
33050 Pacific Coast Hwy.
Malibu, CA 90265
Actress V: 06/17/92

Ross, Tim
c/o WCW/Turner Broad.
One CNN Center, Box 105366
Atlanta, GA 30348-5366
Commentator V: 03/26/93

Rossen, Carol
1119 23rd St. #8
Santa Monica, CA 90403
Actress V: 05/15/92

Rosson Agency
11712 Moorpark St., Ste.204
Studio City, CA 91604
Talent Agency V: 01/24/93

Rossovich, Rick
c/o Paramount Pictures
5555 Melrose Ave., Wilder #214
Los Angeles, CA 90038
Actor V: 05/15/92

Roth, David Lee
3960 Laurel Canyon #430
Studio City, CA 91604
Singer V: 06/17/92

Roundtree, Richard
100 Universal City Plaza
Universal Studios/MCA
Universal City, CA 91608
Actor V: 03/23/92

8721 Sunset Blvd. #202
Los Angeles, CA 90069
Actor V: 04/05/93

8899 Sunset Blvd.
Los Angeles, CA 90069
L.R.U. V: 12/16/92

Rourke, Mickey
8439 Sunset Blvd. #107
Los Angeles, CA 90069
Actor V: 03/26/93

8966 Sunset Blvd.
Hollywood, CA 90069
Alternate V: 01/12/92

Rouse, Suzanne
c/o Dallas Cowboys
One Cowboys Parkway
Irving, TX 75063-4945
Cheerleader V: 08/08/92

Roush, Jack
c/o Roush Racing
P.O. Box 1089
Liberty, NC 27298
NASCAR Owner V: 03/02/92

Rowe, Misty
880 Greenleaf Canyon
Topanga Canyon, CA 90290
Actress V: 03/26/93

Rowe, Misty, contd
161 W. 61 St., #168
New York, NY 10023-7400
Alternate V: 04/22/92

9278 Warbler Way
Los Angeles, CA 90069
L.R.U. V: 02/01/92

Rowell, Victoria
c/o Young and the Restless
7800 Beverly Blvd. #3305
Beverly Hills, CA 90036
Actress V: 06/15/92

Rowland, Betty
217 Broadway
Santa Monica, CA 90405
Burlesque V: 03/16/93

Rowlands, Gena
7917 Woodrow Wilson Dr.
Los Angeles, CA 90046
Actress V: 04/21/92

Roy, Patrick
c/o Montreal Canadiens
2313 St. Catherine St. W.
Montreal, Quebec H3H 1N2
Canada
Hockey V: 11/19/92

Rubenstein, John
10420 Scenario Lane
Los Angeles, CA 90026
Actor V: 06/18/92

Rubinstein, Zelda
8730 Sunset Blvd. #220W
Los Angeles, CA 90069
Actress V: 05/15/92

Ruck, Alan
151 El Camino
Beverly Hills, CA 90212
Actor V: 05/16/92

c/o Lorimar
"Going Places"
3970 Overland Ave.
Culver City, CA 90230
Forwarded V: 12/15/92

Rudd, Ricky
c/o Hendrick Motor Sports
5315 Stowe Lane, P.O. Box 9
Harrisburg, NC 28075
NASCAR Driver V: 03/02/92

Rudie, Evelyn
7514 Hollywood Blvd.
Los Angeles, CA 90046
Actress V: 05/15/92

Rudley, Herbert
c/o Marlyn Rudley
13056 Maxella Ave.#1
Marina del Rey, CA 90292
Actor V: 07/18/92

Runco Jr., Mario
c/o NASA
LBJ Space Center
Houston, TX 77058
Astronaut V: 01/31/92

Rungrun, Todd
2705 Glendower Ave.
Los Angeles, CA 90027
Singer V: 02/01/92

Rush, Barbara
1708 Tropical Ave.
Beverly Hills, CA 90210
Actress V: 03/01/92

Rusk, Dean
c/o University Of Georgia
School Of Law
Athens, GA 30602
Lawyer V: 03/10/92

Russ, William
c/o Stephen J. Cannell Prod.
7083 Hollywood Blvd.
Hollywood, CA 90028
Actor V: 05/15/92

Russell, Betsy
13926 Magnolia Blvd.
Sherman Oaks, CA 91423
Actress V: 03/17/93

P.O. Box 1759
La Jolla, CA 92037
Alternate V: 01/03/92

111 Sweetzer Ave. #3
Los Angeles, CA 90043
Forwarded V: 11/01/92

14411 Riverside Dr. #13
Sherman Oaks, CA 91423
L.R.U. V: 11/01/92

Russell, Jane
2934 Lorita Rd.
Santa Barbara, CA 93108-1632
Actress V: 05/05/92

Russell, Jane, contd
c/o WAIF
67 Irving Pl.
New York, NY 10003
Forwarded V: 03/04/92

Russell, Kimberly
c/o Warner Brothers TV
"Head of the Class"
100 North Pass Rd.
Burbank, CA 91505
Actress V: 12/18/92

Russell, Kurt
1900 Ave. of the Stars #1240
Los Angeles, CA 90067
Actor V: 02/15/93

Russell, Theresa
2 E. Oxford & Cambridge
Old May Bone Rd.
London NW1, England
Actress V: 04/12/92

9255 Sunset Blvd. #505
Los Angeles, CA 90069
L.R.U. V: 07/01/92

151 El Camino
Beverly Hills, CA 90212
L.R.U. V: 07/01/92

Rutherford, Ann
826 Greenway Dr.
Beverly Hills, CA 90210
Actress V: 03/30/92

Rutherford, John
RR 18, Box 340-B
Indianapolis, IN 46234
Race Driver V: 03/01/92

4919 Black Oak Ln.
Ft. Worth, TX 76114
Alternate V: 01/16/92

Rutherford, Kelly
8825 Rangely Ave.
Beverly Hills, CA 90211
Actress V: 06/14/92

148 S. Bedford Dr.
Beverly Hills, CA 90212
L.R.U. V: 06/14/92

Ruttan, Susan
c/o Cynthia Snyder
3518 Cahuenga Blvd. W. #304
Los Angeles, CA 90068
Actress V: 05/02/92

Ruttan, Susan, contd
2677 La Cuesta Dr.
Los Angeles, CA 90046
Alternate V: 03/26/93

c/o 20th Century Fox TV
"L.A. Law"
P.O. Box 900
Beverly Hills, CA 90213
Forwarded V: 01/12/92

Ruttman, Joe
c/o Moroso Racing
3 Knob Hill Rd.
Mooresville, NC 28115
NASCAR Driver V: 03/02/92

Ruzzuto, Phil
912 Westminster Ave.
Hillside, NJ 07205
Baseball V: 12/10/92

Ryan, Marisa
c/o Universal Television
"Major Dad"
100 Univ. City Plz., Bl.426-2E
Universal City, CA 91608
Actress V: 03/02/92

Ryan, Meg
8033 Sunset Blvd. #4048
Los Angeles, CA 90046
Actress V: 01/16/93

8942 Wilshire Blvd.
Beverly Hills, CA 90211
Alternate V: 04/22/92

10153 1/2 Riverside Dr. #116
Toluca Lake, CA 91602-116
Alternate V: 04/22/92

Ryan, Peggy
1821 E. Oakley Blvd.
Las Vegas, NV 89104-3648
Actress V: 05/15/92

Ryan, Tim
220 N. Washington Rd.
Halas Hall
Lake Forest, IL 60045
Football V: 01/12/92

Ryan, Tom K.
c/o King Features
216 East 45th St.
New York, NY 10017
Cartoonist V: 07/17/92

Rydell, Bobby
917 Bryn Mawr Ave.
Narberth, PA 19072
Actor V: 03/04/92

c/o Rudney
919 Conestoga Rd.
Rosemont, PA 19010
Alternate V: 01/12/92

Ryder, Holly
P.O. Box 16678
Beverly Hills, CA 90209-2678
Adult Films V: 01/24/93

Ryder, Winona
c/o CAA
9830 Wilshire Blvd.
Beverly Hills, CA 90212
Actress V: 03/26/93

c/o PMK Inc.
1776 Broadway 8th Fl.
New York, NY 10019
Forwarded V: 03/17/92

S

S.F. Area Stuntmans Assn.
612 Lancaster Way
Redwood City, CA 94061
Production Company V: 03/17/92

S.F. State University
J. Paul Leonard Library
1630 Holloway Ave.
San Francisco, CA 94709
Archive V: 03/20/93

SANTA BARBARA
Dobson Prod.
c/o NBC Burbank
3000 W. Alameda Ave.
Burbank, CA 91523
Production Company V: 03/26/93

SATURDAY NIGHT LIVE
c/o NBC Prod.
Saturday Night Live
30 Rockefeller Plaza
New York, NY 10112
Production Company V: 01/10/92

SAVED BY THE BELL
NBC Prod.
330 Bob Hope Dr.
Burbank, CA 91523
Production Company V: 03/26/93

SECRET SERVICE
103 The East Mall
Toronto, Ontario, Canada
M8Z 5X9
Production Company V: 03/26/93

SEINFELD
c/o Castle Rock
Seinfeld
335 W. Maple Dr. #135
Beverly Hills, CA 90210
Production Company V: 01/07/92

Castle Rock
335 N. Maple Dr. #135
Beverly Hills, CA 90210
Alternate V: 03/26/93

SILK STALKINGS
Stephen J. Cannell Prod.
7083 Hollywood Blvd.
Hollywood, CA 90028
Production Company V: 03/18/93

SIRENS
c/o ABC Prod.
2020 Ave. of the Stars #500
Los Angeles, CA 90067
Production Company V: 04/20/93

SISTERS
Lorimar Television
400 Warner Blvd.
Burbank, CA 91522
Production Company V: 03/26/93

SIXTY MINUTES
c/o CBS Broadcast Center
524 W. 57th St.
New York, NY 10019
Production Company V: 06/15/92

STAR TREK (TNG+DS9)
c/o Parmount Pictures Inc.
5555 Melrose Ave.
Los Angeles, CA 90038
Network Offices V: 03/10/92

STE Representation
9301 Wilshire Blvd. #312
Beverly Hills, CA 90210
Talent Agency V: 03/02/93

STEP BY STEP
c/o Lorimar Prod.
300 S. Lorimar Plaza
Burbank, CA 91505
Production Company V: 04/21/93

SWEATING BULLETS
c/o Kushner-Locke Co.
Sweating Bullets
11601 Wilshire Blvd., 21st Fl.
Los Angeles, CA 90025
Production Company V: 05/15/92

Sabates, Felix
c/o Sabco Racing
P.O. Box 560579
Charlotte, NC 28256
NASCAR Owner V: 03/02/92

Sabatini, Gabriela
2665 S. Bayshore Dr.
Miami, FL 31333
Actress V: 05/15/92

Sacchi, Robert
113 N. San Vicente Blvd. #202
Beverly Hills, CA 90211
Actor V: 02/02/92

Sachs, Andrew
c/o Stone
25 Whitehall
London SW1A 2BS, England
Actor V: 03/17/92

Sadruddin Aga Khan, Prince
Case Postale 6
1211 Geneva 3, Switzerland
Royalty V: 03/02/92

Sagal, Katey
c/o Fox TV
10201 W. Pico Blvd.
Los Angeles, CA 90035
Actress V: 01/12/92

Sagendorf, Bud
c/o King Features
216 East 45th St.
New York, NY 10017
Cartoonist V: 02/04/92

Sager, Carole Bayer
658 Nimes Rd.
Los Angeles, CA 90077
Songwriter V: 03/21/92

Saget, Bob
c/o Lorimar
"Full House"
10201 W. Pico Blvd.
Los Angeles, CA 90035
Actor V: 12/15/90

Saget, Bob, contd
"Funniest Home Videos"
P.O. Box 4333
Los Angeles, CA 90078
Alternate V: 12/15/92

Sahl, Mort
2325 San Ysidro Dr.
Beverly Hills, CA 90210
Comedian V: 06/17/92

Sai Talent Agency
4145 Lankershim Blvd.
Universal City, CA 91602
Talent Agency V: 03/13/93

Saint, Eva Marie
c/o Paul Kohner, Inc.
9169 Sunset Blvd.
Los Angeles, CA 90069
Actress V: 01/06/93

1509 N. Crescent Heights #7
Los Angeles, CA 90046-2405
L.R.U. V: 06/01/92

Saint James, Susan
c/o CAA
9830 Wilshire Blvd.
Beverly Hills, CA 90212
Actress V: 01/16/93

c/o Marlene Fait
854 N. Genesee Ave.
Hollywood, CA 90046
Alternate V: 02/15/92

Sainte-Marie, Buffy
RR1, Box 368
Kapaa, Kauai, HI 96746
Singer V: 12/02/92

Sajak, Pat
3400 Riverside Dr.
Burbank, CA 91505
TV Host V: 01/16/93

1541 N Vine St.
Hollywood, CA 90028
Alternate V: 03/16/92

Salac, Joe
c/o Quebec Nordique
2205 Ave. Colisee
Quebec, Quebec GIL 4W7
Canada
Hockey V: 11/25/92

Saldana, Theresa
c/o BDP
10673 Burbank Blvd.
N. Hollywood, CA 91601
Actress V: 01/16/93

Sales, Soupy
245 E. 35th St.
New York, NY 10016
Comedian V: 04/28/92

Salinger, J.D.
Rural Route #3
Box 176
Cornish Falt, NH 03745
Writer V: 03/02/93

Salk, Dr. Jonas
2444 Ellentown Rd.
La Jolla, CA 92037
Physician V: 06/17/92

Sammer, Mattias
c/o Borussia Dortmund
Westfalenstadion
D-(W) 4600 Dortmund 1
Germany
Actor V: 02/11/93

c/o Romantik Hotel Lennhof
Menglinghauser Str. 20
D-(W) 4600 Dortmund 50
Germany
Forwarded V: 02/01/93

Samms, Emma
335 N. Maple Dr. #360
Beverly Hills, CA 90210
Actress V: 10/13/92

c/o Spelling
1041 N. Formosa Ave.
West Hollywood, CA 90046
Alternate V: 02/13/92

P.O. Box 60257
Los Angeles, CA 90060
Alternate V: 07/24/92

10401 Wyton Dr.
Los Angeles, CA 90024
Alternate V: 01/16/93

P.O. Box 339
Tujunga, CA 91042
Forwarded V: 08/08/92

Samuel Goldwyn Co.
10203 Santa Monica Blvd.
Los Angeles, CA 90067
Production Company V: 03/17/92

San Diego Chargers
San Diego-Jack Murphy Stadium
9449 Friars Rd.
San Diego, CA 92120
Team Offices V: 05/15/92

San Diego Padres
9449 Friars Rd.
San Diego-Jack Murphy Stadium
San Diego, CA 92108
Team Office V: 05/15/92

San Francisco 49ers
4949 Centennial Blvd.
Santa Clara, CA 95054-1229
Team Headquarters V: 02/12/92

San Francisco Giants
Candlestick Park
San Francisco, CA 94124
Team Office V: 05/15/92

San Giacomo, Laura
13035 Woodbridge St.
Studio City, CA 91604
Actress V: 03/22/93

8262 Gould Ave.
Los Angeles, CA 90049
L.R.U. V: 12/02/92

San Jose Sharks
P.O. Box 1240
San Jose, CA 95113
Baseball V: 12/10/92

San Juan, Olga
c/o O'Brien
4845 Willowcrest Ave.
Studio City, CA 91604
Actress V: 05/15/92

Sanda, Dominique
c/o George Beaume
3 Quia Malquais
Paris 75006, France
Actress V: 03/02/92

Sanders Agency
8831 Sunset Blvd. Ste.304
Los Angeles, CA 90069
Talent Agency V: 03/13/93

Sands, Tommy
1047 21st Ave.
Honolulu, HI 96816-4628
Actor V: 02/12/92

Sanford, Isabel
8489 W. 3rd St. #1105
Los Angeles, CA 90048
Actress V: 08/15/92

Sansom, Art
1050 Eire Cliff Dr.
Cleveland, OH 44107
Cartoonist V: 02/04/92

Sansom, Chip
1050 Eire Cliff Dr.
Cleveland, OH 44107
Cartoonist V: 02/04/92

Santana, Carlos
P.O. Box 881630
San Francisco, CA 94188-1630
Singer V: 02/12/92

Santon, Penny
1918 N. Edgemont St.
Los Angeles, CA 90027
Actress V: 05/15/92

Sarandon, Susan
c/o ICM
8942 Wilshire Blvd.
Beverly Hills, CA 90211
Actress V: 03/30/93

1350 6th Ave.
New York, NY 10019
L.R.U. V: 07/01/92

Sarducci, Fr. Guido
c/o Don Novello
P.O. Box 245
Fairfax, CA 94930
Actor V: 04/19/92

Sargent, Dick
7422 Palo Vista Dr.
Los Angeles, CA 90046
Actor V: 02/01/92

Sarnoff Company
12001 Ventura Pl. #311
Studio City, CA 91604
Talent Agency V: 03/19/93

Saskatchewan Archives
University of Regina
Regina, SK S4S 0A2 Canada
Archive V: 03/20/93

Sassoon, Beverly
1520 S. Beverly Glen #202
Los Angeles, CA 90024
Actress V: 05/15/92

Satterfield Jr., Paul
c/o ABC-TV
General Hospital
4151 Prospect Ave.
Hollywood, CA 90027
Actor V: 06/15/92

Saulsbury, Rodney
c/o Young and the Restless
7800 Beverly Blvd.
Beverly Hills, CA 90036
Actor V: 06/15/92

Saunders, Jennifer
c/o Peters
The Chambers, Chelsea Harbour
Lots Road
London SW10 0XF, England
Actress V: 03/20/92

Saunders, John
c/o King Features
216 East 45th St.
New York, NY 10017
Cartoonist V: 04/19/92

Saunders, John R.
Watkins Glen Speedway
Box 500-T
Watkins Glen, NY 14891
NASCAR Official V: 03/02/92

Savage, Fred
c/o New World TV
"The Wonder Years"
1440 S. Sepulveda Blvd.
Los Angeles, CA 90025
Actor V: 12/11/92

P.O. Box 869
Tarzana, CA 91357
L.R.U. V: 07/01/92

Savage, Randy "Macho Man"
P.O. Box 3859
Stamford, CT 06905
Wrestler V: 01/22/92

Savage Agency
6212 Banner Ave.
Los Angeles, CA 90038
Talent Agency V: 03/14/93

Savalas, Telly
c/o Sheraton Hotel
333 Universal City Plz.
Universal City, CA 91608
Actor V: 11/11/92

Savalas, Telly, contd
8942 Wilshire Blvd.
Beverly Hills, CA 90211
  L.R.U. *V: 03/17/92*

Saviano, Josh
c/o New World TV
"The Wonder Years"
1440 S. Sepulveda Blvd.
Los Angeles, CA 90025
  Actor V: 12/11/92

Savoy, Gene
643 Ralston St.
Reno, NV 89503
  Explorer V: 09/17/92

Sawer, Elton
c/o Davis Racing
11 N. Robbins St.
Thomasville, NC 27360
  NASCAR Driver V: 03/02/92

Sawyer, Diane
524 W. 57th St.
New York, NY 10019
  Journalist V: 01/14/92

c/o ABC-TV INC.
77 West 66th St.
New York, NY 10023
  Alternate V: 09/06/92

1965 Broadway
New York, NY 10023
  Alternate V: 03/01/92

c/o ABC News
Prime Time Live
1926 Broadway
New York, NY 10023
  Forwarded V: 12/07/92

Sawyer, Paul
Richmond Int'l Raceway
P.O. Box 9257
Richmond, VA 23227
  NASCAR Official V: 03/02/92

Saxon, John
2432 Banyon Dr.
Los Angeles, CA 90049
  Actor V: 02/24/92

Scacchi, Greta
121 N. San Vicente Blvd.
Beverly Hills, CA 90211
  Actress V: 06/21/92

Scaduto, Al
c/o King Features
216 E. 45th St.
New York, NY 10017
  Cartoonist V: 03/11/93

Scaggs, William R. (Boz)
c/o Slims
333 11th St. 94103
San Francisco, CA 94103
  Singer V: 02/12/92

Scagnetti Agency
5330 Lankershim Blvd. #210
N. Hollywood, CA 91401
  Talent Agency V: 02/19/93

Scales, Prunella
c/o Conway
109 Jermyn St., Eagle House
London SW1 6HB, England
  Actress V: 03/20/92

Scarabelli, Michele
4720 Vineland Ave. #216
N. Hollywood, CA 91602
  Actress V: 03/26/93

Schaal, Wendy
3701 Longview Valley Rd.
Sherman Oaks, CA 91403
  Actress V: 03/26/93

Schaeffer, Paul
c/o CBS-Ed Sullivan Theatre
1697 Broadway
New York, NY 10019
  Musician V: 03/19/93

Schaeffer Agency
10850 Riverside Dr. #505
N. Hollywood, CA 91602
  Talent Agency V: 02/19/93

Schallert, William
14920 Ramos Pl.
Pacific Palisades, CA 90272
  Actor V: 02/15/92

Schecter Company
9300 Wilshire Blvd. #410
Beverly Hills, CA 90212
  Talent Agency V: 02/19/93

Schell, Maria
D-8094 Heberthal
Bei WasserBurgl Inn
Germany
  Actress V: 02/17/93

Schell, Ronnie
1888 Century Park E. #622
Los Angeles, CA 90067
 Actor V: 01/19/92

Schelmerding, Kirk
c/o Childress Racing
P.O. Box 1189, Industrial Dr.
Welcome, NC 27374
 NASCAR Crew V: 03/02/92

Schembechler, Bo
1000 S. State St.
Ann Arbor, MI 48109-2201
 Football Coach V: 01/12/92

Schenk, Otto
Rudolfspltz 6
A-1010 Wein, Austria
 Actor V: 01/19/93

Schiller, Anja
c/o Elan Films
Rudesheimer Str. 11
D-(W) 8000 Munchen 21
Germany
 Actress V: 02/11/93

Schlowitz/Clay/Rose
8228 Sunset Blvd. #212
Los Angeles, CA 90046
 Talent Agency V: 03/11/93

Schirra Jr., Walter M.
c/o NASA LBJ Space Center
Houston, TX 77058
 Astronaut V: 03/03/93

Schmeling, Max
2114 Hollenstedt
Nordheide, Germany
 Boxing V: 02/10/92

Schmidt, Michael J.
P.O. Box 4032
Rydal, PA 19046
 Baseball V: 12/10/92

Schmitt, Harrison H.
P.O. Box 14338
Albuquerque, NM 87191
 Astronaut V: 03/17/92

c/o NASA
LBJ Space Center
Houston, TX 77058
 Alternate V: 01/19/92

Schnarr Agency
8281 Melrose Ave. #200
Los Angeles, CA 90046
 Talent Agency V: 03/17/93

Schneider, John
P.O. Box 2277
Mtn. Lake Park, MD 21550-0677
 Singer V: 03/30/93

P.O. Box 1726
Mechanicsburg, PA 17055
 Alternate V: 01/17/92

Schnetzer, Stephen
c/o NBC-TV
"Another World"
79 Madison Ave., 5th Fl.
New York, NY 91523
 Actor V: 06/15/92

Schoeder, Jochen
Postfach 10 23 46
D-(W) 4630 Bochum 1
Germany
 Actor V: 02/11/93

Schoelen, Jill
1999 Ave. of the Stars #2850
Los Angeles, CA 90067
 Actress V: 05/29/92

Schoen & Associates
606 N. Larchmont Blvd. #309
Los Angeles, CA 90004
 Talent Agency V: 03/17/93

Schoendienst, Alfred Red
331 Ladue Woods Ct.
Crene Coeur, MO 63141
 Baseball V: 02/10/92

Schrader, Ken
c/o Hendrick Motor Sports
5315 Stowe Lane, P.O. Box 9
Harrisburg, NC 28075
 NASCAR Driver V: 03/02/92

Schramm, Tex
c/o Dallas Cowboys
Cowboy Center 1 Cowboys Pkwy.
Irving, TX 75063
 Team Manager V: 01/12/92

Schriver, Maria
321 Hampton Dr. #203
Venice, CA 90291
 Celebrity V: 05/06/92

Schroder, Rick
921 N. Roxbury Dr.
Beverly Hills, CA 90210
Actor V: 03/17/93

Schuck, John
702 California Ave.
Venice, CA 90069
Actor V: 12/10/92

9229 Sunset Blvd.
Los Angeles, CA 90069
L.R.U. V: 12/10/92

Schull, Rebecca
c/o Grub Street Prod.
Wings
5555 Melrose Ave./Wilder RM101
Hollywood, CA 90038
Actress V: 01/07/92

Schultz, Dwight
2824 Nichols Canyon Rd.
Los Angeles, CA 90046
Actor V: 03/17/93

Schulz, Charles
1 Snoopy Place
Santa Rosa, CA 95401
Cartoonist V: 03/16/92

Schumacher, Michael
Forsthausstr. 92
D-(W) 5014 Kerpen-Manheim, Germany
Race Car Driver V: 01/17/93

Schut Agency
11350 Ventura Blvd. #200
Studio City, CA 91604
Talent Agency V: 03/19/93

Schwartz, Scott
4631 Lakeview Canyon Rd.
Westlake Village, CA 91361
Actor V: 04/16/92

Schwartz & Associates
8749 Sunset Blvd.
Los Angeles, CA 90069
Talent Agency V: 04/01/93

Schwartzkopf, Norman
600 N. Westshore Blvd. #1202
Tampa, FL 33609
Soldier V: 03/04/93

Beverly Estates
13100 Mulholland Dr.
Beverly Hills, CA 90210
Alternate V: 02/11/93

Schwartzkopf, Norman, contd
U.S. Military Command Center
Pentagon Building
Washington, DC 20510
Forwarded V: 09/12/92

Schwarzenegger, Arnold
3110 Main St. #300
Santa Monica, CA 90405
Actor V: 01/16/93

P.O. Box 1234
Santa Monica, CA 90406
Alternate V: 06/01/92

Schweickart, Russell L.
c/o NASA LBJ Space Center
Houston, TX 77058
Astronaut V: 03/03/93

67 Issaquah Dock
Waldo Point Harbor
Sausalito, CA 94965
L.R.U. V: 11/01/92

Schygulla, Hanna
c/o ZBF Agentur
Leopoldstr. 19
D-(W) 8000 Munchen 40, Germany
Actress V: 01/17/93

Sci-fi, Fantasy
& Horror Films
334 W. 54th St.
Los Angeles, CA 90037
Academy Office V: 03/17/92

Science Fiction Museum
P.O. Box 18091
Salem, OR 97305-8091
V: 11/16/92

Scofield, Paul
The Gables
Balcome, Sussex, England
Actor V: 02/28/92

Scoggins, Tracy
P.O. Box 2121
Malibu, CA 90265
Actress V: 04/22/92

1041 N. Formosa Ave.
W. Hollywood, CA 90048
Alternate V: 03/13/92

445 N. Bedford Dr.
Beverly Hills, CA 90210
Forwarded V: 05/26/92

Scolari, Peter
930 Hilgard Ave.
Los Angeles, CA 90024
Actor V: 08/15/92

930 Hilgard Ave.
Los Angeles, CA 90024
Actor V: 04/06/93

Scorpions
P.O. Box 5220
3000 Hanover, Germany
Musical Group V: 07/21/92

c/o Rock n' Roll
4009 Pacific Coast Hwy.
Torrance, CA 90505
Alternate V: 01/17/93

Scorsese, Martin
146 W. 57th St. #75B
New York, NY 10019
Director V: 03/04/93

Scott, Danyce
c/o Dallas Cowboys
One Cowboys Parkway
Irving, TX 75063-4945
Cheerleader V: 08/08/92

Scott, David R.
c/o NASA LBJ Space Center
Houston, TX 77058
Astronaut V: 03/03/93

Scott, Fred
1716 Camino Parocela
Palm Springs, CA 92262
Actor V: 06/13/92

1765 E. Ramon Rd.
Palm Springs. CA 92264
Alternate V: 06/13/92

Scott, George C.
3211 Retreat Ct.
Malibu, CA 90265
Actress V: 03/26/93

Scott, Jacqueline
P.O. Box 69405
Los Angeles, CA 90069
Actress V: 06/17/92

Scott, Katherine
12161 Valleyheart Dr.
Studio City, CA 91604-1675
Actress V: 05/15/92

Scott, Lizabeth
P.O. Box 5522
Beverly Hills, CA 90210
Actress V: 03/02/92

P.O. Box 69405
Los Angeles, CA 90069
Alternate V: 06/17/92

Scott, Martha
14054 Chandler Blvd.
Van Nuys, CA 91401
Actress V: 05/15/92

Scott, Melody Thomas
c/o CBS TV/Young & Restless
7800 Beverly Blvd.
Los Angeles, CA 90036
Actress V: 04/17/92

c/o Save the Earth
4881 Topanga Canyon Bl., #201
Woodland Hills, CA 91364
Alternate V: 06/01/92

Scott, Pippa
10850 Wilshire Blvd., Ste.250
Los Angeles, CA 90024
Actress V: 04/16/92

9301 Wilshire Blvd. #312
Beverly Hills, CA 90210
Alternate V: 04/28/92

Scott, Tim
c/o Susan Smith Assoc.
121 N. San Vicente Blvd.
Beverly Hills, CA 90211
Actor V: 02/22/93

Scott, Willard
30 Rockefeller Plz., #304
New York, NY 10112
Commentator V: 05/15/92

Scotti, Vito
5456 Vanadlen Ave.
Tarzana, CA 91356
Actor V: 03/17/93

Scotti Bros.
2114 Pico Blvd.
Santa Monica, CA 90405
Studio HQ V: 02/01/92

Screen Actor Magazine
7065 Hollywood Blvd.
Los Angeles, CA 90028-6065
Publishers V: 03/01/92

Screen Actors Guild (SAG)
7510 Hollywood Blvd.
Hollywood, CA 90028
 Actors Union V: 12/12/92

Screen Children's Agency
12444 Ventura Blvd.
Studio City, CA 91604
 Talent Agency V: 03/17/93

Screen Extras Guild (SEG)
3629 Cahuenga Blvd. W.
Los Angeles, CA 90068
 Actors Union V: 03/17/92

Screen Gems Productions
Columbia Plaza
Los Angeles, CA 91505
 Production Company V: 03/17/92

Scribner, Rick
8904 Amerigo Ave.
Orangeville, CA 95662
 Race Driver V: 03/12/93

Scrimm, Angus
P.O. Box 5193
N. Hollywood, CA 91606-5193
 Actor V: 04/22/92

Scuduto, Al
c/o King Features
216 East 45th St.
New York, NY 10017
 Cartoonist V: 03/12/92

Scully, Vin
1555 Capri Dr.
Pacific Palisades, CA 90272
 Sportscaster V: 05/13/92

Seaborg, Glenn T.
Lawr.-Berkley Lab U.C./CAL
One Cyclotron Rd.
Berkely, CA 94720
 Scientist V: 03/16/92

Seagal, Steven
P.O. Box 727
Los Olivos, CA 93441
 Actor V: 03/26/93

Seagrave, Jocelyn
c/o 'Guiding Light'
51 W. 52nd St.
New York, NY 10019
 Actress V: 11/11/92

Seagraves, Ralph
Rt.10, Box 413A
Winston-Salem, NC 27107
 NASCAR Driver V: 03/02/92

Searfoss, Richard A.
c/o NASA LBJ Space Center
Houston, TX 77058
 Astronaut V: 03/03/93

Seattle Mariners
P.O. Box 4100
The Kingdome
Seattle, WA 98104
 Team Office V: 05/15/92

Seattle Seahawks,
11220 NE 53rd St.ce
Kirkland, WA 98033
 Team Offices V: 05/15/92

Sebastian, John
2431 Briarcrest Rd.
Beverly Hills, CA 90210
 Singer V: 03/13/92

Sedaka, Neil
8787 Shoreham Dr.
Los Angeles, CA 90069
 Singer V: 05/02/92

c/o Sharon Jochimsen
330 W. 58th St., Ste. 4A
New York, NY 10019
 Alternate V: 09/09/92

888 7th Ave., Ste.1905
New York, NY 10019
 Alternate V: 04/22/92

Seddon, Margaret Rhea
c/o NASA LBJ Space Center
Houston, TX 77058
 Astronaut V: 03/03/93

Sedgwick, Kyra
Shoreham Towers
800 West End Ave. Ste.7A
New York, NY 10025-5467
 Actress V: 05/15/92

Sedgworth, Bill
1811 Volusia Ave.
Daytona Beach, FL 32015
 NASCAR Driver V: 03/26/93

Seeger, Pete
P.O. Box 431
Beacon, NY 12508
 Singer V: 02/20/92

Seeger, Pete, contd
c/o Rolling Blunder Review
P.O. Box 657
Housatonic, MA 01236-0657
Alternate V: 03/30/93

c/o Redwood Records
6400 Hollis St., Ste.8
Emeryville, CA 94608
Forwarded V: 02/01/92

Sega, Ronald M.
c/o NASA LBJ Space Center
Houston, TX 77058
Astronaut V: 03/03/93

Segal, Steven
P.O. Box 727
Los Olivas, CA 93441
Actor V: 01/16/93

Segal, Vivienne
c/o Robinson
152 N. Le Doux Rd.
Beverly Hills, CA 90211
Actress V: 05/15/92

Seidenspinner, Dick
c/o Sabco Racing
5901 Orr Rd.
Charlotte, NC 28213
NASCAR Crew V: 03/26/93

Seinfeld, Jerry
2112 Roscomare Rd.
Los Angeles, CA 90077
Actor V: 06/21/92

c/o Castle Rock
Seinfeld
335 W. Maple Dr. #135
Beverly Hills, CA 90210
Forwarded V: 01/07/92

Seizinger, Katja
Rudolf-Epp-Str. 48
D-(W) 6930 Eberbach
Germany
Skiing V: 02/11/93

Seka
c/o Pearl Prod.
840 N. Michigan Ave.
Chicago, IL 60611
Adult Films V: 01/24/93

Sekura Talent Agency
1720 N. La Brea Ave.
Los Angeles, CA 90046
Talent Agency V: 02/12/92

Selected Artists Agency
3575 Cahuenga Blvd. W. 2nd Fl.
Los Angeles, CA 90068
Talent Agency V: 01/26/93

Selleca, Connie
P.O. Box 691632
Los Angeles, CA 90069
Actress V: 03/22/93

c/o Agent
P.O. Box 60257
Los Angeles, CA 90060
Alternate V: 02/12/92

c/o Kippen
8124 W. 3rd St. #204
Los Angeles, CA 90048
Alternate V: 03/16/92

14755 Ventura Blvd. #1-916
Sherman Oaks, CA 91403
Alternate V: 01/16/93

11528 Duque Dr.
Studio City, CA 91604
Forwarded V: 06/14/92

c/o William Morris
151 El Camino Dr.
Beverly Hills, CA 90212
Forwarded V: 03/20/92

c/o CBS-TV
7800 Beverly Blvd.
Los Angeles, CA 90036
Forwarded V: 12/16/92

Selleck, Tom
1761 Potrero Rd.
Hidden Valley, CA 91360
Actor V: 03/18/93

2899 Agoura Rd. #560
Westlake Village, CA 91361-3218
Alternate V: 03/22/93

10560 Wilshire Blvd. #1606
Los Angeles, CA 90024
Alternate V: 03/10/90

c/o Disney Studios
500 S. Buena Vista
Burbank, CA 91521-0001
Alternate V: 01/02/92

c/o Univ. Movie Studios
100 Universal City Plaza
Universal City, CA 91608
Forwarded V: 05/02/92

Selleck, Tom, contd
510 18th St.
Honolulu, HI 96816
L.R.U. V: 01/02/92

Serious, Yahoo
c/o Yahoo Prod.
12-33 E. Crescent St.
McMahons Point
NSW 2060, Australia
Actor V: 07/12/92

Serna, Pepe
1000 Santa Monica Blvd. #305
Los Angeles, CA 90067
Actor V: 09/18/92

2321 Hill Dr.
Los Angeles, CA 90041
Actor V: 04/06/93

Severance, Joan
c/o Stephen J. Cannell Prod.
7083 Hollywood Blvd.
Hollywood, CA 90028
Actress V: 05/15/92

Severeid, Susan
P.O. Box 4171
Malibu, CA 90265
Actress V: 03/20/92

Severn, Jeffrey
1195 Saranap Ave., Ste.16
Walnut Creek, CA 94595
Illustrator V: 12/12/92

Seyler, Athene
Coach House, 26 Upper Mall
Hammersmith, London W6
England V: s//19/es920301/

Seymour, Jane
930 Lilac St.
Montecito, CA 9318-1521
Actress V: 07/16/92

2826 Roscomare Rd.
Los Angeles, CA 90077
Alternate V: 05/15/92

c/o James Sharkey-3rd Fl.
15 Golden Square
London W1R 3AG, England
Alternate V: 02/28/92

St Catherines Court
Batheaston
Bath, Avon, England
Forwarded V: 03/16/92

Seymour, Jane, contd
1849 Sawtelle Blvd. Suite 500
Los Angeles, CA 90025
L.R.U. V: 07/03/92

10390 Santa Monica Bl.#310
Los Angeles, CA 90025
L.R.U. V: 12/02/92

Shalala, Donna
Dept. of Health & Human Services
200 Independence Ave. S.W.
Washington, DC 20201
Head of HHS V: 01/31/93

Shallert, William
14920 Ramos Place
Pacific Palisades, CA 90272
Actor V: 03/04/92

Shamray, Gerry
c/o King Features
216 East 45th St.
New York, NY 10017
Cartoonist V: 02/15/92

Shandling, Garry
Sunset/Gower Studios
1438 N. Gower St. Box 44
Los Angeles, CA 90028
Actor V: 04/14/92

9200 Sunset Blvd.   Ste. 428
Los Angeles, CA 90069
Alternate V: 01/21/92

10201 W. Pico Blvd.
Los Angeles, CA 90035
Forwarded V: 03/02/92

Shane, Nikki
c/o 5K Sales
9420 Reseda Blvd., Ste.836
Northridge, CA 91324
Adult Films V: 01/17/93

Shapira & Associates
15301 Ventura Blvd., Ste.345
Sherman Oaks, CA 91403
Talent Agency V: 01/24/93

Shapiro-Lichtman Agency
8827 Beverly Blvd.
Los Angeles, CA 90048
Talent Agency V: 03/13/93

Sharif, Omar
31/32 Soho Square
London W1V 5DG, England
Actor V: 01/17/93

Sharif, Omar, contd
c/o Correa
18 rue Troyn
F-75017 Paris, France
Alternate V: 01/19/93

c/o New Pentax Films
Via Domenico Amarosa 18
Rome 06198 Italy
Forwarded V: 01/20/93

Sharkey, Ray
c/o Stephen J. Cannell Prod.
7083 Hollywood Blvd.
Hollywood, CA 90028
Actor V: 05/15/92

12424 Wilshire Blvd. #840
Los Angeles, CA 90025
Actor V: 04/01/93

Shatner, William
c/o CBS
1800 Beverly Blvd.
Los Angeles, CA 90036
Actor V: 03/10/92

3674 Berry Ave.
Studio City, CA 91604
Alternate V: 03/07/92

c/o WSF
10940 Moorpark St.
N. Hollywood, CA 91602
Forwarded V: 04/22/92

c/o Shapiro Prod.
Rescue 911
5800 Sunset Blvd.
Hollywood, CA 90028
Forwarded V: 05/15/92

P.O. Box 1366
Hollywood, CA 90078
L.R.U. V: 03/16/92

Shaud, Grant
c/o Warner Bros.
"Murphy Brown"
4000 Warner Blvd.
Burbank, CA 91522
Actor V: 03/02/92

Shaver, Helen
c/o GTG Ent./Culver Studios
9336 W. Washington Blvd.
Culver City, CA 90232
Actress V: 05/15/92

Shaw, Brewster
NASA/LBJ Space Center
Houston, TX 77058
Astronaut V: 01/19/92

Shaw, Martin
200 Fulham Rd.
London SW16, England
Actor V: 03/16/92

Shea, John
c/o GTG Ent./Culver Studios
9336 W. Washington Blvd.
Culver City, CA 90232
Actor V: 05/15/92

Shearer, Mara
c/o A.D. Peters
10 Buckingham St.
London WC2H 6B0, England
Actress V: 03/01/92

Shearer, Rhonda
c/o USA/Up All Night
2049 Century Park E., #2550
Los Angeles, CA 90067
Actress V: 03/30/93

Sheedy, Ally
5451 Marathon St.
Los Angeles, CA 90038
Actress V: 06/12/92

P.O. Box 6327
Malibu, CA 90210
L.R.U. V: 03/03/93

Sheehan, Douglas
4019 Goldfinch #137
San Diego, CA 92103
Actor V: 06/17/92

Sheen, Charlie
29169 Heathercliff
Malibu, CA 90265-4190
Actor V: 03/25/92

c/o Trimark Pictures
2644 20th St.
Santa Monica CA 90405-3009
Alternate V: 01/13/93

6916 Dune Dr.
Malibu, CA 90265
L.R.U. V: 01/02/92

Sheen, Martin
6916 Dune Rd.
Malibu, CA 90265
Actor V: 05/24/92

Sheen, Martin, contd
c/o Contential Film Group
Park St.
Sharon, PA 16146-3090
 Alternate V: 01/20/93

Sheen, Ramon
6916 Dune Dr.
Malibu, CA 90265
 Actor V: 03/20/92

Shefelman, Dan
c/o King Features
216 E. 45th St.
New York, NY 10017
 Cartoonist V: 03/11/93

Shelton, Deborah
1690 Coldwater Canyon Dr.
Beverly Hills, CA 90210
 Actress V: 03/26/93

Shelton, Mike
c/o King Features
216 E. 45th St.
New York, NY 10017
 Cartoonist V: 03/11/93

Shepard, Jewel
P.O. Box 480265
Los Angeles, CA 90048
 Actress V: 03/26/93

Shepard, Sam
c/o Lois Berman
240 W. 44th St.
New York, NY 10036
 Director V: 01/16/93

Shephard Jr., Alan B.
3203 Mercer #200
Houston, TX 77027
 Astronaut V: 05/02/92

c/o NASA
LBJ Space Center
Houston, TX 77058
 Forwarded V: 01/19/92

Shepherd, Cybill
c/o Rogers & Cowan
10000 Santa Monica Blvd.
Los Angeles, CA 90067
 Actress V: 03/20/92

c/o ABC
9911 W. Pico Blvd.
Los Angeles, CA 90035
 Alternate V: 03/13/92

Shepherd, Cybill, contd
16037 Royal Oak Rd.
Encino, CA 91436
 Forwarded V: 02/20/92

2237 Court St.
Memphis, TN 38104
 Forwarded V: 03/19/92

Shepherd, Morgan
c/o McLean Marketing
9307-P Monro Rd.
Charlotte, NC 28270
 NASCAR Driver V: 03/02/92

Shepherd, William M.
c/o NASA
LBJ Space Center
Houston, TX 77058
 Astronaut V: 01/31/92

Shera, Mark
211 S. Beverly Dr. #201
Beverly Hills, CA 90212
 Actor V: 01/20/92

Sheridan, Dinah
c/o Jenny Hanley
30 Chalfont Ct., Baker St.
London NW1, England
 Actor V: 02/01/92

Sheridan, Nicolette
P.O. Box 25578
Los Angeles, CA 90025
 Actress V: 01/16/93

P.O. Box 25578
Los Angeles, CA 90025-0578
 Actress V: 05/15/92

Sherlock, Nancy J.
c/o NASA LBJ Space Center
Houston, TX 77058
 Astronaut V: 03/03/93

Shields, Brooke
P.O. Box 147
Harrington, NJ 07640
 Actress V: 03/13/92

165 E. 62nd St.
New York, NY 10021
 Actress V: 09/30/92

P.O. Box B
Haworth, NJ 07641
 Forwarded V: 05/12/92

Shimmerman, Armin
9200 Sunset Blvd., Ste. 625
Los Angeles, CA 90069
Actor V: 01/03/92

c/o Star Trek-DS9
5555 Melrose Ave.
Hollywood, CA 90036
Alternate V: 02/23/93

Shire, Talia
16633 Ventura Blvd.
Encino, CA 91436
Actress V: 03/26/93

Shirley, Ann
c/o Lederer
7416 Rosewood Ave.
Los Angeles, CA 90036
Actress V: 05/15/92

Shoemaker, Willie
2553 Fairfield Place
San Marino, CA 91108
Trainer V: 02/13/92

Shore, Dinah
P.O. Box 815
Beverly Hills, CA 90213
Singer V: 11/09/92

916 Oxford Way
Beverly Hills, CA 90210
Alternate V: 06/17/92

Short, Martin
15907 Alcoma Ave.
Pacific Palisades, CA 90272
Actress V: 03/26/93

801 Westmount Dr.
Los Angeles, CA 90069
L.R.U. V: 01/02/92

Shorter College
Comm. Arts Dept.
Shorter Hill
P.O. Box 522
Rome, GA 30161
Archive V: 01/20/93

Showbiz Entertainment
6922 Hollywood Blvd. Ste.207
Los Angeles, CA 90028
Talent Agency V: 03/13/93

Showtime Network
1633 Broadway
New York, NY 10019
Network HQ V: 03/01/92

Showtime/Movie Channel
10 Universal City Plz. 31st Fl
Los Angeles, CA 91608
Production Company V: 03/17/92

Shrimpton, Jean
Abbey Hotel
Penzance, Cornwall England
Model, Actress V: 06/19/92

Shriner, Kin
c/o General Hosp./ABC Inc.
4151 Prospect Ave.
Hollywood, CA 90027
Actor V: 03/01/92

Shriver, Loren J.
c/o NASA
LBJ Space Center
Houston, TX 77058
Astronaut V: 01/31/92

Shriver, Maria
231 Hampton Dr. #203
Venice, CA 90291
Celebrity V: 03/01/92

Shue, Elizabeth
217 Turell Ave.
South Orange, NJ 07079
Actress V: 03/26/93

76 South Orange Ave.
South Orange, NJ 07079
Alternate V: 04/18/92

211 S. Beverly Dr. #201
Beverly Hills, CA 90212
L.R.U. V: 06/12/92

Shulman, Ellen L.
NASA/LBJ Space Center
Houston, TX 77058
Astronaut V: 01/19/92

Shumaker Talent Agency
6533 Hollywood Blvd., Ste.301
Hollywood, CA 90028
Talent Agency V: 03/13/93

Sibbet, Jane
c/o Hermans Head
500 S. Buena Vista St.
Burbank, CA 91521
Actress V: 11/11/92

Sibbett, Jayne
570 N. Rossmore #303
Los Angeles, CA 90004
Actress V: 05/15/92

Sidney, Sylvia
9744 Wilshire Blvd. #308
Beverly Hills, CA 90212
Actress V: 03/17/92

Siegel & Associates
7551 Sunset Blvd. #203
Los Angeles, CA 90046
Talent Agency V: 03/19/93

Sievers, Roy
11505 Belle Fontaine Rd.
Spanish Lake, MO 63138
Baseball V: 05/14/92

Sikes, Cynthia
250 Delfern Dr.
Los Angeles, CA 90077
Actress V: 03/20/93

250 N. Delfern Dr.
Los Angeles, CA 90077
Alternate V: 05/15/92

Sikking, James B.
c/o Armstrong Assoc.
5410 Wilshire Blvd.
Los Angeles, CA 90036
Actor V: 04/22/92

c/o Steven Bochco Prods.
Doogie Howser, M.D.
10201 W. Pico Blvd.
Los Angeles, CA 90035
Alternate V: 12/15/92

c/o McCartt
10390 Santa Monica Blvd. #310
Los Angeles, CA 90025
Alternate V: 03/17/92

Silent Network
Box 1902
Beverly Hills, CA 90213
Production Company V: 03/17/92

Silva, Henry
8747 Clifton Way #305
Beverly Hills, CA 90210
Actor V: 04/01/93

Silver, Ron
6116 Tyndall Ave.
Riverdale, NY 10471
Actor V: 03/26/93

Silver Screen Artist Agency
8222 Melrose Ave. #302
Los Angeles, CA 90046
Talent Agency V: 03/14/93

Silver/Kass/Massetti Agency
8730 Sunset Blvd. #480
Los Angeles, CA 90069
Talent Agency V: 02/19/93

Silverman, Jonathan
854 Birchwood Dr.
Los Angeles, CA 90024
Actor V: 03/17/93

Simmons, Gene
6363 Sunset Blvd. #417
Los Angeles, CA 90028
Singer V: 01/16/93

2650 Benedict Canyon
Beverly Hills, CA 90210
L.R.U. V: 12/08/92

Simmons, Jean
9400 Readcrest Dr.
Beverly Hills, CA 90210
Actress V: 05/02/92

Simmons, Richard
1350 Belfast
Los Angeles, CA 90069
Fitness Promoter V: 09/02/92

Simms, Ginny
1578 Murray Canyon Dr.
Palm Springs, CA 92262
Singer V: 06/15/92

Simms, Joan
c/o Mahoney
94 Gloucester Pl., Ground Fl.
London W1V 5DG, England
Actress V: 03/20/92

Simms, Larry
P.O. Box 55
Gray River, WA 98621
Actor V: 06/14/92

Simon, Carly
c/o Arlyne Rothberg, Inc.
135 Central Park West
New York, NY 10023
Singer V: 06/05/92

Simon, Neil
10745 Chalon Rd.
Los Angeles, CA 90024
Playwrite V: 06/07/92

Simon, Paul
462 SD Senate Off. Bldg.
Washington, DC 20510
Politician V: 03/01/92

1619 Broadway, Ste.500
New York, NY 10019
Singer V: 02/03/92

Simon, Simone
5 Rue de Tilsitt
Paris, 75008 France
Actress V: 01/12/92

Simone, Domonique
c/o Five K Sales Co.
9420 Reseda Blvd., #836
Northridge, CA 91324
Adult Films V: 03/03/93

Simpson, O.J.
11661 San Vincente Blvd.
Los Angeles, CA 90049
Actor V: 11/11/92

360 N. Rockingham Ave.
Los Angeles, CA 90049
Alternate V: 03/20/92

Simpson, Walt
17 W. 71st St., #3-D
New York, NY 10023
Artist V: 11/11/92

Simpsons
c/o The Simpsons
10201 W. Pico Blvd.
Los Angeles, CA 90035
Production Company V: 05/02/92

Sinatra, Frank
70588 Frank Sinatra Blvd.
Rancho Mirage, CA 92270
Actor V: 02/23/92

c/o Sintra Enterprises
1041 N. Formosa Ave.
Los Angeles, CA 90069
Alternate V: 09/02/92

Sinatra, Nancy
P.O. Box 69453
Los Angeles, CA 90069
Musician V: 03/26/93

160 Apple Ct.
Luling, LA 70070
Alternate V: 12/11/92

c/o Lambert
P.O. Box 93518
Los Angeles, CA 90093
Alternate V: 02/12/92

9817 Hythe Ct.
Beverly Hills, CA 90210
Forwarded V: 04/19/92

Sinatra Jr., Frank
2211 Florian Pl.
Beverly Hills, CA 90210
Singer V: 03/11/92

Sinbad
c/o Carsey-Warner Co.
"A Different World"
P.O.Box 1-701
14755 Ventura Bl
Sherman Oaks, CA 91403
Actor V: 07/01/93

Sinclair, Madge
P.O. Box 10173
Beverly Hills, CA 90213
Actress V: 02/11/92

8035 Briar Summit Dr.
Los Angeles, CA 90046
Alternate V: 02/19/92

P.O. Box 5617
Beverly Hills, CA 90213
Forwarded V: 12/08/92

Sindell & Elliott
8721 Sunset Blvd. #210
Los Angeles, CA 90069
Talent Agency V: 02/19/93

Sinden, Donald
c/o Agency
60 Temple Fortune Rd.
London NW11, England
Actor V: 01/18/92

c/o Whitehall
125 Gloucester Rd.
London SW7 4TE, England
Alternate V: 03/17/92

Sinden, Jeremy
c/o Agency
388-396 Oxford St.
London W1 9HE, England
Actor V: 03/17/92

Singer, Lori
9830 Wilshire Blvd.
Beverly Hills, CA 90212
Actress V: 01/04/92

330 W. 72nd #10B
New York, NY 10023
Alternate V: 03/26/93

Singer, Marc
11218 Canton Dr.
Studio City, CA 91604
Alternate V: 03/04/93

Singleton, Penny
13419 Riverside Dr. #C
Sherman Oaks, CA 91423
Actress V: 03/17/93

P.O. Box 174
6200 Van Nuys Blvd.
Van Nuys, CA 91401
Alternate V: 01/10/92

Sirtis, Marina
2436 Creston Way
Los Angeles, CA 90068
Actress V: 02/11/92

8942 Wilshire Blvd.
Beverly Hills, CA 90211
Alternate V: 04/10/92

c/o Star Trek-TNG Paramount
5555 Melrose Ave.
Hollywood, CA 90038
Forwarded V: 03/04/92

Sixta, George
c/o King Features
216 East 45th St.
New York, NY 10017
Cartoonist V: 03/13/92

Sjogren, John C.
201 S. Monroe Ave.
Rockford, IL 49341
Medal of Honor V: 02/03/92

Skelton, Red
37-801 Thompson Rd.
Rancho Mirage, CA 92270
Actor V: 05/01/92

Skerritt, Tom
c/o Paramount
"Cheers"
5555 Melrose Ave./Ball RM 105
Hollywood, CA 90038
Actor V: 01/07/92

Slade, Mark
2247 Linda Flora Dr.
Los Angeles, CA 90077
Actor V: 05/02/92

38 Joppa Rd.
Worchester, MA 01602
Forwarded V: 06/14/92

Slaight, Brad
c/o Young and the Restless
7800 Beverly Blvd.
Beverly Hills, CA 90036
Actor V: 06/15/92

Slater, Christian
5871 Allott Ave.
Van Nuys, CA 90401
Actor V: 05/15/92

Slayton, Donald K.
c/o NASA
LBJ Space Center
Houston, TX 77058
Astronaut V: 03/03/93

Slessinger & Associates
8730 Sunset Blvd. Ste.220 West
Los Angeles, CA 90069
Talent Agency V: 03/11/93

Slezak, Erica
ABC-TV
One Life to Live
1330 Ave. of the Americas
New York, NY 10019
Actress V: 03/24/92

Slick, Grace
P.O. Box 69
Mill Valley, CA 94942
Singer V: 06/18/92

Smart, Jean
4545 Noeline Ave.
Encino, CA 91316
Actress V: 03/04/93

c/o Columbia Pictures TV
"Designing Women"
Columbia Plz., Bl.8 #147
Burbank, CA 91505
Forwarded V: 02/03/93

Smith, Alexis
25 Central Park West
New York, NY 10023
Actress V: 03/04/93

c/o Studio Fan Mail
1122 S. Robertson Blvd.
Los Angeles, CA 90035
Alternate V: 06/21/92

1308 N. Flores St.
Los Angeles, CA 90069
L.R.U. V: 07/03/92

Smith, Bee-Be
c/o Carsey-Warner Co.
"A Different World"
P.O.Box 1-701
14755 Ventura Bl
Sherman Oaks, CA 91403
Actress V: 03/01/93

Smith, Bubba
P.O. Box 25578
Los Angeles, CA 90025
Football V: 01/12/92

5178 Sunlight Pl.
Los Angeles, CA 90016
Actor V: 04/01/93

Smith, Buffalo Bob
500 Overlook Dr.
Flat Rock, NC 28731
Celebrity V: 03/26/93

Big Lake
Princeton, ME 04619
L.R.U. V: 06/11/92

Smith, Darwood Kaye
9318 Scotmont Dr.
Tujunga, CA 91042
Actor V: 04/06/93

Smith, David
c/o Childress
P.O. Box 1189 Industrial Dr.
Welcome, NC 27374
Race Crew V: 03/12/93

Smith, Hal
1717 N. Highland Ave. #44
Los Angeles, CA 90028
Actor V: 02/04/92

Smith, Jack
850 W. Main St.
Spartanburg, SC 29301
NASCAR Driver V: 03/02/92

Smith, Jaclyn
c/o 20th Century Fox
10201 W. Pico Blvd.
Los Angeles, CA 90035
Actress V: 01/02/92

P.O. Box 57413
Sherman Oaks, CA 91403
Alternate V: 02/08/93

773 Stradella Rd.
Los Angeles, CA 90077
Alternate V: 06/11/92

Smith, Jaclyn, contd
P.O. Box 57413
Sherman Oaks, CA 91403
Alternate V: 05/02/92

Smith, Jo
Dallas Cowboys
One Cowboys Parkway
Irving, TX 75063-4945
Cheerleader V: 08/08/92

Smith, Kathy
11130 W. Olympic Blvd. #610
Los Angeles, CA 90064
Fitness Expert V: 03/07/92

Smith, Keely
c/o Gen. Hosp./ABC Inc.
4151 Prospect Ave.
Hollywood, CA 90027
Actress V: 03/01/92

Smith, Madolyn
6131 1/2 Glen Oak
Los Angeles, CA 90069
Actress V: 05/15/92

Smith, Maggie
91 Regent St.
London, W1R 8RU England
Actress V: 04/02/92

Smith, Mike
c/o King Features
216 E. 45th St.
New York, NY 10017
Cartoonist V: 03/11/93

Smith, O.B.
Atlanta Motor Speedway
P.O. Box 500
Hampton, GA 30228
NASCAR Official V: 03/02/92

Smith, Ralph
c/o King Features
216 East 45th St.
New York, NY 10017
Cartoonist V: 05/05/92

Smith, Roger
2707 Benedict Canyon Rd.
Beverly Hills, CA 90210
Actor V: 02/17/92

Smith, Ron
c/o Celebrity Look-Alikes
70 Hollywood Blvd. PH1215
Los Angeles, CA 90028
Agency V: 03/03/93

Smith, Taran Noah
c/o Home Improvements
500 S. Buena Vista St.
Burbank, CA 91521
Actor   V: 11/11/92

Smith, Vince
P.O. Box 1221
Pottsville, PA 17901
Singer   V: 01/05/92

Smith, Wendy
2925 Tuna Canyon Rd.
Topanga, CA 90290
Actress   V: 05/15/92

Smith, Will
c/o NBC Prod.
"Fresh Prince of Bel Air"
330 Bob Hope Dr.
Burbank, CA 91523
Actor   V: 01/09/92

Smith, William
3349 Cahuenga Blvd. #2
Los Angeles, CA 90068
Actor   V: 04/26/92

Smith, Yeardley
c/o Hermans Head
500 S. Buena Vista St.
Burbank, CA 91521
Actress   V: 11/11/92

Smith & Associates
121 N. San Vicente Blvd.
Beverly Hills, CA 90211
Talent Agency   V: 03/11/93

Smithers, Jan
2401 Colorado Ave. #160
Santa Monica, CA 90404
Actress   V: 06/17/92

Smithhart, Peggy
5555 Melrose Ave., Wilder #214
Los Angeles, CA 90038
Actress   V: 05/15/92

Smithsonian Archives
Arts & Indust. Bldg., Rm 2135
900 Jefferson Dr. S.W.
Washington, DC 20560
Archive   V: 03/20/93

Smitrovich, Bill
Warner/"Life Goes On"
4000 Warner Blvd.
Burbank, CA 91522
Actor   V: 12/18/92

Smits, Jimmy
110 S. Westgate Ave.
Los Angeles, CA 90049
Actor   V: 03/26/93

211 S. Beverly Dr.
Beverly Hills, CA 90212
Alternate   V: 03/17/92

c/o Fox TV
L.A. Law
P.O. Box 900
Beverly Hills, CA 90213
Forwarded   V: 01/12/92

Smothers, Tom
1976 Warm Springs Rd.
Kenwood, CA 95452
Comedian   V: 08/16/92

Smothers Brothers
8489 W. 3rd St. #1020
Beverly Hills, CA 90211
Comedians   V: 01/02/92

P.O. Box 74130
Los Angeles, CA 90004
L.R.U.   V: 03/02/92

Smythe, Reg
Whitegares, 96 Calidonian Rd.
Hartlepool, Cleveland, England
Cartoonist   V: 02/12/92

Snead, Sam
P.O. Box 544
Hot Springs, VA 24445
Golfer   V: 02/04/92

Snider, Duke
3037 Lakemont Dr.
Fallbrook, CA 92028
Baseball   V: 12/10/92

Snider, Jeremy
c/o Bell-Phillip Prod.
"Bold & Beautiful"
7800 Beverly Blvd., Ste.3371
Los Angeles, CA 90036
Actor   V: 06/15/92

Snodgrass, Carrie
3025 Surry St.
Los Angeles, CA 90027
Actress   V: 05/15/92

Snow, Hank
P.O. Box 1084
Nashville, TN 37202
Singer   V: 01/13/92

Snowden, Van
5751 Camellia
N. Hollywood, CA 91601
Puppet Master *V: 04/16/92*

Snyder, Jimmy (The Greek)
1703 Kaiser
Irvine, CA 92714
Pro Gambler *V: 09/02/92*

Soap Opera Digest
c/o Editor
45 W. 25th St.
New York, NY 10010
Publication *V: 06/15/92*

Soap Opera Now
c/o Editor
1767 Park Ave.
New York, NY 11566
Publication *V: 06/15/92*

Soap Opera People
c/o Editor
50 W. 34th St.
New York, NY 10001
Publication *V: 06/15/92*

Soap Opera Stars
c/o Editor/Daytime TV
355 Lexington Ave.
New York, NY 10017
Publication *V: 06/15/92*

Soap Opera Update
c/o Editor
158 Linwood
New York, NY 10017
Publication *V: 06/15/92*

Soap Opera Weekly
c/o Editor
41 W. 25th St.
New York, NY 10010
Publication *V: 06/15/92*

Soles, P.J.
P.O. Box 2351
Carefree, AZ 85377
Actress *V: 06/18/92*

Somers, Suzanne
190 N. Canon Dr. #201
Beverly Hills, CA 90210
Actress *V: 03/04/93*

10342 Mississippi Ave.
Los Angeles, CA 90025
Alternate *V: 09/10/90*

Somers, Suzanne, contd
24108 Philliprim St.
Woodland, CA 91367
Alternate *V: 11/11/92*

c/o ABC-TV/Step by Step
4151 Prospect Ave.
Los Angeles, CA 90027
Forwarded *V: 12/16/90*

3817 Ocean Front Walk
Venice, CA 90291
L.R.U. *V: 03/03/93*

Sommars, Julie
c/o ABC-TV
4151 Prospect Ave.
Hollywood, CA 90027
Actress *V: 11/11/92*

7272 Outpost Cove Dr.
Los Angeles, CA 90068-2010
Alternate V: 05/15/92

c/o Viacom Prod.
Matlock
100 Universal City Plaza Bl. 448
Universal City, CA 91608
Actress V: 12/01/92

Sommer, Elke
540 N. Beverly Glen Blvd.
Los Angeles, CA 90024
Actress *V: 02/15/92*

Sordi, Alberto
Via Pruso 45
Rome 00184, Italy
Actor *V: 02/28/92*

Sorenson, Paul
8749 Sunset Blvd., #910
Los Angeles, CA 90069
Actor *V: 03/02/92*

Sorice Talent Agency
7540 Balboa Blvd. Ste.1
Van Nuys, CA 91403
Talent Agency *V: 03/17/93*

Sorkin, Arleen
2040 Avenue of the Stars
Los Angeles, CA 90067
Celebrity *V: 01/21/92*

100 S. Doheny Dr. #605
Los Angeles, CA 90048
Alternate V: 05/15/92

Sorkin, Arleen, contd
c/o Vin Di Bona Prods.
"America's Funniest People"
4151 Prospect Ave., Prod.Bldg.
Hollywood, CA 90078
Alternate V: 12/19/92

Sorrells, Robert
c/o Farrell
10500 Magnolia Blvd.
N. Hollywood, CA 91601
Actor V: 03/10/92

Sothern, Ann
P.O. Box 2285
Ketchum, ID 83340
Actress V: 03/23/92

Soul, David
2232 Moreno Dr.
Los Angeles, CA 90039
Actor V: 03/17/93

Southwest Film/Video
Center for Communication Arts
Southern Methodist University
P.O. Box 113 -S.M.U.
Dallas, TX 75275
Archive V: 03/20/93

Southwick, Shawn
12700 Ventura Blvd. #350
Studio City, CA 91604
Actress V: 01/16/93

Spacek, Sissy
c/o CAA
9830 Wilshire Blvd.
Beverly Hills, CA 90212
Actress V: 01/16/93

Spacey, Kevin
7083 Hollywood Blvd.
Hollywood, CA 90028
Actor V: 05/15/92

Special Artists Agency
335 N. Maple Dr. #360
Beverly Hills, CA 91210
Talent Agency V: 04/01/93

Specialty Models Agency
885 Westbourne Dr.
W. Hollywood, CA 90069
Talent Agency V: 04/01/93

Spector, Ron & Phil
7 Maple Crest Dr.
Danbury, CT 06810
Singers V: 01/29/92

Spectre, Phil & Ron, contd
1210 S. Arroyo Parkway
Pasadena, CA 91101
L.R.U. V: 12/01/92

Speed, Lake
c/o NASCAR
1811 Volusia Ave.
Daytona Beach, FL 32015
NASCAR Driver V: 03/02/92

Spelling, Tori
c/o ICM
8942 Wilshire Blvd.
Beverly Hills, CA 91211
Actress V: 02/11/93

Spelling Productions
1041 N. Formosa Ave.
Los Angeles, CA 90046
Production Company V: 03/17/92

Spencer, Bud
c/o Mistral Film Group
24 Via Archimede
I-00187 Rome, Italy
Actor V: 01/17/93

Spencer, Jimmy
P.O. Box 1626
Mooresville, NC 28115
Race Driver V: 03/12/93

c/o NASCAR
1811 Volusia Ave.
Daytona Beach, FL 32015
Alternate V: 03/02/92

Sperber, Wendie Jo
4110 Witzel Dr.
Sherman Oaks, CA 91423
Actress V: 03/26/93

Fox TV
10201 W. Pico Blvd.
Los Angeles, CA 90035
Alternate V: 01/21/92

Spheeris, Penelope
8301 Kirkwood Dr.
Los Angeles, CA 90068
Director V: 04/24/92

Spielberg, David
c/o Stephen J. Cannell Prod.
7083 Hollywood Blvd.
Hollywood, CA 90028
Actor V: 05/15/92

Spielberg, Steven
P.O. Box 6190
Malibu, CA 90264
Director V: 03/23/93

1515 Amalfi Dr.
Pacific Palisades, CA 90272
Alternate V: 05/13/92

c/o Amblin Entertainment
100 Universal Plaza, Bung.#477
Universal City, CA 91608
Forwarded V: 02/20/92

Spillane, Mickey
General Delivery
Marrells Inlet, SC 22117
Author V: 05/22/92

Spiner, Brent
6922 1/2 Paseo del Serra
Los Angeles, CA 90068
Actor V: 06/17/92

c/o Star Trek-TNG Paramount
5555 Melrose Ave.
Hollywood, CA 90038
Forwarded V: 03/04/92

Spinks, Robin
Dallas Cowboys
One Cowboys Parkway
Irving, TX 75063-4945
Cheerleader V: 08/08/92

Spitz, Mark
9171 Wilshire Blvd. #530
Beverly Hills, CA 90210
Olympic Swimmer V: 04/13/92

Sports Channel Pacific
901 Battery St., #204
San Francisco, CA 94111
Production Company V: 11/11/92

Sportscasting Period
9230 Olympic Blvd. #201
Beverly Hills, CA 90212
Talent Agency V: 04/01/93

Spotlight Enterprises
8665 Wilshire Blvd. #410
Beverly Hills, CA 90211
Talent Agency V: 04/01/93

Spotlite/Republic Pictures
12636 Beatrice St.
Los Angeles, CA 90066
Publicity V: 12/15/92

Spring, Sherwood C.
c/o NASA
LBJ Space Center
Houston, TX 77058
Astronaut V: 01/31/92

Springer, Robert C.
c/o NASA
LBJ Space Center
Houston, TX 77058
Astronaut V: 01/31/92

Springfield, Rick
9200 Sunset Blvd. #PH
Los Angeles, CA 90069
Singer V: 12/01/92

Springsteen, Bruce
9922 Tower Ln.
Beverly Hills, CA 90210
Musician V: 03/26/93

2227 Mandeville Canyon Rd.
Los Angeles, CA 90049
L.R.U. V: 05/23/92

Spy Magazine
5 Union Square W.
New York, NY 10003
Publishers HQ V: 03/03/92

St Cyr, Lili
630 1/4 N. Plymouth Blvd.
Los Angeles, CA 90004
Dancer V: 06/21/92

St Duran, Dan
c/o St. Duran Stunts
3774 Robinridge Way
Sacramento, CA 95823
Actor V: 01/02/92

St Jermaine, Saki
c/o Five K Sales Co.
9420 Reseda Blvd., #836
Northridge, CA 91324
Adult Films V: 03/03/93

St Laurent, Michelle
P.O. Box 20191-Cherokee Sta.
New York, NY 10028-9991
Actress V: 03/04/92

St Louis Cardinals
250 Stadium Plaza
Busch Stadium
St. Louis, MO 63102
Team Office V: 05/15/92

St Louis Talent Agency
4109 Backman Ave.
Studio City, CA 91602
 Talent Agency V: 03/29/93

Stack, Robert
321 Saint Pierre Rd.
Los Angeles, CA 91602
 Actor V: 04/21/92

c/o Cosgrove-Meurer Prod.
"Unsolved Mysteries"
4303 W. Verdugo Ave.
Burbank, CA 91505
 Actor V: 01/07/92

Stack, Rosemarie
321 St. Pierre Rd.
Los Angeles, CA 90077
 Actress V: 04/06/93

Stafford, Nancy
c/o Viacom Prod.
Matlock
100 Universal City Plaza Bl. 448
Universal City, CA 91608
 Actress V: 12/01/92

Stafford, Thomas P.
c/o NASA LBJ Space Center
Houston, TX 77058
 Astronaut V: 03/03/93

Staley, Enoch
N. Wilkesboro Speedway
P.O. Box 337
N. Wilkesboro, NC 28659
 NASCAR Official V: 03/02/92

Staley, Joan
24516 Windsor Dr. #8
Valencia, CA 91355-3541
 Actress V: 04/24/92

Stallone, Frank
10668 Eastborne #206
Los Angeles, CA 90025
 Actor V: 03/17/93

Stallone, Jackie
323 San Vicente Blvd. #8
Santa Monica, CA 90402
 Actress V: 04/24/92

Stallone, Sasha
9 Beverly Park
Beverly Hills, CA 90210
 Celebrity V: 04/24/92

Stallone, Sly (Sylvester)
c/o White Eagle Ent.
8800 Sunset Blvd., Ste. 214
Los Angeles, CA 90069
 Actor V: 01/02/92

9750 Wanda Park Dr.
Beverly Hills, CA 90210
 Alternate V: 03/26/93

c/o CAA
9030 Wilshire Blvd.
Beverly Hills, CA 90212
 Alternate V: 07/15/91

c/o Paramount
5451 Marathon Ave.
Hollywood, CA 90038
 Forwarded V: 01/09/92

Stamos, John
c/o Lorimar
"Full House"
3970 Overland Ave.
Culver City, CA 90230
 Actor V: 12/15/92

Stamos, John
ABC-TV
2040 Ave. of the Stars
Los Angeles, CA 90067
 Forwarded V: 01/16/93

Stamp, Terence
c/o Duncan Heath
162 Wardour St.
London W1, England
 Actor V: 02/28/92

Stander, Lionel
13176 Boca de Canon Lane
Los Angeles, CA 90049
 Actor V: 06/20/92

Stang, Arnold
P.O. Box 786
New Canaan, CT 06840
 Actor V: 04/24/92

Stanley, Florence
c/o Jacobs-Henson Prod.
Dinosaurs
4024 Radford Ave., Bldg.2, Rm.11
Studio City, CA 91604
 Actress V: 06/15/92

P.O. Box 48876
Los Angeles, CA 90048
 Alternate V: 04/24/92

Stanton, Harry Dean
14527 Mulholland Dr.
Los Angeles, CA 90077
Actor V: 03/01/92

Stapleton, Jean
635 Perugia Way
Los Angeles, CA 90024
Actress V: 02/12/92

Stapleton, Maureen
15 W. 70th St.
New York, NY 10023
Actress V: 07/23/92

c/o Morgan
1 Bolton Dr.
Lenox, MA 01240-2541
Alternate V: 04/24/92

Star Talent Agency
1050 N. Maple
Burbank, CA 91505
Talent Agency V: 03/29/93

Star Trek Official Fan Club
c/o Paramount Pictures
P.O. Box 111000
Aurora, CO 80011
Fan Club V: 03/10/92

Star Weekly
660 White Plains Rd.
Tarrytown, NY 10591
Publishers V: 03/01/92

Starr, Kay
223 Ashdale Place
Los Angeles, CA 90077
Singer V: 06/11/92

Starr, Ringo
Rocca Bella
24 Ave. Princess Grace
Monte Carlo, Monaco
Musician V: 03/17/93

Starwil Talent
6253 Hollywood Blvd. #730
Los Angeles, CA 90028
Talent Agency V: 03/02/93

Stasha
7095 Hollywood Blvd.
Hollywood, CA 90028
Adult Films V: 01/24/93

State Hist. Society of WI
816 State St.
Madison, WI 53706
Archive V: 03/20/93

Statler Brothers
P.O. Box 2703
Staunton, VA 24401
Singer V: 03/12/92

Status Quo
c/o Quarry Prod.
113-17 Wardone St.
London W1, England
Band V: 03/15/93

Staubach, Roger
6750 LBJ Freeway Suite 1100
Dallas, TX 75240
Football V: 04/01/92

Steel, Amy
888 7th Ave. #1602
New York, NY 10019
Actress V: 05/16/92

Steele, Barbara
442 S. Bedford
Beverly Hills, CA 90212
Actress V: 03/26/93

Steele, Danielle
P.O. Box 1637/Murray Hill Sta.
New York, NY 10156
Author V: 03/02/92

Steele, Selena
9555 Cozycroft Ave., Ste.A
Chatsworth, CA 91311
Adult Films V: 01/24/93

Steele, Tommy
13 Burton St.
London, W1X 8JY England
Actor V: 03/23/92

Steenburgen, Mary
151 El Camino
Beverly Hills, CA 90212
Actress V: 03/30/93

c/o Tri Star Pictures
3400 Riverside Dr.
Burbank, CA 91505
Forwarded V: 12/17/92

Steenburgen, Mary
8942 Wilshire Blvd.
Beverly Hills, CA 90211
Actress V: 07/01/92

Steiger, Rod
6324 Zumirez Dr.
Malibu, CA 90265
Actor V: 03/17/93

c/o Image Organization
9000 Sunset Blvd. Ste. 915
Los Angeles, CA 90069
Alternate V: 12/14/92

Stein, Pamela Jean
8560 Sunset Blvd.
Los Angeles, CA 90069
Playboy Playmate V: 03/24/92

2275 E. Bay Dr. #101B
Clearwater, FL 34624
Forwarded V: 07/21/92

Steinberg, David
c/o Agency
801 Westmount Dr.
Los Angeles, CA 90069
Comedian V: 02/01/92

Stephens, Robert
113 Wardour St.
London W1, England
Actor V: 03/01/92

Stephenson, Jan
6300 Ridglea Place #1118
Ft. Worth, TX 76116
Golfer V: 02/04/92

Sterling, Alicyn
P.O. Box 6603
Los Angeles, CA 90066
Adult Films V: 01/24/93

Sterling, Robert
121 S. Bentley Ave.
Los Angeles, CA 90049
Actor V: 05/01/92

Stern, Barry
P.O. Box 6653
Chicago, IL 60606-0653
Musical Group V: 01/11/92

Stern, Daniel
"The Wonder Years"
1440 S. Sepulveda Blvd.
Los Angeles, CA 90025
Actor V: 12/11/92

Stern, Howard
600 Madison Ave.
New York, NY 10022
TV/Radio DJ V: 03/14/93

Stern, Isaac
211 Central Park W.
New York, NY 10024
Violinist V: 11/11/92

Stern Agency
11755 Wilshire Blvd. #2320
Los Angeles, CA 90025
Talent Agency V: 03/15/93

Sternahagen, Frances
152 Sutton Manner Rd.
New Rochelle, NY 10805
Actress V: 04/24/92

Stevens, Andrew
1122 S. Robertson Blvd.
Los Angeles, CA 90035
Actor V: 03/18/93

Stevens, Brinke
8033 Sunset Blvd., Ste. 556
Hollywood, CA 90046
Actress V: 01/12/92

Stevens, Cat
c/o Yusuf Islam
3 Furlong Rd.
London, N7 8LA England
Singer V: 07/01/92

Stevens, Connie
243 Delfern
Los Angeles, CA 90024
Actress V: 02/16/92

9551 Cherokee Ln.
Beverly Hills, CA 90210-1705
Alternate V: 07/01/92

c/o Betty Moran
2500 Gaither St.
Hillcrest Heights, MD 20031
Forwarded V: 04/21/92

Stevens, Craig
25 Central Park West
New York, NY 10023
Actor V: 03/05/93

Stevens, Fisher
c/o William Morris Agency
151 El Camino
Beverly Hills, CA 90212
Actor V: 03/20/93

Stevens, K.T.
147 Gretna Green Way
Los Angeles, CA 90049
Actress V: 04/24/92

Stevens, Rise
930 Fifth Ave.
New York, NY 10021
Actress V: 04/24/92

Stevens, Shadoe
10430 Wilshire Blvd. #2006
Los Angeles, CA 90024
Actress V: 03/26/93

Stevens, Stella
c/o StellaVisions-Rex Mail Co.
6520 Selma Ave.#649
Hollywood, CA 90028
Actress V: 01/22/92

P.O. Box 226
Carlton, WA 98814
Alternate V: 06/05/92

930 Fifth Ave.
New York, NY 10021
Alternate V: 04/24/92

2180 Coldwater Canyon
Beverly Hills, CA 90210
Forwarded V: 07/01/92

Stevenson, Parker
4875 Louise Ave.
Encino, CA 91316
Actor V: 03/26/93

Stewart, James
9201 Wilshire Blvd. #201
Beverly Hills, CA 90210
Actor V: 07/07/92

918 N. Roxbury Dr.
Beverly Hills, CA 90210
Forwarded V: 04/28/92

P.O. Box 90
Beverly Hills, CA 90213
L.R.U. V: 06/01/92

Stewart, Patrick
9 Cork St.
London W1, England
Actor V: 03/16/92

c/o Star Trek-TNG Paramount
5555 Melrose Ave.
Hollywood, CA 90038
Alternate V: 03/04/92

7449 Melrose Ave.
Los Angeles, CA 90046
Forwarded V: 03/21/92

Stewart, Payne
390 N. Orange Ave., Ste.2600
Orlando, FL 32801-1642
Golfer V: 02/04/92

Stewart, Peggy
11139 Hortense St.
N. Hollywood, CA 91602
Actress V: 04/12/92

Stewart, Robert L.
c/o NASA LBJ Space Center
Houston, TX 77058
Astronaut V: 03/03/93

Stewart, Rod
391 Carolwood Dr.
Los Angeles, CA 90077
Singer V: 12/17/92

Stiers, David Ogden
3827 Ronda Vista Pl.
Los Angeles, CA 90027
Actor V: 02/04/92

c/o Viacom Prod.
"Perry Mason"
100 Universal City Plaza Bl. 448
Universal City, CA 91608
Forwarded V: 12/01/92

Stills, Stephen
19816 Haynes St.
Woodland Hills, CA 91367
Singer V: 06/14/92

Stock, Barbara
13421 Chelteham Dr.
Sherman Oaks, CA 91423
Actress V: 01/12/92

Stockwell, Dean
535 Concha Loma Dr.
Carpenteria, CA 93013
Actor V: 03/26/93

Quantum Leap
100 Universal City Plaza
Universal City, CA 91608
Forwarded V: 01/12/92

Stockwell, Guy
4924 Cahuenga Blvd.
N. Hollywood, CA 91601
Actor V: 04/01/93

Stone, Dee
23035 Cumorah Crest Dr.
Woodland Hills, CA 91364
Actress V: 02/14/92

Stone, Oliver
3110 Main St. #210
Santa Monica, CA 90405
Actor *V: 03/22/93*

c/o Ixtlan
321 Hampton Dr. #105
Venice, CA 90219
Alternate *V: 03/26/93*

Stone, Sharon
P.O. Box 7304
N. Hollywood, CA 91603-7304
Actress *V: 06/21/92*

c/o Dorthy Stone
9830 Wilshire Bl.
Beverly Hills, CA 90212
Forwarded *V: 04/22/92*

c/o Tri-Star Pictures
3400 Riverside Dr.
Burbank, CA 91505
Forwarded *V: 03/30/93*

Stone, Sheila
c/o Pin-up Prod.
409 N. Pacific Coast Hwy.#492
Redondo Beach, CA 90277
Adult Films *V: 01/24/93*

Stone Manners Talent Agency
8091 Selma Ave.
Los Angeles, CA 90046
Talent Agency *V: 03/13/93*

Stonehenge Productions
10202 W. Washington Blvd.
Culver City, CA 90232
Production Company *V: 03/17/92*

Storch, Larry
336 West End Ave. #17F
New York, Ny 10023
Actor *V: 06/17/92*

Storm, Gale
308 N. Sycamore Ave. #104
Los Angeles, CA 90036
Actress *V: 03/03/92*

Storm, Jim
c/o Bell-Phillip Prod.
"Bold & Beautiful"
7800 Beverly Blvd., Ste.3371
Los Angeles, CA 90036
Actor *V: 06/15/92*

Stoyanov, Michael
c/o Blossom
500 S. Buena Vista St.
Burbank, CA 91521
Actor *V: 11/11/92*

Straight, Beatrice
30 Norfolk Rd.
Southfield, MA 01259
Actress *V: 04/24/92*

Strasberg, Susan
c/o Gladys Hart
1244 11th St. A
Santa Monica, CA 90401
Actress *V: 01/07/92*

732 Millich Dr. #B
San Jose, CA 95117
Alternate *V: 08/15/92*

135 Central Park West
New York, NY 10023
Forwarded *V: 03/26/93*

Strassman, Marcia
1111 Las Pulgas Pl.
Pacific Palisades, CA 90272
Actress *V: 04/24/92*

Streep, Meryl
C/o CAA
9830 Wilshire Blvd.
Beverly Hills, CA 90212
Actress *V: 01/16/93*

c/o Agency
40 W. 57th St.
New York, NY 10019
Alternate *V: 05/02/92*

c/o Michael Ovitz
1888 Century Park E. Ste.1400
Los Angeles, CA 90067
Alternate *V: 06/15/92*

Street, Rebecca
c/o Seabaugh
291 Amalfi Dr.
Santa Monica, CA 90402
Actress *V: 04/24/92*

Streisand, Barbara
301 N. Carolwood Dr.
Los Angeles, CA 90077
Singer/Actress *V: 03/26/93*

521 Fifth Ave.
New York, NY 10017
Alternate *V: 02/03/92*

Strickland, Amzie
1329 N. Ogden Dr.
Los Angeles, CA 90046
Actress V: 04/24/92

Strickland, Gail
7280 Caverna Dr.
Los Angeles, CA 90068
Actress V: 04/24/92

Strickland, Hut
5254 Pit Road South
Harrisburg, NC 28075
NASCAR Driver V: 03/02/92

Stricklin, Hut
c/o Johnson & Assoc.
Rt.1, Box 161a
Rhonda, NC 28670
Alternate V: 03/12/93

Stroud, Don
c/o Diamond Artists
9200 Sunset Blvd.
Los Angeles, CA 90001
Actor V: 02/18/92

Struthers, Sally
9229 Sunset Blvd. #520
Los Angeles, CA 90069
Actress V: 03/17/93

181 N. Saltair
Los Angeles, CA 90049
Alternate V: 06/17/92

c/o Dinosaurs
500 S. Buena Vista St.
Burbank, CA 91521
Forwarded V: 11/11/92

Stuart, Anna
c/o NBC-TV
"Another World"
79 Madison Ave., 5th Fl.
New York, NY 91523
Actress V: 06/15/92

Stuart, Gloria
884 S. Bundy Dr.
Los Angeles, CA 90049
Actress V: 06/17/92

Studio Fan Mail
1122 S. Robertson Blvd.
Los Angeles, CA 90035
Celebrity Services V: 03/01/92

Studio Make-Up Academy
(Sunset Gower Studios)
1438 N. Gower St.
Mail Box 14, Bldg.5, Rm.308
Hollywood, CA 90028
Make-up V: 04/16/92

Stunt Action Coordinators
21828 Lassen Ste. E
Chatsworth, CA 91311
Production Company V: 03/17/92

Stuntman's Assn. of M.P.
4810 Whitsett Ave.
N. Hollywood, CA 91607
Production Company V: 03/17/92

Stuntwoman's Assn. of M.P.
202 Vance St.
Pacific Palisades, CA 90272
Production Company V: 03/17/92

Sturm Talent Agency
19725 Sherman Way #200
Canoga Park, CA 91306
Talent Agency V: 02/14/93

Stutzman, Mark
100 G St.
Mt. Lake Park, MD 21550
Artist V: 11/11/92

Style Models & Artists
12377 Lewis St. Ste.101
Garden Grove, CA 92640
Talent Agency V: 02/18/93

Suchet, David
c/o Brunskill
169 Queen's Gate
London SW7 5EH, England
Actor V: 03/17/92

Sues, Alan
1492 Second Ave.
New York, NY 10021
Actress V: 03/27/93

Sullivan, Barry
14687 Round Valley Dr.
Sherman Oaks, CA 91403
Actor V: 08/02/92

Sullivan, Danny
891 Washington Rd.
Grosse Point, MI 48230
Race Driver V: 01/09/92

Sullivan, Kathryn
c/o NASA
LBJ Space Center
Houston, TX 77058
Astronaut V: 01/19/92

Sullivan, Susan
c/o Grant
8500 Wilshire Blvd., Ste. 520
Beverly Hills, CA 90211
Actress V: 03/20/92

Sullivan, Susan
8642 Allenwood Dr.
Los Angeles, CA 90069
Actress V: 04/24/92

Summers, Angela
553 N. Pacific Coast Hwy.#B-282
Redondo Beach, CA 90277
Adult Films V: 01/24/93

Summers, Dana
c/o King Features
216 East 45th St.
New York, NY 10017
Cartoonist V: 06/17/92

Sunset-Gower Studios
1438 N. Gower St.
Los Angeles, CA 90028
Production Company V: 03/17/92

Super Bloopers
c/o Dick Clark Prod.
Super Bloopers
3003 W. Olive
Burbank, CA 91505
Production Company V: 01/07/92

Surovy, Nicolas
8942 Wilshire Blvd.
Beverly Hills, CA 90211
Actor V: 11/22/92

Susan Geller Associates
335 N. Maple #254
Beverly Hills, CA 90210
Talent Agency V: 03/20/93

Sutherland, Donald
c/o J/P/M Inc.
760 La Cienega Blvd. #300
Los Angeles, CA 90069
Actor V: 01/02/92

Sutherland, Kiefer
520 11th St.
Santa Monica, CA 90402
Actor V: 06/27/92

Sutton, Grady
1207 N. Orange Dr.
Los Angeles, CA 90038
Comedian V: 08/02/92

Sutton-Barth-Vennari
145 S. Fairfax Ave. Ste.310
Los Angeles, CA 90036
Talent Agency V: 02/18/93

Suzman, Janet
c/o Wm. Morris
31 Soho Square
London W1, England
Actress V: 02/28/92

Svenson, Bo
801 Greentree Rd.
Pacific Palisades, CA 90272
Actor V: 03/04/92

Swaggart, Jimmy
P.O. Box 2550
Baton Rouge, LA 70821-2550
Religious Leader V: 02/21/92

Swanson, Kristy
9000 Sunset Blvd. #1200
Los Angeles, CA 90069
Actress V: 12/16/92

330 N. Screenland Dr. #128
Burbank, CA 91506
L.R.U. V: 12/01/92

Sward, Anne
c/o As The World Turns CBS-TV
524 W. 57th St.
New York, NY 10019
Actress V: 01/11/92

Swayze, Patrick
c/o Wm. Morris
151 El Camino
Beverly Hills, CA 90212
Actor V: 12/16/92

9016 Wilshire Blvd. Ste. 500
Beverly Hills, CA 90211
Alternate V: 01/04/92

1033 Gayley Ave. #208
Los Angeles, CA 90024
Alternate V: 01/16/93

Sweet Hearts of the Rodeo
P.O. Box 121885
Nashville, TN 37203
Musical Band V: 02/10/93

Sweetin, Jodie
c/o Lorimar
"Full House"
3970 Overland Ave.
Culver City, CA 90230
Actress V: 12/15/92

Swenson, Inga
3475 Cabrillo Blvd.
Los Angeles, CA 90066
Actress V: 03/26/93

Swift, Clive
c/o PTA
Bugle House, 21a Noel St.
London W1V 3PD, England
Actor V: 03/17/92

Swit, Loretta
24216 Malibu Rd.
Malibu, CA 90265
Actress V: 03/30/93

151 S. El Camino Dr.
Beverly Hills, CA 90212
Alternate V: 01/16/93

Sylvia
c/o Moress
1209 16th Ave. S.
Nashville, TN 37212
Singer V: 07/03/92

Syms, Sylvia
c/o Brown
47 West Square
London SE11 4SP, England
Actress V: 03/20/92

Szigeti, Cynthia
464 N. Spalding #6
Los Angeles, CA 90036-2293
Actress V: 06/14/92

T

TBS Super Station
c/o Cable Network News
1050 Techwood Dr. N.W.
Atlanta, GA 30318
Network HQ V: 03/01/92

TEENAGE NINJA TURTLES
Murakami-Wolf-Swenson Prod.
4222 West Burbank Blvd.
Burbank, CA 91505
Production Company V: 03/18/93

TODAY, DATELINE NBC
NBC News
30 Rockefeller Plaza
New York, NY 10112
Production Company V: 03/26/93

TONIGHT
NBC
3000 W. Alameda Ave.
Burbank, CA 91523
Production Company V: 03/26/93

TONIGHT SHOW
c/o NBC Prod.
The Tonight Show
3000 W. Alameda Ave.
Burbank, CA 91523
Production Company V: 01/10/92

TOP COPS
c/o Grosso-Jacobson Prod.
767 Third Ave., 15th Fl.
New York, NY 10017
Production Company V: 05/15/92

TORKELSONS
Walt Disney Prod.
c/o CBS/MTM
4024 Radford Ave., Admin. Bldg, Ste.310
Studio City, CA 91604
Production Company V: 03/26/93

TV Guide
100 Matsonford Rd.
Radnor, PA 19088
Publishers V: 03/01/92

Tabori, Kristoffer
P.O. Box 1139 Station B
London, Ont., Canada N6A 5K2
Celebrity V: 03/02/92

Taft Entertainment
3330 Cahuenga Blvd.
Los Angeles, CA 90068
HQ Offices V: 04/22/92

Takei, George
4368 W. 8th St.
Los Angeles, CA 90005
Actor V: 06/17/92

Talbert, Billy
c/o U.S. Banknote Co.
345 Hudson St.
New York, NY 10014
Tennis V: 02/18/92

Talbot, Lyle
149 Fairmont St.
San Francisco, CA 94131
Actor V: 01/12/92

Talbot, Nita
3420 Merrimac Rd.
Los Angeles, CA 90049
Actress V: 06/17/92

Talent Bank
1680 N. Vine St. Ste.721
Los Angeles, CA 90028
Talent Agency V: 01/14/93

Talent Group
9250 Wilshire Blvd. #208
Beverly Hills, CA 90212
Talent Agency V: 01/14/93

Tamblyn, Russ
c/o ABC/Capitol Cities
2040 Ave. of the Stars
Los Angeles, CA 90067-4785
Actor V: 04/16/92

c/o Beakle & Debord
10637 Burbank Blvd.
N. Hollywood, CA 91601
Alternate V: 04/01/92

2310 6th St. #2
Santa Monica, CA 90405
Alternate V: 04/23/92

1833 Stanford Ave.
Santa Monica, CA 90404
Forwarded V: 04/16/92

Tambor, Jeffrey
5526 Calhoun Ave.
Van Nuys, CA 91401
Actor V: 03/26/93

Tampa Bay Buccaneers
One Buccaneer Place
Tampa, FL 33607
Team Offices V: 05/15/92

Tandy, Jessica
63-23 Carlton St.
Rego Park, NY 11374
Actress V: 03/01/92

Tannen & Associates
1800 N. Vine St. #120
Los Angeles, CA 90028
Talent Agency V: 02/27/93

Tara, Suzanne
c/o ABC-TV
General Hospital
4151 Prospect Ave.
Hollywood, CA 90027
Actress V: 06/15/92

Tarkington, Fran
Tower Place Suite 444
3340 Peachtree Rd. N.E.
Atlanta, GA 30326
Actor V: 03/25/92

Tatler Magazine
c/o Vogue House
Hanover Sq.
London, W1R 0AD London
Entertainment V: 03/03/92

Taylor, Bob
c/o Dallas Times/Herald
1101 Pacific Ave.
Dallas, TX 75202
Cartoonist V: 10/18/92

c/o King Features
216 East 45th St.
New York, NY 10017
Alternate V: 07/18/92

Taylor, Buck
c/o Gerler-Stevens
3349 Cahuenga Blvd., W. Ste.1
Los Angeles, CA 90068
Actor V: 01/02/92

c/o Gerler-Stevens
2899 Agoura Rd., Ste. 275
Westlake Village, CA 91361
Alternate V: 01/02/92

206 Via Colinas
Westlake Village, CA 91362
Alternate V: 01/02/93

Taylor, Cheri
P.O. Box 711
Redondo Beach, CA 90277
Adult Films V: 01/24/93

Taylor, Clarice
35 Hamilton Terr.
New York, NY 10031
Actress V: 03/17/93

Taylor, Dub
21417 Gaona St.
Woodland Hills, CA 91364
Actor V: 05/13/91

Taylor, Elizabeth
700 Nimes Rd.
Los Angeles, CA 90024
Actress V: 06/14/92

c/o Sharon Leigh
P.O. Box 487
Sunland, CA 91041-0487
Alternate V: 02/12/91

Taylor, Holland
c/o Lorimar
"Going Places"
3970 Overland Ave.
Culver City, CA 90230
Actress V: 12/15/92

Taylor, Jackie Lynn
115 Thorn St.
San Diego, CA 92103
Actress V: 04/24/92

Taylor, Lauren Marie
c/o ABC-TV 'Loving'
77 W. 66th St.
New York, NY 10023
Actress V: 10/09/92

Capital Cities/ABC. Inc.
320 W. 66th St.
New York, NY 10023
Alternate V: 10/09/92

Taylor, Meshach
969 Mt. Curce Ave.
Altadena, CA 91001
Actor V: 03/26/93

c/o Columbia/Mozark
Designing Women
Columbia Plaza, Prod.Bl.8,#147
Burbank, CA 91505
Forwarded V: 02/03/93

Taylor, Rip
9021 Melrose Ave. #308
Los Angeles, CA 90069
Actor V: 07/22/92

Taylor, Rod
2375 Bowmont Dr.k E. #1400
Beverly Hills, CA 90210
Actor V: 08/20/92

Taylor-Young, Leigh
1279 Beverly Estates Dr.
Beverly Hills, CA 90210
Actress V: 03/17/93

Teague, Brad
c/o NASCAR
1811 Volusia Ave.
Daytona Beach, FL 32015
NASCAR Driver V: 03/02/92

Tedrow, Irene
5763 Corteen Pl.
North Hollywood, CA 91602
Actress V: 06/17/92

Teed, Dick
45 Taylor St.
Windsor, CT 06095
Baseball V: 10/11/92

Telemundo
1740 Broadway, 18th Fl.
New York, NY 10019
Network HQ V: 03/01/92

Television Arts & Sciences
3500 W. Olive #700
Burbank, CA 91505
Academy Office V: 03/17/92

Teller, Edward
UC/Livermore National Lab.
P.O. Box 808
Livermore, CA 94550
Scientist V: 03/16/92

Templeton, Christopher
c/o Young and the Restless
7800 Beverly Blvd.
Beverly Hills, CA 90036
Actor V: 06/15/92

Tenant, Victoria
P.O. Box 5617
Beverly Hills, CA 90210
Actress V: 02/18/92

c/o Steve Martin
10000 Santa Montica Bl.
Los Angeles, CA 90062
Forwarded V: 02/18/92

c/o Hatton & Baker
18 Jermyn St.
London SW1Y 6HN, England
Forwarded V: 03/20/92

Tenney, Jon
c/o Orion
"Equal Justice"
1888 Century Park East
Los Angeles, CA 90067
Actor V: 12/18/92

Tennille, Toni
P.O. Box 262
Glenbrook, NV 89413
Singer V: 03/04/93

Tenuta, Judy
332 E. Euclid Ave.
Oak Park, IL 60302
Actress V: 03/23/93

Terrell, Tony
c/o CBS-TV/Guiding Light
51 W. 52nd St.
New York, NY 10019
Actor V: 01/17/92

Tesh, John
5555 Melrose Ave.
Los Angeles, CA 90038
Actor V: 03/17/93

Tewes, Lauren
13858 Sunset Blvd.
Pacific Palisades, CA 90036
Actress V: 02/18/92

Texas Rangers
P.O. Box 1111
Arlington Stadium
Arlington, TX 76010
Team Office V: 05/15/92

Thagard, Norman E.
c/o NASA LBJ Space Center
Houston, TX 77058
Astronaut V: 03/03/93

Thatcher, Margaret
11 Dulwich Gate
Dulwich, London SE12, England
Former English P.M. V: 04/05/92

Thaw, John
c/o Redway
16 Berners St.
London W1P 3DD, England
Actor V: 03/17/92

The Agency
10351 Santa Monica Blvd. #211
Los Angeles, CA 90025
Talent Agency V: 09/01/92

Theisman, Joe
5912 Leesburg Pike
Falls Church, VA 22041
Football V: 12/10/92

Thicke, Alan
10505 Sarah St.
N. Hollywood, CA 91602
Actor V: 03/27/93

c/o Warner Bros. TV
"Growing Pains"
4000 Warner Blvd.
Burbank, CA 91522
Forwarded V: 12/03/92

Thinnes, Roy
8016 Willow Glen Rd.
Los Angeles, CA 90046
Actor V: 03/26/93

Thomas, Betty
c/o ICM
8942 Wilshire Blvd.
Beverly Hills, CA 90211
Actress V: 03/20/92

3585 Woodhill Canyon
Studio City, CA 91604
Actress V: 04/24/92

Thomas, Carmen
c/o ABC-TV/All My Children
1330 Ave. of the America's
New York, NY 10019
Actress V: 01/17/92

Thomas, Dave
c/o Wendy's Int'l
P.O. Box 256
4288 W. Dublin Granville
Dublin, OH 43011
Founder V: 01/12/92

Thomas, Donald A.
c/o NASA LBJ Space Center
Houston, TX 77058
Astronaut V: 03/03/93

Thomas, Gareth
c/o Belfrage
60 St. James's St.
London SW1A 1LE, England
Actor V: 03/17/92

Thomas, Heather
1433 San Vicente Blvd.
Santa Monica, CA 90402
Actress V: 03/11/93

9000 Sunset Blvd. #315
Los Angeles, CA 90069
Forwarded V: 07/03/92

Thomas, Heather, contd
606 Hanley Ave.
Los Angeles, CA 90049
L.R.U. V: 12/16/92

Thomas, Isiah
c/o Detroit Pistons
Pontiac Silverdome
1200 Featherstone Rd.
Pontiac, MI 48057
Basketball V: 11/11/92

Thomas, Jonathon
c/o Home Improvements
500 S. Buena Vista St.
Burbank, CA 91521
Actor V: 11/11/92

Thomas, Marlo
420 E. 54th St. #22F
New York, NY 10022
Actress V: 03/23/93

9830 Wilshire Blvd.
Beverly Hills, CA 90212
Forwarded V: 12/12/92

Thomas, Phillip Michael
12156 W. Dixie Hwy.
Miami, FL 33161
Actor V: 03/26/93

2951 S. Bayshore Dr.
Coconut Grove, FL 33275
L.R.U. V: 05/29/92

Thomas, Richard
4834 Bonville Ave.
Los Angeles, CA 90047
Actor V: 01/16/92

5261 Cleon Ave.
N. Hollywood, CA 91601
Forwarded V: 08/20/92

Thomas-Scott, Melody
c/o CBS-TV/Young&Restless
7800 Beverly Blvd. #330
Los Angeles, CA 90036
Actress V: 01/21/92

Thompkins, Angel
P.O. Box 5069
Beverly Hills, CA 90210
Actress V: 11/11/92

Thompson, Bobby
122 Sunlit Dr.
Watchung, NJ 07060
Baseball V: 05/14/92

Thompson, Lea
7966 Woodrow Wilson Dr.
Los Angeles, CA 90046
Actress V: 06/01/92

P.O. Box 16894
Baltimore, MD 21206
L.R.U. V: 10/10/92

Thompson, Linda
6342 Sycamore Meadows
Malibu, CA 90265
Actress V: 11/11/92

Thompson, Sada
P.O. Box 490
Southbury, CT 06488-0490
Actress V: 04/24/92

Thompson Agency
6381 Hollywood Blvd. #640
Los Angeles, CA 90028
Talent Agency V: 02/27/93

Thorne-Smith, Courtney
9301 Wilshire Blvd. #312
Beverly Hills, CA 90210
Actress V: 02/12/92

Thornton, Kathryn C.
NASA/LBJ Space Center
Houston, TX 77058
Astronaut V: 01/19/92

Thornton, Sigrid
c/o Umbrella Film Services
75-83 High St.
Prahar, Melbourne
Victoria 3181, Australia
Actress V: 02/12/93

Thornton, Sigrid
10202 W. Washington Blvd.
Culver City, CA 90232
Alternate V: 04/16/92

Thornton & Associates
5657 Wilshire Blvd. #290
Los Angeles, CA 90036
Talent Agency V: 02/27/93

Thorton, William E.
NASA/LBJ Space Center
Houston, TX 77058
Astronaut V: 03/03/93

Thuot, Pierre J.
NASA/LBJ Space Center
Houston, TX 77058
Astronaut V: 01/31/92

Thurman, Uma
9057 Nemo St. #A
W. Hollywood, CA 90069
Actress V: 12/15/92

Tianna
c/o 5K Sales
9420 Reseda Blvd., Ste.836
Northridge, CA 91324
Adult Films V: 01/17/93

Tibbets, Paul W.
5574 Knollwood Dr.
Columbus, OH 43232
Soldier V: 02/01/92

Ticotin, Rachel
14231 Margate St.
Van Nuys, CA 91404
Actress V: 04/24/92

Tiegs, Cheryl
2 Greenwich Plaza #100
Greenwich, CT 06830
Actress V: 06/21/92

829 Park Ave. #7B
New York, NY 10021
Alternate V: 02/01/92

1185 Park Ave.
New York, NY 10128
Alternate V: 05/02/92

c/o Ford Agency
344 E. 59th St.
New York, NY 10072
Forwarded V: 07/01/92

Tiffany
13659 Victory Blvd. #550
Van Nuys, CA 91401
Singer V: 03/26/93

P.O. Box 604
San Francisco, CA 94191
Alternate V: 05/04/92

Tillis, Mel
809 18th Ave. S. Dr.
Nashville, TN 37203
Singer V: 04/18/92

Tillis, Pam
c/o Mike Robertson Mgmt.
1232 17th Ave.
Nashville, TN 37212
Actress V: 01/22/93

Tilly, Jennifer
c/o MTA
9320 Wilshire Blvd. 3rd Fl.
Beverly Hills, CA 90212
Actress V: 04/22/92

Timmins, Cali
c/o NBC-TV
"Another World"
79 Madison Ave., 5th Fl.
New York, NY 91523
Actress V: 06/15/92

Tiny Tim
c/o Morse Theatrical Agency
354 Broadway
Providence, RI 02909
Singer V: 04/10/92

27 W. 72nd St.
New York, NY 10023
Alternate V: 02/11/92

Tippit, Jack
c/o King Features
216 East 45th St.
New York, NY 10017
Cartoonist V: 09/01/92

Tisherman Agency
6767 Forest Lawn Dr. #115
Los Angeles, CA 90068
Talent Agency V: 04/01/93

Title, Y.A.
310 S. Lafayette St.
Marshall, TX 75670
Football V: 03/17/92

Todd, Ann
c/o Agent
Seagrove Cottage, Walkerswick
Suffolk, England
Actress V: 02/17/92

Todd, Hallie
c/o Lorimar
"Going Places"
3970 Overland Ave.
Culver City, CA 90230
Actress V: 12/15/92

Todd, Richard
Chinham Farm
Farington
Oxfordshire, England
Actor V: 01/20/93

Todd, Russell
c/o NBC-TV
"Another World"
79 Madison Ave., 5th Fl.
New York, NY 91523
Actor   V: 06/15/92

Toguri, Iva
851 W. Belmont Ave.
Chicago, IL 60613
Tokyo Rose   V: 12/11/92

Tolsky, Susan
10815 Acama St.
North Hollywood, CA 91601
Actress   V: 06/15/92

Tombaugh, Clyde
P.O. Box 306
Mesilla Park, NM 88047
Scientist   V: 03/23/92

Tomei, Marisa
c/o Carsey-Warner Co.
"A Different World"
P.O.Box 1-701
14755 Ventura Bl.
Sherman Oaks, CA 91403
Actress V: 01/07/93

Tomita, Tamlyn
c/o Artists Group
1930 Century Park W. #403
Los Angeles, CA 90067
Actress   V: 02/23/93

Tomlin, Lily
P.O. Box 27759
Los Angeles, CA 90027-0759
Actress   V: 04/24/92

Tomlinson, Barry
c/o King Features
216 E. 45th St.
New York, NY 10017
Cartoonist   V: 03/11/93

Tomlinson, David
c/o Disney Productions Ltd.
31-32 Soho Sq.
London W1, England
Actor   V: 03/01/92

Tompkins, Angel
c/o A.G.
1930 Century Park W. #403
Los Angeles, CA 90067
Actress   V: 04/20/92

Topol
236 Grays Inn Rd.
London WC1X 8HB, England
Actor   V: 02/28/92

Topol, Chaim
108 Dizengoff St.
Tel Aviv, Isreal
Actor   V: 10/18/92

Topping, Lynne
1680 N. Vine St. #1003
Hollywood, CA 90028
Actress   V: 01/16/93

Torme, Mel
151 El Camino
Beverly Hills, CA 90212
Singer   V: 01/16/93

1734 Coldwater Canyon
Beverly Hills, CA 90210
Alternate   V: 04/23/92

Torn, Rip
130 W. 42nd St. #2400
New York, NY 10036
Actor   V: 03/26/93

Toronto Blue Jays
P.O. Box 7777
Adelaide St. Post Office
Exhibition Stadium
Toronto, Ont., Canada M5C 2K7
Team Office   V: 05/15/92

Torres, Liz
7800 Beverly Blvd.
Los Angeles, CA 90036
Actress   V: 04/16/92

1711 N. Ave. 53
Los Angeles, CA 90042
Alternate V: 04/24/92

303 S. Crescent Heights
Beverly Hills, CA 90211
Alternate   V: 07/19/92

Torrey, Rich
c/o King Features
216 East 45th St.
New York, NY 10017
Cartoonist   V: 04/21/92

Totten, Bob
13819 Riverside Dr.
Sherman Oaks, CA 91403
Director   V: 01/21/92

Totter, Audrey
1851 Midvale Ave. #2
Los Angeles, CA 90025
Actress V: 06/20/92

1945 Glendon, Ste.305
Los Angeles, CA 90025
Alternate V: 04/24/92

Touchstone TV & Films
5064 Fan Mail
500 S. Buena Vista St.
Burbank, CA 91521
Viewer Services V: 11/02/92

Towers, Constance
2415 Century Hill
Los Angeles, CA 90067
Actress V: 06/17/92

Townsend, Robert
3000 Durand Dr.
Los Angeles, CA 90068
Actor V: 04/06/93

Trachta, Jeff
c/o Bell-Phillip Prod.
"Bold & Beautiful"
7800 Beverly Blvd., Ste.3371
Los Angeles, CA 90036
Actor V: 06/15/92

Trachte, Don
c/o King Features
216 East 45th St.
New York, NY 10017
Cartoonist V: 02/18/92

Tratloft, Hannes
10 Werder Strasse
757 Baden Baden, Germany
Knights Cross V: 03/03/92

Travalena, Fred
P.O. Box 260171
Encino, CA 91426-0171
Actor V: 05/29/92

4515 White Oak Place
Encino, CA 91316
Forwarded V: 03/04/92

P.O. Box 171
Encino, CA 91316
L.R.U. V: 05/12/92

Travanti, Daniel J.
4024 Radford Ave.
Studio City, CA 91604
Actor V: 03/29/92

Travanti, Daniel J., contd
14205 Sunset Blvd.
Pacific Palisades, CA 90272
Alternate V: 04/05/93

9220 Sunset Blvd. #202
Los Angeles, CA 90069
Alternate V: 01/06/92

Travers, Bill
c/o Belfrage
68 St James St.
London SW1A 1LE, England
Actor V: 04/20/92

Cherry Tree Cottage
Cold Harbour, Dorking
Surrey RH5 6HA, England
Alternate V: 02/28/92

Travis, Lib
P.O. Box 121137
Nashville, TN 37212
Celebrity V: 03/26/93

Travis, Randy
P.O. Box 121137
Nashville, TN 37212
Singer V: 03/26/93

1610 16th Ave. South
Nashville, TN 37213
Alternate V: 03/01/92

Travolta, Ellen
5832 Nagle Ave.
Van Nuys, CA 91401
Actress V: 07/31/92

Travolta, Joey
4975 Chimineas Ave.
Tarzana, CA 91356
Actor V: 03/17/93

Travolta, John
P.O. Box 491246
Los Angeles, CA 90049
Actor V: 06/02/92

1504 Live Oak Lane
Santa Barbara, CA 93105
Alternate V: 04/01/93

Rancho Tajiguas
Sunburst Farms, Hwy. 101
Santa Barbara, CA 92103
Alternate V: 06/24/92

Trebek, Alex
1541 N. Vine St.
Hollywood, CA 90028
Celebrity V: 03/03/92

7966 Mulholland Dr.
Los Angeles, CA 90046
Forwarded V: 03/03/92

Treff, Alice
Bonner Str. 1
D-(W) 1000 Berlin 33
Germany
Actress V: 01/19/93

Trever, John
c/o King Features
216 E. 45th St.
New York, NY 10017
Cartoonist V: 03/11/93

Trevino, Lee
5757 Alpha Rd. Ste.620
Dallas, TX 75240-4668
Golf V: 03/30/93

14901 Quorum Dr. Ste.170
Dallas, TX 75240
Alternate V: 03/21/92

1221 Abrams Rd., Ste.327
Richardson, TX 75081
Alternate V: 09/02/92

Trevor, Claire
Hotel Pierre
2 E. 61st St.
New York, NY 10022
Actress V: 01/19/92

Trevor, John
c/o King Features
216 East 45th St.
New York, NY 10017
Cartoonist V: 03/02/92

Trickle, Dick
c/o Stavola Racing
P.O. Box 339
Harrisburg, NC 28705
NASCAR Driver V: 03/02/92

Trillin, Calvin
c/o King Features
216 East 45th St.
New York, NY 10017
Writer V: 05/24/92

Trimark Pictures
2901 Ocean Park Blvd. #123
Santa Monica, CA 90405-2956
Studio Offices V: 12/12/92

2644 30th St.
Santa Monica, CA 90405-3009
Alternate V: 12/12/92

Trintignant, Jean-Louis
10 Ave. George-V
F-75008 Paris, France
Actor V: 02/11/93

Triola, Michelle
23215 Mariposa de Oro
Malibu, CA 90265-4909
Actress V: 04/24/92

Tritt, Travis
P.O. Box 440099
Kennesaw, GA 30144
Singer V: 12/28/92

Troup, Bobby
16074 Royal Oaks St.
Encino, CA 91316
Actor V: 08/06/92

Trucks, Virgil Fire
2156 Gatson Valley Dr.
Birmingham, AL 35235
Baseball V: 03/30/93

36 Santarem Circle
Punta Gorda, FL 33983
Alternate V: 03/30/93

P.O. Box 59267
Homewood, AL 35259
Forwarded V: 04/12/92

Trudeau, Garry
4900 Main St.
Kansas City, MO 64112
Cartoonist V: 02/12/92

4400 Johnson Dr.
Fairway, KS 66205
L.R.U. V: 05/29/92

Trudy, Natalie
6140 Lindenhurst Ave.
Los Angeles, CA 90048
Actress V: 07/14/92

Truly, Richard H.
c/o NASA LBJ Space Center
Houston, TX 77058
Astronaut V: 03/03/93

Truman, Margaret
c/o Merideth
830 Park Ave.
New York, NY 10028
 Author V: 03/25/92

Trump, Donald
725 5th Ave.
New York, NY 10022
 Business V: 06/08/92

Trump, Ivana
c/o Mille
1100 Palm Beach Blvd.
Palm Beach, FL 33480
 Celebrity V: 05/29/92

725 5th Ave.
New York, NY 10022
 Forwarded V: 07/14/92

Tucker, Michael
c/o 20th Century Fox TV
L.A. Law
P.O. Box 900
Beverly Hills, CA 90213
 Actor V: 01/12/92

2183 Mandeville Canyon
Los Angeles, CA 90049
 Alternate V: 03/20/92

Tucker, Regina
Dallas Cowboys
One Cowboys Parkway
Irving, TX 75063-4945
 Cheerleader V: 08/08/92

Tucker, Tanya
8012 Brooks Chaple Rd. Ste.73
Brentwood, TN 37027
 Singer V: 03/30/93

5200 Maryland Way #103
Brentwood, TN 37027
 Alternate V: 12/12/92

200 Chapple Blvd.
Brentwood, TN 37027
 Forwarded V: 04/22/92

Tully, Susan
265 Liverpool Rd.
London N1 1LX, England
 Actress V: 03/20/92

Tune, Tommy
50 E. 89th St.
New York, NY 10128
 Singer V: 03/20/92

Turner, Janine
c/o Cine-Nevada Inc.
"Northern Exposure"
3000 Olympic Blvd., Ste.2575
Santa Monica, CA 90404
 Actress V: 05/15/92

Turner, Kathleen
73 County Rd. 39A, Ste.2700
Southhampton, NY 11968
 Actress V: 03/30/93

P.O. Box 5617
Beverly Hills, CA 90213
 Alternate V: 06/14/92

c/o Gersh Agency
130 W. 42nd St.
New York, NY 10036
 Forwarded V: 05/05/92

Turner, Morrie
c/o King Features
216 East 45th St.
New York, NY 10017
 Cartoonist V: 05/14/92

Turner, Tina
14755 Ventura Blvd. #10710
Sherman Oaks, CA 91403
 Singer V: 01/16/93

151 El Camino
Beverly Hills, CA 90212
 Alternate V: 03/08/92

Turner Home Entertainment
c/o Publicity
420 5th Ave., 7th Fl.
New York, NY 10018
 Production Office V: 12/12/92

Turner Network TV
One CNN Center
P.O. Box 105366
Atlanta, GA 30348
 Network HQ V: 03/01/92

Tushingham, Rita
c/o London Mgmt.
235 Regent St.
London W1, England
 Actress V: 07/13/92

Tweed, Shannon
9300 Wilshire Blvd. #410
Beverly Hills, CA 90212
 Actress V: 01/16/93

Twentieth Century Artists
c/o 20th Cent. Artists
14724 Ventura Blvd. 5th Fl.
Sherman Oaks, CA 91403
Talent Agency V: 02/23/93

Twentieth Century Fox
P.O. Box 900
Beverly Hills, CA 90213
Network HQ V: 03/01/92

Twentieth Century Fox
10201 W. Pico Blvd.
Los Angeles, CA 90035
Distributor V: 03/17/92

Twiggy
4 St. George's Houses
15 Hannover Sq.1
London, W1R 9AJ England
Actress V: 01/12/92

Twitty, Conway
1 Music Village Blvd.
Hendersinville, TN 37075
Singer V: 11/11/92

Tyler, Beverly
c/o Jordan
14585 Geronemo Trail
Reno, NV 89511
Actress V: 07/14/92

Tylo, Hunter
c/o Bold & Beautiful
7800 Beverly Blvd., Ste.3371
Los Angeles, CA 90036
Actor V: 06/15/92

Tylo, Michael
c/o ABC-TV/All My Children
1330 Ave. of the America's
New York, NY 10019
Actor V: 01/17/92

Tyrrell, Susan
826 Amoroso Pl.
Venice, CA 90219
Actress V: 03/26/93

Tyson, Mike
c/o Indiana Youth Center
727 Moon Rd.
Plainfield, IN 46168
Boxer V: 09/27/92

Tyson, Richard
3000 W. Alameda
Burbank, CA 91523
Actor V: 11/22/92

U

U.S. Dept. of Defense
Motion Picture Media Record Center
HqAAVS/DOSD
Norton AFB, CA 92409
Archive V: 03/20/93

U2
c/o Wasted Talent
321 Fulham Rd.
London SW10 9QL, England
Band V: 03/15/93

UBU Productions
5555 Melrose Ave.
Hollywood, CA 90038
Production Company V: 03/17/92

UCLA Film & Television Archive
1015 N. Cahuenga Blvd.
Hollywood, CA 90038
Archive V: 03/13/93

UNI
605 Third Ave, 12th Fl.
New York, NY 10158
Network HQ V: 03/01/92

UNSOLVED MYSTERIES
Cosgrove-Meurer Prod.
4303 W. Verdugo Ave.
Burbank, CA 91505
Production Company V: 03/26/93

UP ALL NIGHT
2049 Century Park E., #2550
Los Angeles, CA 90067
Production Office V: 03/30/93

US Magazine
1 Dag Hammerskjold Plaza
New York, NY 10017
Publishers V: 03/01/92

USA Network
1230 Ave. of the Americas
New York, NY 10020
Network HQ V: 03/01/92

1900 Ave. of the Stars #1290
Los Angeles, CA 90067
Alternate V: 03/17/92

USA Today TV
9336 W. Washington Blvd.
Culver City, CA 90230
Production Company V: 03/17/92

Udonte, Gean Maria
c/o NC
Viale Bruno Buozzi 53
Rome 00197, Italy
 Actress *V: 02/28/92*

Uggams, Leslie
9255 Sunset Blvd. #404
Los Angeles, CA 90069
 Singer *V: 04/06/92*

151 El Camino Dr.
Beverly Hills, CA 90212
 Alternate *V: 08/15/92*

30 W. 50th St. #10-A
New York, NY 10023
 L.R.U. *V: 07/13/92*

Ullman, Liv
15 W. 81st St.
New Nork, NY 10024
 Actress *V: 05/12/92*

9196 Sunset Blvd.
Los Angeles, CA 90069
 Alternate *V: 03/22/92*

Ullman, Tracy
c/o McKeown
13555 D'Este Dr.
Pacific Palisades, CA 90272
 Actress *V: 03/26/93*

10201 W. Pico Blvd. Bungalo 9
Los Angeles, CA 90035
 Forwarded *V: 11/10/92*

Underwood, Blair
c/o 20th Century Fox TV
L.A. Law
P.O. Box 900
Beverly Hills, CA 90213
 Actor *V: 01/12/92*

Unitas, Johnny
c.o Nat'l Circuits
4820 Seton Dr.
Baltimore, MD 21215
 Football *V: 03/25/92*

United Fan Club Service
8966 Sunset Blvd.
Hollywood, CA 90069
 Service *V: 05/04/92*

United Fan Mail
9056 Santa Monica Blvd. #100
Hollywood, CA 90069
 Fan Service *V: 02/23/93*

United Talent Agency
9560 Wilshire Blvd. 5th Fl.
Beverly Hills, CA 90212
 Talent Agency *V: 03/29/93*

Universal City Studios
100 Universal City Plaza
Universal City, CA 91608
 Distributor *V: 03/17/92*

Universal Fan Mail
14842 Strathern St.
Van Nuys, CA 91402
 Services *V: 03/17/92*

Universal Press Synd.
4900 Main St.
Kansas City, MO 64112
 Artists *V: 11/11/92*

Universal Television
100 Universal Studios Plaza
Universal City, CA 91608
 Production Company *V: 03/17/92*

Unser, Bobbie
7700 Central Ave. S.W.
Albuquerque, NM 87105
 Race Driver *V: 01/17/92*

Urban, Matt
352 Wildwood
Holland, MI 49423
 Medal of Honor *V: 02/05/92*

Urich, Robert
c/o Look Up Prod.
4000 Warner Blvd. Pro.Blg.2
Burbank, CA 91522
 Actor *V: 07/25/92*

15930 Woodvale Rd.
Encino, CA 91316
 Alternate *V: 05/11/92*

24 Phillip St.
Andover, MA 01810
 Forwarded *V: 04/13/92*

Ustinov, Peter
c/o Wm. Morris Agency
147 Wardour St.
London W1, England
 Actor *V: 07/12/92*

c/o JY Publicity
100 Edbury St.
London SW1W 9QD, England
 Alternate *V: 03/17/92*

Ustinov, Peter, contd
11 Rue de Silly
92 100 Boulogne, France
Alternate V: 05/11/92

Utay, William
c/o Warner/Night Court
4000 Warner Blvd., Office 12A
Burbank, CA 91521
Actor V: 01/12/92

VH-1/Video Hits 1
1515 Broadway/MTV Network
New York, NY 10019
Production Company V: 01/12/92

V

Vaccaro, Brenda
14423 Dickens. St. #3
Sherman Oaks, CA 91423
Actress V: 03/26/93

2965 Hutton Dr.
Beverly Hills, CA 90210-1104
L.R.U. V: 01/05/92

Vadim, Vanessa
316 Alta Ave.
Santa Monica, CA 90402
Actress V: 07/14/92

Vale, Jerry
621 N. Palm Dr.
Beverly Hills, CA 90210
Singer V: 03/24/92

Vale, Virginia
c/o Artists Mgmt. Inc.
4039 Edenhurst Ave.
Los Angeles, CA 90039
Actress V: 01/22/92

Valen, Nancy
10000 Santa Monica Bl. Ste 305
Los Angeles, CA 90067
Actress V: 03/30/92

Valentine, Karen
145 W 67th St. #42H
New York, NY 10023
Actress V: 04/22/92

Vallely, Tannis
Warner/Head of the Class
100 North Pass Rd.
Burbank, CA 91505
Actress V: 12/18/92

Vallely, Tannis, contd
142 S. Clark Dr. Ste.103
Los Angeles, CA 90048
Actress V: 07/14/92

Valley, Paul Michael
c/o NBC-TV
Another World
79 Madison Ave., 5th Fl.
New York, NY 91523
Actor V: 06/15/92

Valli, Alida
Viale Liegi 42
00100 Rome, Italy
Actress V: 07/14/92

Valli, Frankie
26 Oaktrail Rd.
Englewood, NJ 07631
Singer V: 01/20/93

Van Amerongen, Jerry
c/o King Features
216 East 45th St.
New York, NY 10017
Cartoonist V: 09/20/92

Van Ark, Joan
c/o CBS-TV
7800 Beverly Blvd.
Los Angeles, CA 90036
Actress V: 04/01/92

10950 Alta View Dr.
Studio City, CA 91604
Forwarded V: 07/21/92

Van Cleef Talent Agency
7319 Beverly Blvd. #7
Los Angeles, CA 90036
Talent Agency V: 03/02/93

Van Damme, Jean-Claude
P.O. Box 4149
Chatsworth, CA 91311
Actor V: 03/17/92

Van Devere, Trish
3211 Retreat Ct.
Malibu, CA 90265
Actress V: 06/15/92

Van Doren, Mamie
8340 Rush St.
Rosemead, CA 91770
Actress V: 09/06/92

Van Doren, Mamie, contd
428 31st St.
Newport Beach, CA 92663
Alternate V: 04/21/93

Van Dyke, Dick
151 El Camino Dr.
Beverly Hills, CA 90212
Actor V: 04/03/92

4335 Marina City Dr. #1046
Marina del Rey, CA 90292
Alternate V: 02/21/92

21315 Mariposa de Oro
Malibu, CA 90265
Forwarded V: 12/11/92

Van Dyke, Jerry
c/o Universal TV
Coach
100 Universal Plaza, Bung.78
Universal City, CA 91608
Actor V: 12/18/92

606 Larchmont Blvd. Ste. 309
Los Angeles, CA 90004
L.R.U. V: 05/04/92

Van Halen, Eddie
10100 Santa Monica Blvd. #2460
Las Angeles, CA 90067
Musician V: 03/18/93

Van Hoften, James D.
c/o NASA LBJ Space Center
Houston, TX 77058
Astronaut V: 03/03/93

Van Patten, Dick
13920 Magnolia Blvd.
Sherman Oaks, CA 91423
Actor V: 03/02/92

c/o GTG Ent./Culver Studios
9336 W. Washington Blvd.
Culver City, CA 90232
Alternate V: 05/15/92

Van Patten, Jimmy
13920 Magnolia Blvd.
Sherman Oaks, CA 94123
Actor V: 12/11/92

Van Patten, Joyce
1321 N. Hayworth #C
Los Angeles, CA 90046
Actress V: 06/17/92

Van Patten, Vincent
13920 Magnolia Blvd.
Sherman Oaks, CA 94123
Actor V: 06/15/92

Van Peebles, Mario
40 W. 57th St.
New York, NY 10023
Actor V: 01/05/93

Van Valkenburgh, Deborah
2025 Stanley Hills Dr.
Los Angeles, CA 90046
Actress V: 03/26/93

Van Vooren, Monique
165 E. 66th St.
New York, NY 10021
Actress V: 01/19/93

Vanderbilt TV News Archive
Vanderbilt University
Heard Library
Nashville, TN 37240-007
Archive V: 03/20/93

Vanity
151 El Camino
Beverly Hills, CA 91202
Actress V: 02/18/92

Varney, Jim
1221 McGovock St.
Nashville, TN 37203
Actor V: 05/18/92

Vartan, Sylvie
706 N. Beverly Dr.
Beverly Hills, CA 90210
Actress V: 07/14/92

Vaughan, Peter
c/o Agency
388-396 Oxford St.
London W1 9HE, England
Actor V: 03/17/92

Vaughn, Robert
162 Old West Mountain Rd.
Ridgefield, CT 06877
Actor V: 01/12/92

Vavasseur, Kevin
c/o Carsey-Warner Co.
A Different World
P.O.Box 1-701
14755 Ventura Bl
Sherman Oaks, CA 91403
Actor V: 07/01/92

Veach, Charles Lacey
c/o NASA
LBJ Space Center
Houston, TX 77058
Astronaut V: 01/31/92

Vel Johnson, Reginald
c/o Lorimar Telepictures Prod.
Family Matters
3970 Overland Ave.
Culver City, CA 90230
Actress V: 12/15/92

9229 Sunset Blvd. #311
Los Angeles, CA 90069
Actor V: 03/20/92

Velez, Eddie
10661 Whipple St.
N. Hollywood, CA 91602
Actor V: 03/20/92

Venable, Evelyn
141 S. Gretna Green Way
Los Angeles, CA 90049
Actress V: 07/14/92

Ventures
P.O. Box 1646
Burbank, CA 91507
Musical Group V: 01/04/92

Verdon, Gwen
91 Central Park West
New York, NY 10023
Actress V: 06/11/92

Verdugo, Elena
P.O. Box 2048
Chula Vista, CA 92012
Actress V: 04/22/92

Verhoeven, Lis
Strenstr. 17
D-(W) 8000 Munchen 22
Germany
Actress V: 01/19/93

Vernon, John
15125 Mulholland Dr.
Los Angeles, CA 90077
Actor V: 06/17/92

Vestron Pictures
2121 Ave. of the Stars #600
Los Angeles, CA 90067
Production Company V: 03/17/92

Vetri, Victoria
P.O. Box 69793
Los Angeles, CA 90069
Actress V: 06/24/92

13111 Ventura Blvd. #204
Los Angeles, CA
Forwarded V: 06/16/92

Viacom Productions
100 Universal City Plaza Bl.69
Universal City, CA 91608
Network HQ V: 03/10/92

Vickers, Yvette
P.O. Box 664
Pinon Hills, CA 92372
Actress V: 03/26/93

c/o Gavin Kern
780 Hollywood Blvd.
Los Angeles, CA 90028
Alternate V: 03/09/93

Vidal, Gore
2562 Outpost Dr.
Los Angeles, CA 90068
Humorist V: 03/23/92

Vidmark Entertainment
2901 Ocean Park Blvd. #123
Santa Monica, CA 90405
Distributor V: 03/17/92

Vigoda, Abe
1215 Beverly View Dr.
Beverly Hills, CA 90210
Actor V: 04/19/92

Villard, Tom
1999 Ave. of the Stars #2850
Los Angeles, CA 90067
Actor V: 01/03/93

Villechaize, Herve
P.O. Box 1305
Burbank, CA 91507
Actor V: 03/11/92

Villiers, James
Paramount House
162 Wardour St
London W1V 3AT, England
Actor V: 03/17/93

Vilsmaier, Joseph
Franz-Pruller-Str. 12
D-(W) 8000 Munchen 80
Germany
Director V: 02/01/93

Vincent, Jan Michael
P.O. Box 7000-690
Redondo Beach, CA 90277
 Actor V: 03/26/93

P.O. Box 4475
N. Hollywood, CA 91607
 Forwarded V: 01/14/92

P.O. Box 4399
N. Hollywood, CA 91607
 L.R.U. V: 01/02/92

Vincz, Melanie
520 2nd St.
Manhattan Beach, CA 90266-6515
 Actress V: 03/24/92

Viner, Michael
12711 Ventura Blvd. #250
Studio City, CA 91604
 Screenwriter V: 01/16/93

Vinton, Bobby
1905 Cold Canyon Rd.
Calabasas, CA 91302
 Singer V: 01/27/93

P.O. Box 906
Malibu, CA 90265
 Alternate V: 01/05/92

Vinton, Wil
1400 N.W. 22nd Ave.
Portland, OR 97210
 Claymation Creator V: 04/22/92

Viper/Vixen
c/o Bearly Decent Ent.
8231 Delongpre Ave. #1
W. Hollywood, CA 90046-3729
 Actress V: 05/18/92

Viscardi, John
c/o ABC-TV/One Life to Live
New York, NY 10023-6298
 Actor V: 06/21/92

Visitor, Nana
10390 Santa Monica Blvd. #300
Los Angeles, CA 90025
 Actress V: 02/23/93

c/o Star Trek-DS9
5555 Melrose Ave.
Hollywood, CA 90036
 Alternate V: 02/23/93

Visser, Lesley
c/o CBS-TV Sports Dept.
51 W. 52nd St.
New York, NY 10019
 Commentator V: 01/25/93

Vista Films
8439 Sunset Blvd. #200
Los Angeles, CA 90069
 Production Company V: 03/17/92

Vitti, Monica
Via F.38, Siacci
Rome 00197, Italy
 Actress V: 02/28/92

Voight, Jon
13340 Galewood Dr.
Sherman Oaks, CA 91423
 Actor V: 03/17/93

620 Vollambrosa
Pasadena, CA 91107
 L.R.U. V: 03/21/92

Voltz, Nedra
615 Tulare Way
Upland, CA 91786
 Actress V: 06/17/92

Von Oy, Jenna
c/o Witt/Thomas
"Blossom"
846 N. Cahuenga Blvd. Bldg.K
Hollywood, CA 90038
 Actress V: 01/17/92

c/o Blossom
500 S. Buena Vista St.
Burbank, CA 91521
 Alternate V: 11/11/92

Von Sydow, Max
Strandvegen B
114-56 Stockholm, Sweden
 Actor V: 11/22/92

Voss, James S.
c/o NASA
LBJ Space Center
Houston, TX 77058
 Astronaut V: 01/31/92

Voss, Janice E.
c/o NASA LBJ Space Center
Houston, TX 77058
 Astronaut V: 03/03/93

Vuono, Carl
Department of the Army
Office of the Chief of Staff
Washington, DC 20310
Soldier V: 07/14/92

W

WALTER AND EMILY
Witt, Thomas, Harris Prod.
1438 N. Gower
Bldg. 42, 3rd Fl.
Hollywood, CA 90038
Production Company V: 03/26/93

WHAT HAPPENED?
Hearst Entertainment
c/o Valencia Studios
26030-100 Ave. Crocker
Valencia, CA 91355
Production Company V: 03/14/93

WINGS
Grub St. Prod.
5555 Melrose Ave.
Wilder Bldg., Room 101
Hollywood, CA 90038
Production Company V: 03/26/93

WONDER YEARS
c/o New World TV
"The Wonder Years"
1440 S. Sepulveda Blvd.
Los Angeles, CA 90025
Production Company V: 12/11/90

Waalkes, Otto
c/o Russl Musikverlag
Papenhuderstr. 61
D-(W) 2000 Hamburg 76, Germany
Actor V: 01/17/93

Waddill, Carla
c/o Dallas Cowboys
One Cowboys Parkway
Irving, TX 75063-4945
Cheerleader V: 08/08/92

Wadkins, Bobby
P.O. Box 673
Richmond, VA 23206
Golf V: 09/02/92

Waggoner, Lyle
4450 Balboa Ave.
Encino, CA 91316
Actor V: 06/25/92

Wagner, Fred
c/o King Features
216 East 45th St.
New York, NY 10017
Cartoonist V: 04/24/92

Wagner, Jack
c/o General Hosp./ABC Inc.
4151 Prospect Ave.
Hollywood, CA 90027
Actor V: 03/01/92

1750 N. Beverly Dr.
Beverly Hills, CA 90210
Alternate V: 06/15/92

c/o General Hospital
1438 N. Gower
Hollywood, CA 90028
Alternate V: 07/31/92

Wagner, Jane
P.O Box 27700
Los Angeles, CA 90027
Writer V: 07/14/92

Wagner, Kate
1500 Old Oak Rd.
Los Angeles, CA 90049
Actress V: 07/14/92

Wagner, Lindsay
P.O. Box 188
Pacific Palisades, CA 90272
Actress V: 03/26/93

P.O. Box 5002
Sherman Oaks, CA 91403
Alternate V: 11/11/92

c/o ICM
8942 Wilshire Blvd.
Beverly Hills, CA 90211
Alternate V: 03/30/93

Wagner, Robert
1500 Old Oak Rd.
Los Angeles, CA 90077
Actor V: 06/17/92

151 El Camino
Beverly Hills, CA 90212
Alternate V: 01/16/93

Wahl, Ken
c/o Stephen J. Cannell Prod.
7083 Hollywood Blvd.
Hollywood, CA 90028
Actor V: 05/15/92

Wahl, Ken, contd
6622 Portshead Dr.
Malibu, CA 90265
 Alternate V: 01/14/92

c/o Terry Newton
1950 Sawtelle Blvd., Ste. 250
Los Angeles, CA 90025
 Alternate V: 04/22/92

Wain, Bea
9955 Durant Dr. Ste.305
Beverly Hills, CA 90212
 Actress V: 07/14/92

Wain Agency
1418 N. Highland Ave. Ste.102
Los Angeles, CA 90028
 Talent Agency V: 03/02/93

Waits, Tom
P.O. Box 498
Valley Ford, CA 94972
 Singer V: 01/06/93

Walden, Robert
1450 Arroyo View Dr.
Pasadena, CA 91103
 Actor V: 06/17/92

Waldheim, Kurt
Presseabteilung der Osterrich
Hofburg, Bellariator, A-1014
Wien, Austria
 Diplomat V: 03/16/92

Waldhorn, Gary
c/o London Mgmt.
235-241 Regent St.
London W1A 2JT, England
 Actor V: 03/17/92

Walken, Christopher
142 Cedar Rd.
Wilton, CT 06897
 Actor V: 02/01/92

Walker, Bree
c/o KCBS-TV
6121 Sunset Blvd.
Los Angeles, CA 90028
 Personality V: 11/11/92

Walker, Chris
c/o Agency
388 Oxford St.
London W1, England
 Actor V: 02/13/92

Walker, Clint
10113 Joerschke Dr. #202
Grass Valley, CA 95945
 Actor V: 01/11/92

Walker, David M.
NASA/LBJ Space Center
Houston, TX 77058
 Astronaut V: 03/03/93

Walker, Mort
61 Studio Ct.
Stamford, CT 06903
 Cartoonist V: 03/04/92

241 E. 45th St.
New York, NY 10017
 Alternate V: 02/12/92

Walker, Nancy
3702 Eureka Dr.
Studio City, CA 91604
 Actress V: 06/17/92

Walker, Robert, Jr.
20828 Pacific Caost Hwy.
Malibu, CA 90265
 Actor V: 03/26/93

Walker, Tonja
4138 Augusta Dr.
Crown Point, IN 46307
 Actress V: 03/18/92

c/o General Hosp./ABC Inc.
4151 Prospect Ave.
Hollywood, CA 90027
 Alternate V: 02/01/92

c/o 'One Life to Live'
77 W. 66th St.
New York, NY 10023
 Alternate V: 11/11/92

Wallace, David
c/o Gen. Hosp./ABC TV
4151 Prospect Ave.
Hollywood, CA 90027
 Actor V: 03/01/92

Wallace, Dee
23035 Cumorah Crest Dr.
Woodland Hills, CA 91364
 Actress V: 03/14/92

Wallace, George
141 El Camino Dr. #7205
Malibu, CA 90265
 Comedian V: 02/02/93

Wallace, Kenny
c/o Sabco Racing
6013 Victory Ln.
Harrisburg, NC 28075
NASCAR Driver V: 03/02/92

Wallace, Rusty
c/o Penske Racing
6 Knob Hill Rd.
Mooreville, NC 28115
NASCAR Driver V: 03/02/92

Wallach, Eli
90 Riverside Dr.
New York, NY 10024
Actor V: 02/24/92

Walley, Debra
1923 Olivera Dr.
Agoura, CA 91301
Actress V: 05/17/92

31 1/2 24th Ave.
Venice, CA 90291-4301
L.R.U. V: 06/25/92

Walsh, Kay
4 Ovington Gardens
London SW3 1L5, England
Actress V: 11/22/92

Walston, Ray
423 S. Rexford Dr.
Beverly Hills, CA 90212
Actor V: 04/24/92

Walter, Jessica
10530 Strathmore Dr.
Los Angeles, CA 90024
Actress V: 03/04/92

c/o Dinosaurs
500 S. Buena Vista St.
Burbank, CA 91521
Forwarded V: 11/11/92

Walter, Tracey
257 N. Rexford Dr.
Beverly Hills, CA 90210
Actor V: 01/04/92

c/o S.T.E.
9301 Wilshire Blvd.
Beverly Hills, CA 90210
Alternate V: 03/10/92

Walters, Barbara
2029 Century Pk.E., #940
Los Angeles, CA 90067
Interviewer V: 02/01/92

Walters, Barbara, contd
2020 Ave. of the Stars
Century City, CA 90067
Alternate V: 02/01/92

c/o ABC News
20/20
1926 Broadway
New York, NY 10023
Alternate V: 12/07/92

33 W. 60th St.
New York, NY 10023
Forwarded V: 02/01/92

Walters, Bunny
10560 Wilshire Blvd. #403
Los Angeles, CA 90024
Actress V: 07/31/92

Walters, Laurie
4450 Kensington Rd. #5
Los Angeles, CA 90066
Actress V: 07/14/92

Walton, Jill
c/o Young and the Restless
7800 Beverly Blvd.
Beverly Hills, CA 90036
Actress V: 06/15/92

Waltrip, Darrell
c/o Darwal Inc.
6780 Hudsdeth Rd.
Harrisburg, NC 28705
NASCAR Driver V: 03/02/92

P.O. Box 855
Franklin, TN 37065
Alternate V: 03/01/92

Waltrip, Michael
47 Rolling Hills Rd.
Mooresville, NC 28115
NASCAR Driver V: 03/02/92

Walz, Carl E.
NASA/LBJ Space Center
Houston, TX 77058
Astronaut V: 03/03/93

Wanamaker, Sam
354 N. Croft
Beverly Hills, CA 90211
Actor V: 01/22/92

Wane, Taylor
P.O. Box 572229
Tarzana, CA 91357-2229
Adult Films V: 01/24/93

Wang, Dr. Taylor
c/o Jet Prop. Lab/Cal-Tech
4800 Oak Grove Dr.
Pasadena, CA 91109
Astronaut V: 01/09/92

Wapner, Judge Joseph A.
c/o The Peoples Court
1717 N. Highland Ave. 10th Fl.
Hollywood, CA 90028
TV Personality V: 10/15/92

16616 Park Lane Pl.
Los Angeles, CA 90049
Alternate V: 05/04/92

Ward, Burt
1559 Pacific Coast Hwy. #815
Hermosa Beach, CA 90254
Actor V: 03/26/93

8484 Wilshire Blvd., Ste.550
Beverly Hills, CA 90211
L.R.U. V: 01/05/92

Ward, Sela
2102 Century Park Lane #202
Los Angeles, CA 90067
Actress V: 02/09/93

Ward, Simon
c/o Agency
388 Oxford St.
London W1, England
Actor V: 05/29/92

Warden, Jack
23604 Malibu Colony Dr.
Malibu, CA 90265
Actor V: 03/03/92

Warden, Veronica
P.O. Box 68
Sierra Madre, CA 91024
Actress V: 05/18/92

Warfield, Marsha
P.O. Box 691713
Los Angeles, CA 90069
Actress V: 07/14/92

Marsha Warfield Show
12711 Ventura Blvd. Ste.430
Studio City, CA 91604
Alternate V: 01/17/92

Warner/Night Court
4000 Warner Blvd., #12A
Burbank, CA 91521
Forwarded V: 01/17/92

Waring, George
c/o Joseph & Wagg
Studio 1, Tunstall Rd.
London SW9 8BN, England
Actor V: 03/17/92

Warlock, Billy
6822 Lasaine Ave.
Van Nuys, CA 91406
Actor V: 03/20/92

Warner, David
c/o Leading Artists
68 Saint James St.
London SW1A 1LE, England
Actor V: 02/13/92

Warner, Malcolm-Jamaal
1301 The Colony
Heartsdale, NY 10530-1725
Actor V: 03/20/92

Warner Brothers Film
15821 Ventura Blvd. #685
Encino, CA 91436
Distributor V: 03/17/92

Warner Brothers TV
4000 Warner Blvd. 1st Fl.
Burbank, CA 91522
Distributor V: 03/17/92

Warner Hollywood Studios
1041 N. Formosa Ave.
Los Angeles, CA 90046
Production Company V: 03/17/92

Warren, Jennifer
1675 Old Oak Rd.
Los Angeles, CA 90049
Actress V: 08/03/92

Warren, Lesley Ann
8730 Sunset Blvd. PH-W
Los Angeles, CA 90069
Actress V: 02/28/92

Warren, Michael
c/o Bressler
15760 Ventura Blvd.
Encino, CA 91436
Actor V: 03/17/92

Warrick, Ruth
903 Park Ave.
New York, NY 10021
Actress V: 07/14/92

Warwick, James
c/o Burnett
Grafton House, Ste. 42-43
2-3 Golden Square
London W1R 3AD, England
Actor V: 03/17/92

Warwick, Richard
388-396 Oxford St.
London W1, England
Actor V: 03/20/93

Washington, Denzel
c/o Wm. Morris
151 El Camino Dr.
Beverly Hills, CA 90212
Actor V: 03/17/92

4701 Sancola Ave.
N. Hollywood, CA 91602
Actor V: 03/26/93

c/o Answer Fan
1112 First St. #134
Coronado, CA 92118
Alternate V: 03/17/92

Washington Redskins
P.O. Box 17247
Dulles Int'l Airport
Washington, DC 20041
Team Offices V: 05/15/92

Wass, Ted
c/o Witt/Thomas
"Blossom"
846 N. Cahuenga Blvd. Bldg.K
Hollywood, CA 90038
Actor V: 01/17/92

c/o Blossom
500 S. Buena Vista St.
Burbank, CA 91521
Actor V: 11/11/92

Waterman, Dennis
388 Oxford St.
London W1, England
Actor V: 02/18/92

Waterson, Bill
Universal Press Synd.
4900 Main St.
Kansas City, MO 64112
Cartoonist V: 11/11/92

Wathan, John
P.O. Box 419969
Kansas City, MO 64141
Baseball Manager V: 01/16/93

Watkins, Dana
c/o Dallas Cowboys
One Cowboys Parkway
Irving, TX 75063-4945
Cheerleader V: 08/08/92

Watson, Doug
c/o Another World NBC-TV
30 Rockefeller Plaza
New York, NY 10112
Actor V: 01/12/92

Watson, Tom
Commerce Tower #1313
911 Main
Kansas City, MO 64105
Golf V: 09/02/92

Waugh Talent Agency
4731 Laurel Canyon Blvd. Ste.5
N. Hollywood, CA 91607
Talent Agency V: 03/15/93

Wayans, Kim
c/o A Different World
P.O.Box 1-701
14755 Ventura Bl
Sherman Oaks, CA 91403
Actress V: 07/02/92

Wayne, David
868 Napoli Dr.
Pacific Palisades, CA 90272
Actor V: 11/11/92

Wayne, Fredd
11846 Ventura Blvd. #100
Studio City, CA 91604
Writer V: 01/16/93

Wayne, Michael
9570 Wilshire Blvd. #400
Beverly Hills, CA 90212
Actor V: 01/03/93

Wayne, Patrick
10502 Whipple St.
N. Hollywood, CA 91602
Actor V: 03/01/92

Weather Channel
2600 Cumberland Parkway
Atlanta, GA 30339
Production Company V: 11/11/92

Weathers, Carl
7083 Hollywood Blvd.
Los Angeles, CA 90028
Actor V: 08/15/92

Weathers, Dave
Chiefs/MacArthur Stadium
Syracuse, NY 13208
Baseball V: 02/03/92

Weaver, Dennis
P.O. Box 983
Malibu, CA 90265
Actor V: 12/02/92

25006 Malibu Rd.
Malibu, CA 90265
Alternate V: 02/17/92

P.O. Box 983
Malibu, CA 90265
Alternate V: 04/16/92

Weaver, Patty
c/o Young & Restless
7800 Beverly Blvd.
Beverly Hills, CA 90036
Actress V: 06/15/92

5009 Hayvenhurst Dr.
Encino, CA 91316
Actress V: 07/14/92

Weaver, Sigourney
200 W. 57th St. #1306
New York, NY 10019-3211
Actress V: 08/02/92

12 W. 72nd St.
New York, NY 10023
Alternate V: 11/11/92

Webb, Richard
13330 Chandler Blvd.
Van Nuys, CA 91401
Actor V: 11/22/92

Webb Enterprises
7500 Devista Dr.
Los Angeles, CA 90046
Talent Agency V: 03/13/93

Weber, Steven
c/o Grub Street Prod.
Wings
5555 Melrose Ave./Wilder RM101
Hollywood, CA 90038
Actor V: 01/07/92

Weber Jr., Bob
c/o King Features
216 East 45th St.
New York, NY 10017
Cartoonist V: 03/07/92

Weber Sr., Don
c/o King Features
216 East 45th St.
New York, NY 10017
Cartoonist V: 04/01/92

Wedgeworth, Ann
822 S. Robertson Blvd. #200
Los Angeles, CA 90035
Actress V: 03/26/93

2121 Ave. of the Stars #410
Los Angeles, CA 90067
L.R.U. V: 02/02/92

Weems, Pricilla
c/o Columbia/Mozark
"Designing Women"
Columbia Plz, Pro.Bl.8,#147
Burbank, CA 91505
Actress V: 02/03/93

Weibring, D.A.
1316 Garden Grove Ct.
Plano, TX 75075
Golf V: 09/02/92

Weigel, Teri
P.O. Box 1232
Pacific Palisades, CA 90272
Adult Films V: 01/24/93

Weiner, Scott
c/o Miller-Boyett
Family Man
9336 W. Washington Blvd.
Culver City, CA 90232
Actor V: 05/15/92

Weintraub, Jerry
11111 Santa Monica Blvd.
Los Angeles, CA 90038
Producer V: 01/16/93

Weiskopf, Tom
5412 E. Morrison Ln.
Paradise Valley, AZ 85253
Golf V: 01/06/92

Weist, Diane
320 Central Park W.
New York, NY 10025
Actress V: 07/14/92

Weitz, Bruce
3061 Lake Hollywood Dr.
Los Angeles, CA 90068
Actor V: 11/26/92

Weitz, Paul J.
c/o NASA LBJ Space Center
Houston, TX 77058
Astronaut V: 03/03/93

Welch, Raquel
P.O. Box 270707
San Diego, CA 92198
Actress V: 06/25/92

134 Duane St. #400
New York, NY 10013
Alternate V: 03/26/93

c/o J.H.E.
16536 Gabarda Rd.
San Diego, CA 92128
Alternate V: 04/05/93

c/o JHE
P.O. Box 26472
Prescott Valley, AZ 86312
Forwarded V: 05/01/92

Weld, Tuesday
300 Central Park W., Ste.14E
New York, NY 10019
Actress V: 12/01/92

Weldon, Joan
67 E. 78th St.
New York, NY 10021
Actress V: 11/11/92

Weller, Peter
853 7th Ave. #9A
New York, NY 10019
Actor V: 04/18/92

Wells, Clyde
c/o King Features
216 East 45th St.
New York, NY 10017
Cartoonist V: 03/15/92

Wells, Dawn
11684 Ventura Blvd. #364
Studio City, CA 91604
Actress V: 06/01/92

P.O. 291817
Los Angeles, CA 90029
Alternate V: 03/26/93

Wells, Kitty
264 Old Hickory Blvd.
Madison, TN 37115
Singer V: 05/25/92

Wells, Kitty, contd
1302 Saunders Ave.
Nashville, TN 37115
Forwarded V: 01/27/92

Wells, Tori
22647 Ventura Blvd. #378
Woodland Hills, CA 91364
Adult Films V: 01/24/93

Wences, Senor
204 W. 55th St., #701
New York, NY 10019
Ventriloquist V: 04/21/92

c/o Hotel Andalucia Plaza
Apdo./P.O. Box 21
Nueva Andalucia, Marbella
Costa Del Sol, Spain
Alternate V: 04/16/93

Wenders, Wim
Potsdamerstr. 199
D-(W) 1000 Berlin 30, Germany
Director V: 01/17/93

Wendlinger, Karl
Salurner Str. 31
A-6330 Kufstein
Austria
Race Driver V: 02/01/93

Wendt, George
c/o Paramount
Cheers
5555 Melrose Ave./Ball RM105
Hollywood, CA 90038
Actor V: 01/07/92

9200 Sunset Blvd. Ste. 428
Los Angeles, CA 90069
Alternate V: 01/21/92

Wesley, Kassie
c/o CBS-TV/Guiding Light
51 W. 52nd St.
New York, NY 10019
Actress V: 01/17/92

221 W. 26th St.
New York, NY 10001
Alternate V: 01/17/92

West, Adam
Box 3446
Ketchum, ID 83340-3440
Actor V: 01/29/92

612 El Cerco
Pacific Palisades, CA 90272
L.R.U. V: 04/14/92

West, Jerry
P.O. Box 10
Inglewood, CA 90306
 Lakers Manager V: 02/03/92

3900 W. Manchest Blvd.
Inglewood, CA 90305
 Alternate V: 12/10/92

Westbrook, Danniella
c/o Young Mgmt.
Rossmore Rd.
London NWI 6NJ, England
 Actress V: 06/26/92

Western Visuals
15745 Stagg St.
Van Nuys, CA 91406
 Reader Services V: 12/15/92

Westheimer, Ruth
900 W. 190th St.
New York, NY 10025
 Sex Therapist V: 11/26/92

Westmoreland, James
8019 1/2 W. Norton Ave.
Los Angeles, CA 90046
 Actor V: 11/14/92

Wetherbee, James D.
NASA/LBJ Space Center
Houston, TX 77058
 Astronaut V: 01/31/92

Wethers, Googie
1740 Puttwater Rd.
Bay View, Australia NSW 2104
 Actress V: 03/15/93

Wettig, Patricia
11850 Chaparal St.
Los Angeles, CA 90049
 Actress V: 11/26/92

Whaley-Kilmer, Joanne
P.O. Box 362
Tesuque, NM 87574-0362
 Actress V: 11/26/92

Whalum, Kirk
P.O. Box 61116
Houston, TX 77208
 Musician V: 12/12/92

Wheaton, Wil
c/o Star Trek-TNG Paramount
5555 Melrose Ave.
Hollywood, CA 90038
 Actor V: 03/04/92

Wheaton, Wil, contd
c/o Wilpower
Box 12567
La Crescenta, CA 91214
 Alternate V: 04/22/92

Wheel of Fortune
c/o Merv Griffin Enterprises
Beverly Hilton Hotel
9860 Wilshire Blvd.
Beverly Hills, CA 90210
 Production Company V: 06/16/92

Wheeler, H.A. "Humpy"
Charlotte Motor Speedway
P.O. Box 600
Concord, NC 28026-0600
 NASCAR Driver V: 03/02/92

Whelchel, Lisa
P.O. Box 469
Mt. Pleasant, TX 75445
 Actress V: 04/18/92

11906 Shoshone Ave.
Granada Hills, CA 91344
 Actress V: 11/26/92

1623 Greenfield #2
Los Angeles, CA 90025
 L.R.U. V: 03/03/93

Whitaker, Christine
200 N. Robertson Blvd. #219
Beverly Hills, CA 90211
 Actress V: 03/19/92

Whitaker Agency
12725 Ventura Blvd. Ste.F
Studio City, CA 91604
 Talent Agency V: 03/13/93

Whitcomb, Bob
c/o Whitcomb Racing
9201 Garrison Rd.
Charlotte, NC 28208
 NASCAR Owner V: 03/02/92

White, Betty
P.O. Box 3713
Granada Hills, CA 91344-0713
 Actress V: 07/14/92

506 N. Carmelita Ave.
Los Angeles, CA 90049
 Alternate V: 03/01/92

c/o Golden Palace
846 N. Cahuenga Blvd. Bldg.G
Hollywood, CA 90038
 Alternate V: 01/17/92

White, Jack
Regerstr. 18-20
D-(W) 1000 Berlin 19
Germany
Composer V: 01/19/93

White, Jaleel
c/o Lorimar
Family Matters
3970 Overland Ave.
Culver City, CA 90230
Actor V: 12/15/92

White, Vanna
3400 Riverside Dr.
Burbank, CA 91505
Model V: 01/16/93

8306 Wilshire Blvd. #75
Beverly Hills, CA 90211
Alternate V: 10/10/92

2600 Larmar Rd.
Los Angeles, CA 90068
Forwarded V: 11/10/92

Whitelaw, Billie
c/o Joy Jameson Ltd.
7 West Eaton Place Mews
London SW1, England
Actress V: 04/03/92

c/o Duncan Heath
162 Wardour St.
London W1, England
Alternate V: 02/28/92

Whiting, Barbara
c/o Smith
1085 Waddington St.
Birmingham, MI 48009
Actress V: 11/26/92

Whiting, Margaret
41 W. 58th St. Ste.5A
New York, NY 10019
Actress V: 03/24/92

Whitman, Slim
1300 Division St. #103
Nashville, TN 37203
Singer V: 01/12/92

Whitman, Stuart
c/o PM Entertainment
16780 Schoenborn St.
Sepulveda, CA 91343
Actor V: 03/14/93

Whitman, Stuart, contd
721 N. La Brea Ave.
Los Angeles, CA 90038
L.R.U. V: 12/15/92

Whitmore, James
c/o Paramount Film Studios
5555 Melrose Ave.
Los Angeles, CA 90038
Actor V: 12/17/92

4990 Puesta del Sol
Malibu, CA 90265
Actor V: 03/20/92

Whitney, Grace Lee
c/o Page Lewis
2611 Silverside Rd.
Wilmington, DE 19810
Actress V: 02/13/92

P.O. Box 1786
Burbank, CA 91507
Alternate V: 02/03/92

Whoppers, Wendy
8605 Allisonville Rd. #282
Indianapolis, IN 46250
Adult Films V: 01/24/93

Wicker, Brooke
Dallas Cowboys
One Cowboys Parkway
Irving, TX 75063-4945
Cheerleader V: 08/08/92

Wickes, Mary
2160 Century Park E. #503
Los Angeles, CA 90067
Actress V: 06/17/92

Wickham Jr., John A.
AFCEA 4400 Fair Lakes Ct.
Fairfax, VA 22033-3899
Soldier V: 04/07/92

Widmark, Richard
c/o ICM
8942 Wilshire Blvd.
Beverly Hills, CA 90211
Actor V: 06/02/92

Wight, James A.
c/o James Herriot
23 Kirkgate, Thirsk
North Yorkshire, England
Author V: 06/09/92

Wight, James A., contd
c/o James Herriot
Thirlby, Thirsk
North Yorkshire, England
Forwarded V: 06/09/92

Wilby, James
Marmont Mgmt/Langham House
302/308 Regent St.
London W1R 5AL, England
Actor V: 03/02/92

Wilcox, Paula
c/o Burnet
Grafton House, Ste. 42-43
2-3 Golden Square
London W1R 3AD, England
Actress V: 03/20/92

Wilcutt, Terrence W.
c/o NASA LBJ Space Center
Houston, TX 77058
Astronaut V: 03/03/93

Wilder, Billy
10375 Wilshire Blvd.
Los Angeles, CA 90024
Director V: 06/17/92

Wilder, Don
c/o King Features
216 East 45th St.
New York, NY 10017
Cartoonist V: 04/01/92

Wilder, Gene
9350 Wilshire Blvd. #400
Beverly Hills, CA 90212
Actor V: 09/06/92

Wilder, Yvonne
5450 Topeka Dr.
Tarzana, CA 91356
Actress V: 11/26/92

Wilding, Michael
c/o Guiding Light CBS-TV
51 W. 52nd St.
New York, NY 10019
Actor V: 01/12/92

Wilhelmina Artists Reps.
8383 Wishire Blvd. #650
Beverly Hills, CA 90211
Talent Agency V: 02/14/93

Wilke, Robert J.
12550 Otsego St.
N. Hollywood, CA 91607
Actor V: 04/01/92

Wilkins, Dominique
c/o Atlanta Hawks
100 Techwood Dr. NW
Atlanta, GA 30303
Basketball V: 04/05/93

Wilkinson, June
3653 Fairesta St.
La Crescenta, CA 91214
Actress V: 03/25/92

5154 Tyrone Ave.
Sherman Oaks, CA 91423
Forwarded V: 03/01/92

Willaims, Treat
215 W. 78th St. #10A
New York, NY 10024
Actor V: 03/26/93

William Morris Agency
151 El Camino
Beverly Hills, CA 90212
Talent Agency V: 01/24/93

Williams, Alice
c/o Dallas Cowboys
One Cowboys Parkway
Irving, TX 75063-4945
Cheerleader V: 08/08/92

Williams, Amir
c/o Carsey-Warner Co.
A Different World
P.O.Box 1-701
14755 Ventura Bl
Sherman Oaks, CA 91403
Actor V: 07/01/92

Williams, Andy
c/o Moon River Theatre
2500 W. Highway 76
Branson, MO 65616
Singer V: 12/12/92

816 N. La Cienega Blvd.
Los Angeles, CA 90069
Alternate V: 01/21/92

Williams, Barbara
15760 Ventura Blvd. #1730
Encino, CA 91436
Actress V: 01/12/92

Williams, Billy Dee
1240 Loma Vista Dr.
Beverly Hills, CA 90210
Actor V: 06/04/92

Williams, Billy Dee, contd
9200 Sunset Blvd. Ste.530
Los Angeles, CA 90069
Alternate V: 06/01/92

605 N. Oakhurst Dr.
Beverly Hills, CA 90210
Forwarded V: 07/02/92

Williams, Cara
146 S. Peck Dr.
Beverly Hills, CA 90212
Actress V: 03/20/92

Williams, Cindy
c/o Sterling/Winters
1900 Ave. of Stars, Ste.739
Los Angeles, CA 90067
Actress V: 01/02/92

709 19 St.
Santa Monica, CA 90402-3025
Alternate V: 05/18/92

500 South Buena Vista St.
Burbank, CA 91521
Forwarded V: 11/22/92

7023 Birdview Ave.
Malibu, CA 92065
Forwarded V: 11/22/92

Williams, Donald E.
c/o NASA LBJ Space Center
Houston, TX 77058
Astronaut V: 03/03/93

Williams, Edy
1638 Bluejay Way
Los Angeles, CA 90069
Celebrity V: 03/02/93

1717 Sunset Plaza Dr.
Los Angeles, CA 90069
L.R.U. V: 06/01/92

Williams, Emlyn
123 Doverhouse St.
London SW3, England
Actor V: 03/01/92

Williams, Esther
9377 Readcrest
Beverly Hills, CA 90210
Actress V: 03/21/92

Williams, Greg
1680 Vine St. Ste. 604
Hollywood, CA 90028
Puppeteer V: 03/17/92

Williams, Hershal W.
Rt.1, Box 38-C
Ona, WV 25545
Medal of Honor V: 03/01/92

Williams, Jo Beth
3529 Beverly Glenn Blvd.
Sherman Oaks, CA 91423
Actress V: 04/16/92

c/o E. Ralston
35 Heather Way
Ventura, CA 93004
L.R.U. V: 03/03/93

Williams, John
1560 E. Valley
Santa Barbara, CA 93108
Composer V: 05/03/92

c/o Boston Pops Orch.
301 Massachusettes Ave.
Boston, MA 02115
Alternate V: 02/12/92

Williams, K.C.
P.O. Box 57556
Sherman Oaks, CA 91413-7556
Adult Films V: 01/24/93

Williams, Kellie Shanygne
c/o Lorimar
Family Matters
3970 Overland Ave.
Culver City, CA 90230
Actor V: 12/15/92

Williams, Mary Alice
30 Rockefeller Plaza
New York, NY 10020
Commentator V: 06/17/92

Williams, Mason
3097 Floral Hill Rd.
Eugene, OR 97403
Musician V: 08/09/92

Williams, Robin
1100 Wall Rd.
Napa, CA 94550
Actor V: 04/13/92

1108 Lincoln Way
San Francisco, CA 94122
Alternate V: 02/23/93

4426 19th Ave.
San Francisco, CA 94152
Forwarded V: 03/18/92

Williams, Tonya Lee
c/o Young and the Restless
7800 Beverly Blvd.
Beverly Hills, CA 90036
Actress V: 06/15/92

Williams, Treat
215 W. 78th St., Ste.10-A
New York, NY 10024
Actor V: 01/21/93

Williams, Van
1630 Ocean Park Blvd.
Santa Monica, CA 90405
Actor V: 03/26/93

Williams, Vanessa
Rt. 100
Millwood, NY 10546
Actress V: 03/16/93

Williams Jr., Hank
P.O. Box 850
Paris, TN 38242
Singer V: 12/11/92

Williamson, Nicol
388 Oxford St.
London W1, England
Actor V: 02/02/92

Willis, Bruce
c/o William Morris Agency
151 El Camino Dr.
Beverly Hills, CA 90210
Actor V: 12/17/92

1122 S. Robertson Blvd.
Los Angeles, CA 90035
Alternate V: 02/25/92

Wilson, Demond
Church of God in Christ
Ft. Washington, MD 20022
Actor V: 03/20/92

Wilson, Dorothy
330 W. Hwy. 246, Space 129
Buellton, CA 93427
Actress V: 11/26/92

Wilson, Elizabeth
9301 Wilshire Blvd. #312
Beverly Hills, CA 90210
Actress V: 01/20/92

Wilson, Flip
21970 Pacific Coast Hwy.
Malibu, CA 90265
Actor V: 01/21/92

Wilson, Frank
NC Motor Speedway
P.O. Box 500
Rockingham, NC 28379
NASCAR Official V: 03/02/92

Wilson, Gahan
c/o Michelle Urry, Cartoon Ed.
747 Third Ave.
New York, NY 10017
Cartoonist V: 05/23/92

919 Michigan Ave.
Chicago, IL 60611
Forwarded V: 08/23/92

Wilson, John
c/o Sabco Racing
5901 Orr Rd.
Charlotte, NC 28213
NASCAR Crew V: 03/26/93

Wilson, Pete
State Capitol Bldg.
Sacramento, CA 95814
Politician V: 01/02/92

Wilson, Rick
c/o Petty Enter.
311 Branson Mill Rd.
Randleman, NC 27317
NASCAR Driver V: 03/02/92

Wilson, Woody
c/o King Features
216 E. 45th St.
New York, NY 10017
Cartoonist V: 03/11/93

Wilson Agency
5410 Wilshire Blvd. Ste.227
Los Angeles, CA 90036
Talent Agency V: 02/18/93

Wincott, Jeff
3880 Fredonia Dr. #8
Los Angeles, CA 90068
Actor V: 03/20/92

Windom, William
6535 Langdon Ave.
Van Nuys, CA 91406
Actor V: 03/14/92

c/o Universal TV
"Murder She Wrote"
100 Universal Plz., Bl.507
Universal City, CA 91608
Alternate V: 02/03/93

Windsor, Barbara
c/o Peter Rogers Prod.
Pinefood Film Studio
Iver Heath
Bucks., SLO 0NH, England
Actress V: 03/15/93

Windsor, Marie
9501 Cherokee Lane
Beverly Hills, CA 90210
Actress V: 04/07/92

Winfield, Paul
5693 Holly Oak Dr.
Los Angeles, CA 90068
Actor V: 03/26/93

10000 Santa Monica Blvd. #305
Los Angeles, CA 90067
Alternate V: 01/07/92

Winfrey, Oprah
P.O. Box 909715
Chicago, IL 60690
Celebrity V: 02/10/93

c/o Harpo Prod.
110 N. Carpenter
Chicago, IL 60607
Alternate V: 03/03/93

35 E. Wacker, Ste.1782
Chicago, IL 60601
L.R.U. V: 01/02/92

Winger, Debra
P.O. Box 4306
Malibu, CA 90265
Actress V: 09/27/92

P.O. Box 1368
Pacific Palisades, CA 90272
L.R.U. V: 10/10/92

Wingert, Dick
c/o King Features
216 East 45th St.
New York, NY 10017
Cartoonist V: 05/01/92

Winkler, Henry
5555 Melrose Ave.
Hollywood, CA 90038-3197
Production Company V: 03/17/92

Winningham, Mare
9560 Topanga Canyon Blvd.
Suite 103
Chatsworth, CA 91311
Actress V: 11/14/92

Winningham, Mare, contd
12256 La Maida St.
N. Hollywood, CA 91607
L.R.U. V: 10/10/92

Winston, George
c/o Windham Hill Rec.
P.O. Box 9388
Stanford, CA 94309
Musician V: 02/01/92

Winter, Alex
9350 Wilshire Blvd #324
Beverly Hills, CA 90212
Actor V: 01/16/93

Winter, Edward
4359 Havenhurst Ave.
Encino, CA 91436
Actor V: 06/17/92

Winter, Sterling
12636 Beatrice St.
Los Angeles, CA 90066
Artists Agency V: 12/15/92

Winters, Jonathan
755 Romero Canyon Rd.
Santa Barbara, CA 93108
Actor V: 01/04/92

4310 Arcola Ave.
Toluca Lake, CA 91602
Alternate V: 06/17/92

Winters, Shelley
c/o Gladys M. Hart
1244 11th St. #A
Santa Monica, CA 90401
Actress V: 01/03/93

457 N. Oakhurst Dr.
Beverly Hills, CA 90210
Alternate V: 02/21/92

c/o Jay Julien
1501 Broadway
New York, NY 10010
Alternate V: 02/28/92

Wintersole, William
c/o Young and the Restless
7800 Beverly Blvd.
Beverly Hills, CA 90036
Actor V: 06/15/92

Wirth, Billy
8730 Sunset Blvd. #220W
Los Angeles, CA 90210
Actor V: 01/17/93

Wisdom, Norman
19 Denmark St.
London W2, England
Actor V: 02/28/92

Wise, Robert
315 S. Beverly Dr. #214
Beverly Hills, CA 90212
Film Producer V: 01/20/92

Wisenthal, Simon
Dokumentationszentrum
1010 Wien, Saltztorgasse
Austria 6/IV/5
Nazi Hunter V: 02/07/93

Wisoff, Peter J.
c/o NASA LBJ Space Center
Houston, TX 77058
Astronaut V: 03/03/93

Withers, Googie
c/o Thames TV
306-316 Euston Rd.
London NW1 3BB, England
Actor V: 03/22/92

Withers, Jane
2208 Live Oak Drive West
Los Angeles, CA 90068
Actress V: 06/17/92

Witt, Katarina
Zwechaur Str. 12
Karl Marx Stadt, Germany
Olympian V: 02/21/92

Witt\Thomas Productions
500 S. Buena Vista St.
Burbank, CA 91521
Production Company V: 03/17/92

Witt\Thomas\Harris
846 N. Cahuena Blvd.
Hollywood, CA 90038
Production Company V: 03/17/92

Witter, Karen
c/o Harry Gold
3500 W. Olive, Ste.1400
Burbank, CA 91505
Actress V: 02/01/92

c/o ABC One Life to Live
77 W. 66th St.
New York, NY 10023
Alternate V: 03/14/93

Wojciehowicz, Alex
105 Silway Dr.
Forked River, NJ 08731
Football V: 03/17/92

Wolf, David A.
c/o NASA LBJ Space Center
Houston, TX 77058
Astronaut V: 03/03/93

Wolfe, Michael
c/o Arsenio Hall
5555 Melrose Ave.
Hollywood, CA 90038
Musician V: 01/12/92

Wolfe, Tom
c/o Farrae/Strauss
19 Union Sq. W.
New York, NY 10003
Author V: 05/22/92

Wolfman Jack
P.O. Box 38
Belvedere, NC 27919
Personality V: 01/12/92

Women in Film
6464 Sunset Blvd. #660
Hollywood, CA 90028
Production Company V: 03/17/92

Women in Show Business
P.O. Box 2535
N. Hollywood, CA 91602
Production Company V: 03/17/92

Women of the M.P. Industry
11701 Texas Ave.
Los Angeles, CA 90025
Production Company V: 03/17/92

Wonder, Stevie
4616 Magnolia Blvd.
Burbank, CA 91505
Singer V: 04/01/89

Wood, Eddie
c/o McLean Marketing
9307-P Monro Rd.
Charlotte, NC 28270
NASCAR Crew V: 03/02/92

Wood, Glen
c/o McLean Marketing
9307-P Monro Rd.
Charlotte, NC 28270
NASCAR Owner V: 03/02/92

Wood, Judith
1300 1/4 N. Sycamore
Los Angeles, CA 90028
Actress V: 11/26/92

Wood, Len
c/o McLean Marketing
9307-P Monro Rd.
Charlotte, NC 28270
NASCAR Crew V: 03/02/92

Woodard, Alfre
c/o STE
9301 Wilshire Blvd. #312
Beverly Hills, CA 90210
Actress V: 01/17/93

Woods, James
760 La Cienega Blvd.
Los Angeles, CA 90069
Actor V: 11/10/89

1612 Gilcrest Dr.
Beverly Hills, CA 90210
Forwarded V: 03/14/92

Woodward, Edward
c/o Universal Television
"Over My Dead Body"
100 Univ. Plz., BL.480 Fl.3
Universal City, CA 91608
Actor V: 05/16/92

10 E. 40th St. #2700
New York, NY 10016
Alternate V: 11/26/92

c/o McCartt
10390 Santa Monica Blvd. #310
Los Angeles, CA 90025
Alternate V: 04/18/92

28 Berkeley Square
London, England
Forwarded V: 08/19/92

Woodward, Joanne
1120 Fifth Ave. #1C
New York, NY 10128-0144
Actress V: 03/30/93

477 Madison Ave.
New York, NY 10022-5800
L.R.U. V: 05/26/92

Woodward, Morgan
2111 Rockledge Rd.
Hollywood, CA 90068
Actor V: 01/15/92

Wooley, Sheb
Rt.3, Box 231
Sunset Island Trail
Gallantine, TN 37066
Comedian V: 03/20/92

Wopat, Tom
12245 Morrison St.
North Hollywood, CA 91607
Actor V: 06/17/92

Worden, Alfred M.
129 Commodore
Jupiter, FL 334777
Astronaut V: 01/04/92

c/o BF Goodrich Aerospace
5353 52nd St., S.E.
P.O. Box 873
Grand Rapids, MI 49588-0873
Alternate V: 05/18/92

c/o NASA
LBJ Space Center
Houston, TX 77058
Forwarded V: 01/19/92

World Class Sports
9171 Wilshire Blvd. #404
Beverly Hills, CA 90210
Talent Agency V: 01/14/93

Worley, Joanne
4714 Arcola Ave.
N. Hollywood, CA 91602
Actress V: 11/26/92

Woronov, Mary
5350 1/4 Beverly Blvd.
Los Angeles, CA 90004
Actress V: 11/26/92

Wray, Fay
2160 Century Park E. #1901
Los Angeles, CA 90067
Actress V: 05/18/92

2526 Taler Way
Los Angeles, CA 90036
L.R.U. V: 11/26/92

2080 Century Park E. #406
Los Angeles, CA 90067
L.R.U. V: 05/29/92

Wright, Corbina
1326 Dove Meadow Rd.
Solvang, CA 93463
Actress V: 11/26/92

Wright, Jenny
245 W. 104th St.
New York, NY 10025-4249
Actress V: 11/26/92

Wright, Michelle
1207 17th Ave. S. 3rd Fl.
Nashville, TN 37212
Singer V: 03/30/93

Wright, Robin
P.O. Box 2630
Malibu, CA 90265
Actress V: 01/16/93

Wright, Rudy
P.O. Box 19519
San Diego, CA 92119
Director V: 11/26/92

Wright, Samuel E.
500 S. Buena Vista St.
Burbank, CA 91521
Actor V: 11/11/92

Wright Talent Agency
6533 Hollywood Blvd. #201
Hollywood, CA 90028
Talent Agency V: 01/14/93

Writers & Artists Agency
924 Westwood Blvd. 9th Fl.
Los Angeles, CA 90024
Talent Agency V: 02/27/93

Writers Guild of America
9845 Beverly Blvd.
Beverly Hills, CA 90211
Guild Office V: 01/12/92

Writers Society of America
11684 Ventura Blvd. #868
Studio City CA 91604
Production Company V: 03/17/92

Wuhl, Robert
10590 Holman Ave.
Los Angeles, CA 90024
Actor V: 03/26/93

Wyatt, Jane
651 Siena Way
Los Angeles, CA 90077
Actress V: 01/11/92

Wyatt, Shannon
8949 Falling Creek Ct.
Annadale, VA 22003
Actress V: 11/11/92

Wyatt, Sharon
1801 Ave. of the Stars #1250
Los Angeles, CA 90067
Actress V: 01/16/93

c/o "General Hosp."/ABC Inc.
4151 Prospect Ave.
Hollywood, CA 90027
Alternate V: 03/01/92

c/o ABC TV-"General Hospital"
1438 N. Gower St.
Los Angeles, CA 90028
Forwarded V: 09/03/92

Wyler, Gretchen
15115 Weddington St.
Van Nuys, CA 91411
Actress V: 04/13/92

Wyman, Jane
P.O. Box 540148
Orlando, FL 32854
Actress V: 01/02/92

P.O. Box 540148
Orlando, FL 32854
Alternate V: 11/26/92

Wyndham, Victoria
c/o NBC-TV
Another World
79 Madison Ave., 5th Fl.
New York, NY 91523
Actress V: 06/15/92

Wyner, George
c/o MEW
151 N. San Vincente Blvd.
Beverly Hills, CA 90211
Actor V: 07/24/92

3450 Laurie Place
Studio City, CA 91604
Alternate V: 06/17/92

Wynette, Tammy
1222 16th Ave. S.
Nashville, TN 37212
Singer V: 01/20/92

P.O. Box 540148
Orlando, FL 32854
Singer V: 11/26/92

Wyss, Amanda
9000 Sunset Blvd #1200
Los Angeles, CA 90069
Actress V: 01/16/93

Y

YOUNG & RESTLESS
7800 Beverly Blvd. Ste. 3305
Los Angeles, CA 90036
Fan Assistance V: 05/12/92

Yankovic, "Weird" Al
8842 Hollywood Blvd.
Los Angeles, CA 90069
Singer V: 02/16/93

Yarborough, Cale
1801 Volusian Ave.
Daytona Beach, FL 32015
Race Driver V: 06/23/92

724 Scott Dr.
Fredericksburg, VA 22405
Alternate V: 01/03/92

c/o Yarborough Racing
9617 Dixie River Rd.
Charlotte, NC 28270
Alternate V: 03/02/92

Yarborough, William
1801 Volusia Ave.
Dayton Beach, FL 32015
Race Driver V: 03/01/92

Yasbeck, Amy
2170 Century Park E. #1111
Los Angeles, CA 90067
Actress V: 11/26/92

Yates, Bill
c/o King Features
216 East 45th St.
New York, NY 10017
Cartoonist V: 04/11/92

Yates, Cassie
10100 Santa Monica Blvd. #700
Los Angeles, CA 90067
Actress V: 01/16/93

Yeager, Chuck
P.O. Box 128
Cedar Ridge, CA 95924
Test Pilot V: 04/21/92

Yeager, Jeana
614 Sandydale Rd.
Nipomo, CA 93444
Astronaut V: 02/03/92

Yearwood, Trisha
P.O. Box 65
Monticello, GA 31064
Singer V: 03/26/93

1112 N. Sherbourne Dr.
7800 Beverly Blvd.
Los Angeles, CA 90027
Singer V: 04/05/93

Yeltsin, Boris
4 Straya Ploschad
Moscow, USSR
Politician V: 03/03/92

Yoakam, Dwight
15840 Ventura Blvd. #465
Encino, CA 91436
Musician V: 01/16/93

York, Brittany
c/o Playboy Ent.
8560 Sunset Blvd.
Los Angeles, CA 90069
Playmate V: 11/11/92

York, Francine
14333 Addison St. #315
Sherman Oaks, CA 91423
Actress V: 07/31/92

c/o Carroll
120 S. Victory Blvd. #104
Burbank, CA 91502
Alternate V: 01/16/93

York, John
ABC/General Hospital
4151 Prospect Ave.
Hollywood, CA 90027
Actor V: 06/15/92

York, Michael
9100 Cordell Dr.
Los Angeles, CA 90069
Actor V: 05/23/92

c/o Duncan Heath
162 Wardour St.
London W1, England
Alternate V: 02/28/92

3425 Knox Pl.
Bronx, NY 10467
Alternate V: 05/04/92

York, Susannah
388 Oxford St.
London, W1 England
Actress V: 06/17/92

York, Susannah, contd
c/o Jeremy Conway
109 Jermyn St.
London SW1Y 6HN, England
Alternate V: 02/28/92

Young, Alan
33872 Barcellona Pl.
Dana Point, CA 92629
Actor V: 03/26/93

c/o Geordie Prod.
24843 Del Prado, Ste. 522
Dana Point, CA 92629
L.R.U. V: 02/28/92

Young, Bob
c/o King Features
216 East 45th St.
New York, NY 10017
Cartoonist V: 03/13/92

Young, Bruce
c/o ABC-TV
"General Hospital"
4151 Prospect Ave.
Hollywood, CA 90027
Actor V: 06/15/92

Young, Burt
c/o NBC
3000 W. Alameda Ave.
Burbank, CA 91523
Actor V: 01/19/92

708 N. Roxbury Dr.
Beverly Hills, CA 90210
L.R.U. V: 01/02/92

Young, Chris
5959 Triumph St.
Commerce, CA 90040-1688
Actor V: 12/08/92

Young, Corey
c/o General Hosp./ABC Inc.
4151 Prospect Ave.
Hollywood, CA 90027
Actor V: 03/01/92

Young, Dean
c/o King Features
216 East 45th St.
New York, NY 10017
Cartoonist V: 01/07/92

Young, Faron
1300 Division St. #102
Nashville, TN 37203
Singer V: 05/18/92

Young, Faron, contd
P.O. Box 526
Old Hickory, TN 37138
Alternate V: 06/15/92

1512 Hawkins
Nashville, TN 37203
Forwarded V: 05/22/92

Young, Jesse Colin
c/o Keauhou
P.O. Box 325
Pt. Reyes Sta., CA 94956
Singer V: 04/22/92

P.O. Box 130
Pt. Reyes Sta., CA 94956
Alternate V: 06/21/92

Young, John W.
c/o NASA
LBJ Space Center
Houston, TX 77058
Astronaut V: 01/19/92

Young, Loretta
c/o Studio Fan Mail
1122 S. Robertson Blvd.
Los Angeles, CA 90035
Actress V: 06/21/92

c/o Lewis
1705 Ambassador Dr.
Beverly Hills, CA 90210
L.R.U. V: 05/01/92

Young, Lyman
c/o King Features
216 East 45th St.
New York, NY 10017
Cartoonist V: 07/24/92

Young, Neil
75 Rockefeller Plaza
New York, NY 10019
Singer V: 02/01/92

Young, Sean
300 Mercer St. #7-E
New York, NY 10003
Actress V: 02/02/92

Yulin, Harris
c/o GTG Ent./Culver Studios
9336 W. Washington Blvd.
Culver City, CA 90232
Actor V: 05/15/92

Yune, Johnny
11574 Iowa Ave. #114
Los Angeles, CA 90025
Actor V: 04/18/92

Z

ZBF Agentur
Jenfelder Allee 80
D-(W) 2000 Hamburg 70, Germany
Talent Agency V: 02/27/93

Leopoldstr. 19
D-(W) 8000 Munchen 40, Germany
Alternate V: 02/27/93

Ordensmeisterstr. 15-16
D-(W) 1000 Berlin 42, Germany
Alternate V: 02/27/93

ZZ TOP
P.O. Box 19744
Houston, TX 77024
Band V: 05/20/92

Zabitowsky, Fred W.
P.O. Box 660
Pembroke, NC 28372
Medal of Honor V: 02/05/92

Zabriski, Grace
1536 Murray Dr.
Los Angeles, CA 90069
Actress V: 11/26/92

Zadeh & Associates
11759 Iowa Ave.
Los Angeles, CA 90025
Talent Agency V: 02/27/93

Zadora, Pia
23720 Malibu Colony Rd.
Malibu, CA 90265
Actress V: 03/18/93

8 Beverly Park
Beverly Hills, CA 90210
Alternate V: 03/19/93

c/o Zadora Enterprises Inc.
888 7th Ave. 44th Floor
New York, NY 10019
Forwarded V: 01/02/92

Zane, Lisa
1722 N. Serrano #4
Los Angeles, CA 90027
Actress V: 11/26/92

Zapata, Carmen
6107 Ethel Ave.
Van Nuys, CA 91405
Actress V: 06/17/92

Zappa, Dweezil
P.O. Box 5265
N. Hollywood, CA 91606
Actor V: 01/16/93

Zappa, Frank
P.O. Box 5418
N. Hollywood, CA 91616
Musician V: 01/16/93

7885 Woodrow Wilson Dr.
Los Angeles, CA 90046
Alternate V: 06/17/92

Zappa, Moon Unit
345 N. Maple Dr. #183
Beverly Hills, CA 90210
Singer V: 01/16/93

Zee, Ona
2523A Folsom St.
San Francisco, CA 94110
Adult Films V: 01/24/93

Zefferelli, Franco
9247 Swallow Dr.
Los Angeles, CA 90069
Director V: 03/26/93

Zeigler, Larry
6209 Dartmoor Circle
Orlando, FL 32819
Golfer V: 09/02/92

Zeman, Jacklyn
c/o ABC-TV
"General Hospital"
4151 Prospect Ave.
Hollywood, CA 90027
Actress V: 06/15/92

Zeotrope
P.O. Box 608005
Chicago, IL 60626
Musical Group V: 01/09/92

Zerbe, Anthony
245 Chateaux Elise
Santa Barbara, CA 93109
Actor V: 08/22/92

Zetterling, Mai
28 Charring Cross Rd.
London W1, England
Actress V: 02/28/92

Ziegler, Bill
c/o King Features
216 East 45th St.
New York, NY 10017
 Cartoonist V: 02/20/92

Ziegler, Jack
c/o New York Magazine
25 W. 43rd St.
New York, NY 10036
 Cartoonist V: 04/12/93

Zimbalist, Stephanie
151 El Camino
Beverly Hills, CA 90212
 Actress V: 01/16/93

4024 Radford Ave.
Studio City, CA 91604
 Alternate V: 04/01/92

c/o Sharon Leigh
P.O. Box 487
Sunland, CA 91041-0487
 Alternate V: 02/20/92

Zimbalist Jr., Efrem
4750 Encino Ave.
Encino, CA 91316
 Actor V: 04/27/92

Zimmer, Norma
661 Wood Lake Dr.
Brea, CA 92621
 Singer V: 11/26/92

Zinc, Tom
c/o WCW/Turner Broad.
One CNN Center, Box 105366
Atlanta, GA 30348-5366
 Pro Wrestler V: 03/26/93

Zmed, Adrian
23500 Daisy Trail
Calabasas, CA 91302
 Actor V: 04/02/92

4322 Bakman Ave.
Studio City, CA 90068
 Alternate V: 06/19/92

Zorina, Vera
10 Gracie Square
New York, NY 10028
 Actress V: 11/26/92

2128 N.E. Halsey Cir.
New York, NY 10028
 L.R.U. V: 11/26/92

Zuckerman, Pinchas
173 Riverside Dr.
New York, NY 10024
 Concert Violinist V: 04/19/92

Zuniga, Daphne
8033 W. Sunset Blvd. #3535
Los Angeles, CA 90046-2427
 Actress V: 04/22/92

c/o Constellation
P.O. Box 1249
White River Jct., VT 05001
 Alternate V: 06/29/92

9200 Sunset Blvd. #25
Los Angeles, CA 90069
 Forwarded V: 02/04/92

TV PROGRAM LATE ENTRIES

FAMILY MATTERS
FULL HOUSE
HANGING w/MR. COOPER
c/o Lorimar
300 S. Lorimar Plaza
Burbank, CA 91505
 Production Offices V: 03/09/93

DOOGIE HOUSER
c/o Bochco/Fox TV
10201 W. Pico Blvd.
Los Angeles, CA 90035
 Production Office V: 04/22/93

COMMISH
c/o Cannell
555 Brooksbank Ave.
N. Vancouver, BC V7J 3S5
Canada
 Production Office V: 04/13/93

ROOM FOR TWO
c/o Warner TV
4000 Warner Blvd.
Burbank, CA 91533
 Production Office V: 04/12/93

YOUNG INDIANA JONES
c/o Paramount TV
5555 Melrose Ave.
Los Angeles, CA 90038
 Production Office V: 04/11/93

**Christensen's Ultimate Movie, TV, and Rock & Roll Directory
and Christensen's Autograph Facsimile Book
Cardiff by-the-sea Publishing
6065 Mission Gorge Rd.
San Diego, CA 92120**

These books are the ultimate working tools. They are absolutely necessary to help build ones reference library. The address book contains over 40,000 celebrity addresses. The facsimile book carries over 6000 celebrity replications. This is for the beginner as well as the knowledgeable journeyman in this field.

This is an encyclopedic listing of celebrity addresses, memorabilia listings, and photographic reproductions. It is the most extensive directory of its kind ever published.

The purpose of this directory is to assist the millions of fans from all walks of life who want to write to their favorite celebrities, no matter what field of entertainment they're in.

This directory can be most useful in requesting an autographed photo of your favorite movie star, sending a birthday greeting to your favorite sports celebrity, requesting a TV script from the actual writer, and so many more things, the list is endless.

Looking for other books, autographs for sale, photos, posters, collectibles, records, dealers, baseball cards, audio or video cassettes, baseball cards, or other collectibles? This book is full of listings and dealers who carry many of these items.

This book is highly recommended by everyone we have talked to, and we list it first as **our** ultimate first listing. It was there in the beginning for us before we began Celebrity Access-The Directory and a year hasn't gone by without our continued support of such a fine book.

Don't forget about their hit second book, "Celebrity Autographs." This is one of the most valuable tools a collector can have. The thousands of celebrity signature examples reproduced from documents, cards, and letters, will help one sort out the secretary signed items from the real thing. If you are a novice collector, this could save you thousands of dollars when purchasing questionable autographs. We hope a Volume II will follow this book.

Child Stars Magazine
P.O. Box 55328
Stockton, CA 95205-8828
(209) 942-2131

Child Stars Magazine. This is a magazine for film and TV buffs featuring stories, interviews, and news briefs about past and present child stars. This is a slick illustrated magazine. It is brought to you by the same person who created and recently sold, "The Autograph Collectors Magazine," which in its years of circulation has brought the hobby of autograph collecting into the lives of tens of thousands of people.

It will feature columns like, where are they now, addresses so one may write them, obituaries, and lots of photos.

This full size magazine will have a color cover and quality coated paper inside. The subscriptions will be quarterly, with a minimum of 5,000 copy circulation guaranteed.

As always, there will be lots of ads from dealers featuring posters, lobby cards, stills, videos, autographs, and much more of your favorite child stars.

Collectors Connection & Registry
Ralph D. Vogel, President
P.O. Box 54
So. San Francisco, CA 94083-0054
(415) 598-9871 (Cal)
(800) 777-1078 (US)

Collectors Connection & Registry, is a service oriented publication to put collectors and sellers in contact with each other in all areas. This is done with their packed updated annual directory and for a more specialized or current listing you may access their massive computer locator network by phone for free. This special oversized paperback directory is almost 200 pages of collecting information. The service is nation wide.

The Bare Facts Video Guide
by Craig Hosada
P.O.Box 3255
Santa Clara, CA 95055

The Bare Facts Video Guide. This book helps the researcher and fan alike, to find the scenes, films, and magazines where their favorite actor or actress can be found with little or no clothing on. This oversized paperback which has already caught the attention of Playboy, and is completely updated annually. This is a really a gold mine of thorough information. A 450+ pages and a must for the videophile.

Argent Express. Here is the source for those of you whom are seeking a "Western" link to the film industry. Hank's specialty is TV's Gunsmoke, but he works in all areas of western history, films, radio, photo's, advertizing, and ephemera. He is a researcher, collector, seller, and you can tell he's one of the good guys by his white hat.

Magazines:
The Autograph Review
305 Carlton Rd.
Syracuse, NY 13207
   This fantastic mini-magazine, is full of current information leaning heavily towards sports with some information on film stars. Sports interviews are here as well. This is certainly worth the subscription.

The Eclectic Marketeer
10108 Worrell Pl.
Glenn Dale, MD 20769
   This homemade newsletter is really fun with quizzes, mystery photos, give-aways, contests, celebrity interviews, and more. Well worth the small annual dues and certainly one of a kind.

Autograph and Manuscript Organizations:
Universal Autograph Collectors Club
Penn and Quill Magazine
2 Catalpa Rd.
Providence, RI 02906

The Manuscript Society
The Manuscript Society Magazine
350 N. Niagara St.
Burbank, CA 91505

Newspapers:
Movie Collectors World
P.O. Box 309
Frazier, MI 48026
   This is a super huge monthly paper which contains information on where to fulfill all your film collecting needs. Aside from the articles, one will find the largest assortment of dealers anywhere.
The paper is a huge two section, cornucopia for collectors. This is for serious collectors. We use it ourselves.

Jim Weaver's Address Lists
405 Dunbar Dr.
Pittsburgh, PA 15235

This list comes out several times a year with star addresses and his own unique category listings (Horror, Sex Symbols, etc.).
They also include updated addresses, bad address warnings, deaths, and new additions. Worth having to complete your reference library.

"V.I.P. Address Book"
by James M. Wiggins
c/o Assoc. Media Comp. Ltd.
P.O. Box 10190
Marina del Rey, CA 90295-8864

This award winning book has a place on our shelves. Unlike the others it covers famous people in all areas of interest, with an easy to read and follow text. Hollywood, sports, science, military, the arts-- almost everything. We recommend it often as a companion to the others we have listed. Also published are their 6 annual updates.

Autograph Price Guides:
Price Guide to Autographs
P.O. Box 685
Enka, NC 28728

Fan Clubs and Fans:
Fandom Directory
7761 Astrella Ct.
Springfield, VA 22152-3133

If you are a collector, dealer, publisher, convention organizer, or just a fan, you can be listed FREE! This directory is huge. Loaded with collectors and cross-referenced with their areas of interest. They've been around serving the collector for a long time, and used by all sorts of professionals.

National Association of Fan Clubs
"The Fan Club Directory"
c/o Linda Kay
P.O. Box 7487
Burbank, CA 91510

Join the only International Fan Club Association representing all fan clubs, in all fields of entertainment, The benefits are many, including the sharing of information with other fan clubs, helpful suggestions a fan club which meets your needs, how to start your own fan club, and much more. Annually they publish an incredible fan club directory. Please write for membership fees.

<u>**Rare Video, Film, and Music Dealers:**</u>
Videobrary
6117 Carpenter Ave.
N. Hollywood, CA 91606

Eddie Brandt's
Saturday Matinee Video
6310 Colfax Ave.
N. Hollywood, CA 91606

Village Music
9 E. Blithdale Ave.
Mill Valley, CA 94941

<u>**Unsigned Celebrity Photographs, Books, Posters, and Memorabilia:**</u>
Sy Sussman Photo's
2962 South Mann St.
Las Vegas, NV 89102

The Bijou Collectibles
P.O. Box 201
Fullerton, CA 92632

Hollywood Poster
Gallery
5150 Mae Anne
Ste.213-200
Reno, NV 89523

Collectors Book Store
1708 N. Vine St.
Hollywood, CA 90028

Cinema Collectors Store
1507 Wilcox Ave.
Hollywood, CA 90028

Hollywood Book and
Poster Co.
6349 Hollywood Blvd.
Hollywood, CA 90028

Flash Photos
4718 Canehill Ave.
Lakewood, CA 90713

Farrell's Celebrity Photos
14731 Nelson Way
San Jose, CA 95124

<u>**Reference Books:**</u>
"Wanted To Buy"
by Collector Books
P.O. Box 3009
Paducah, KY 42001

"Ill Buy That"
Dr. Tony Hyman
by Treasure Hunt Publications
P.O. Box 699
Claremont, CA 91711

"The Film Encyclopedia"
by Ephraim Katz

"The Complete Directory To Prime Time Network TV Shows/The Complete Directory To Prime Time Stars"
by Brooke & Marsh

Leonard Maltin's
"TV Movie and Video Guide"

Your own Public Library

<u>**Autographs:**</u>
Celebrity Access
Buy & Sell Autographs & Collections
Authentication & Appraisal Service
Reference Books
Movie Memorabilia
(send 2 S.A.S.E. and mark each "Info 94" to be notified of future magazine and catalog projects)
20 Sunnyside Ave., Ste.A241
Mill Valley, CA 94941
(415) 389-8133

NOTES